STREETS OF HOPE

THE FALL AND RISE
OF AN URBAN NEIGHBORHOOD

P9-BBT-456

PETER MEDOFF AND HOLLY SKLAR

SOUTH END PRESS   BOSTON, MA

Cover by Geneva Design
Cover mural by the DSNI Youth Committee
Cover photos by Carren Panico
Text design and production by the South End Press collective
Photos © Gertrudes Fidalgo, pp. 36 (except Farrier), 66 bottom, 88 top; Rick Jurgens, 36 (Farrier); Ros Everdell, 114 top left and bottom, 244 bottom; Leah Mahan, 243 bottom; Craig Bailey, 244 top; all others DSNI

Library of Congress Cataloguing-in-Publication Data

Medoff, Peter, 1957-
    Streets of hope : the fall and rise of an urban neighborhood / by Peter Medoff and Holly Sklar.
        p.   cm.
    Includes bibliographical references and index.
    ISBN 978-0-89608-482-7 (pbk.)

    1. Urban renewal—Massachusetts—Boston—Case studies.   2. Community development corporations—Massachusetts—Boston—Case studies.   3. Neighborhood—Massachusetts—Boston—Case studies. I. Sklar, Holly, 1955-   . II. Title.
HT177.B6M44   1994
307.76'09744'61—dc20   94-4613
                                             CIP

www.southendpress.org

TABLE OF CONTENTS

Acknowledgments   v

Maps   vii

Introduction   1

People With Solutions • "Re-Membering"

1. Remembering   7

Divided Development • Boom and Bust • Segregated Suburbanization • Urban Renewal, Urban Removal • Rising Poverty in the "New Boston" • Redlining, Blockbusting and Loan-Sharking • Trashed and Burned • "That Neighborhood Doesn't Matter"

2. Creating the Dudley Street Neighborhood Initiative   37

Searching for a New Beginning • The Riley Foundation • Making a Difference • Dudley Advisory Group • Boundaries • "Organization of Organizations" • BRA Dudley Square Plan: Renewed Fears of Displacement • "We Don't See the Community Here": Bringing the Neighborhood Into the Dudley Street Initiative • New Governance Structure: Resident Majority • First Elections • The Board Takes Charge • Hiring Staff • Passing the Baton

3. Don't Dump On Us: Organizing the Neighborhood   67

Knocking on Neighbors' Doors • "Don't Dump On Us" • Cleaning Up • Friction • Cultivating Resources • "Don't Dump On Us" II: Trash Transfer Stations • Turning Point

4. Planning an Urban Village   89

Bottom-Up Planning: Forging a Partnership with the City • Greater Roxbury Neighborhood Authority (GRNA) • Choosing Consultants • Planning Begins • Community Design • Urban Village • Completing the Plan • The Master Plan for Dudley Revitalization • Celebration and City Support

5. Controlling the Land Through Eminent Domain   115

Expanding Staff and Outside Support • Critical Mass through Eminent Domain • Development Without Displacement • Convincing the City: Keys to the Vault • Dudley Neighbors, Inc. • Town Common • The Mayor • "Take a Stand, Own the Land" • BRA Hearing • The Drama of the BRA Decision • Precedent?

6. Land and Housing Development: The Triangle and Beyond — 145

Financing the Land: Ford Foundation Loan • Triangle Build-Out Plan • Closing in on the Land and the Loan • $2 Million • Community Land Trust: Preserving the Affordability of Quality Housing • Beyond the Triangle: Tenant Organizing, Co-ops and Orchard Park Redevelopment • Homebuyers and Banks

7. Holistic Development: Human, Economic, Environmental — 169

Human Development • Agency Collaborative • Dudley PRIDE • Neighborhood Greening • Transition • Moving on Economic Development • "Economics With People In Mind" • Economics Without People In Mind • Understanding Economic Trends That Undermine Community Development • Declaration of Community Rights

8. The Power of Youth — 203

Risky Stereotypes • Whose "Culture of Violence"? • Pride and Prejudice • Part of the Solution • Dudley's Young Architects and Planners • Designs and Dreams • Reclaiming a Park • A Youth Leader's Story • "Guilty of Being Black" • Give the Kid a Record • "United We Stand, Divided We Fall"

9. Pathfinders — 245

Rebuild Dudley and L.A. • "Together, We'll Find the Way" • From Dumping Ground to Breaking Ground • "A Vision With a Task" • Building on Neighborhood Assets • Nurturing Diversity, Unity and Neighborhood Leadership • The Importance of Youth • Organize, Organize, Organize • Creating Vision and Political Will • Controlling the Real Estate Market • Comprehensive Community Revitalization • Building on Success • Community-Foundation Partnership • Avoiding Premature Partnerships • Local Community-Government Partnership • Community-Federal Government Partnership • Community

Box: DSNI's Declaration of Community Rights	202
Notes	289
List of Interviews	317
Appendix A: Census Data Tables	319
Appendix B: Declaration of Community Rights in Spanish and Cape Verdean	322
Index	325
About the Authors	339

ACKNOWLEDGMENTS

Our warm thanks to the board, staff and members of the Dudley Street Neighborhood Initiative who gave so generously of their time, knowledge and memories. Special thanks to everyone we interviewed, whose names appear in a separate list. Your words enriched us and this book. Thank you Paul Bothwell for such eloquent remembering during your personal struggle of "re-membering."

Three foundations provided generous funding. Thank you Newell Flather, Naomi Tuchmann, Phil Hall and the Riley Foundation trustees for encouraging the writing of this book and providing sustained financial support and other assistance. Thank you also Rebecca Riley, Kavita Ramdas and the John D. and Catherine T. MacArthur Foundation, and Nancy Andrews, Mark Elliott and the Ford Foundation.

We are grateful to the following people who critiqued the draft manuscript and/or have engaged with one or both of us in ongoing conversations about DSNI, community development and government policy: Ros Everdell, Jodi Kretzmann, Ché Madyun, John McKnight, Andrea Nagel, Gus Newport, Steve Perkins, Mat Thall, Bill Traynor and Paul Yelder. Also Mimi Abramovitz, Najwa Abdul-Tawwab, Sue Beaton, Lisa Chapnick, Pierre Clavel, John E. Davis, Gertrudes Fidalgo, Newell Flather, Nancy Green, Laura Henze, Sue Karant, Mel King, Mark Lipman, Leah Mahan, Melinda Marble, Bill Slotnik, Diane Stephenson, Gail Sullivan, Ellen Teninty, Clayton Turnbull and Ro Whittington.

Our thanks to Jarrett Barrios, Virginia Bullock and Bonnie Wolf for research assistance during parts of 1990-92; Gertrudes Fidalgo for help with photographs; John Demeter for suggesting the title, "Streets of Hope"; Rolf Goetze and the BRA for compiling Dudley census data; the Public Facilities Department Research and Development Unit for preparing the maps; Marc Sawyer and Liz DiFranza of Geneva Design for the cover; Carren Panico for the cover photographs; Do Mi Stauber for index preparation; Margaret Kelner and Tricia Horn for proofreading; and the Winthrop Group for interview transcription. Thanks also to Tollie Miller, Cyndi Koebert, Mike Kozu and Jason Webb. Finally, thank you Cynthia Peters and South End Press for publishing this book in record time.

For the residents of the Dudley Street neighborhood.

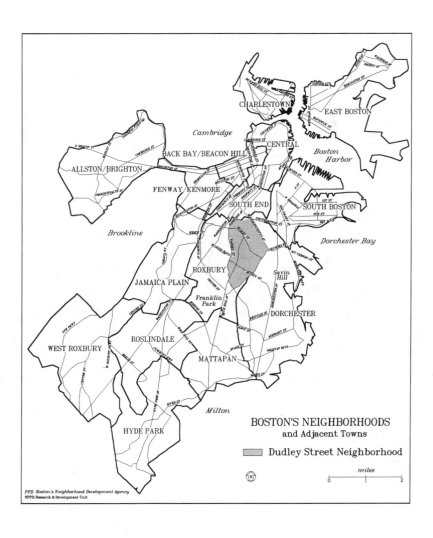

CHARLESTOWN

EAST BOSTON

Cambridge

CENTRAL

BACK BAY/BEACON HILL

Boston Harbor

ALLSTON/BRIGHTON

FENWAY/KENMORE

SOUTH END

SOUTH BOSTON

Brookline

Dorchester Bay

ROXBURY

Savin Hill

JAMAICA PLAIN

Franklin Park

DORCHESTER

ROSLINDALE

WEST ROXBURY

MATTAPAN

Milton

HYDE PARK

BOSTON'S NEIGHBORHOODS
and Adjacent Towns

Dudley Street Neighborhood

miles

0   1   2

PFD Boston's Neighborhood Development Agency
NPPD: Research & Development Unit

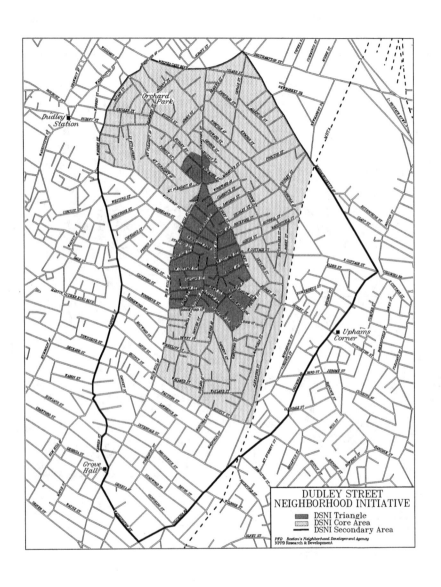

DUDLEY STREET
NEIGHBORHOOD INITIATIVE

DSNI Triangle
DSNI Core Area
DSNI Secondary Area

PFD   Boston's Neighborhood Development Agency
NPPD Research & Development

INTRODUCTION

Long Boston's most impoverished area, the Dudley Street neighborhood is living an extraordinary story of community rebirth shaped by the dreams of ordinary people of different races and generations. This inner city neighborhood, like so many around the country, was treated like an outsider city—separate, unequal and disposable. The resident-led Dudley Street Neighborhood Initiative (DSNI) is rebuilding it with the power of pride, organizing and a unified vision of comprehensive community development.

For years, Dudley has looked as if an earthquake had struck, leveling whole sections. Streets crisscross blocks of vacant lots where homes and shops used to be. In the summer, the lots bloom with violet wildflowers, nature's gift to a community working to rebuild against great odds.

The earthquake that hit Dudley was neither natural nor sudden. Instead, in a pattern repeated nationally, a thriving urban community was trashed and burned. It was redlined by banks, government mortgage programs and insurance companies in a self-fulfilling prophecy of White flight, devaluation and decline. While tax money subsidized the building of segregated suburbia and upscale "urban renewal," inner city neighborhoods like Dudley were stripped of jobs, homes and government services.

The distance between downtown Boston and downtrodden Dudley could not be measured by the less than two miles between them. One area reflected privilege and reinvestment, the other prejudice and disinvestment.

Beginning in the 1950s, disinvestment, abandonment and arson turned Dudley homes, yards and businesses into wasteland.* By 1981, one-third of Dudley's land lay vacant. It became a dumping ground for trash from around the city and state. The dumping wasn't legal, but the violators came and went without fear of the law, blighting the neighborhood with toxic chemicals, auto carcasses, old refrigerators, rotten meat and other refuse. Adding insult to injury, Dudley became an illegal dumping ground for debris from housing and other construction elsewhere around Boston.

Ché (pronounced Shay) Madyun, longtime president of the Dudley Street Neighborhood Initiative, first moved to Dudley in 1976. For two years she and her family lived in the home of community activist Jessie Farrier in the historic Mt. Pleasant section of Dudley, an area with numerous longtime homeowners, many of them African American. Farrier's son had been a classmate of Madyun at Emerson College. Farrier encouraged Madyun to register to vote for the 1977 election in which John O'Bryant became the first Black person elected to the Boston School Committee in the twentieth century.

Originally from Alabama, Farrier has lived in the Dudley neighborhood since 1950. She committed herself to staying and making things better as more and more houses burned down around her. Every New Year's Day, Farrier has an open house to which all are welcome. In her plant-filled living room, pictures of her children and grandchildren are mingled with her awards for community work. "I didn't buy this house to sell it," Farrier asserts. "As long as any of my children are in Boston, I want them to be in this house here."[1]

In 1978, Ché Madyun and her family moved to a larger place in the Cottage Brook Apartments on Dudley Street. "Fire engines used to run up and down the street every night," Madyun recalls. "You could always smell smoke, and I used to get real afraid [thinking] that our building was going to get burned also. I remember when the building behind us burned—directly behind us—and the smoke was coming inside and the windows were closed. It was scary...Cars used to get burned a lot, but mostly it was houses. And then, of course, eventually

---

* Throughout this book, Dudley refers to the Dudley Street neighborhood as defined by DSNI boundaries (see earlier map), not to the Dudley Station commercial district that borders the neighborhood.

they got torn down." Fire trucks were a familiar sight, but not other city services. "I don't remember seeing any street cleaners," she says.

As her three children grew older, Madyun went "to great lengths" to take them "all over the city so they could get involved in different activities, and I used to think it was a shame I always had to go so far away." A talented dancer herself, Madyun took her children to music, dance and swimming programs in the South End and other Boston neighborhoods.

"Everything was over there, over there, over there," she recalls. "There was nothing ever in here."

Today, Madyun and her family live in a new cooperative purchased partly with "sweat equity." Her children have participated in DSNI's Youth Committee, summer programs and multicultural festivals and helped design a planned community center. In the future, no parent will have to lament, "Everything was over there, over there…nothing ever in here."

PEOPLE WITH SOLUTIONS

The unnatural earthquake didn't destroy the whole Dudley neighborhood. Many homes remained, some businesses survived. Newcomers moved in—some from across town, others from down South or across the ocean. Old-timers and newcomers—White, Black, Latino and Cape Verdean—joined together to rebuild their neighborhood with the power of hope and pride, organizing and community-controlled development.

The Dudley population is poorer and younger than that of Boston as a whole. Unemployment is at least twice as high and per capita income is half that of the larger city. Dudley's official poverty rate—more than one out of three residents—is nearly twice Boston's average. Over a third of Dudley residents are under 18 years old. One out of two Dudley children lives below the official poverty line—a line set well below what is actually needed to buy adequate food, housing and other necessities.[2]

Though it is Boston's most underemployed and economically impoverished neighborhood, Dudley is also richly diverse and industrious. The DSNI story challenges those who mask disinvestment and discrimination in slanderous, scapegoating stereotypes about an "underclass culture of poverty." As one major study put it, "Areas of concentrated poverty emerge from much of the historical and contemporary underclass literature as monolithic islands of despair and degradation."³ The stereotypical inner city neighborhood is full of hoodlums and not neighborly. It's stereotypically a savage jungle where the heroic, hardworking few, if any, struggle onward amid the many presumed to be hooked on crime, drugs and government "handouts." Stereotypers might count DSNI members among the heroic, but DSNI members are not few; they are many. As Dudley residents demonstrate, poor people are not generically lacking in values. Their government often is.

Terms like "underclass" and "persistent poverty" imply that poverty persists in spite of society's commitment to end it. In reality, the economic system reproduces poverty no matter how persistently people are trying to get out or stay out of poverty. Since 1973, reports the Children's Defense Fund, "most of the fastest increases in poverty rates occurred among young white families with children, those headed by married couples, and those headed by high school graduates. For all three groups, *poverty rates more than doubled in a single generation*, reaching levels that most Americans commonly assume afflict only minority and single-parent families."⁴ (Italics in original.)

The DSNI story challenges those who see inner city residents as people who have only problems, not solutions. It shows how effective community development begins by recognizing and reinforcing the resources within the community. It encourages low-income neighborhood residents to take stock of their varied individual and community assets and think boldly as they envision the future together.

DSNI is an intergenerational organization, with elders and teenagers among its diverse leadership. The DSNI story encourages others to nurture the positive power of inner city youth who are too often feared and expected to fail. Dudley's young people are playing an increasingly dynamic and inspirational role in the Dudley Street Neighborhood Initiative.

Beginning in the 1980s with a "Don't Dump on Us" campaign to clean up the vacant lots and close down illegal trash transfer stations, DSNI organized hundreds of residents, forged a new sense of neighborhood identity and power and forced city government to respond. DSNI then turned the traditional top-down urban planning process on its head. Instead of struggling to influence a process driven by city government, Dudley residents and agencies became visionaries, created their own bottom-up "urban village" redevelopment plan and built an unprecedented partnership with the city to implement it. DSNI made history when it became the nation's first neighborhood group to win the right of eminent domain and began transforming Dudley's burnt-out lots from wasteland to wealth controlled by the community. Launched with the strong backing of the local Riley Foundation, DSNI developed a growing network of public and private sector supporters.

Organizing is the renewable energy that powers DSNI and community development. DSNI's campaigns are punctuated with summary slogans: "Don't Dump On Us," "Take a Stand, Own the Land," "Building Houses and People Too," "Dudley PRIDE—People and Resources Investing in Dudley's Environment," "Unite the Community, Celebrate Our Diversity," "Economics With People In Mind." Like quilters, the people of Dudley are working together, mixing old fabric and new, to create something warm and beautiful.

The Dudley neighborhood still has many vacant lots, many people without jobs or sufficient income, many children being shortchanged by society. Yet every year, Dudley residents see more of their holistic vision of community development become reality.

DSNI's challenge is enormous. It is striving to assure fair opportunity for people long treated as disposable, at a time when more and more people are being dispossessed of secure livelihoods. It is striving to build a sustainable, mutually beneficial, multicultural community, at a time when so many others choose divisiveness over diversity. The people of Dudley are pathfinders, guided by a vision of the future in which no one is disposable.

"RE-MEMBERING"

DSNI activist Paul Bothwell has lived in Dudley since 1976—a White church worker who arrived with his family after so many Whites had left. In October 1990, Bothwell was riding his bicycle when he was hit by a stolen car on the run in Dudley Station. "My head and face were crushed," he explained almost two years later. "It's just been devastating...and I'm still slowly in the rebuilding process. A lot of what has gone on through this recovery process, which was miraculous in itself, has been related to or has come from the effect of head injury on my brain and on my psyche and everything else...What it feels like inside is terrible, terrible dismemberment where you're terribly fractured psychically, mentally, spiritually, emotionally and physically as well. Just terribly fractured."

Bothwell describes his recovery process as a long, step-by-step process of being "*re-membered*. That is...the broken pieces, the scattered pieces...little by little, are being picked up and re-membered. What comes out is something different. I'm not the same as before and I never will be the same as before. It's different."

"I think that same thing has happened" in Dudley, says Bothwell. "That's why I tell my story so much...This community wasn't shattered in 1972 on July 4th or something. It was a long process of dismemberment. Literally, it was torn limb from limb and heart from heart and person from person...I think it rested at that place being terribly dismembered for quite a long period of time. There were some little spurts of hope, but it rested dismembered.

"I think that DSNI [was] able to identify the heart of the community and start with that. It...began to pull the heart back together again and began to get something that people could say, 'Hey, that's me! That's what I feel! Little by little, what I feel in this community begins to matter.' That's the first time that's ever happened. Somehow, the heart began to grow and grow. Very little by little, pieces of this community have sort of re-membered again, pulled back together. It's not whole by any means yet. You dream and hope it will be, whatever wholeness means and can be. It's being re-membered...It will come out different than it was before...It will reflect who is here now. That's the way it ought to be. It's great...It's a process of finding its way."

Bothwell cites an African proverb he learned while growing up in Zaire: "'Together we find the way.' Nobody knows the way. 'We ought to go this way. We ought to go that way.' The fact of the matter is that together, we find the way. It's a process...There are lots of ups, lots of downs, lots of wrong turns and everything else. Together, we'll find the way. I feel that's what's happening with DSNI. Together, we'll find the way."

1

REMEMBERING

The Dudley Street neighborhood straddles the historic towns of Roxbury and Dorchester that were founded over a century before the American Revolution. In 1630, a decade after the Pilgrims crossed on the Mayflower, more than 1,000 English immigrants sailed to the Massachusetts Bay Colony to lead off the Great Migration of Puritans. Lord Dorchester was among their patrons. Some settlers traveled inland from a place Native Americans called Mattapannock (Columbia Point) to build homes and a meeting house near the junction of East Cottage and Pleasant Streets, just a few blocks from today's Dudley neighborhood.[1] The colonizers looked to the nearby fort on Savin Hill to keep Native Americans from effectively resisting their displacement. The town of Roxbury was established in 1630 near what is now Dudley Station. In 1639, the nation's first public school opened on Pleasant Street in Dorchester.

The Puritan Council for Life, theocratic rulers of Church and State, included the first governors of the Massachusetts Bay Colony: John Winthrop, John Endicott and Thomas Dudley. Governor Winthrop famously declared that the Puritans' Bible Commonwealth would "be like a city upon a hill. The eyes of all people are upon us." He also proclaimed, "In all times some must be rich, some poor, some high and eminent in power and dignity; others mean and in subjection."[2] The self-righteous Puritan "Saints" banished and hanged Quakers and other "blasphemers" and considered Native Americans to be heathen savages.

Winthrop declared that Indian land could be taken because the Indians had not "subdued" the land and therefore had only a "natural right" to it, not a "civil right." A "natural right" had no legal standing in the colonial domain.[3] Native Americans lost their land and their lives. Today, less than 1 percent of the Dudley population—like that of the larger United States—is American Indian.

In 1747, King George's Royal Governor William Shirley, later the commander in chief of British forces in North America, erected a governor's mansion that still stands on the street bearing his name in the core of the Dudley neighborhood. The mansion was later the home of William Eustis, governor of the state of Massachusetts in the 1820s and secretary of war during the War of 1812 with Great Britain. The history of the neighborhood echoes in streets with names like Dudley, Shirley, Eustis and Winthrop.

DIVIDED DEVELOPMENT

For a long time, Roxbury was connected to largely waterlocked Boston by a narrow neck of land running—where Washington Street is now—between Back Bay and South Cove. Wealthy Bostonians built country estates and summer homes on the hilltops of Roxbury and North Dorchester. Around 1800, Amos Upham built a grocery store at the Dorchester junction of what is now Dudley Street and Columbia Road to serve those traveling by horse between their country homes and Boston. Today, that end of Dudley Street leads into the Uphams Corner commercial center.

As Boston grew, bays and other bodies of water were filled in and "the outlying districts became more accessible, the people spread out and at the same time were localized in distinctive areas...The more numerous middle-class found its outlet in the developing suburbs, first in the South End, where they forced out a small, poorer population, then in South Boston, and finally, in Roxbury and Dorchester...By 1845 residential areas were well fixed. The very wealthy either remained on Beacon Hill or moved to the rural suburbs, Roxbury or Cambridge. The middle classes scattered in the South Cove, in South Boston or in the outskirts. Finally, large districts were available at low rents in the North and West Ends."[4]

Roxbury's "geography divided the town's settlement into two parts: the highlands, the steep uplands south of Dudley Street; and lower Roxbury, the intown lowlands that stretch from the South End to Dudley Street."[5] The Roxbury highlands—bounded roughly by Dudley and Washington Streets and Blue Hill Avenue, with Franklin Park to the south—was an affluent community throughout the nineteenth century.

Roxbury's "first major development was from 1840 to 1870 when less expensive versions of Boston townhouses and detached single and two family houses were constructed along Dudley Street."[6] Dudley Street was an important traffic artery, running from Roxbury Crossing through Lower Roxbury to Uphams Corner in North Dorchester. Lower (northern) Roxbury was a New England mill town with textile mills, tanneries, lumber yards, printing firms, foundries and shops, and an increasingly Irish working-class community.

The Irish first immigrated in large numbers to Boston during Ireland's devastating potato famine and land evictions beginning in 1845. By 1880, Boston was home to almost 65,000 Irish immigrants, many of them Catholic peasants driven from the land.[7] In 1888, the Irish ascended to political power in Boston, electing a succession of Irish American mayors beginning with Hugh O'Brien and Rose Kennedy's father, John "Honey Fitz" Fitzgerald. The long-ruling Yankee elite known as the "Boston Brahmin" continued to dominate economically.

Roxbury was annexed to Boston in 1868; Dorchester followed a year later. Between 1870 and 1900, Roxbury experienced its greatest growth, with large-scale residential development, much of it lower-middle-class construction, as streetcar service—first horse-driven, then electric trolley—was extended into the area and the bays between Roxbury and the city of Boston were filled.[8]

The expansion of streetcar railway service enabled higher-income Bostonians to move further out of the city into increasingly class-segregated suburbs with larger lots of land for homes. By the 1890s, writes Sam Warner in *Streetcar Suburbs*, "the census showed the special suburban process of ethnic integration and income segregation. Early twentieth century observers called the inner suburbs the 'zones of emergence.' Here, first and second generation immigrant families moved from their original ethnic centers and began to take their place in the general life of the American middle class. In the 1870's and 1880's the Irish were Roxbury's largest emergent group. In the 1890's substantial numbers of Jews and Canadians began leaving the working class quarters of the old city."[9] Few Jews lived in Boston before the 1840s, when several hundred Germans immigrated. The Puritans had made clear that Jews, like Quakers, were not welcome. Beginning in the

1880s, some 75,000 Russian Jews, fleeing the anti-Semitic pogroms, settled in Boston.

A city of Boston profile of Roxbury notes that "Jewish families moved into the southern area replacing earlier residents who were predominantly Irish. At about the same time, black families first moved into the northern area."[10] For Black residents, Roxbury would become a zone of disinvestment.

Blacks have a long history in Boston. Some of Boston's earliest Black residents came in chains, others to find and fight for freedom. African slaves were in Boston at least as early as 1638 when a ship named *Desiré* brought them from Providence Island in the Bahamas. The New England slave trade increased in 1644 when an association of Boston "businessmen" sent three ships to Africa "for gold dust and Negroes."[11] Colonial Boston was also home to a smaller number of free Blacks. Bostian Ken, who owned a house and farm in Dorchester in 1656, was reportedly the first Black landowner in Massachusetts. Crispus Attucks, an escaped slave, became the first martyr of the American Revolution when he was killed by British soldiers in the Boston Massacre of 1770 while leading a group of colonists. Crispus Attucks Place is just below the intersection of Dudley and Washington Streets. Slavery was abolished in Massachusetts in 1780 with a Declaration of Rights added to the state constitution. In the early 1830s, the first American-born woman to lecture in public, Maria Stewart—also considered the United States' first Black political writer—championed the rights of Blacks and women from the pulpit of Boston's African Meeting House on Beacon Hill. The New England Anti-Slavery Society was founded there in 1832 and later hired the great abolitionist leader Frederick Douglass, who escaped from slavery in 1838; Douglass also became the nation's leading male proponent of women's rights.

Boston was reportedly the most segregated northern city in 1850. For much of the nineteenth century, most Blacks lived in parts of Beacon Hill and the West End; in 1865, according to census data—which historically undercounted the Black population, especially escaped slaves—only 83 Blacks lived in Roxbury and Dorchester.[12] During the Civil War, Boston's 54th Massachusetts regiment (immortalized in the film *Glory*) was the first Black unit organized in the North. Boston's ghetto conditions worsened in the late 1800s. Black men and women were largely restricted to domestic service, manual labor and the lowest-paid manufacturing jobs, whatever their skill and schooling.[13]

BOOM AND BUST

In the early twentieth century, the descendants of immigrants turned on the newest European immigrants in the area around Uphams Corner in Dorchester. In the words of a city profile, "With the coming of World War I, anti-immigrant feelings and the fear of everything foreign increased. With the influx of working class people moving into the triple-deckers [three-story, multifamily units], the disappearance of most vacant land, and the increase in immigrants, many of the older upper-middle class residents panicked in 1920, leaving for suburbs further to the south."

Still, the area around Uphams Corner, at the junction of five streetcar lines, flourished. The Strand Theatre opened in 1918 to wide acclaim as "New England's most beautiful theatre," featuring vaudeville performers and, later, first-run movies. During the 1920s, Cifrino's Market (later Uphams Corner Market and Elm Farm) was the world's first and, for many years, largest supermarket.[14]

St. Patrick's Church has been part of the changing Dudley neighborhood for over 100 years. The present church, an elaborate brick edifice on the crest of the hill at Dudley and Magazine Streets, was dedicated in 1891. The St. Patrick's parish, the third parish in the archdiocese of Boston, was founded just outside Dudley in 1836 by Irish immigrants. When the original wooden church was constructed on Northampton Street, parishioners guarded it from attack by members of the anti-Catholic, anti-immigrant Know-Nothing Party. A special 1986 issue of St. Patrick's paper, *The Patrician*, looked back on the history of the church and the Dudley neighborhood, calling it "a Rainbow of Catholic experience." The church "opened its doors sometimes widely, and sometimes with hesitance and caution to: the arrival and integration of Irish and Italian Catholics in 1920; the arrival and integration of Irish, Italian, and Black Catholics in the 1950s; the arrival and integration of Irish, Italian, Black and Hispanic Catholics in the 1960s; and the arrival and integration of Irish, Italian, Black, Hispanic, and Cape Verdean Catholics in the 1970s."[15]

Irish parishioner Tom Lyons recalled growing up in Dudley in the 1930s:

> Gaslight cast flickering shadows along our street. Trolleys—we called them streetcars—clanged back and forth to Dudley Station and we drank our Cherry Coke, milkshakes or frappes at a drugstore fountain...

Harrington's Market, Alice's Coffee Shop, Bill's Barbershop lined the block on Dudley St. across from the church. There were a fur shop and Kingsbury Press a few steps away toward Dudley Station. Honen's Drugstore at the corner of Dunmore and Hampden Streets and Freedman's Drug Store at Blue Hill and Mt. Pleasant Aves. served as bookends for the church, and growing up in Roxbury we spent many days and nights, doing what kids nowadays call "hanging out" in front of them.

If there is one word, one thought that rises above all, as the mind drifts back, it's the feeling that in Roxbury, in St. Patrick's Parish, there was a lot of caring for us young people from parents, priests, nuns, friends and neighbors.[16]

St. Patrick's parishioner Margarita Sturniolo, an Italian American, moved to Dudley in January 1921 and taught school for 40 years. Her Irish American friend Sophia McCarthy, also a St. Patrick's parishioner, moved to the neighborhood in the 1920s. McCarthy's family owned a grocery store. Sturniolo and McCarthy, both stalwart neighborhood activists, remember a thriving neighborhood with shops of all kinds, homes with flower gardens and good schools. And they remember when the neighborhood was burned, figuratively and literally, beginning in the 1950s.

"I was afraid that my house would go up in smoke," Sturniolo recalls. Most of her old friends are gone now, she says. "They either die off or they move away." The population in the Dudley core area* dropped by more than half between 1950 and 1980, when it leveled off. The 1990 core area population—based on a more precise census delineation of the neighborhood than that of earlier years—is 12,000. Dudley's White population plummeted after 1950, when it was 95 percent, to 79 percent in 1960, 45 percent in 1970 and 16 percent in 1980, including Whites of Hispanic origin. In 1990, the non-Hispanic White population was 7 percent.**

During the 1940s and 1950s, the mechanization of southern agriculture and mining displaced millions of people from their liveli-

---

* DSNI divides the neighborhood into core and secondary areas, as explained in Chapter Two (see earlier map). Because the smaller core area—with about half the Dudley population—is the primary focus of DSNI, census statistics refer to the core unless stated otherwise.

**Based on available census data, Black and White population figures for 1950-1980 include a small but growing number of White and Black Hispanics. Figures for 1990 distinguish non-Hispanic Whites and Blacks from Latinos.

hoods. Large numbers of African Americans migrated from the segregated South to northeastern cities like Boston, where discrimination was also rampant. Boston's population of color rose from 3 percent in 1940 (when nearly one out of four Boston residents was foreign-born) to 9 percent in 1960 and 16 percent in 1970.[17] Roxbury's racial composition shifted from majority White to predominantly Black. Malcolm X lived in Roxbury in the 1940s and, in 1954, he helped found Temple 11 on Intervale Street in the Dudley neighborhood. Within the Dudley core area, the Black population rose from 5 percent in 1950 to 20 percent in 1960 and 53 percent in 1970, including Blacks of Hispanic and Cape Verdean origin. In 1990, the non-Hispanic Black population was 50 percent, including Cape Verdeans.

"Excluded from the suburban jobs and housing," writes Mel King in his study of Black community development in Boston, Blacks faced job segregation "reinforced by educational segregation," housing segregation and "gerrymandering of the Black population in such a way as to assure that they had no political voice. This systematic denial of jobs, housing, education and political representation by the Boston power structure came to full development in the creation of the 'ghetto,' for the image of the ghetto allowed the ruling elite to blame the Black community for what they had systematically imposed upon us."[18]

Latinos and Cape Verdean immigrants became a significant part of the Dudley population during the 1960s and 1970s. According to a 1981 report, about half the Latinos who moved into Dudley came directly from Puerto Rico. A significant number were displaced from Boston's South End, as discussed below.[19] Dudley's Latino population more than doubled from 12 percent in 1970 to 28 percent in 1980 and about 30 percent in 1990. Today, a majority of Dudley's Latino residents are of Puerto Rican origin, followed by Dominican, then Honduran, Guatemalan, Cuban and Mexican.

Cape Verde is an island nation off the coast of West Africa that won independence from Portugal in 1975. Cape Verdean immigrants first arrived in Massachusetts, in the port of New Bedford—south of Boston—in the late eighteenth century. Most Cape Verdeans are Catholic, and by the mid-1960s, writes the Reverend Pio Gottin, "the new influx of Cape Verdean immigrants was supplanting the earlier Italian and Irish immigrants" within Dudley's St. Patrick's parish. "St. Patrick's is today the center of the Cape Verdean Apostolate of the Archdiocese of Boston as well as a point of reference for all Cape

Verdeans in New England."[20] Today, Cape Verdeans make up an estimated 25 percent of Dudley's core area population.[21]

Business directories show 1950-era Dudley Street and Blue Hill Avenue to be lined with residences, businesses, municipal buildings, union halls and social clubs. By 1970, address after address is listed vacant. The number of private businesses on Dudley Street (from Warren Street to the railroad tracks) dropped from 129 in 1950 to 79 in 1960, 49 in 1970 and 26 in 1980. On Blue Hill Avenue (from Dudley to Quincy Streets) the number fell from 210 in 1950 to 150 in 1960, 74 in 1970 and 47 in 1980.[22] As of 1993, there were about 32 businesses on Dudley Street and 28 on Blue Hill Avenue. Many of the businesses—now owned by Blacks, Latinos and Cape Verdeans as well as Whites—are small groceries, restaurants and auto-related enterprises.

SEGREGATED SUBURBANIZATION

White flight from Dudley and areas like it around the country was promoted by government policies that subsidized segregated suburbanization and disinvested in inner city communities. When Whites moved out, so did private and public investment in everything from schools and housing to business and street repair, creating a self-fulfilling prophecy of disinvestment and decay wrongly blamed on newcomer people of color.

As the twentieth century began, industry left cities to set up mass assembly plants where manufacturers could pay lower taxes and land prices and avoid labor unions. Federal policies to encourage suburban growth were strengthened in the 1930s in an effort to jump start the economy out of depression. The Federal Housing Administration (FHA) was created in 1934 to provide guaranteed mortgages for new construction. The "G.I. Bill" of 1944 provided Veterans Administration (VA) loan guarantees to subsidize home mortgages for returning veterans, almost all in suburbia—where most new wartime industrial capacity was also located. The FHA and VA programs insured about one-third of all homes purchased in the 1950s. Federal transportation spending was targeted to highway construction, favoring suburbia and the auto industry at the expense of urban mass transit.

The FHA and the real estate industry promoted racial segregation as the key to neighborhood stability and housing values. A report prepared for the FHA in 1933 ranked 15 racial and ethnic groups according to the impact of their presence on property values—values reflecting prejudice. English, Germans, Scotch, Irish and Scandinavians were classified as having the most favorable impact, "Negroes" and Mexicans the most detrimental.[23] In the FHA's 1938 *Underwriting Manual* for banks, one of the guidelines for loan officers read: "Areas surrounding a location are [to be] investigated to determine whether incompatible racial and social groups are present, for the purpose of making a prediction regarding the probability of the location being invaded by such groups...A change in social or racial occupancy generally contributes to instability and a decline in values."[24] Restrictive covenants were one means of stemming the "invasion."

"All through the 1930s and 1940s," explains political scientist Dennis Judd, "F.H.A. administrators advised and sometimes required developers of residential projects to draw up restrictive covenants against nonwhites as a condition of obtaining F.H.A.-insured financing. Since areas that were all black were considered even worse credit risks than mixed neighborhoods, the policy closed almost all African-Americans out of the federally insured market and excluded them from the new suburbs altogether."[25] One model restrictive covenant required that builders and lenders pledge that "no persons of any race other than [race to be inserted] shall use or occupy any building or any lot, except that this covenant shall not prevent occupancy by domestic servants of a different race domiciled with an owner or tenant."[26] The exception, needless to say, was not designed for hypothetical White servants of Black homeowners.

The U.S. Supreme Court ruled that racial covenants could not be enforced in the 1948 case of *Shelley v. Kraemer*, but de facto segregation continued. "Between 1946 and 1959, less than 2 percent of all the housing financed with the assistance of federal mortgage insurance was made available to blacks," writes Judd. "In 1960, not a single African-American could be counted among the 82,000 residents of Long Island's Levittown [New York]. The situation was typical."[27]

A 1968 National Commission on Urban Problems deplored the "tacit agreement among all groups—lending institutions, fire insurance companies, and FHA"—to "redline" inner city neighborhoods, denying them credit and insurance. The commission reported that up until the summer of 1967, "FHA almost never insured mortgages on homes in slum districts, and did so very seldom in the 'gray areas' which surrounded them. Even middle-class residential districts in the central cities were suspect, since there was always the prospect that they, too, might 'turn' as Negroes and poor whites" moved in.[28]

The 1977 edition of *The Appraisal of Real Estate*, published by the American Institute of Real Estate Appraisers, still included "prevailing nationalities, infiltration" among the criteria for assessing neighborhoods. Institute training materials provided this appraisal example: "The neighborhood is entirely Caucasian. It appears that there is no adverse effect by minority groups."[29]

As of 1989, Blacks accounted for only 7 percent of those living in the nation's suburbs, where real estate steering also reinforces segregation within suburbia. In 1991, 51 percent of Whites lived in the suburbs and only 26 percent in central cities. The majority of Blacks—56 percent—remained in central cities while only 27 percent lived in suburbs.[30] In 1960, per capita income was 5 percent higher in a sample of cities than in their surrounding suburbs. By 1987, suburban per capita income was 59 percent higher than in the cities.[31] Housing discrimination remains pervasive. According to a 1991 Department of Housing and Urban Development (HUD) report of fair housing testing audits in 25 U.S. cities, Blacks encounter discrimination more than half of the time.[32]

Segregated suburbanization took a toll on Boston and other cities as population and jobs moved away, leaving a weaker economy and tax base behind. In the 1950s, Route 128 around Boston became a suburban magnet for high-tech industries.[33] In 1929, Boston's per capita income exceeded that of the metropolitan area by over $2,200. The trend reversed in 1959 and, by 1980, the metro area's per capita income was nearly $1,500 greater (adjusting for inflation) than Boston's. "The City's economy lost much of its production capacity in textiles, leather, and food processing, and no substantial new manufacturing took its place," explains a Boston Redevelopment Authority report. "At the same time, much retail trade followed the population shifts to the suburbs" and the rise of shopping malls. The service industries, especially hospitals and universities, doubled their share of Boston's earned income to 29 percent. But there were not enough jobs and they often paid poorly.[34]

"As the wave of suburbanization...swept over the country," observes a city report, "Boston [was] sorely impacted, but Roxbury was devastated." Once an industrial center for food processing, apparel and leather goods, manufacturing employment in Roxbury dropped from over 20,000 jobs in 1947 to 4,000 jobs in 1981.[35] Many of Roxbury's manufacturing jobs are in the New Market Industrial Area, a portion of which is in Dudley. By 1980, Dudley's unemployment rate, then over

12 percent, was twice Boston's overall rate. The 2 to 1 ratio remained as Dudley's official unemployment rate topped 16 percent in 1990, not counting jobless people too discouraged to keep actively looking for work and those working part-time jobs only because they could not find full-time employment.

URBAN RENEWAL, URBAN REMOVAL

In an effort to meet rising expenses, increase tax revenues—a problem exacerbated by cities' large portion of tax-exempt educational, religious and other institutions—and reverse urban decline, Boston and other cities responded with massive urban renewal projects. City planners bulldozed lower-income neighborhoods in desirable locations to make way for office and retail complexes, large public buildings such as Boston's Government Center, and upscale housing and hotels. While many Whites made new homes in subsidized suburbia, inner city Blacks and Latinos, and low-income Whites, were hit by a wave of "slum clearance" urban renewal projects. Often, "slum clearance" meant the destruction of bustling racially mixed working-class neighborhoods and small businesses.

Instead of the "decent home and a suitable living environment for every American family," promised by the Housing Act of 1949, residents of low-income neighborhoods, including poor and elderly Whites, were often left with less housing, higher rents, fewer businesses and scarcer jobs than before. Segregation worsened as many dislocated Whites moved to blue-collar suburbs. Displaced Blacks typically had no choice, because of housing and economic discrimination, but to move into ghetto neighborhoods and ghettoized public housing.

Urban renewal got a bad reputation early in Boston when the working-class West End neighborhood was demolished to make room, in part, for luxury housing overlooking the Charles River. The 47-acre West End was home to a diverse population of Italian American (the largest ethnic group), Jewish, Polish, Irish, Black and other residents. A newspaper columnist called the West End a vice-ridden slum and a cesspool, typifying the view of the urban renewers.[36] "By the summer of 1960," writes Herbert Gans in *The Urban Villagers*, chronicling West End community life, "only rubble remained where two years ago had lived more than 7,000 people."[37] When the rubble became "first-class" housing, shopping and office space, it was out of reach for the former West Enders who had lost homes, jobs, businesses and strong social networks.[38] Where West Enders once lived, the Charles River Park complex advertises itself to commuters with the slogan: "If You Lived Here, You'd Be Home Now."

Under "New Boston" Mayor John Collins, Ed Logue became director of the Boston Redevelopment Authority (BRA) in 1960 with the backing of a group of city power brokers known as "The Vault." Called The Vault because it met in the boardroom of the Boston Safe Deposit and Trust Company, the group formed in 1959 with some 16 members, including the chief officers of the four largest commercial banks, two largest retailers, two largest industrial firms, the leading law firm, the city's public utility and the third largest insurance company.[39]

The BRA, established in 1957, was responsible for urban renewal and planning activities in the city. Logue produced "The 90 Million Dollar Development Program for Boston." The BRA's *1965-1975 General Plan for the City of Boston* stated that the policy of the Development Program is "to promote stability in the size of Boston's population while increasing the diversity of its composition so that it more nearly reflects the composition of the Region's population as a whole. This would, of course, entail a reversal of present trends towards increasing proportions of low-income groups and non-whites in the core City."[40] In 1970, Boston's population was 16 percent people of color, while the metropolitan area population—the program's "diversity" model—was only 6 percent.

Logue's BRA promised that neighborhoods would be rehabilitated with the input and without the displacement of existing residents. Mayor Collins asserted, "I would expect that neighborhood communities would have a key partnership role in the preparation and carrying out of renewal plans. I would call it planning *with* people instead of planning for people."[41] The problem, illustrated by Roxbury and South End urban renewal, is that the city wanted to plan *with* like-minded people, mainly middle-class homeowners, while planning displacement *for* low-income residents.

Roxbury's Washington Park Urban Renewal project received federal approval in 1963. Its boundaries were enlarged from 186 acres to 502 acres (bounded generally by Washington, Dudley, Warren and Seaver Streets) after a 1961 BRA study concluded that over half the residential homes in the original smaller area should be demolished. Since that was far above the clearance level seen as politically viable after the destruction of the West End, the Washington Park boundaries were extended southward to include sounder housing between Townsend Street and Franklin Park, thus diluting the overall demolition percentage (to a still-high 35 percent) without reducing clearance in the original target area. The Washington Park area was 71 percent Black and 29 percent White in 1960. Poor Blacks were not invited to participate in Washington Park urban renewal planning. They were considered the "blighting influence" whose removal was part of the renewal process strongly supported by many middle-class Blacks. Numerous low-rent dwellings were eliminated without replacement. Of those displaced, 1,275 families and hundreds of individuals were eligible for public housing, but the only publicly aided housing included in the renewal area were 200 units for the elderly.[42]

Logue called Washington Park "the most successful of our renewal programs, and the one that caused the least grief."[43] A later report by the BRA and the Roxbury Planning and Zoning Advisory Committee commented, "the Urban Renewal process was a negative experience for the residents of Roxbury. The legacy left by Urban Renewal is the scars of vacant land, abandoned buildings, a fear of displacement and gentrification, and a fear of lack of control over the future of one's own community."[44]

When DSNI began in the 1980s, members often voiced the sentiment, "We don't want to be another South End." The South End Urban Renewal Plan was adopted in 1965. The South End was developed from 1850 to 1875 on partially filled land and, in the words of a city profile, "it was briefly a genteel enclave before attracting immigrant workers finding work nearby," beginning with the Irish. "By the turn of the century, the South End had become the largest lodging house district in the United States." It "gained a reputation as a haven for 'dens of vice'...In 1898, South End social worker Robert Woods coined the term 'the city wilderness' to describe the district. Although still containing a working class family population, most Bostonians associated the area with alcoholism, prostitution, and drug traffic." Continuing a historical pattern, the outsiders' stereotype of "vice-ridden slums" masked the vitality and diversity of multiracial working-class communities. "After its first 100 years," the South End profile continues, "the relative harmony in this neighborhood of gracious but decaying brick bowfronts and rowhouses was shattered by three powerful external forces: the construction of the Prudential Center on adjoining railyards, urban renewal, and an awakening of new interest in inner city neighborhoods."[45]

At the time of urban renewal, the South End was one of Boston's only multiracial, multiethnic neighborhoods. It was also its densest and poorest, with mostly pre-1900 housing, much of it needing renovation. The South End's location, a few minutes' walk from downtown, and rows of tree-shaded brownstones made it a potential gold mine of gentrification by the so-called "urban pioneers." As political scientist John Mollenkopf writes, "Though redlined in the 1950s, it did not take a real estate genius to see that with financing and rehabilitation loan funds, the South End's 'faded elegance' had tremendous market potential."[46]

Although a goal of the Boston General Plan quoted above was "a reversal of present trends towards increasing proportions of low-income groups and non-whites," city planners could not, in Mollenkopf's words, "acknowledge to those about to be displaced, or perhaps even to themselves, that they were engaged in highly regressive social engineering. Renewal entrepreneurs resolved this bind largely by denying it. Official agency plans systematically underestimated the likely displacement and overestimated housing alternatives for those displaced." They "thus made many promises which by their nature were bound to be broken."[47]

The BRA's original plan was modified in consultation with neighborhood institutions and homeowner associations in the South End Urban Renewal Committee. Residents in the Castle Square area, for example, won an increase in the number of low-income units to be constructed, with residents getting first priority. But neighborhood tensions rose as the BRA's demolition work outstripped its promises of relocation and affordable housing. The tension wasn't over whether to renew the South End, but how and for whom. Three new groups struggled to gain more community control: the South End Tenants Council, which spawned the Tenants Development Corporation to successfully rehabilitate housing; the Emergency Tenants Council, later called Inquilinos Boricuas en Acción (Puerto Rican Tenants in Action); and an umbrella group, Community Assembly For a United South End (CAUSE), whose bylaws specified a membership of 60 percent tenants, mirroring the South End population.

Through a range of actions, including demonstrations and negotiations, these groups were able to win some important battles while losing the war against urban removal. On April 26, 1968, just a few weeks after the assassination of Martin Luther King Jr., CAUSE members took over the BRA's South End site office and blocked Mayor Kevin

White from entering. One of CAUSE's leaders was educator and community organizer Mel King, a lifelong South End resident and future state representative and Boston mayoral candidate. King writes that two days later, he and other CAUSE members "approached the Fitz-Inn parking lot bounded by Dartmouth, Columbus and Yarmouth Streets, directly across from my house. The lot was the site of a choice parcel of land which had been earmarked for development by the BRA. Its sound, handsome brick row houses had been razed, and the lots paved for parking, until its resale value would net enough profit to suit its owner." One hundred families were dislocated. The site was a "symbol of all we have been fighting against for so long." The demonstrators blocked the site, and after 23 were arrested, community support grew and a spontaneous "Tent City" emerged.[48] After 20 more years of battles with city government, a mixed-income development was finally built on the site, with two-thirds of its units affordable to low- and moderate-income tenants. It is called Tent City.

The South End had become home for Boston's Latino community when Puerto Ricans began to settle there in the 1950s. After more than five years of struggle, the BRA, then led by Hale Champion, granted the Emergency Tenants Council the right to develop the 30-acre Parcel 19, where many Puerto Ricans lived. It was, says Mel King, "the first housing construction program in the nation to be developed and controlled by a community group on such a large scale."[49] In 1973, the Emergency Tenants Council, committed to moving beyond "building housing to building community," restructured itself as the tenant-controlled Inquilinos Boricuas en Acción (IBA). IBA developed Parcel 19 into Villa Victoria, a housing complex with a community plaza, commercial development and social services. Today, writes Miren Uriarte of the Mauricio Gastón Institute for Latino Community Development and Public Policy at the University of Massachusetts at Boston, Villa Victoria is "the symbolic center of Boston's Latino community," but "the gentrification of the South End and the rise in the cost of housing" have made the larger South End neighborhood "inaccessible as a permanent settling place for Latinos."[50]

As BRA demolition went forward, abandonment and private market rehabilitation removed many more low-rent units from the housing stock. Between 1960 and 1980, an estimated 25,000 people relocated from the South End while 19,000 newcomers moved in, many of them White young professionals. Though still multiracial, by 1985 the South End was a microcosm of polarization with both gentrification and deepening poverty, trendy restaurants and hunger and homeless-ness. The South End's median income (half earn below the median, half earn above it) was higher than the city's, but so was its unemployment rate, and one-third of all families in the South End lived in poverty. The lodging houses were supplanted by condominiums. At the start of South End urban renewal, the shells of South End row houses could be purchased for as little as $5,000 while solid structures sold for about $20,000. By 1979, the average property value had increased to $110,000 and, in 1985, it was $320,000, almost triple the city average.[51] Dudley resident Sophia McCarthy remembers when the South End was full of boarding houses where people with limited income could rent a decent room. "Now they have no place!...No wonder they have street people."

By the end of Ed Logue's tenure at the BRA, development projects involving about 3,223 acres of city land "had demolished 9,718 low-rent units while constructing only 3,504 new units, of which only 982 were federally subsidized. Some twenty-two-thousand low-income individuals were thus displaced...[Logue] also built the BRA from a staff of seventeen and a budget of $250,000 into a 700-strong parallel government with an annual cash flow of $25 million by the time he left in 1967."[52]

Mollenkopf observes that neighborhood activism of the 1960s and 1970s "ended large-scale clearance projects, drastically revised traditional planning practices by creating citizen review and participation procedures, and created a new policy emphasis on preservation and rehabilitation." However, "just as neighborhoods had won some influence over" urban development programs, "the Nixon administration began its onslaught against them...From 1973 to 1975, economic recession and Nixon's New Federalism pushed subsidized housing projects toward bankruptcy, halted the construction of additional projects, terminated urban renewal, and made it impossible for local agencies and officials to deliver on their promises."[53] Even if they wanted to.

Reagan's and Bush's New Federalism made Nixon's look like liberalism. Appropriations for HUD's subsidized housing programs dropped 81 percent, after adjusting for inflation, between fiscal years 1978 and 1991. By 1989, only one out of three of the 7.5 million renters with incomes below the official poverty line received a rental subsidy from any governmental housing program or lived in public housing. Meanwhile, there was a sharp increase in federal housing subsidies that primarily benefit middle- and upper-income families, namely mortgage interest and property tax deductions. In fiscal year 1990, direct spending on federal low-income housing assistance programs totaled $18.3 billion. More than four times as much was spent through the tax code in the form of homeowner deductions, amounting to some $78.4 billion, disproportionately benefiting those with higher incomes.[54]

RISING POVERTY IN THE "NEW BOSTON"

Under urban renewal and other programs, the cities—drained of manufacturing jobs as corporations sought cheaper labor and land, lower taxes and greater government subsidies elsewhere—redeveloped their downtowns to serve the private and public service sector: finance, insurance, real estate (together abbreviated as FIRE, which was appropriate for the Dudley neighborhood), law, advertising, management consulting, hospitals, universities, etc. By 1985, only 8 percent of Boston's workers were employed in manufacturing and the majority worked in services.[55] The service economy is increasingly polarized between relatively few high-income earners and many earning low wages, often in dead-end jobs. So too, the cities are being polarized between affluent professionals and the poor employed, underemployed and unemployed.

In the words of a BRA report, "By 1985, Boston's downtown area had achieved a high degree of economic health and vitality." However, "the benefits of rejuvenation did not spread throughout the city. A premise of the 'New Boston' movement was that the benefits of private investment would flow to all of Boston. On the contrary, Boston in 1985, had persistent poverty, pockets of unemployment, and a serious shortage of decent, affordable housing units." The official poverty rate rose from 16 percent in 1970 to 20 percent in 1980; one out of every four families with children under 18 lived in poverty. In 1984, the White poverty rate was 13 percent, while 29 percent of Blacks, 40 percent of Asians and 50 percent of Latinos lived below the official poverty line. Many working poor had jobs paying too little to provide an adequate standard of living. "Unemployment and underemployment continued to plague willing and able adults," reported the BRA, "especially minorities and teenagers." Boston's overall official unemployment rate was 6 percent in 1980 and 1985, but the rate for people of color rose from 9 percent to 12 percent—four times higher than the White unemployment rate.

"Private investment flowed to commercial projects or to luxury rental condominium units and 'market rate' units that were beyond the means of much of Boston's population," the BRA report observed. "In too many instances, downtown investment, its new jobs, and its related pressure on a limited housing stock displaced neighborhood residents who could not keep up with rising rents." The result was deeper poverty and homelessness.[56] Boston's median monthly contract rent shot up 25 percent, after adjusting for inflation, between 1980 and 1985. It increased 47 percent in the South End, 50 percent in Mattapan and 15 percent in Roxbury.[57]

In 1985, Blacks represented 21 percent of the resident Boston workforce, but only 12 percent of professional, technical and managerial employees—with an average full-time weekly wage of $359—and 34 percent of service workers, earning an average $161; Latinos were 4 percent of professional, managerial and technical employees and 10 percent of service workers. Black-owned firms with paid employees accounted for less than 1 percent of the total business establishments in Boston and tended to be small, with 6 employees average per firm compared to the city average of 24 employees. There were only a handful of firms in such fields as finance, insurance, real estate and wholesale trade. As a BRA report explains, Black and other "minority-owned businesses have played key roles in residential development and small commercial projects in neighborhood commercial districts. However, the bulk of development in Boston has been large office, hotel and retail projects carried out by White-owned businesses."[58]

REDLINING, BLOCKBUSTING AND LOAN-SHARKING

As urban renewal removed lower-income people from areas where the city was investing, continued disinvestment strangled the redlined neighborhoods where most people of color lived, or could move to. Redlining is the practice by which lenders and insurers brand certain neighborhoods as areas where they will not lend or supply insurance—or, more subtly, offer loans and insurance only at exorbitant premiums and interest rates. Redlining denies residents, however qualified, the mortgages, insurance, home-improvement and home-equity loans so essential for a secure home and retirement. College educations are often financed by the kind of home-equity loans absent in redlined areas. Loans and insurance needed for the start-up, expansion and protection of local businesses are also denied.

As Charles Finn, the author of an important study of mortgage lending for the Boston Redevelopment Authority, puts it, "Banks, as an important source of capital, play a pivotal but often invisible role in determining whether a community will thrive or decline...Mortgage and construction lending decisions are often made based upon expectations about neighborhood growth or decline—expectations about risk. Thus, banks' expectations of neighborhood growth or decline often become reality—a 'self-fulfilling prophecy.' Without a steady flow of credit, neighborhoods deteriorate. Economic opportunities for residents of these neighborhoods are reduced, even during periods of economic growth. During periods of economic decline, disinvested neighborhoods suffer disproportionately."[59]

The Dudley area was affected not only by typical redlining, elaborated later, but by a reverse form of redlining through which, for a short period, mortgages *were* made available for Blacks, but only in specific areas of Roxbury, Dorchester and Mattapan. The program was known as BBURG (Boston Banks Urban Renewal Group), a bank consortium created at city behest in 1963 to provide FHA-insured home ownership and rehabilitation loans in and around the Washington Park Urban Renewal Project. BBURG took on a new size and significance in 1968 when it opened a mortgage-processing office on Warren Street.

A 1979 BRA report observes, "[BBURG] loans to low income homeowners in the early 1970's, current bank requirements for FHA insured mortgages and unwillingness of banks to give conventional mortgages have adversely affected [the Dudley neighborhood] by discouraging middle income homeowners. Furthermore, the change in racial/ethnic composition, although gradual, has contributed to the perception of realtors and bankers that the Dudley neighborhood is not viable financially, thus further promoting disinvestment. The result of these attitudes has been the demise of a good portion of residential structures through abandonment."[60]

Authors Hillel Levine and Lawrence Harmon explain what happened under BBURG: "Under the guise of expanding homeownership opportunities for the city's black community, the heads of twenty-two Boston savings banks were complicit in establishing a carefully limited and well-defined inner-city district within which, and only within which, blacks could obtain the attractive, federally insured housing loans....Incredibly, the area selected for heightened loan activity skirted the predominantly Irish and Italian working-class neighborhoods and, less surprisingly, the suburbs where the bankers themselves lived. Falling exclusively within the B-BURG line, however, was almost the entirety of Boston's Jewish community, an unprofitable neighborhood for the city's bankers because so many of the residents had paid off their mortgages."[61]

In 1960, there were still about 7,500 Jews living in the neighborhood above Franklin Park later subject to Washington Park urban renewal and tens of thousands more in Dorchester and Mattapan. "By forcing blacks with homeownership aspirations to compete in a limited geographic area, the B-BURG bankers created an eruption of panic selling, blockbusting, street violence, and rage," write Levine and Harmon. In much of Roxbury, Dorchester and Mattapan, "more than fifty years of Jewish settlement were overturned during a two-year period from 1968 to 1970. Jews sold their homes to unscrupulous speculators for less than market value while blacks, eager to participate in the 'American Dream,' were forced to pay inflated prices."[62]

An anonymous realtor described for a real estate journal how blockbusting was used in the late 1960s. White fright was orchestrated into White flight and "whole areas went from white to black in a matter of months."

> I first heard about blockbusting when I decided I wanted to buy and sell property in Dorchester...
>
> We were told, you get the listings any way you can. It's pretty easy to do: just scare the hell out of them! And that's what we did.
>
> We were not only making money, we were having fun doing what we were doing...we would try to outdo each other with the most outlandish threats that people would believe, and chuckle about them at the end of the day. Some of the milder things were: property values are going down, you're going to get a thousand dollars less next month than this. Market values really didn't decline that much. They did decline slightly, but the thousand dollars a month, or whatever figure you picked—that was something you pulled out of the air....
>
> We weren't subtle about it. You'd say, how would you like it if they rape your daughter, and you've got a mulatto grandchild?...I even used it once on a son, the little boy would get raped. Whatever worked, I would try to use...
>
> I had direct contact with people who were more blatant than I ever dreamed of being. There were instances of housebreaks that were arranged only to scare people out....I don't think anybody to this day is aware that anybody arranged this. Nobody was ever arrested for it, convicted of it, or anything else...

What we did back then, I don't really consider that bad. We hurt people who were asking to be hurt...It was their idea to run. We fueled the fire. In my own defense, I lived in Dorchester and sold the house next door to a black family, and then I lived there for the next five years. The black family left, though, after the white kids in the neighborhood got together and stoned their house night after night.[63]

FHA "windshield inspections" would hurt sellers by undervaluing good properties being bought by speculators and hurt buyers by overvaluing rundown properties. A 1971 survey found that 65 percent of the houses sold under the BBURG program needed major repairs within two years of purchase. Negligence was compounded with corruption. The head FHA appraiser for Boston, Joseph Kenealy, was accused by the Justice Department in 1971 of having "blatantly engineered" appraisals to enrich himself and his family who were heavily involved in speculation through property and mortgage deals.[64]

For many Blacks, the American dream became a nightmare. As Levine and Harmon explain, "B-BURG buyers were far more likely to lose their homes through foreclosure and abandonment than to realize capital gains on their purchases. With little or no down payment, the new buyers enjoyed no equity. For those who had difficulty meeting mortgage and upkeep costs and who had no reserves to cover the needed repairs that inefficient or corrupt FHA appraisers had failed to report, it was often more prudent to walk away than to persevere." Later studies revealed that "more than one-half of all B-BURG purchasers would lose their homes by 1974. The effect on the city's black community would be devastating." The bankers, meanwhile, made money on mortgage-processing fees while passing on all the costs of foreclosure to the federal government.[65]

In the mid-1970s, Congress responded to the crisis of redlining and disinvestment with the 1975 Home Mortgage Disclosure Act, the 1976 Equal Credit Opportunity Act and the 1977 Community Reinvestment Act. As the Finn report for the BRA explains, "The ultimate effects of restricted credit availability on neighborhoods, it was generally agreed, are physical neighborhood decline, reduced housing values, crime, and reduced opportunities for socioeconomic mobility." The Community Reinvestment Act "emphasizes the continuing, affirmative obligation of federally-regulated banks to meet the credit needs of the communities in which they do business, including minority and low- and moderate-income neighborhoods. It does not ask banks to make risky loans. Rather, it requires fair banking practices."[66]

Practices remained unfair. Banks around the country continued discriminating and disinvesting while federal bank regulators rubber stamped their supposed compliance with the Community Reinvestment Act for more than two decades.[67] Between 1978 and 1988, banks closed 40 percent of their branch offices in Roxbury, Dorchester and Mattapan while adding branches in White areas of Boston. A 1989 survey found that Boston's 12 largest lending institutions had five times more offices in White areas than in predominantly Black or Latino areas with the same total population.[68]

Finn's study for the BRA found that between 1981 and 1987, mortgage lending by banks in Boston neighborhoods—using city Neighborhood Statistical Areas—"demonstrates a pattern of marked racial disparity. Comparing neighborhoods with similar median family incomes, the ratio of mortgage loans per 1,000 housing units in white and minority neighborhoods was 2.9 to 1." The lending gap increased to 3.4 to 1 when government-guaranteed mortgage loans were subtracted. The Neighborhood Statistical Areas with the lowest and second-lowest lending levels overall were Dudley/Brunswick-King (with 17 loans per 1,000 housing units) and Sav-Mor (25 loans per 1,000 units), which encompass a large section of the Dudley neighborhood.* The citywide average was 70 loans per 1,000 units. The average number of loans in neighborhoods with a majority of people of color—including the former BBURG areas—was 35, while the average number of loans in White neighborhoods with comparable incomes was 102.[69]

The Finn study also found that "while banks appear to be reluctant to lend in minority neighborhoods, where housing is relatively affordable, they clearly participated in and facilitated the wave of condominium conversion that Boston experienced in the 1980's. In lower-income white neighborhoods bank mortgage capital has gone overwhelmingly to those neighborhoods with high levels of rental-to-condominium conversions—the city's gentrifying neighborhoods. Rental-to-condominium conversion has eroded Boston's affordable rental stock and displaced many families unable to afford a condominium unit."[70] During the early 1980s, the market converted an average of "nearly 2,700 private apartments that were formerly affordable rentals, into over 2,700

---

* The Finn study compared 60 Boston Neighborhood Statistical Areas (NSAs). The Dudley/Brunswick-King NSA is bounded by Blue Hill Avenue, Magazine Street, the railroad tracks and Washington Street. The adjacent Sav-Mor NSA is bounded by Blue Hill Avenue, Dudley Street and Warren Street.

condos, dwarfing all assistance efforts to create more affordable housing." In 1985, "there were 4,525 conversions, more than during the entire decade of the 1970s."[71]

A 1991 Federal Reserve Board study, analyzing 1990 Home Mortgage Disclosure Act (HMDA) data, found racial lending disparities around the country, with Blacks and Latinos rejected twice as often as White applicants, regardless of income. The Boston lending gap was 3 to 1. A crucial 1992 report by the Boston Federal Reserve that systematically controlled for the largest range of financial, employment and other lending variables confirmed the widespread bias that the banks had kept trying to rationalize away. The report (discussed more fully in Chapter Six) found that Blacks and Latinos "were two to three times as likely to be denied mortgage loans as whites. In fact, high-income minorities in Boston were more likely to be turned down than low-income whites."[72]

Adding to the discriminatory picture, some of the same banks denying conventional mortgages and home-improvement loans in predominantly Black neighborhoods were colluding with con-artist contractors who provided financing for repair work at sky high interest rates of 24, even 40 percent. Second mortgages were taken out with or without the homeowners' approval—using tactics such as hiding second mortgage agreements in a stack of contracts and loan documents or forging signatures—and the contractors then sold the loans to banks. To keep their homes, owners then had to pay the extortionist loans even when, as was often the case, the repair work was shoddy or never completed. Many lost their homes to foreclosure before the scam became a public scandal in 1991. Some of the banks benefiting from the loan-sharking cited their purchase of second mortgages in minority communities as evidence they were fulfilling the mandates of the Community Reinvestment Act.[73]

As for insurance redlining, a 1993 congressional hearing documented its continued role. "Insurance is the invisible key to economic advancement," observed Rep. Joseph Kennedy, whose district includes a portion of Dudley. "The industry has used it to lock tight the door of economic opportunity for millions of consumers. The evidence presented to this Subcommittee clearly suggests a pattern of massive, nationwide discrimination against low-income and minority Americans...The message that insurance companies are sending to low-income and minority consumers is crystal clear: you are irresponsible, you are dangerous, and you don't deserve insurance. Solely because of the color of their skin, the size of their paycheck, and the address of their home, millions of Americans must pay more in premiums for less coverage, take their chances with shadowy unregulated and underfunded companies, or go without any insurance at all and face financial disaster as a daily fact of life."[74] Racist redlining and government irresponsibility has endangered inner city residents and communities.

TRASHED AND BURNED

"Most of the problems of Roxbury today," Sam Warner wrote in 1962, "are not primarily housing problems, but the problems of urban society as a whole. The houses of Roxbury are but vestiges of an earlier, rapidly changing society which built to the measure of the moment and then left its remains for others to use as best they could."[75] As best they could in the face of redlining and other disinvestment and discrimination.

In the words of a BRA report, Roxbury, North Dorchester and Mattapan, "Boston's principal neighborhoods of concentration of minorities,...experienced an exaggerated version of the city's era of throw-away housing, flowing from the population loss and the outflow of industry and jobs, 1950-1980, and an inequitable property tax system, in operation until 1983, with significantly higher effective tax rates for poorer neighborhoods. The result was large-scale housing abandonment and attrition."[76]

Arson is another factor. DSNI board member Bob Haas, formerly an engineer working for a Route 128 corporation, bought his home in the Uphams Corner area in 1970. He recalls what it was like to look across the railroad tracks deeper into the Dudley neighborhood and see houses burning: "They were burning down very quickly. You could go up after dinner onto the roof of this house and watch them burn down just any night you wanted to watch. And it was scary because the sparks would blow right over from these fires and we [feared] that sooner or later one of [our] houses would catch. But I was interested also in the underlying causes of this kind of thing. What could...make it so that so many houses had burned down so quickly when [so] many people needed housing?"

A 1985 report by the City of Boston Arson Prevention Commission outlined "three socio-economic matrixes for arson." The "Appreciating Matrix in which the value of property in an area is increasing in relation to the incomes of traditional residents" corresponds to urban renewal/redevelopment areas. "This creates economic pressure for the dislocation of lower income residents. A classic example of this is the conversion of a rooming house to condominiums. A fire is of financial benefit to the developer under these circumstances because: 1) it drives out low-income residents without the cost of waiting for attrition and without the potential political resistance to mass evictions, 2) it does the work of gutting the building for rehabilitation, 3) insurance provides tax-free, interest-free financing for the rehabilitation of the structure."

In 1981, Roxbury's Highland Park neighborhood was dubbed "The Arson Capital of the Nation." Most of the fires, the Arson Commission notes, "were directly related to increased speculation due to the Southwest Corridor Project," the massive redevelopment project centered around the relocated mass transit Orange Line (which used to run through Dudley Station) and extending from the South End through Roxbury and Jamaica Plain. The Arson Commission says, "Many of the buildings that were burned were among the approximately 75 abandoned buildings that local residents attempted to save for low-income housing and community-based activities. When frightened residents, ignored then by Mayor [Kevin] White, appealed" to the state for assistance, they "learned that Highland Park's fire statistics were the highest in the Commonwealth."

"The second socio-economic matrix for arson is the Depreciating Matrix," explains the Arson Commission. "This is characterized by the long-term erosion of mortgage availability and the exodus of stable-income residents. This leads to a steady decline in property values and a sense of entrapment for the remaining residents. Often, depreciating areas reflect a sense of racial or class 'frontier' moving towards them. In these areas, arson is an easy solution to the problem of declining housing values and services." A solution, that is, for absentee landlords and residents and businesses willing and able to burn their way out of neighborhoods like Dudley.

The Arson Commission's third matrix is the "Tension Matrix," which is "characterized by sustained struggle between appreciating and depreciating forces. In these areas, long-term low- and moderate-income residents are impacted by declining housing values and services for them, while, at the same time, profits are made in housing speculation aimed at outside moderate- to high-income people. In this matrix, we find both 'rehabilitation' fires and 'selling to the insurance company' fires."[77]

A detailed BRA examination of the Dudley portion of the Dudley/Brunswick-King Neighborhood Statistical Area showed the devastation of housing in the area. In 1973, over 57 percent of the housing units in the center of the Dudley neighborhood required repairs in excess of $1,000, an enormous sum for an area where well over a third of the families earned less than $5,000 a year. Between 1947 and 1976, 2,200 housing units in 648 buildings were demolished, wiping out nearly half of the 1947 housing stock. Because of the relatively high taxes and the difficulty Dudley homeowners had in getting home-improvement financing for their aging houses and would-be owners had in getting mortgages, Dudley has seen a rise in abandonment, absentee-owned buildings and vacant lots.

As the BRA report explains it, "These absentee landlords have the financial capability to purchase properties with cash. A large number of these absentee landlords are real estate trusts whose trustees live outside of Boston. The majority of these absentee landlords have been receiving rents from their tenants without either bringing these properties up to the Housing Code or paying their taxes. Although there are presently few City owned buildings in the area there are many vacant parcels which belong to the City. By the time the City of Boston has been able to acquire these buildings through the lengthy foreclosure process only a badly vandalized, often burnt shell remains." The annual demolition rate rose from 6.9 structures during 1947-59, to 27.8 structures during 1960-69 and 40 structures per year during 1970-76. Between 1970 and 1975, 735 housing units were lost while new construction brought only 187 units (structures may have multiple units).

The result then was approximately 840 vacant lots covering 177 acres of land in the heart of the Dudley neighborhood. "Abandonment, if allowed to proceed unchecked," warned the BRA report, "can spread like cancer, taking whole city blocks."[78] The "cancer" continued to spread.

Dudley's weedy wasteland of vacant lots became a dumping ground for trash, a breeding ground for rats and a hiding place for criminal activity. "Often the most pervasive dumping has been done by City contractors," the BRA report stated. As the land once used for housing was allowed to become wasteland, so too were the parks and playgrounds. "There is a scarcity of adequate recreational facilities in terms of staff, programs, equipment and maintenance in the Dudley area," the report noted. Denison House, "which provided some after-school programs for youth, burned down in the fall of 1975." The Mary Hannon Playground "is in shambles."[79]

"THAT NEIGHBORHOOD DOESN'T MATTER"

Paul Bothwell bucked the White flight trend and moved to Dudley from the South End in 1976. He worked in the ministry of an evangelical Baptist church and became immersed in neighborhood affairs. The more involved he became, the more he saw that communities don't just deteriorate by themselves. "It's not something that's just sheer chance. It's not because people are stupid," says Bothwell. "This was really part of much, much larger forces that are at work and they may or may not be consciously malicious...This is the result of city policy, of other kinds of large-scale things that systematically cripple or dismember a community." Some neighborhoods are "fed." Others are bled.

Bothwell recalls what it was like to try to help people get bank loans when redlining was "in full force and explicit." The bankers would say, "Listen. Banks would be fools to invest money in that neighborhood to these kind of people...That's not what banks are for." Bothwell adds, "They didn't seem to [have] any huge guilt in saying that to us." He found it to be infuriating, demeaning and devastating.

Bothwell saw buildings burn and the land empty. He remembers the April 1976 four-alarm fire that destroyed four buildings on Dennis Street and damaged seven others on Stafford Street and Blue Hill Avenue. Arson was suspected in the abandoned building where the fire started.[80] Bothwell says, "The streets were just crawling with people saying, 'Hey! What in the world are we going to do now? Where are we going to go now?'"

Bothwell and a small group of residents began meeting together to address immediate problems, such as getting a quicker response from the Fire Department, and the longer-range problem of housing. They knew that residents couldn't do it alone and "began to shape proposals for what might be ways in which we, the community, could team up with the city." They focused on a triangle area bounded by Dudley, Blue Hill and West Cottage. "That's the farthest that any of us could even hope for or focus on...That area was becoming increasingly burned down and vacant...There was this desperate sense of 'How could we preserve what's still here?' And then later, 'How could we do something about renewing or rebuilding this vacant land?' Our initial attempts to go to the city with some of these proposals were just laughed at."

With the city, says Bothwell, "There was the sense of '17 years from now, you're scheduled for urban renewal,' which was going on in the South End at that time. They were always tearing things down...They never would take us seriously...We were trying...to figure out some way to build some sort of a land trust...that would place control of the land in the hands of community people...I think the city, either as a stall or whatever, said, 'Listen. As long as you're talking about land...' They thought we were talking about gardening and that kind of stuff. They hooked us up with the U.S. Department of Agriculture to have somebody work on agricultural issues." Fortunately, says Bothwell, the Agriculture Department contact "had a good head on him and a real vision for rebuilding communities and neighborhoods. He began to meet with us regularly [and] help us to formulate a plan." He also provided small amounts of funding to facilitate the planning.

Bothwell and about ten others worked on the project for some two years. Every six months or so they'd have a community meeting at the Jesus Helps Church. The city, says Bothwell, moved from neglect to being "clearly and openly resistant to working with us." The residents finally had a meeting with city officials to present their plans and propose a partnership. "This guy from the Department of Agriculture was with us...It was really doable, we thought. They listened and listened. Then they started to laugh—literally. They just laughed...One of them stood up and...he says, 'This city don't make partnerships with nobody! We don't need partnerships! We don't make partnerships! We do what we want to do and we'll do it in our time!' It was that up front."

When people heard what happened at the next community meeting "they were just really in a rage," says Bothwell. "Enough people had invested enough in this process at that point that they really owned it, they had some blood involved in it...Discouragement is understating it. There was a sense of fatalism, kind of like, 'Hey, we should have known this all along...This is what this city is like.' So that, I think, was quite a significant turning point, at least in mentality, for what was possible and what was not."

Still, Bothwell and the others tried to enlist city support. "We said, 'All right, okay. No partnership.' We were really crawling on our knees. No partnership. Just help us out!...They as much as said, 'That neighborhood doesn't matter to us. What's going on there doesn't matter.'"

Blocked on the housing front, Bothwell and the others tried in desperation to turn some of the vacant land along Dennis Street into a big soccer field. They asked the city to close off part of Winthrop Street, which was "burned out, vacant, devastated, everybody dumping their trash there and everything else...The city stalled and hemmed and hawed and went round and round and sent people out to look and [said] they had to do some more studying on it. We'd push them and push them. Finally, the decision was no, they weren't going to close the street because they don't close streets for nobody. 'If we start doing this for you, somebody else somewhere is going to want the street closed to make this or that! We're going to have this city all chopped up into pieces because everybody wants streets closed!' Nobody used the street. It's covered with a thousand tons of sheet rock and metal and everything the trucks have dumped there, but they're not going to close the street. And they wouldn't let you do anything without it officially closing." At that point, Bothwell's group lost hope. "It was like this sense of having no allies. People were really powerless."

A 1979 BRA report asserted, "The Dudley neighborhood is typical of many lower income areas in that City services are inadequate, in part, because of the lack of a well organized community." The report continued, "Apathy seems pervasive among both residents and those responsible for street cleaning and garbage collecting. A cleanliness and hygiene campaign should be undertaken to raise neighborhood consciousness about trash and debris disposal stressing how residents, street cleaners and garbage collectors can all cooperate and contribute towards a better looking neighborhood." In even more condescending fashion, the report encouraged the formation of neighborhood associations, saying, "In order to form such organizations members of these neighborhoods must be committed and willing to come to meetings as well as convince others to join."[81]

It was the city, not residents, which had disinvested in the neighborhood and was unwilling to commit to its improvement. That would change in the 1980s with the creation of the Dudley Street Neighborhood Initiative.

Sophia McCarthy (l) and Margarita Sturniolo (r) taking a break during a DSNI community planning meeting at the Shirley-Eustis House, May 1989.

Left: Jessie Farrier and Adalberto Teixeira (behind) at DSNI's salute to Gus Newport at the Strand Theatre, April 1992.
Below: Newell Flather (l) and Nelson Merced (r) at the 1993 DSNI open house.

Paul Bothwell at the 1991 DSNI annual meeting.

CREATING THE DUDLEY STREET NEIGHBORHOOD INITIATIVE

In 1981, students from Roxbury Community College (RCC), then located on Dudley Street near St. Patrick's Church, did a small survey of residents and students in the area around the college. Housing and arson were the top problems mentioned. "Poor street lighting, rats, lack of garbage collection, abandoned cars all add to the impression of an extremely depressed area, in which islands of freshly-painted, spruced up homes and apartment buildings may be found," the report observed. At the same time, residents and students described the neighborhood as friendly and warm. They "praised their community for its racial harmony and tolerance." There was a sense of "pride in the neighborhood, a determination to fight outside encroachment, arson & abandonment, and a determination to keep the area livable."

Among those quoted in the survey was a White woman on Shirley Street. She said, "Our family has seen it all happen. They tore down house after house. They talked about urban renewal and they built those damn infill houses.* We didn't see any renewal. We saw a catastrophe. But we stayed. And now there are new people—black people, Spanish [speaking], Portuguese [Cape Verdean]. You know what, I see them and I see my father and mother struggling, proud of their little house in this neighborhood. I have to say I like what I see of these other people."[1]

SEARCHING FOR A NEW BEGINNING

Following the study, RCC participants organized a neighborhood meeting—interpretation was provided in Spanish and Portuguese—attended by many of the groups that would later be part of the Dudley Street Neighborhood Initiative, including La Alianza Hispana, Roxbury Multi-Service Center, St. Patrick's Church, Orchard Park Tenants Association, WAITT House and the Mt. Pleasant Neighborhood Association.[2] The meeting resulted in a loose "Dudley Neighborhood Coalition" that never really got off the ground. At that point, the coalition lacked both consensus and resources.

Among the coalition participants was La Alianza Hispana Director Nelson Merced, a Puerto Rican-born community activist who would later become the first Latino elected to the Massachusetts State Legislature. "I went to a few of those meetings," he recalls vaguely. "It was basically about crime issues and stuff like that, but it was very weak, and didn't really get going."

La Alianza Hispana, a multiservice agency, commissioned an in-depth study of Dudley by MIT graduate students in planning and architecture assisted by Professor Tunney Lee. The December 1981 report, *From the Ground Up*, was prepared by Total Studio, a class in environmental design. La Alianza Hispana wanted the report to help guide Nuestra Comunidad Development Corporation, a community development corporation it had newly established with the Hispanic Office of Planning and Evaluation (HOPE). *From the Ground Up* emphasized the need to build on the strengths of community residents and agencies, organize residents around immediate needs and reclaim the vacant land as a "potential asset" by cleaning it up and putting the

---

* Boarded-up boxy brick structures scattered around the neighborhood originally intended to fill in some vacant lots with public housing, but abandoned, half-finished after developers went bankrupt and funding dried up.

open space to use as urban gardens, parks and play areas. It suggested acquiring the land through a land trust for housing and other longer-term neighborhood development.[3]

In February 1984, La Alianza Hispana and Nuestra Comunidad Development Corporation organized a "Community Search Conference" with the technical support of the MIT Department of Urban Studies and Planning. It was a strategic planning conference of "community stakeholders and activists." In a discussion of Dudley trends, Search Conference participants highlighted common themes: Dudley is "a neighborhood in flux," which "seems to function under a system of managed chaos." It is a community "under siege" by external forces and "on the defensive, protecting scarce human and physical resources from being coopted or lost altogether." Dudley is "fragmented," particularly among ethnic groups and within many families. It is "disenfranchised," without meaningful access to the local political system and financial capital. Among the conference ideas for future action was that of a "Constitution for Development," whose elaboration would bring the community together around a shared vision, change its image as a high-risk investment area and establish community standards and priorities for housing, employment and other issues.[4]

In spring 1984, not long after the Community Search Conference, Nelson Merced was seeking funds to renovate the facilities of La Alianza Hispana, which is housed in the old police and fire stations on Dudley Street just across the street from St. Patrick's Church. Under Merced's leadership, La Alianza had become the largest Latino educational and social service agency in the Boston area. They couldn't let the building fall apart.

Along with the paint and plumbing, Merced wanted to replace the stained, threadbare carpet that he saw as a symbol of the downtrodden Dudley community. He approached the Boston-based Riley Foundation, one of the few local foundations to provide capital improvement grants for inner city organizations. Merced knew that Riley Foundation personnel got out into the community to visit grantees and he hoped to take the trustees and staff on a neighborhood tour and discuss ideas for improving the area.

THE RILEY FOUNDATION

The Riley Foundation was founded in 1972 as a charitable trust from the estate of philanthropist Mabel Louise Riley, heir to a family fortune made during New England's textile heyday. Although the Riley Foundation is able to make grants throughout Massachusetts, the trustees have focused their attention on the city of Boston with particular emphasis on its poorest neighborhoods, especially those that have struggled to nourish a multiracial community. Reflecting Mabel Louise Riley's dedication to children, the foundation has made improving the lives of children a theme that runs throughout its grant support in the areas of social services, community development, youth programs, education, the arts and the urban environment. Newell Flather, the foundation's administrator, believes that "Riley's ultimate mission for the Dudley Initiative, to improve the quality of life of the families living in the Dudley community, is...essentially a children's project."

The Riley Foundation is one of Massachusetts' larger private foundations—though modest by national standards—with grants totaling about $1.5 million a year. People often think Riley is bigger than it is because its average grant size is twice that of Boston's larger foundations and it has a reputation as an innovative, risk-taking foundation. Indeed, as Riley Trustee Andrew Bailey emphasizes, Riley is careful not to overcommit its grant resources so that it can be in a financial position to respond to special needs and unusual opportunities. In the 1970s, for example, Riley took a lead role in responding to the racial violence challenging court-ordered school desegregation and in supporting efforts to improve public education. At the time the Riley Foundation visited La Alianza Hispana in 1984, it was actively looking for an innovative new project initiative to support.

Riley is governed by a board of three individual trustees and a representative of the Boston Safe Deposit and Trust Company, the foundation's financial manager. The three grantmaking trustees— Andrew Bailey, Douglas "Doad" Danner and Robert Holmes Jr.—are lawyers in the prestigious Boston law firm of Powers & Hall, established in 1897. Though traditionally conservative corporate lawyers in many respects, Bailey, Danner and Holmes have used their grantmaking power to improve opportunities for those most hurt by society's inequalities. Newell Flather has been the foundation's primary staffperson since its inception—first as an employee of the Boston Safe Deposit and Trust Company and then as a principal in Grants Management Associates, an innovative company he and two colleagues, Ala Reid and Mary Phillips, started to provide grantmaking, administration and consulting services to foundations and individual donors. Flather's experience in Ghana as a member of the first group of Peace Corps volunteers in 1961, his familiarity with the displacement of Black homeowners during Philadelphia urban renewal in 1969 and his role as a founding trustee of Oxfam-America, which works to end hunger and promote grassroots development in the Third World, helped solidify his commitment to racial and economic justice.

Unlike most charitable foundations, Riley's staff and trustees have a practice of making field visits to applicants and grantees. "Kicking the tires," trustee Andrew Bailey calls it.

MAKING A DIFFERENCE

Early in the morning on April 12, 1984, trustee Doad Danner drove Newell Flather, Bob Holmes and Andrew Bailey to Roxbury, a short ride from Powers & Hall. They visited two other organizations before arriving at La Alianza Hispana at the intersection of Dudley Street and Blue Hill Avenue. Though the trustees had been in Dudley before, Bob Holmes recalls, "It's the first time that we really had a good look at it." On the way to La Alianza they recognized the name of a warehouse storing Powers & Hall files. Holmes didn't know then how familiar Dudley would become.

Nelson Merced gave the Riley visitors a tour of La Alianza, including the classroom space where worn, dirty carpeting covered the floor. Newell Flather can still recall how Merced explained why La Alianza needed funds for new carpeting. Among the many services the agency provided were adult English language classes. Merced's case, says Flather, was you can't help "bring people into the mainstream" if negative conditions make them "feel they're second-rate." He "felt that as a sign of respect for the people who were learning the language, a carpet would have significant symbolic value." As it turned out, the carpet became a jumping off point for a much larger initiative to bring respect to the people of Dudley and stop their treatment as second-class citizens by government and the private sector.

After touring La Alianza, Flather and the trustees met with Merced and Melvyn Colón, the director of Nuestra Comunidad Development Corporation. Merced's presentation of agency plans and neighborhood conditions was reinforced by his references to a wall map and aerial photograph—blowups of those prepared during the La Alianza His-pana-MIT *From the Ground Up* project—which, in Flather's words, "graphically illustrated the story of disinvestment. The combination of Merced's easy style, obvious experience and well-articulated expressions of concern were very convincing, and his determination to bring about change had a gripping effect on the gathering."

Over half the area around La Alianza was colored in gray. "What's all the gray?" Holmes asked. "Is that new housing?" On the contrary, Merced explained, that was vacant land, used as a dumping ground for abandoned cars and trash instead of needed housing. Melvyn Colón talked about Nuestra Comunidad's mission to develop affordable housing in Dudley. There was enough gray space to keep busy many community development corporations.

"I think we were all astonished at how much vacant land there was," says Holmes. "So, we suggested [Merced] take us around...You know, a picture is worth a thousand words." It was a picture of torched buildings and torched dreams.

Merced showed the Riley people a street that "looked like Beirut"—as if it had been bombed. He remembers the trustees commenting, "I can't believe this! In the middle of Boston, an area like this!" Holmes says he "knew the area had a lot of problems, but I didn't realize that it had been neglected as much as it had." He called it "negative space, a place defined by neglect."

In the taxi going back to Powers & Hall the trustees were upset. They were "bumping and bouncing" over the potholes, recalls Flather. "It was raining out. It was cold and gray...It was at that worst period after the snows have gone but spring has not yet come that we made that trip. Nothing in New England looks beautiful at that time of year. Dudley looked particularly sad."

Flather says the trustees felt, "Sure, they had made plenty of good grants, but they were not solving many real problems." The culture of grantmaking in Boston and around the country was to spread money around, a little bit here, a little bit there. Riley had bucked that culture somewhat by making its grants larger and fewer. Still, the staff and trustees wondered, "Are we really making a difference?" Riley had established itself before as a "leadership foundation" in school desegregation and urban environment. It provided ongoing "leadership and leverage," says Flather, through its willingness to "give the first boost of support to somebody," especially inner city organizations led by people of color.

"How could Riley consider itself a leadership foundation if there was a community like Dudley?" challenged Holmes on the way back from La Alianza. "What was the point of fixing up Alianza when the neighborhood was falling apart?"

Flather pointed out that Dudley was the most disadvantaged area in the city. "Why not see if we can't focus our money right there," Holmes suggested. The other trustees and Flather agreed.

At their grantmaking meeting the next day, the trustees approved a $30,000 capital improvement grant for La Alianza Hispana, but, as a symbol of their intention to make a significant contribution to rebuilding the neighborhood, they earmarked no funds for replacing the worn carpet. As recorded in the minutes, "Discussion centered on the development of a one or two year plan for the Riley Foundation with the objective of focusing the Foundation's grant funds in one area of the City, or perhaps on one specific problem, in order to effect change." The trustees decided to consider that "if funds are to be focused in one place, the depressed area of Roxbury/Dorchester should be a high priority."

The trustees also suggested "providing long term support for an organization to free it from major financial concerns allowing leadership to concentrate on program building rather than fundraising."[5] They were thinking long-range and large-scale and they wanted a potential grantee to be able to operate that way.

Flather was authorized to study the appropriate area Riley should focus on and define the major problems and opportunities in that area. Three months later, Flather and research associate Nancy Condit presented their report, *The Dudley Initiative*, to the Riley trustees. Drawing on earlier studies such as *From the Ground Up*, they wrote, "Clearly Dudley is among the hardest hit areas in Boston....Approximately 30% of the land in Dudley is vacant, excluding streets...The vacant land has a blighting effect. Business decline...has been accelerated by the population loss. The remaining population and the new immigrant population is characterized by low *income*, low *education* levels and high *unemployment*." (Italics in original.) "Housing," the report concluded, "is the greatest need and the most important priority facing Dudley."[6]

In preparing their report, Flather and Condit interviewed numerous people from nonprofit agencies, foundations, business and government. "Virtually all persons interviewed viewed the Riley initiative as bold, if not brave. While none was in any way negative, all indicated that...[it] would involve very high risk."[7]

Father Walter Waldron, who was based for 18 years in the South End, recalls talking to Flather within months after coming to St. Patrick's Church in February 1984. Flather "explained what the Riley Foundation wanted to do, which basically was to put a good deal of their money into one project that would have a dramatic impact on the area" and leverage other funding and support. "I told him I thought it was a great idea if it could work." Waldron was among those who would help get DSNI going.

The Flather-Condit report provided the Riley trustees with a funding scenario for Dudley in which new grant outlays would reach $2 million by mid-1989. That wasn't far off the mark, as it turned out. At the trustees' meeting on July 18, 1984, though La Alianza Hispana and Nuestra Comunidad were described as "the two top agencies through which Riley could work in the Dudley community," the "trustees agreed that the undertaking will require a lot of players, including the city, and would require total cooperation on the part of all Dudley agencies and a special emphasis on bringing all agencies and races to work together." Riley staff met further with Dudley area agencies to gauge their interest and "discuss the formation of a Riley/Dudley Advisory Board which may include a staff member from each agency."[8]

DUDLEY ADVISORY GROUP

Nelson Merced began meeting with the leaders of other agencies to discuss the Riley Foundation's growing interest in the area. They included Nuestra Comunidad Development Corporation Director Melvyn Colón; Ricardo Millett of the Roxbury Multi-Service Center (RMSC), a large agency providing a wide range of social services and community development programs for the Greater Roxbury community; Valerie Gregory from the Cape Verdean Community House (now defunct), the only organization then serving Cape Verdeans in Boston; Father Walter Waldron of St. Patrick's Church; and Sisters Pauline O'Leary and Mary Rogers from WAITT House (We're All In This Together), a small agency linked to the Sisters of Charity and St. Patrick's Church, emphasizing multicultural harmony and empowerment through adult education.

Merced recalls most people in the early meetings being "kind of skeptical, but open-minded. Remember, at this point, not many people thought of that [vacant] land as a resource. I mean, it wasn't until probably the end of that year that the attitudes towards the land switched from a liability...to an asset."

The Riley Foundation invited Dudley area organizations to a September 17 meeting at the Shirley-Eustis House, the historic governor's mansion just off Dudley Street. Surrounded by a low stone wall, the mansion with its large green lawn is a stark contrast to adjacent weedy vacant lots long used for illegal dumping. The Shirley-Eustis House was a symbol of how close the neighborhood was to the doors of power, yet how difficult it was to enter them.

To the Riley Foundation, the Shirley-Eustis House represented a resource for Dudley residents. The Foundation had helped restore the mansion with a $25,000 grant in 1981 (it later helped restore the nearby historic Eliot Burying Ground where Governors Thomas and Joseph Dudley are entombed). When Riley was approached for another grant by the Shirley-Eustis House in 1982, one of the trustees responded, "We can't help you for your own sake. Our only grantmaking interest in the Shirley-Eustis House is its location in this neighborhood and what you can do for the people here." Riley's next grant did not come until 1992, when it gave the Shirley-Eustis House money to purchase adjacent vacant land to create a park open to the neighborhood. By then, the Riley Foundation had invested heavily in Dudley.

In planning the September 1984 meeting, Flather wanted to make sure that Riley would be viewed as neutral with regard to area agencies. Riley didn't want the initiative dominated by La Alianza Hispana or any other agency. The Shirley-Eustis House was considered neutral space. It had the convenience of a large meeting room, and the inconvenience of no heat. To chair the meeting, Flather decided to bring in a skilled outside facilitator on the advice of Janet Taylor, then executive director of the Associated Grantmakers of Massachusetts, and Ala Reid, who helped found Grants Management Associates. The facilitator was Bill Slotnik, director of the Community Training and Assistance Center (CTAC), a technical assistance agency that has received regular support from Riley and other local foundations. What began with a call from Flather to Slotnik to facilitate "just one meeting" became a long relationship between CTAC and the Dudley initiative.

Flather was aware, says Slotnik, that if he chaired the meeting the dynamic would have been one of "groups playing to a foundation." Merced provided an introduction to the meeting and Flather welcomed people on behalf of the Riley trustees. Then Flather made what Slotnik calls an important symbolic gesture—he "took himself away from the head table and sat in the outer area." Flather plays down the significance of that gesture. "Quite honestly, I feel more comfortable sitting back...in my chair, so that's why I do it." The important point, Flather says, is that "the Riley trustees made it clear that they were there to listen and learn, and that was really the posture they took."

What followed was a wide-ranging discussion of the neighborhood's problems and priorities for action, including the need to acquire land, develop and rehabilitate housing, help tenants organize, provide job training, involve youth in the planning process, build a broad base of support and "conduct planning on development, services, resources, models and open space."[9]

Riley's involvement provided an obvious incentive for the participants to suspend skepticism, forge a consensus and act on it. As Merced observes, "There was a clear statement from the Riley Foundation and from its trustees that they were interested in doing something in a major way. They didn't know what it was, but they were willing to go through a process to find out." The participation of their officers was ample evidence of the seriousness of Riley's commitment. "So even though they hedged their bets so that just in case this whole thing fell apart they had an out...it was pretty much understood that they were going to give money. So it was in everybody's best interest...to make sure that happened."

The "Dudley Advisory Group"[10] moved quickly. From the first meeting on, there was an effort to rotate responsibility and, in particular, make sure the initiative was not seen as either "Latino dominated" or "Black dominated." As a continuing facilitator, Slotnik's methodology "was to give different people a chance to be on center stage, not only for ego purposes but to really have the leadership base of this group be as broad and as diverse as possible."

On October 15, 1984, with 22 people in attendance, the Dudley Advisory Group voted unanimously "to establish an organization" and set up an ad hoc governance committee to define its structure. The group also voted to define the organization's geographic area, based on task force recommendations.

Bob Holmes recalls, "There was a sense that this was a long shot, but we might be able to actually do something. Maybe not go all the way, but do something" more than had been done before. It was like "a venture capital deal," says Holmes. "You don't hit a home run every time, you don't expect to. You take a chance."

BOUNDARIES

The drawing of geographic boundaries was a controversial matter that might have split a less committed group. It reflected the turf and race issues that often define—and undermine—neighborhood politics.

By some accounts, the methodology was poor when it came to approving the boundaries. The group proceeded by voting on the smallest geographic region proposed and then voted on additions to that region one by one, with the boundaries widening as long as there were majority votes in favor. Nelson Merced says, "There was a big motivation to try to focus in on the vacant land." He felt that making the boundaries too wide would be "watering down the resources that we had for the purpose of developing the vacant land." Melvyn Colón acknowledges that when it came to the region later called the "core" area, "There was a sense of advocating. This was the area that Nuestra and La Alianza had been working with, and knew a lot about in their studies." To some people it looked like a classic case of some agencies, in this case the Latino-run agencies, protecting their turf at the expense of others.

A key question was whether to draw one of the core area boundaries at Quincy Street. Though geographically logical, since Quincy was a major through street, it left out the office of Roxbury Multi-Service Center (RMSC), two blocks further south. Serving the Greater Roxbury area, RMSC's clientele is largely African American, though it provides multilingual services for Latinos and others, such as a rape crisis center. In 1970, RMSC leaders had created the autonomous La Alianza Hispana to better meet the needs of the area's growing Latino population. Though RMSC's service area includes all of Dudley, the physical exclusion of the office from the core area raised a perception of "Latino domination" that would linger.

Bill Slotnik recalls that RMSC's representatives to the Dudley Advisory Group, Ricardo Millett and Shelley Hoon, never made a big issue of RMSC's relationship to the boundaries. "I think they were legitimately there, as were many people, wanting to see something happen that could benefit the community. If they could be a help to it, that would be great. But they didn't see…the Riley cash register ringing in the background. So their approach was pretty much, 'If this is what somebody wants, we're not going to fight it.'" However, says Slotnik, "some other people there were very indignant about that and felt that it was a real mistake and would be seen as a real slap to the Black community."

"It wasn't just the boundaries on the map," Ricardo Millett said later. "It was also the boundaries in our heads."[11] "It was a vote that was essentially mishandled," asserts Melvyn Colón. "I don't know how we came around to it, but finally we agreed that this was the area," with Quincy Street as one of the boundaries. And then Newell Flather proposed to accommodate wider boundaries by creating a "secondary area," extending, for example, to Grove Hall and Uphams Corner. Others questioned the idea, says Colón, but in deference to Riley they passed the proposal without much discussion. It was an atypical moment in Riley's ongoing relationship with DSNI. Especially after control passed from the agency-led Dudley Advisory Group to an elected, resident-majority board, Flather and the Riley trustees deferred to a DSNI process in which Riley was a key outside supporter, not a decision maker.

Flather explains that he recognized "the core area by itself was going to take an extraordinary effort and extraordinary resources. But I think I felt from the foundation's point of view that to leave out the secondary area left us" without sufficient geographical area, population or institutions. "It left out potential allies and resources...I was thinking from a funder's point of view that the larger area would serve as more of an attraction to other funders we were going to [need]. I thought it was important, while not getting carried away, that we be as inclusive as possible." The Riley Foundation saw "a potentially vibrant commercial district" in struggling Uphams Corner and had an interest in the historic Strand Theatre, Dorchester Bay Economic Development Corporation and other Uphams Corner nonprofits, some of which had been involved in the Dudley initiative from the beginning.

The Dudley Advisory Group approved the following definitions of the core and secondary areas, which guide DSNI today (see the map at the front of the book for boundaries):

> 1. The inner configuration will be the core area. As such, it will be the first priority for focusing efforts in physical development, business development and services.

> 2. The surrounding area will be incorporated into the overall planning for services and, through phasing, will be a secondary area of emphasis.[12]

"ORGANIZATION OF ORGANIZATIONS"

The Dudley Advisory Group approved a governance structure on November 28 that was expected to last "for the period of time up to the point of there being a community consensus on an overall action plan for the core area. Then, the governance structure will be reviewed and reconsidered." The governance structure, it turned out, didn't make it past the first community-wide meeting.

The governance structure approved by the advisory group reflected their view of the emerging Dudley entity as, in Nelson Merced's words, an "organization of organizations." While there was recognition of the need for community support, the priority at that point was not participation by community residents, but building trust among the participating agencies and community activists. There was to be a 23-member governing board, "broadly representative of the community," with: 4 community members from the core area (Black, Cape Verdean, Hispanic, White); 5 nonprofit agencies from the health and human service fields; 2 other nonprofit organizations or groups; 2 representatives each from community development corporations, small businesses, the broader business community and religious community; 2 others determined by the board to enhance racial/ethnic/age/sex representation, skills or resources; and 1 official each from the city and state.

With boundaries and governance structure in hand, the advisory group turned its attention to the first community meeting. According to the Ad Hoc Community-Wide Meeting Committee, "This meeting will be geared to building on the consensus already achieved, to bringing more people in to where the process currently is."[13] It was assumed that the meeting, which would inform and sign up initial organization members, would be followed two weeks later by another community meeting to elect the board—a board that would overlap greatly with the advisory group.

As Merced explains it, "We were going to have a community-wide meeting to announce this coalition, and we were going to do wide...outreach to make sure people got there, and therefore we used a church because it was the biggest room we had in the community...We would then proceed to an election...That thing was scheduled like bang, bang, which was really optimistic. I mean, it just showed to a certain extent that everyone was sort of on the same wavelength. We're going to elect ourselves to this board, and then we'll bring in some other community folks, so you don't need to spend that much time."

The advisory group unanimously approved the name, the Dudley Street Neighborhood Initiative, on January 16, 1985. A month later, DSNI was the subject of a *Boston Globe* article titled, "Change is in the air along Dudley Street." RMSC Director Ricardo Millet was quoted saying, "If this works, I think we can prove that neighborhood-based planning is viable. So far as I'm concerned, it's already been successful in bringing people together to the table. We've transcended the barriers, both ethnic and language."[14]

BRA DUDLEY SQUARE PLAN: RENEWED FEARS OF DISPLACEMENT

There was another kind of change in the air along Dudley Street as the Boston Redevelopment Authority's "Dudley Square Plan" was leaked to the press before DSNI's first community meeting. The city was so startled by the backlash to the plan that they tried to deny its existence, a moot point when copies of the draft were distributed around Boston. The BRA's "Strategy for Neighborhood Revitalization" centered around Dudley Station, Roxbury's primary commercial center. The BRA plan extended into DSNI's target area, from the Orchard Park public housing development to an envisioned Shirley-Eustis Park and Moreland Street Historical District.

"For a third of a century," the draft BRA plan began, "an ebb tide of negative factors—population loss, housing abandonment, uncoordinated government policies, private disinvestment, etc.—have combined to reduce Roxbury from a populous, thriving, industrial neighborhood integrated with the City economy, to an isolated shadow of its former self. In addition, race continued to be a significant factor limiting social access and economic opportunity. By 1980, the per capita income of the Dudley Square residents was one of the lowest in the nation, on a par with the poorest counties in Mississippi, or Indian Reservations of the West."

The BRA proposed a "New Town" strategy with a $750 million complex of office towers, hotels, housing, historical parks and light manufacturing in the northern Dudley area. The plan called for building high-, moderate- and low-income housing—with "home ownership opportunities for families with incomes as low as $20,000."[15] That wasn't very low. Boston's median family income was only $22,200 in 1984; in Roxbury, one out of two families earned under $11,750.[16] Many saw the "New Town" strategy as the old "urban removal."

Income was far lower at the Orchard Park public housing development for which the BRA proposed "rehabilitation...under a co-op home ownership program for present tenants, and renovation of Dearborn School into condominiums and a community center." In 1984, the average per capita income in Boston Public Housing Authority (BHA) developments—housing many White families—was $2,156. Orchard Park was then home to 600 Black and Latino families, most of them headed by women. A 1985 survey found that in Orchard Park and other BHA developments, most of the single mothers were involuntarily unemployed or underemployed—at part-time, low-wage jobs, for example—because they could not find adequate child care; another major factor was the lack of job training and placement assistance. As the survey report put it, the "findings contradict the often held image of low income people who have no interest in becoming self-sufficient or improving the lives of their children."[17]

The BRA plan would more likely lead to displacement of Orchard Park tenants than the child care, employment and fair wages supporting home ownership. "Everybody was suspicious of the BRA and the city," says Sarah Flint, then chair of the Orchard Park United Tenants Association (now known simply as the Orchard Park Tenants Association). "We had heard rumors that there was a plan...that totally wiped out Orchard Park and put condominiums. You know, these are our homes. We have been living there for years, and we were like, 'No, wait a minute. Hold on! We have to find out more about this.'" The tenant association began organizing intensively and, as seen later, Orchard Park subsequently developed a resident-led renewal plan.

The BRA's Dudley Square plan promised "citizen participation," but weakly defined it, for example, as public attendance at open meetings to discuss particular projects and the establishment of a "Planning and Development Advisory Committee." This non-resident-oriented committee would have "five members selected from governmental agencies, five members from organizations, and five members from businesses who have demonstrated special concern for the Dudley area." Though the BRA plan promised 12,000 jobs and affirmative action, it acknowledged that Roxbury residents—disproportionately unemployed—were at a disadvantage in terms of training, education and job experience.

The BRA admitted that its strategy "could lead to displacement of existing residents, the gentrification of existing single-family neighborhoods, and jobs for 'new' residents at the expense of current residents." It warned that "The paradox of increasing poverty amidst growing wealth, which has been characteristic of the City's economy for the past decade, could also occur in the Dudley Square area."

The BRA plan claimed, "Roxbury's era of throw-away housing and castaway land is over. Values of residential and nonresidential property are rising...Private market forces are moving with the new tide."[18]

Dudley residents wondered if they would be cast away with a new tide of speculation and gentrification. Some of them had been displaced by the previous tidal wave of South End urban renewal. The new Dudley Street Neighborhood Initiative appeared more urgent than ever.

"WE DON'T SEE THE COMMUNITY HERE": BRINGING THE NEIGHBORHOOD INTO THE DUDLEY STREET INITIATIVE

Almost 200 people came to St. Patrick's Church on Saturday morning, February 23, 1985, for DSNI's first community-wide meeting. The hall resembled a makeshift mini United Nations. Cape Verdean and Spanish-speaking residents were given headphones through which they could listen to simultaneous translations.

Chosen for its central location and large meeting space, St. Patrick's continues to provide a home for many DSNI events. Seen with hindsight, however, the church architecture highlighted the gap between the agencies and residents at that first community meeting. "We set ourselves up," says Nelson Merced. Dudley Advisory Group members, "all these people in business suits," sat at a long table on a platform in front of the alter. What an image, comments Merced. "It was like the Last Supper!"

Bill Slotnik, who cochaired the meeting with Melvyn Colón, uses a similar analogy. "You look like the apostles up there with Christ in back of you. And you're all sitting there, and you're up higher than everybody, where they're used to seeing, you know, the representatives of God speak." Fortunately, residents didn't treat them that way.

After introductions, there was a review of the initiative's background and priorities. "In the next five years, Roxbury and North Dorchester will change," Merced told the meeting. "That confronts us with the three questions: Who will change the community? Who will benefit from this change? And how will this change come about?" The BRA's Dudley Square Plan was on a lot of minds. Stephen Johnson of the Greater Roxbury Development Corporation declared that the BRA's outreach to the community "has been insulting and offensive."[19]

Numerous issues were raised in the open discussion that followed, including: "the need to translate development issues into a form that is easily understood by the average citizen, the importance of developing jobs for neighborhood residents, the need to benefit all the racial groups involved in the area, the need for coordination relative to other Initiatives [e.g., the Greater Roxbury Neighborhood Authority, discussed later], the importance of community residents being directly involved in the Initiative, the need to prevent what has happened in the South End from happening in the Dudley Street neighborhood, the need for the community to gain control of the land in order to stop outside developers from transforming the land in ways that would be unresponsive to the needs of the community."[20]

The pivotal moment in the meeting came after presentation of the governance structure and board nomination procedure. Some residents angrily challenged the legitimacy of the proposed board in which only a minority of seats (4 out of 23) were specifically designated for residents—though it was assumed by the organizers that some of the other slots would be filled by people who were also residents. To some residents, the new Dudley Street Neighborhood Initiative looked like the failed efforts of the past that made false promises in the name of a community that wasn't really represented.

In Slotnik's words, "All hell broke loose" after Ricardo Millett finished the board presentation. "We don't see the community here!" was the common theme. The meeting's convenors began losing control. This was clearly not going to be a meeting that simply ratified a pre-existing consensus.

"Who the hell are you people and what do you want?" demanded Earl Coleman, a longtime neighborhood resident and hospital lab technician. "Who is Riley? Why should we trust you?"

Though not everyone was so skeptical, people were expressing real concern for their futures and for the neighborhood. The initiative, says Merced, "was perceived as a major undertaking—when you had all the community organizations and executive directors sitting before you in front of the church with a major foundation." People worried, "Were they going to build skyscrapers and displace people? There was a lot of fear."

In his conception of an "organization of organizations" Merced recalls being "motivated by speed and expediency." He thought the organizations were sufficiently representative of the community. "It wasn't really until we got to that meeting that people told us, 'No, you guys are not representative of the community.' I think it was a surprise to everybody." It shouldn't have been such a surprise. Merced acknowledges, "We only represented very small sections of the community...I didn't have any illusion that Alianza was representative of the community because I always had a hard time trying to get clients to be part of the board, although we had people [who] lived in the community on the board." At the DSNI meeting, "the issue of direct representation was brought to the floor by the community. I think the community was blaming the human service organizations for the conditions in which the community was in."

Earl Coleman, Fadilah Muhammad, Ché Madyun and other residents challenged the whole assumption that this was a neighborhood initiative. "How many of you people up there live in this neighborhood?" Madyun asked the panel. Slotnik remembers one person raising a hand. Others saw no hands go up. The anger built.

Ché Madyun was then a parent coordinator with METCO (Metropolitan Council for Educational Opportunity), a desegregation program begun in the 1960s for Black children to attend school in the suburbs. She first heard about the Dudley initiative when her friend and supervisor at METCO, Qasim Abdul-Tawwab—who is married to DSNI activist Najwa Abdul-Tawwab—told her about the February 17 *Boston Globe* article on DSNI; he thought it would interest her since he knew she wanted better housing for her family. After reading the article, Madyun decided to "go check this out and see what they're doing. Because the thing that alarmed me when I read the article was I felt like we were going to have displacement like the South End...and I felt like I needed to stay involved so I would know what was going on." Madyun says she "wasn't extremely aware, but it was kind of obvious that they were building these things called condos...I knew they were expensive and they were putting people out. I knew that there were more homeless people on the street than there ever had been and I said, 'Well, who am I to be any different than these people?'

What do you do, go wave your bachelor's degree and say, 'Hey, look, I've got a bachelor's degree—let me move in?'" She went to the meeting with feelings of both "hope and fear."

At the meeting, Madyun questioned how the initiative could be community-based if it was not resident-controlled. She also asked, "How can we nominate people to represent us when we don't know each other?...I don't know whether I should vote for them or not."

Fadilah Muhammad, a neighborhood resident active with the local American Muslim Mission, brought the meeting to a crossroads of continued confrontation or cooperation between agency representatives and residents. Instead of speaking from the floor mike facing the initiative organizers at the table in front, Muhammad turned around and talked to the residents in the "audience." Slotnik remembers it as a "superb job of public speaking...It was clear that what she was doing was denying the legitimacy of these people...It was also saying that the people whose voices need to be heard are the 200 people who are in this room."

The organizers needed to stop the Us versus Them momentum from building. Bob Holmes thought that those saying the neighborhood was not represented were making sense. He decided to jump in. Here was a conservative blond-haired corporate lawyer in an expensive suit—who not only lived outside Dudley, he lived in affluent suburban Duxbury—speaking from the heart. Slotnik remembers him saying, "I want to tell you a little bit about who I am. I'm Bob Holmes...I'm not from this neighborhood...I probably know less about Roxbury and North Dorchester than anybody in the room...I work for a corporate law firm. I'm a trustee of the Riley Foundation. I'm probably what a lot of you think of when you think of the downtown interests. And if you want to turn this neighborhood around, it can't just be done by...the residents, and not with agencies." He told them that funders would want to see agency involvement. "They want to give money to somebody they know and have some relationship with. If you're going to make a difference in this neighborhood, the only way to do it is to have everybody work together...I don't know how to deal with the tension here, but if everybody isn't working together you can't accomplish it." Today, Holmes doesn't remember what he said. "No, it was happening real fast, and it's like catching a pass, I guess. You just do it."

Holmes provided the breathing space for meeting participants to move down the road of cooperation. Fadilah Muhammad reiterated,

"We're talking about the community's role in this." Slotnik then proposed taking two straw polls to see how people felt on the issue of community control. There was overwhelming consensus that both the general membership and governing board "be modified so as to ensure that 51% or more" of their members be residents from the core or secondary areas.[21]

At that point DSNI clearly took the road to community control. A previously scheduled follow-up meeting was recast as an open meeting where the consensus for resident leadership would be translated into a new governing structure. The DSNI convenors made clear, says Holmes, "We want to go forward. We don't want to go back...Please come."

"Well, okay," thought Ché Madyun. "I'm going to come and put my input in there and see where this thing goes." She explains, "I've always told my children, if you don't like something, you just don't sit around and wait for somebody to do it for you. You can help to change it yourself."

Many other residents felt the same way. The openness and responsiveness demonstrated at the first community meeting remained constant sources of DSNI strength.

NEW GOVERNANCE STRUCTURE: RESIDENT MAJORITY

A few nights later some 70 people, most of them residents, crowded into the governance structure committee meeting at La Alianza Hispana. Residents showed they were going to assume the responsibility for community control they had demanded at the St. Patrick's meeting.

At "the first meeting or two," Madyun remembers "people venting frustration at all the different [groups and programs] that have come in the neighborhood saying what they're going to do for us and then leaving with nothing done or things being worse, like the Model Cities program and some other ones." Longtime Dudley residents "had some serious history that they were expressing." They made clear that the future of Dudley would not be shaped without them.

For many African Americans, Madyun observes, there was an undercurrent of fear that given the strong founding roles played by La Alianza Hispana and Nuestra Comunidad Development Corporation,

DSNI would benefit the Latino community at the expense of others. This undercurrent remained for quite some time, even after DSNI began expanding its membership and found that African Americans were joining in large numbers while Latino residents were underrepresented. African Americans urged each other to participate strongly in the meetings. Madyun found their participation mattered as she saw Nelson Merced, who chaired many of the meetings, "really try to address…the different fears and concerns that everybody had." He earned Madyun's respect because that "is something that I've never seen in any kind of leadership—I don't care whether they're White, Black, green, purple, yellow or orange. Usually people get in there and they just try to push their agenda, and that's it. So that helped me stay also. Because if I just thought this person was just going to try to push their agenda anyway, I don't know if I'd still be here today." Instead she saw cooperation.

The expanded governance committee voted to recommend a revised DSNI governing structure strengthening resident participation. In the new structure, the general membership included "(a) residents from the core and secondary areas, (b) organizations (religious, commercial, non-profit, neighborhood associations, community groups) within the core geographic area, (c) organizations in the secondary area that provide services to the core area—participation being from executives, board chairs or others having decision-making authority—and (d) at-large members (e.g., community leaders, resource people, et al.) designated by the Governing Board."

Instead of a 23-member governing board with only 4 designated community slots, there would be a 31-member board, with a resident majority—a minimum of 12 community members and 4 additional spots designated for residents. The multiracial, multiethnic character of DSNI was reaffirmed. Equal minimum representation was provided for the neighborhood's four major cultures—Black, Cape Verdean, Latino and White—rather than representation based simply numerically on Dudley's population.[22] Equal minimum representation was chosen to strengthen collective action and underscore the common stake of all people in rebuilding Dudley. The Riley Foundation, the dollars behind DSNI at this point, never sought a seat on the board and, in keeping with the spirit of community control, it never occurred to DSNI members to propose that they do.

The board structure presented then, which still governs DSNI, is as follows:

- 12 Community members (Black, Cape Verdean, Latino, White) from the core area

- 5 Nonprofit agencies from the Health and Human Service fields [from the core area]

- 2 Community development corporations from the core area

- 2 Small businesses from the core area

- 2 Broader business community [members]

- 2 Religious community [members] from the core area

- 2 Other (determined by the Board, using criteria of racial/ethnic/age/sex representation, skills or resources)

- 2 Nonprofit organizations or groups from the secondary area

- 1 City official

- 1 State official

On March 7, DSNI held a second community-wide meeting at St. Patrick's Church which was even larger than the first. This time, Nelson Merced and the other meeting facilitators avoided the Us versus Them appearance of a raised podium and spoke from floor mikes. The meeting debated two governing structures: the 31-member board recommended by the governance committee (and presented by resident Earl Coleman) and a 19-member board proposed by a small group of residents that would have limited the nonprofit agencies to one agency caucus slot and ensured a resident majority without enlarging the board. After extensive debate the 31-member board was strongly approved. Though some proponents of the smaller board dropped out of DSNI after that, others such as Ché Madyun ran for the new board.

FIRST ELECTION

The governing board election took place on April 27 after weeks of intensive organizing and a "Meet the Candidates Night." Resident Gail Latimore participated in the effort to inform the neighborhood and encourage people to vote. "There was a lot of excitement," says Latimore. "Given that nothing like that had really happened in the community in a long, long time," she says, "the fact that we actually got people out I think was a major accomplishment."

The election was held at St. Patrick's during the day on Saturday to maximize turnout. With sunny spring weather, it was "the ideal day for an election," says CTAC's Bill Slotnik. To prevent any individual candidates or groups from swinging the election with people who had not yet participated in the DSNI process, voting eligibility was restricted to residents who had attended one of the large DSNI community meetings. Members could use various forms of identification to establish residency, including, for example, a driver's license, rent receipt, Medicare card and utility bill. More than 100 people voted.[23]

"There were master lists of who had been at the first two community meetings and therefore were allowed to vote," recalls Slotnik. "And there was this Cape Verdean couple that came in…[They] lived about a mile away from [St. Patrick's] and they didn't have a car…[The] woman insisted that she had been in the meeting, [but] she didn't show up on any of the charts…She was so insistent and yet the ruling had to be that she couldn't vote because her name didn't show up on something. At which point, after having walked a mile from her apartment to the church, she got up, left her husband there, walked home and walked back with" her copy of a mailing DSNI had sent out, showing "she had to have been involved." Slotnick says that they checked the original community meeting sign-in sheets and found that "the husband's name had been written and then the woman's name had been written" and people preparing the master list "had seen that as one name, rather than two names." Seeing the woman affirm her right to vote, with "determination and no bitterness," strengthened Slotnik's "sense that there was a real potential to this community process here."

Before entering the voting area, DSNI members could study blowups of the ballot and seek further assistance from election personnel speaking different languages. The actual voting area was blocked off. Once people cast their ballots, including candidates, they had to leave the voting area. After the voting closed, every ballot was counted twice. Two of Slotnik's colleagues who had no connection to Dudley were paid to count the ballots so there would be no question regarding impartiality. If the counts for any slot were not identical, says Slotnik, "we recounted all the ballots again twice. Because the last thing you want in something like this is for somebody or an agency to lose by one or two votes," demand a recount and find inaccuracies. It would "call the whole thing into question."

During the ballot count, recalls Slotnik, Ché Madyun was sitting on the other side of the room, "being very patient, not pushy, just wanting to see what the results were." When the count was completed, "I said, 'Che, you got the second highest vote count'" in the heavily contested voting for one of the four slots designated for African Americans. She "perks up her eyes and she goes 'All right!' Then she just takes her bag, grabs her kids, and walks out. Doesn't say another word." This was another sign "that things were being done right," says Slotnik. "You had people revved up and...taking it very seriously who hadn't been involved before [DSNI], and who could see a role for themselves."

THE BOARD TAKES CHARGE

DSNI's newly elected board met for the first time on May 6, 1985. The first board included early Dudley Advisory Group members such as Nelson Merced from La Alianza Hispana, Melvyn Colón from Nuestra Comunidad Development Corporation, Shelley Hoon from Roxbury Multi-Service Center, Sister Pauline O'Leary from WAITT House and Father Walter Waldron from St. Patrick's Church. It included people who became involved during the first two community meetings, such as African Americans Ché Madyun, Fadilah Muhammad and Earl Coleman, who all successfully challenged DSNI to live up to its promise of community control; Tubal Padilla, a Puerto Rican activist who worked with the state Office for Children; Bob Haas from Dorchester Bay Economic Development Corporation, a White resident of the secondary area in Uphams Corner; two Cape Verdean brothers, Manuel and Ulisses Gonçalves, both teachers; African American resident Lloyd Harding of the Roxbury Community Land Trust; Betty Brickley, a longtime White resident who lived on Dudley Street; Esteban Soto Jr., the son of the minister of a local Latino church; and Gail Latimore, an African American resident who later became head of planning for Action for Boston in Community Development (ABCD). Latimore's mother, Lessie Spann, also served on the DSNI board in later years.

The board decided to have two cochairs, one from the community, the other from an agency. Fadilah Muhammad and Nelson Merced were elected. Members committed themselves to weekly board meetings until the end of June and then biweekly board meetings in addition to committee meetings (the full board presently meets monthly).

To address the issue of Riley Foundation support, the board decided to invite a representative from Riley to a meeting. Riley administrator Newell Flather attended the board meeting on June 3 and expressed Riley's commitment to the improvement of the community and readiness, if solid DSNI plans were developed, to "provide basic support to get the operation started; provide funds which can be leveraged; and provide a blocking back to bring contacts and serve as a marketing tool for the group."[24] At the DSNI board's request, Riley also arranged for one of its personnel, Lauress Wilkins, to provide DSNI with interim staff support.

Much of DSNI's work is done through committees open to general members as well as the board. By June 10, four committees were functioning: Nominations, Land Use, Planning and Communications. The latter three reported on their activities as follows:

Land Use: As its general goal, the Land Use Committee has determined to promote the development of all parcels of vacant lots in the Initiative's target area. The Committee will meet with a representative of the City to address three issues: 1) provision of manpower for cleanup of vacant lots; 2) appointment of residents to be responsible for maintenance of those lots; and 3) discussion of interim uses of the lots until permanent plans are in place. Also, the Committee is considering negotiating with the City for a property disposition policy which would address DSNI's land control concerns.

Planning: Preliminary plans for the Committee's activities include: 1) conducting a needs assessment (possibly through a survey designed and implemented by a consulting firm) in the community; and 2) designing and implementing a plan of action through which DSNI can address those community needs. [The Committee] emphasized the importance of continued input from community residents in the planning process.

Communications: The Committee has identified as its priority activities: 1) to provide timely and accurate information internally and externally; and 2) to provide transportation and other resources which would facilitate attendance at community meetings. The Committee hopes to help the Board to increase general membership, to work toward the enhancement of the image of the neighborhood, and to concretize the Board's credibility in the larger community.[25]

On July 27, the board had an all-day retreat facilitated by CTAC to discuss operational issues and develop the goals of a comprehensive development plan. In a letter dated August 26, 1985, DSNI formally submitted a proposal to the Riley Foundation to fund the first six months of a staffed operation. The proposal specified the full-time positions of project director, organizer (trilingual or bilingual) and secretary (bilingual). In October, the Riley Foundation provided DSNI with its first grant of $70,000.

By then Newell Flather had spoken with numerous foundation audiences about DSNI. "People would say, 'This is wonderful. How much of your resources has it taken?'" A year and a half into the process, Flather could still reply, "It's the largest grant we never made." Until October 1985, Riley staff and trustees had invested a lot of time, energy and caring into the initiative, but no grant dollars. The relationship between Riley and DSNI, built on something more than money, was already unusual for a foundation and low-income neighborhood. It was built on growing trust and mutual respect as well as substantial resources over time. By mid-1989, Riley support for DSNI and other Dudley area grantees would surpass the $2 million originally projected and keep on rising.

HIRING STAFF

In the hiring of its first director DSNI reached another crossroads between agency domination or resident control. The two finalists for the position were both White males, but they had different backgrounds and organizing approaches.

Peter Medoff had grown up in the Boston area, but had worked primarily in New York City as a tenant organizer and in Hartford, Connecticut, as director of the Citizens Research Education Network, which provided research and organizing assistance to community groups. He combined a masters degree in urban planning with over five years of organizing experience. Medoff had his first interview with the full DSNI board at WAITT House on February 13, 1986. Board members sat in a circle and the agency representatives fired off most of the questions. With his background in organizing, Medoff emphasized the need for DSNI to be guided by a strategy of organizing the community. To create a plan and encourage investment without building a strong community, he argued, would only invite the type of speculation and displacement that residents were already worried about. Most of the residents listened quietly and Medoff didn't sense much enthusiasm. At that moment DSNI appeared to be driven by agency professionals.

The other candidate had worked as a consultant for Oficina Hispana, a social service agency in the Jamaica Plain neighborhood of

Boston. He was far better known in Boston and had close ties with many social service agencies. A majority of the board—but not the two-thirds majority needed to hire—supported him after the first round of interviews, though some resident board members saw him as too close to the agencies. Medoff was supported mainly by residents on the board who saw him as an experienced advocate for community control. Since the board was split and some members felt they needed more information to make a final decision, a second round of interviews was scheduled for March 3. During Medoff's interview, where residents were still relatively quiet, some concern was raised about connections he had with some members of the Flynn administration from his previous work.

While Mayor Ray Flynn would prove responsive to DSNI, his administration was not generally seen as a friend to the Black community. Flynn, a former city councilor and state representative from the conservative White neighborhood of South Boston where he grew up, had in the 1970s angered many in the Black community with his opposition to school busing. In 1974, Judge Arthur Garritty ruled that the Boston School Committee had "knowingly carried out a systematic program of segregation affecting all of the city's students, teachers and school facilities and [had] intentionally brought about and maintained a dual school system. Therefore, the entire school system of Boston is unconstitutionally segregated."[26] Busing was one of the remedies chosen to achieve desegregation in a city whose neighborhoods were heavily segregated. Boston was soon appearing on newscasts nationwide as court-ordered busing faced heated, sometimes violent opposition by White groups such as ROAR (Restore Our Alienated Rights).

In the 1983 mayoral election, Ray Flynn faced Mel King, the first Black candidate to win Boston's nonpartisan mayoral preliminary election and run as one of two finalists in the general election. A lifelong resident of the South End and a state representative from 1973 to 1982, King had a long history as a progressive activist for civil rights and economic justice—domestic and international. King led the fight in the Massachusetts Legislature to divest the state of investments in South Africa. During the mayoral campaign he promoted measures to link neighborhood economic development to downtown growth. King's campaign was rooted in the multiracial Boston Rainbow Coalition he led—predating Jesse Jackson's National Rainbow Coalition. Flynn, who campaigned as an economic populist promising to share downtown wealth with Boston's neighborhoods, was supported by many White progressive activists from such groups as the Massachusetts Tenants Organization and Massachusetts Fair Share even though he maintained his antibusing and antiabortion positions.

King's campaign boosted voter registration and turnout by people of color. He received 90 percent of the Black vote and carried Latino and Asian precincts. He also received 20 percent of the White vote. While this was a higher percentage of the White vote than Harold Washington received to win the Chicago mayoralty that year, a poll showed racism to still be a major factor in Boston: "One-third of the white voters interviewed would not vote for a black candidate under any circumstances, no matter how appealing the candidate's proposals happened to be."[27]

Some DSNI board members were concerned that Medoff would be swayed by his relationships with officials in the Flynn administration who were considered disrespectful of and unresponsive to the concerns of people of color and hostile to anyone they perceived as tied to Mel King. While Medoff's relationships with Flynn associates could open doors for the neighborhood, that access would be harmful if it were used to perpetuate the White "good old boys" network rather than empower people of color from the Dudley neighborhood.

Medoff convinced the board of his commitment not only to expanded community participation, but genuine community control. He began working on March 10, 1986 in shared office space at the back of Nuestra Comunidad Development Corporation. Soon after, as if to confirm earlier suspicions, he received calls from city officials asking him about issues in Roxbury, even though others, especially people of color whom the administration seemed to ignore, were far more experienced and knowledgeable. Medoff responded by politely redirecting the callers to more appropriate sources while maintaining the relationships for the future. The challenge of balancing insider access with critical independence would be a continuing one for DSNI.

At the beginning of April, DSNI was awarded a Fair Housing Award by the city of Boston. It was a quick lesson in politics. DSNI had not done any housing work yet, had no real office and was just getting its staff in place. In fact, after calling DSNI to tell them about the award, Boston Fair Housing Commission staffer Cynthia Koebert asked for informational material about DSNI, since no one at the commission knew anything about it. The Flynn administration, it seemed, needed a Roxbury group to recognize that was not considered hostile. Again, DSNI would learn from this early experience and go on to build a reputation as an independent group that could work with the city without being co-opted and realize, rather than sell out, its goals of community control.

PASSING THE BATON

As the staff began taking shape, DSNI went through some significant leadership changes. In February 1986, Nelson Merced, who had played so pivotal a role in creating DSNI and had been elected its first president, resigned from the board. He also left La Alianza Hispana and became deputy director for Policy and Planning in the city's Public Facilities Department. When Merced resigned, Melvyn Colón of Nuestra Comunidad became acting president. By then, Fadilah Muhammad had needed to reduce her participation in DSNI, and in April she dropped off the board so she could devote more time to her family.

In November 1986, the DSNI board unanimously approved a new slate of officers. Ché Madyun became president and Melvyn Colón became vice president. Colón continued to chair board meetings until the following fall, when Madyun, who had never chaired an organization before, felt ready to take on that role.

Madyun resisted being nominated as president. She insists she didn't know "anything about being a president. I really didn't know anything about what a board of a nonprofit organization was supposed to do—so why should I be president?" Colón, Medoff and many residents urged her to accept the nomination. Finally, Madyun agreed, thinking she would be a temporary "figurehead" president until new board elections. Far from being a figurehead, Madyun has been a dynamic leader who repeatedly won reelection. She enrolled in a two-year management program at Lesley College focusing on nonprofit organizations, with a particular interest in the arts. She also became an experienced public speaker, increasingly in demand as DSNI gained a national reputation. All while working at METCO and then the Strand Theatre, raising three children, being an active member of her mosque and, in 1992, doing "sweat equity" for her new cooperative home on Magnolia Street.

The transition from Colón to Madyun as president was symbolic of DSNI's shift from an agency-driven to resident-driven alliance. In the words of Orchard Park's Sarah Flint, when "Ché became president I said, 'Wow, it is going to be all right. It is really in the control of the community.'"

Illegal dumping and abandoned cars. View from Dennis Street looking down Winthrop Street, July 1986. Site of new DSNI homes (l) and community center (r).

1990 DSNI neighborhood cleanup.

DON'T DUMP ON US: ORGANIZING THE NEIGHBORHOOD

Organizing is the renewable energy that powers DSNI. As DSNI's first director, Peter Medoff advocated blending campaigns for immediate victories with a long-range, Think Big strategy. While short-term victories were essential, Medoff believed that DSNI's sustaining strength would come from the participatory process of creating a long-term vision for the neighborhood. Through organizing, DSNI would build up people's expectations of what is desirable and doable. With united community willpower behind it, DSNI could create the political will necessary to make the city a partner in implementing the Dudley neighborhood's bold development agenda. DSNI would not be afraid to use confrontation to achieve its objectives, nor would it be afraid to cooperate with people or institutions who didn't share the whole agenda. It recognized both the power of numbers and the importance of building personal relationships.

DSNI's first full-time community organizer was Andrea Nagel, whose family had moved to the United States from Chile when she was eight years old. Nagel had attended some DSNI meetings while working as a community outreach worker for Oficina Hispana in Jamaica Plain.

When the DSNI organizer job opened, she was ready to leave her social service position to "really get out into the community and address some of the root causes" of issues that concerned her. On her first day of work, April 14, 1986, Nagel went with Medoff and some board members to look for donated furniture and supplies for the new DSNI office that would be opening in May at 385 Dudley Street, a storefront owned by Nuestra Comunidad.

On April 16, DSNI held a community meeting at La Alianza Hispana attended by some 75 people. While the primary business on the agenda was finalizing DSNI's bylaws, the major focus of the meeting was the problem of arson. DSNI invited representatives of the Boston Arson Prevention Commission to speak. The commission's controversial 1985 report documenting a new wave of arson in the Dudley area had recently been made public. The arson rate was even higher than that earning Roxbury's Highland Park neighborhood the title "Arson Capital of the Nation" in 1981.

Focusing on the Sav-Mor neighborhood (bounded by Blue Hill Avenue, Dudley Street and Warren Street) in DSNI's secondary area, the Arson Commission reported, "Many of the buildings which have burned in this area [in 1985] were among the approximately 75 abandoned buildings which area residents would like to see developed by and for local, low-income residents. Other fires have occurred in buildings currently occupied by low-income tenants that appear destined for Condo Conversion."

"It is obvious," the commission bluntly stated, "that this increase in serious fires in the Sav-Mor area is directly related to the increased speculation due to the [BRA] Dudley Square Revitalization Plan." The Arson Commission characterized the area as fitting its "Tension Matrix," described earlier as a mix of both appreciating and depreciating forces.[1] As speculation increased, homeowners in the Dudley Station area reported "the almost daily receipts of slips under the door from realtors urging them to sell; in classic blockbusting fashion, some of these slips allude to the threat of an influx of Latinos in traditionally black neighborhoods."[2]

Mayor Flynn and Boston Redevelopment Authority officials criticized the Arson Commission report but, as City Councilor David Scondras, chair of the council's arson committee, noted, Flynn himself wrote in a February 1984 *Boston Globe* op-ed, "redevelopment arson takes place in areas targeted for major improvements. Buildings which do not fit into these plans, but might otherwise be saved for affordable housing, are often burned to facilitate land clearance."[3]

KNOCKING ON NEIGHBORS' DOORS

The DSNI staff's first priority was getting to the streets, knocking on doors and looking for clear, winnable issues that could begin to build residents' sense of their own power. During April and May 1986, Nagel and Medoff knocked on hundreds of doors, talking to residents about their fears and hopes for the neighborhood. Beginning with lists of people who had attended DSNI meetings, they also approached local neighborhood associations such as the Mt. Pleasant Neighborhood Association.

Nagel recalls, "Folks were excited and wanted to know what was happening. I spent a lot of time at the beginning visiting people in their homes. There was so much history and a lot of people had been struggling in this neighborhood for so long...Their stories would go on and on and on. It was clear that people cared. Contrary to what was commonly thought, people certainly cared about where they lived and bettering their lives and their children's lives. And they not only cared, but they had already been doing things about it. In some cases, I came across veteran activists. After spending hours with them and learning about battles they had fought in the past, I knew they would be part of DSNI. I'm talking about people like Jessie Farrier, Margarita Sturniolo, Sophia McCarthy and Mildred Daniels.* They are pillars of strength in this neighborhood.

"I also came across people who were afraid and others who had lost hope altogether. I remember talking to people through their doors—yelling to hear each other or communicating through the peep hole...There were others who opened their doors and talked about how nothing they could do would make a difference. I remember asking myself, 'How can I at least help to spark hope in this case?'...At times the negativity was really alarming. And it's because people had just lost hope or were very cynical about anything really changing. They had seen too much come down or had heard too many broken

---

* DSNI member Mildred Daniels is the founder of the Mt. Pleasant Tot Lot and longtime active member of the Mt. Pleasant-Vine Neighborhood Association.

promises. So it was going to be up to DSNI to create the conditions for them to be part of something successful."

DSNI staff and members were able to reach some people who were very cynical at first. Paul Bothwell, whose earlier efforts to move city government into constructive action had left him discouraged, is a good example. "He was very negative and very unbelieving," says Nagel. "That's certainly the way I felt," says Bothwell, recalling how he reacted to DSNI with "a good deal of despair and cynicism." Bothwell changed his mind as he watched DSNI in action and began to get personally involved. "Little by little [I had] a sense of real wonder and hope. I just really began to...marvel that maybe communities can be empowered enough that something can change fundamentally." Bothwell became a strong resident activist on the Development Committee and was later elected to the DSNI board.

Common themes emerged from the door-knocking visits, which then guided the early organizing campaigns. "Everyone talked about the garbage, everyone talked about the crime and everyone talked about how the city treats people here," says Nagel. They complained about the illegal dumping on vacant lots and the city's dismal garbage collection and street cleaning. They talked about how the city gave poor neighborhoods like Dudley poor service. Tenants complained of bad building conditions and landlord neglect. In general, residents wanted the lots cleaned, abandoned cars towed, recreational areas maintained, more effective policing, better city services and enforcement of housing and health codes.

"DON'T DUMP ON US"

Responding to resident priorities, DSNI planned an organizing campaign called "Don't Dump On Us." The immediate objectives were to clean up and fence off vacant lots in the Dudley area—there were more than 1,300—and enhance the neighborhood's image as well as its health and safety. The longer-range objective was to transform people's thinking—from seeing the lots as health-threatening eyesores to seeing them as potential spaces for homes, businesses, community services, parks and playgrounds. The "Don't Dump On Us" campaign was a unifying campaign, bringing together public housing tenants, homeowners and businesspeople in the common pursuit of making the neighborhood a better place in the present, while pointing to a vision for long-term revitalization. Originally planned as a short-term organizing effort, "Don't Dump On Us" was an organizing priority for many years, targeting vacant lots, abandoned cars and the illegal trash transfer stations operating in the neighborhood.

"Don't Dump On Us" always meant more than simply eliminating physical trash. It meant stop trashing the community in every way. Dudley's reputation and its people had been dumped on for years—by media who largely ignored the neighborhood, except to portray it as a haven for drug dealing; by politicians who collected votes and taxes from the neighborhood, but provided little or no services; by banks who redlined and discriminated, denying people a fair opportunity to buy and maintain their homes and businesses. "Don't Dump On Us" meant stop blighting, disrespecting and shortchanging the community.

The "Don't Dump On Us" kickoff event was a community meeting and speakout attended by city officials. On the evening of Wednesday, June 18, 1986, DSNI's office was buzzing with activity and anticipation as the organization's first action-oriented community-wide meeting was about to take place. Leaflets had been dropped at hundreds of homes; follow-up phone calls had been made during the previous two nights; several city officials had been invited to attend and had confirmed; hundreds of "Don't Dump On Us" buttons had been produced in three languages; rides, child care, refreshments and translations had all been arranged to make the meeting as accessible as possible. Still, there were a lot of nervous DSNI staff and members wondering how many people would show up.

The event was a terrific success. Over 100 residents crowded the basement of St. Patrick's Church along with politicians such as then City Council President Bruce Bolling (Boston's first Black City Council president) and city officials from various departments. The meeting was an important first step in building the credibility of DSNI with city officials. They were clearly taken aback by the size and character of the crowd.

For an hour, one resident after another came to the microphone and gave graphic examples of garbage and debris—from old tires and refrigerators to rotten vegetables and sides of beef—being illegally dumped all over the neighborhood, with little being done to clean it up or prevent it from happening again. Della Jones, a Winthrop Street resident, declared, "The terrible thing that has happened to our house is that the mice have taken over." City officials stated that rats outnumbered humans three to one in the Dudley Street neighborhood.

Residents demanded that the dumping stop and the trash transfer stations be replaced by housing and jobs.

A city official slipped out quietly to call Mayor Flynn and inform him of what was happening. Toward the end of the meeting, a commotion was heard in the back of the hall. The mayor had suddenly arrived to address the crowd. Though not invited originally, Flynn decided to come in response to the size and dynamism of the meeting. For many residents, it was their first time in the same room with a mayor of their city. Flynn would return many times in the years ahead.

Flynn had run for mayor as the "neighborhood candidate" and had promised early in his first term—beginning in 1984—to clean up all the city's vacant lots. For Dudley, it was an empty promise until that community meeting. In his impromptu speech to DSNI, Flynn committed the city to "provide funds and any kind of help necessary" to clean the lots.

The local media, including three television stations, gave DSNI extensive coverage. "We are tired of being dumped on," the next day's Boston Globe quoted Orchard Park resident Joan Porter. "Who wants to live with rats? Who wants to live with filth? Who wants to live with disease? Dump some good things, if you're going to dump. Dump some money in the area."[4]

CLEANING UP

A week later Mayor Flynn issued a press release appropriately titled "City Responds to Community." It began, "The Flynn Administration, working in concert with the Dudley Street Neighborhood Initiative, will be implementing a program," beginning with 61 of the worst "vacant lots that have been illegally dumped upon." The mayor committed the city to cleaning up the lots, erecting wooden poles and concrete barriers to keep dumpers out and fully prosecuting anyone dumping illegally (mainly that meant fining the dumpers and putting tax liens on private property used for dumping). Residents were encouraged to call the city's new 725-DUMP hotline to report illegal dumping. Flynn also pledged the city's material support for a neighborhood cleanup planned by DSNI.

The June 18 community meeting was one of DSNI's earliest lessons in power politics. Residents saw that by coming together in large numbers and demanding what they were rightfully entitled to, they could change their neighborhood for the better. The mayor responded in both words and deeds. Residents' ability to achieve immediate action from a city government that had for so long not represented them laid the foundation for achieving longer-range, more difficult goals.

On Saturday, July 19, over 100 residents participated in the neighborhood cleanup under cloudy skies. The city contributed rakes, shovels and T-shirts just as they did for cleanups in other neighborhoods, but they also committed about 25 employees and heavy equipment such as front-end loaders and dump trucks. Mayor Flynn showed up to kick off the event, which received significant publicity. DSNI gave out balloons and refreshments at the Dudley and East Cottage gathering site and turned the cleanup into a minifestival.

Even as they contributed to cleaning up the lots, some employees of the city Public Works Department dumped some trash of their own in the form of racist stereotypes. After handing out 100 rakes and shovels to local residents, one of the city employees snidely remarked, "We won't be seeing those tools again." They weren't even planning to return at the end of the day to pick them up. But when they did return at 5 P.M., there were 96 rakes and shovels there to greet them and the astonishment was plain on their faces. The following Monday, three more tools were returned. And, as if to punctuate the point, a Cape Verdean woman arrived at DSNI's office on Tuesday with her adolescent son in hand. The boy held a rake with a broken handle. He apologized for breaking it and left it with the other tools.

As part of the "Don't Dump On Us" campaign, DSNI also began tackling the problem of abandoned cars which made parts of Dudley look like car wreckers' lots. Massachusetts has one of the nation's highest car theft rates. Car thieves stole cars from around the city, stripped them and dumped them in Dudley. Car owners dumped their cars there to collect insurance fraudulently or avoid paying wreckers' fees. As hundreds of abandoned, often burnt-out cars accumulated the city seemed to ignore them, but the residents would not.

DSNI began to gather lists of cars and demanded that the city tow them out of the neighborhood. At first the city was slow to respond. Residents in the Virginia-Monadnock Neighborhood Association in the Uphams Corner area stepped up their action. Association President Bob Haas recounted what they did in the first multilingual edition of DSNI's newsletter, published in fall 1986: "Residents saw an accumulation of 28 vehicles on their streets, 12 alone on a one-block stretch of Monadnock St. They made a computerized listing of the abandoned cars and gave it to the police and other city officials. When still no cars were towed they went to the *Boston Globe*, which covered the problem on September 3 with photographs of the wrecks. Within two weeks 16 vehicles were removed." By late 1986, with Dudley residents pressing the city with lists of cars, tow trucks began spending more time in Dudley. Still the process was slow, and the next year DSNI became more creative—and more effective.

The 1987 mayoral campaign provided the opportunity for one of DSNI's most successful tactics. DSNI staff and members reasoned that having abandoned cars with RAY FLYNN FOR MAYOR bumper stickers plastered all over them would be a political embarrassment. They would remind everyone of Flynn's responsibility for the eyesores and prod the city into action. So that summer, a DSNI member called Flynn's campaign office in Roxbury posing as a campaign volunteer and asked for 200 bumper stickers. The campaign office was eager to oblige. During the next couple of nights the stickers were strategically placed on abandoned cars throughout the neighborhood. As predicted, within days all the cars miraculously disappeared. And abandoned car removal remained better after that.

FRICTION

DSNI's neighborhood leadership was tested in August 1986 when ACORN (Association of Community Organizations for Reform Now), a national multi-issue organizing group, chose Dudley as one of its target neighborhoods. By the time ACORN first expanded into Massachusetts in 1980, it had already developed a reputation among progressive organizers and funders for not working in coalition with other organizations. In Boston it was seen as invading the turf of Massachusetts Fair Share.[5] By 1986, ACORN had created a nonprofit development arm and wanted the city of Boston to give it some land to develop. Since the city was moving slowly on this demand, ACORN decided to set up a "tent city," erecting a small village of tents on a city-owned vacant lot. Without even bothering to contact DSNI, ACORN chose a lot on Dudley Street in the heart of DSNI's core area.

DSNI members were angry not only because ACORN, seen as an outsider to the neighborhood, had focused on Dudley Street without first contacting DSNI, which had been so carefully structured to empower residents and break the pattern of outsider-agency domination. But also, DSNI (as discussed in Chapter Four) had successfully negotiated with the city to have it *stop* disposing of vacant land until the neighborhood was able to complete a comprehensive redevelopment plan and exercise community control. At the August 4 DSNI board meeting, board members expressed concern "about ACORN wanting to develop on Dudley Street without any experience and without being involved in the planning process."[6] After angry exchanges between ACORN and DSNI supporters, a scaled-down version of the event took place with little fanfare. The city of Boston kept its word to DSNI and refused to dispose of any city-owned vacant land before DSNI's comprehensive plan was created.

DSNI had other conflicts with ACORN. ACORN's organizing approach included a door-to-door canvas asking money for memberships. Several DSNI members reported that they were made to believe that ACORN canvassers were actually from DSNI.

More tension arose during DSNI's campaign to have a commuter rail line running through the neighborhood open a local station for easy access to downtown. The Midlands rail corridor was the eastern boundary of DSNI's core area, running adjacent to the Uphams Corner neighborhood. It was used by trains carrying suburban commuters into downtown Boston. But Dudley residents could only see the trains shoot by at high speed without ever stopping. With the elimination of Roxbury's elevated Orange Line, taken down in May 1986, the Dudley Street neighborhood was left with only limited bus service to downtown. Many in Dudley believed that the Massachusetts Bay Transportation Authority (MBTA) didn't want the trains to stop in neighborhoods where people of color were in the majority because that would lessen ridership from the mostly White suburbs. In 1987, however, after a series of meetings with the MBTA, and with the strong backing of the city Transportation Department, transit officials agreed to open a station on Dudley Street as well as one in Mattapan. DSNI had done door-knocking and held several meetings on the issue. Just as a neighborhood victory was imminent, ACORN scheduled a couple of meetings of their own and proceeded to claim responsibility for the success in the local press. A year later, after failing to win resident support to be designated the developer of a lot in DSNI's secondary area, ACORN stopped their activities in Dudley.

Also during summer 1986, DSNI began having informal discussions with Local 26 of the Hotel and Restaurant Employees International Union about potential joint projects. Local 26 had a long history of progressive organizing transcending traditional workplace issues. Its membership was composed primarily of people of color earning relatively low wages. Numerous Local 26 members lived in the Dudley area and some of them were members of DSNI, though they did not participate actively. Local 26 had identified housing as the number-one need of its members and decided to seek contributions for a housing fund from employers during its next contract negotiations. The union was also interested in using pension funds to develop affordable housing for its members and others in the Dudley neighborhood.

Since DSNI and Local 26 were two of the strongest multiracial organizing groups in Boston, with overlapping memberships, an alliance offered tremendous potential to effectively combine workplace and community agendas. DSNI could galvanize community support for the union's organizing drives and housing development plans and provide assistance in finding appropriate sites for development within the context of the DSNI neighborhood plan. For DSNI, Local 26 represented a potential resource of millions of dollars for housing development. Further, Local 26 offered to help Dudley residents fill job openings in unionized hotels. DSNI could provide a connection to the union for inactive Local 26 members who lived in the Dudley area, and Local 26 could help DSNI organize union members who lived in Dudley but were not yet DSNI members. To start, DSNI and Local 26 identified overlapping members and made presentations at each other's membership meetings. Plans were drawn up for a neighborhood job fair with representatives from local hotels. In November 1986, DSNI members joined in a series of actions against a local nonunion hotel, the Back Bay Hilton, to show broad-based community support for the Local 26 organizing drive.

The relationship soured as Local 26 began to implement its development agenda in the DSNI area—without adapting it to DSNI's comprehensive planning process and long-range timetable. The union had identified a large city-owned lot on Dacia Street for which it wanted to be a codeveloper with Nuestra Comunidad Development Corporation. Local 26 saw the project as a necessary step to obtaining access to Hotel and Restaurant Employees International pension funds and building momentum for their upcoming battle to include an unprecedented housing benefit in hotel contracts. Local 26 would take care of much of the financing and organizing while Nuestra Comunidad would be responsible for project management and design. They needed to convince the neighborhood and the city to designate the team as developers of the site. The organizations were a mismatch. Local 26 was one of the most aggressive groups in Boston, famous for its rapid-fire, confrontational organizing tactics. Development is a notoriously slow process and Nuestra Comunidad was just putting together a track record; its first construction project, which took much longer to complete than originally proposed, met with considerable local criticism over the design of the houses.

DSNI decided not to sidetrack its own development agenda by playing a significant part in the Dacia project. As problems arose in the Dacia process, DSNI did not meet Local 26's expectation that it would play a cleanup role. To make matters worse, opposition to the Local 26-Nuestra Comunidad project was fueled by a small group of people who portrayed DSNI and Nuestra Comunidad as a Hispanic conspiracy to take over the neighborhood. The Dacia lot was eventually awarded to another team made up primarily of minority developers who had the backing of City Councilor Bruce Bolling, the representative for the district; unfortunately, their Dacia houses, completed in 1989, did not fulfill the design and quality commitments made to the community or the city. Though DSNI and Local 26 continued to explore avenues of cooperation over financing and developing housing and sometimes worked in coalition together with other groups—such as a later antiredlining campaign—the goal of a far-reaching alliance between a powerful union and community group died an early death.

In contrast to the rhetorical charges of Latino domination leveled by opponents of DSNI and Nuestra Comunidad, as DSNI's organizing picked up steam, Latino participation lagged behind their numbers in the Dudley population. Melvyn Colón, former DSNI president and Nuestra Comunidad director, says he purposely downplayed Latino organizing: "I didn't want [DSNI] to become perceived as a Latino agency so I sort of never focused on the need to organize within the Latino communities."

Over the years, DSNI tried and succeeded in increasing Latino involvement and leadership, but organizing among Latinos remained relatively difficult. The Latino population is even younger (with a median age of 22) and poorer than the larger Dudley population, with fewer homeowners and more vulnerable tenants. There are also tensions among Puerto Ricans, the largest Latino ethnic group in Dudley; Dominicans, the next largest; and Hondurans, Guatemalans and others. Miren Uriarte, senior researcher at the Mauricio Gastón Institute for Latino Community Development and Public Policy of the University of Massachusetts-Boston, believes that the combination of differing places of origin, the geographical dispersion of Latinos across the city, and severe financial conditions, has made organizing Latinos in Boston particularly difficult.[7]

"I think part of it is history," says DSNI board member Arnaldo Solís. "African Americans have been burned a lot here in this neighborhood, and they've been living in Roxbury for quite a while now, so they know the history, and what has been attempted before, and when they saw that this [DSNI] was going on, they saw it as an opportunity to finally do something...The Latino community is relatively young in Boston, and particularly so in Roxbury." Solís continues, "There is some tension between the Latino community and the Black community, and I think that tension has been created from the outside...[There] was the constant publicity about how rapidly the Latino community is growing, and how the Latino community will eventually surpass the African American community, and what that means in terms of political clout and economic [clout] as well...There are some politicians or some so-called leaders within the Hispanic [and African American] communities that are playing into that and are using it for their own interest." Others feel "that the Latino community should work together with the Black community because we share a lot of similar needs and, therefore, we are a stronger force together than separate." Working together, of course, is what DSNI stands for.

CULTIVATING RESOURCES

In September 1986, DSNI held its first multicultural neighborhood festival at the Ralph Waldo Emerson Elementary School on Dudley Street. Though the event was sparsely attended by adults, several hundred children and teenagers participated in a variety of activities ranging from face painting to relay races and performances by local musical groups. The enthusiastic response from young people underscored the great need and potential for youth-centered activities in the neighborhood, a potential that DSNI would more fully develop in later years.

By fall 1986, DSNI was working intensively with five neighborhood associations it had helped create or strengthen. On Brook Avenue, for example, DSNI helped residents push the city Inspectional Services Department to tear down a house destroyed by fire. On Leyland and Julian Streets, DSNI organizers worked with residents to revitalize community gardens in cooperation with the Boston Natural Areas Fund, which owned the gardens, and Boston Urban Gardeners. The Leyland Street garden gazebo had become a hangout for drug use and drinking, and the corner across the street, East Cottage and Dudley, was a major drug-dealing site—many of the buyers were Whites from around the city and suburbs, a subject addressed in Chapter Eight. DSNI worked with the Leyland Street Crime Watch to hold meetings with the police and other city officials, leading to a greater police presence at the corner and several arrests. The first meeting of the Woodville Area Neighborhood Association (WANA) focused on the "Don't Dump On Us" campaign, but many other issues soon emerged. For example, WANA members decided to improve safety at an accident-prone intersection, where they feared a child would be hit by a speeding car. They met with officials from the Department of Public Works and collected signatures in support of placing a stop sign at the intersection. Within months, a stop sign appeared. WANA's first president, Cynthia Lopes-Jefferson, was elected to the DSNI board, and many members became active participants in DSNI's neighborhood planning efforts.

On November 5, DSNI hosted a group of local foundations. It was the first significant attempt to bring foundations other than Riley into the process of revitalizing the neighborhood. The Riley Foundation deserved recognition for the dedicated work and resources they were putting into the project. On the other hand, DSNI and Riley personnel wanted the message to go out that the Riley Foundation could not be the sole support for DSNI. The Funders Day was sponsored by Associated Grantmakers of Massachusetts (AGM), an umbrella organization for local foundations, which had taken the unusual step months earlier to act as the fiscal conduit for Riley's first grant to DSNI because DSNI had not yet secured its own tax-exempt status. AGM invited its entire membership to tour Dudley and hear a presentation about DSNI activities. Following the presentation at La Alianza Hispana, the group of about 30 funders walked over to the Shirley-Eustis House, the governor's mansion-turned-museum, for a reception and informal discussion. The president of the museum regaled the group with a history of the house, portraying the time of its heyday as the good ol' days. The fact that the ancestors of many of the mansion's current neighbors would have been slaves at that time seemed lost on the museum president.

One of the goals of Funders Day was to address the concern of many DSNI agency members that DSNI would end up raising money for itself at the expense of other agencies in the neighborhood.

Traditionally, agencies compete for often severely limited resources and stake claims to particular geographic areas or population groups. DSNI had to show that fundraising did not have to be a zero-sum game. Instead, foundations would channel more money into the neighborhood if the agencies worked together, strengthening not only DSNI, but each individual agency's ability to fund its operations. Literature about various agencies was included in a packet given to the funders and, following the formal presentation, agency leaders had a chance to talk informally with foundation officials, most of whom they had not met before. By most accounts, the event was a huge success. Funders left with genuine enthusiasm about DSNI and the efforts to revitalize Dudley, and local agencies developed new relationships with funders.

Numerous agencies clearly benefited from the Riley Foundation's strong commitment to Dudley. Before DSNI's formation, in fiscal year (FY) 1984 (June 1, 1983 to May 31, 1984), Riley made two Dudley-related grants totaling $90,000, including $30,000 for La Alianza Hispana. In FY 1985, as the Dudley initiative was evolving, the grants increased to $266,500 for ten projects. In FY 1986, when DSNI received its first grant of $70,000, funding for nine other Dudley-related projects totaled $285,000. In FY 1987, total grants doubled to $593,000 for 13 projects, not including direct DSNI support. By May 1989, Riley's cumulative total of Dudley-related grants had passed $2.3 million, including $414,500 in direct support to DSNI. By the end of FY 1993, Riley's Dudley-related grants would top $3.2 million, including a cumulative total of nearly $950,000 for DSNI.[8] Over the years, Riley's support of DSNI would be bolstered by many other local and national foundations.

The Riley Foundation took a strategic approach to grants in the Dudley area. For example, it used large grants to Morgan Memorial Goodwill Industries as leverage to open doors for residents. The purpose of the grants was to help Morgan Memorial move its headquarters to a site in DSNI's core area in the Crosstown Industrial Park across the street from the Orchard Park public housing development. In May 1986, Newell Flather and Peter Medoff were invited as observers to attend a Morgan Memorial meeting at which plans would be presented to the "community," largely meaning agency heads, developers and others associated with the project. Few residents were in attendance. As the plans went up on the screen, Flather was struck by the stark image of a brick wall facing the windows of Orchard Park. It was "clearly a fortress," he says. "There was no way for the community to get into the place [without walking] around this entire huge building."

The plans called for a Morgan Memorial Goodwill store. "They're all over the city," says Flather, "and they're like any other retail shop where clothing and appliances are sold. And any retailer knows that if you have street space, you want windows...[to attract people] to come in and shop." Yet Morgan Memorial plans showed only second-story windows. "They were to let light in," says Flather, but "you couldn't see in, and we objected."

At a different meeting in Orchard Park, recalls Sarah Flint, Tenants Association leader Edna Bynoe angrily insisted to Morgan Memorial personnel, "We don't want anything looking like a prison." Morgan Memorial responded to the criticism by adding windows to the store and headquarters, as well as a door in the wall facing Orchard Park. While the wall facing the housing development still appears somewhat as a fortress and the door generally remains locked to the public, community access was increased and Morgan Memorial developed a good relationship with Orchard Park; later, Orchard Park tenants organizer Steve Ambush became the chaplain at Morgan Memorial. Morgan Memorial opened its building up to Orchard Park Tenants Association annual meetings and other Dudley community events and joined in DSNI's human services agency collaborative.

"DON'T DUMP ON US" II: TRASH TRANSFER STATIONS

In June 1987, DSNI turned up the heat on a problem that residents had been complaining about for years: the illegal trash transfer stations that were breeding grounds for rats, mosquitoes, odors and disease. Trash transfer stations handle massive amounts of refuse, separating it into piles of different materials and eventually transferring it for final disposal. Five transfer stations operated in the Dudley area, more than anywhere else in the city. Two of them were covered operations, licensed and monitored by the Department of Health and Hospitals. The other three were unlicensed, open-air facilities and major health hazards to the community.

The nauseating stench and noise from these operations were frequently unbearable. Many families kept their windows closed even in sweltering summer heat. Others, recalls Andrea Nagel, opened their windows to seek some relief from the oven-like heat, only to deal with their kids vomiting from the stench. Residents described rats "the size of dogs." Two of the sites were near Mason Elementary School. Trucks rumbled up and down the blocks, back and forth to the trash stations. Children had to watch out for the trucks as they walked by the dumps on their way to school. Sometimes they stopped to play in the trash where seagulls were flying around. A Cape Verdean couple, Olivia and Jose Barros, lived with their family on East Cottage Street, adjacent to an illegal block-long trash station on Robey Street run by AFL Disposal Company. Many blamed the dump when their young son was rushed to the hospital, where he spent a week recovering from a serious infection.

Ray Flynn had made an appearance in the neighborhood during his 1983 mayoral campaign and promised to shut down the illegal trash transfer stations. He renewed that pledge at DSNI's June 1986 "Don't Dump On Us" meeting at St. Patrick's Church. After the hospitalization of the Barros child, the neighborhood demanded action, not words. DSNI members and staff met with the city's Public Works and Law Departments. They were told that the city was in court with the operators and could not act without a judge's ruling. The legal cases had dragged on for years with seemingly endless appeals. At the same time, city health inspectors regularly cited the operations for numerous violations. The fines were so low, however, that the operators paid them and kept right on doing business. DSNI representatives also met with Flynn's chief environmental policy analyst, Robert Bauman, who expressed sympathy and an eagerness to work with DSNI, but offered no solutions.

An internal report issued in May 1987 by the city's Office of Environmental Affairs said that AFL Disposal Company had "almost continuously violated the law with impunity for four years."[9] AFL Disposal was owned by Anthony Lepardo, a Milton resident who, along with members of his family, owned several properties around Dudley. The Lepardos had a reputation for property speculation and dealing in drugs and stolen goods and had intimidated many residents in the past. Anthony Lepardo was arrested in 1986 and charged with receiving stolen goods, but was never indicted. He would later be convicted after being indicted with his son Frank on charges of heading a $155 million drug-smuggling ring—among other things, authorities alleged that in 1981 Lepardo used AFL Disposal to store drugs.[10]

Angry neighbors of the illegal transfer stations began meeting with DSNI organizers Andrea Nagel and Marvin Martin to discuss strategy for shutting them down—Martin, an experienced African

American organizer who formerly worked for Massachusetts Fair Share in the Roxbury area, was a member of the DSNI staff from November 1986 to mid-1988. The campaign against the transfer stations brought residents from the nearby Orchard Park housing development together with homeowners and tenants around the neighborhood. DSNI decided to organize a demonstration to stop trucks from entering the trash station run by K & C (Kouns and Clifford) Disposal and then hold a march to Lepardo's AFL Disposal sites. Organizers knocked on the doors of homes near the trash stations and enlisted the participation of many people who had not previously joined DSNI.

This type of direct action was a new strategy for many in the neighborhood. Some residents were not eager to "cause trouble," fearing they would further alienate the city officials who had long ignored them. Cape Verdeans especially had little experience, much less success, in taking to the streets to demand their rights. Longtime DSNI board member Maria-Goreth Fidalgo, whose family had emigrated from Cape Verde when it was still under Portuguese rule, says that in the experience of people who lived under colonization, "When you ask for something, most likely you won't get it." Older people who had immigrated before Cape Verde gained independence in 1975 were most inhibited by the disempowering effects of colonization. On the other hand, the close-knit nature of the Cape Verdean community facilitated grassroots organizing.

Slowly, DSNI members were raising their expectations of government and confidence in direct action. Board member Alice Gomes, who helped organize the protest at the transfer stations—one of which was a block from her house—declared, "We were fed up and we just said, 'No more!' We won't live in this filth."[11]

The demonstration was set for 10 A.M. on Tuesday, July 8—three days before the annual neighborhood cleanup. While no one wanted to risk arrest, DSNI members decided they would block the entrance to K & C Disposal until police ordered them to move. Though it was a difficult time to recruit large numbers of marchers, the action was scheduled for midmorning on a weekday because it was the time of busiest truck traffic. It would also give reporters plenty of time to meet deadlines for the evening news shows and the next day's papers.

By 10 A.M., about 100 people had gathered in front of the gates. They set up a picket line with a giant banner proclaiming "We've Had Enough of Your Garbage." Signs demanded, "Don't Bury Us Alive," "Don't Dump On Us" and "We Want a Healthy Community." Protesters, many of them wearing surgical masks and gas masks, circled the entrance chanting "Shut 'em down." Speaker after speaker recounted the horrors of living next to the trash stations and criticized the city for not shutting them down. Orchard Park Tenants Association Chair Sarah Flint and other residents described how their children would have to walk by the dumps to get to school each morning. Olivia Barros told of her son's illness. Father Walter Waldron described the impact on his parishioners. Other residents spoke of the sickening smells and rats. Huge trucks loaded with trash approached the gates and only after long delays would the demonstrators move enough to let them pass.

Finally, the crowd began their half-mile march to AFL Disposal. There, several more speakers rose to demand that the city shut down the dumps. Jose Barros told reporters, "They tell us to sell the house. But we're not gonna sell it, because if you sell the house, the problem's gonna stay here. We want *them* to go away."

City Council President Bruce Bolling, the only elected official to join the demonstrators, suggested to thunderous applause that the residents visit Mayor Flynn with some of the trash if he didn't take immediate action. Several residents promised to do just that if Flynn didn't act within a week. Flynn Environmental Policy Analyst Robert Bauman told reporters at the demonstration, "The city just can't walk up and put padlocks on their gates."[12]

The event was covered by all major media in the city. Responding to the negative publicity, Flynn had an aide call DSNI the next morning and schedule a meeting. On the morning of July 14, a group of DSNI members and staff rode public transit together down to City Hall. No one knew what to expect. Over 15 administration officials greeted them in the mayor's office. This was the first time DSNI representatives had entered the inner halls of power in City Hall. It was both intimidating and exhilarating.

Mayor Flynn came bounding into the room. Flynn was already familiar with DSNI from previous organizing campaigns and from the relationship—discussed in Chapter Four—that DSNI had built with the Public Facilities Department. His support in the past had been instrumental to cleaning up the vacant lots. "What's going on?" he immediately asked the DSNI representatives. They again recounted the horror of living with the trash stations and closed by stating "enough is enough." Flynn asked his staff for a report on what they were doing. The lawyers began explaining the ins and outs of the slow court process. Cutting off a lawyer in mid-sentence, Flynn shouted, "I don't want to hear any more legal stuff. I want them shut down now!"

DSNI members left City Hall feeling pleasantly surprised at Flynn's strong response. As Orchard Park's Sarah Flint puts it, "It is something to be a registered voter. But when you actually exercise those rights…and get things done you find out, yes, there is definitely something to doing advocacy work, but not doing it by yourself." She adds, "You don't know unless you try if you can accomplish anything."

On July 21, DSNI attended a meeting of the city Health and Hospitals Commission where testimony was presented about the trash transfer stations, including the dumping of asbestos. The commission decided to enforce a state statute allowing the closure of businesses cited as threats to public health. The next day, city health officials ordered the illegal trash stations to cease and desist operations within 24 hours or the city would padlock the gates. The trash stations ignored the order.

Anthony Lepardo angrily huffed to reporters, "I don't need no permits. From my property to another piece of property, I do not need permits." He blamed the trash on other illegal dumpers and local residents. "It's all gypsy rubbish," he declared, "including from the people next door."[13]

On July 23, Mayor Flynn led a team of city officials in padlocking the gates. "This is a public health menace to all the people who live in the area," Flynn told a crowd of DSNI members and reporters. "I'm sure there will be a legal challenge to what we are doing, but we'll stand behind the community 100 percent to keep these illegal transfer stations closed down forever." A newly inspired Robert Bauman told reporters, "If Anthony Lepardo trespasses here again, we will bust him for it."

Olivia Barros declared, "Our children live and play here. The people that dump the trash have no respect for anyone else. Now that they are closed, we'll make sure that they stay closed and clean."[14] Crews from the Department of Public Works began cleaning the sites. When the owners of K & C cut through the padlock and attempted to resume operations, the city ordered a round-the-clock police guard. Attempts to beat the city in court this time were unsuccessful. The *Boston Globe* ran an August 4 editorial praising the mayor's role in shutting down the trash stations. DSNI showed that turning up the heat on city government can bring mutually beneficial light.

"The squeaky wheel gets the oil," says Sophia McCarthy, a longtime Dudley resident and board member active in the trash station campaign. "So we squeak." To push the metaphor further, before DSNI could become enough of a "squeaky wheel" in the ears of city officials to prompt action, it had to organize residents into a vehicle whose wheels were turning together with enough power to move the neighborhood and then the city.

TURNING POINT

Father Walter Waldron of St. Patrick's Church says the trash transfer station campaign "tested the mettle of DSNI—of how it was going to be able to work, both with the people and with the political forces downtown." DSNI demonstrated a "commitment to stay the distance. It wasn't just a show [to] give certain people publicity." Waldron says, "I think when some of the trash folks were trashed—closed down—that it then became [acceptable] to believe that if they could be changed, well, then, [so could] other things."

For Cape Verdeans especially, recalls former DSNI organizer Adalberto Teixeira, the campaign against the trash transfer stations was a turning point. "People finally said, 'Hey, if we stick together we might be able to get things done here.'" Cape Verdeans had a special interest in DSNI efforts around housing. Cape Verdean families often doubled up to accommodate lower-income relatives or new immigrants not yet able to afford their own places. In addition, numerous Cape Verdean businesspeople had opened small stores on Dudley Street and were committed to strengthening the neighborhood's economic vitality.

Prior to DSNI's emergence, local organizations and city government had all but ignored the small but growing Cape Verdean community. The local Cape Verdean Community House was ineffective and closed in fall 1989. DSNI's bylaws mandated Cape Verdean representation on the board and empowered Cape Verdeans not only in Dudley, but in the larger city.

Adalberto Teixeira, a longtime Dudley resident who became a DSNI organizer in May 1987, cohosted a Cape Verdean radio show and was well known in the community. He would announce community events on the show, including those sponsored by DSNI. He recalls how after a radio announcement, people would show up the next morning at the DSNI office with problems ranging from housing violations to unemployment. "They came for anything *but* the issue that I had mentioned on the radio show. But they came, and one way or the other they started relating to me and to DSNI. Some people even thought that DSNI was one of the small old little City Halls in Roxbury."

DSNI helped Cape Verdeans press the city to establish the position of Cape Verdean liaison in the mayor's Office of Neighborhood Services. The liaisons to different neighborhoods and constituencies function both as advocates for the communities they represent to City Hall and advocates for the mayor's agenda to those constituencies. In November 1988, the Cape Verdean community working with DSNI experienced both a victory and a loss. The mayor agreed to hire a Cape Verdean resident to be his liaison to the community. The person he picked was DSNI organizer Adalberto Teixeira.

DSNI, says Teixeira, told Cape Verdeans, "'You count...You are a member. Here is your membership card'...And people carry that little membership card in their wallets with pride. I still have mine."

Dudley residents had come a long way from demands at the first DSNI community meeting that they should make up a majority of the board to assuming formal leadership and asserting their power in shaping the staff, building a solid membership base, organizing the successful "Don't Dump On Us" campaign and undertaking the comprehensive planning explored in Chapter Four. They would go on to achieve a level of community control over development that no neighborhood-based organization had ever won before.

1991 DSNI annual meeting and board election at St. Patrick's Church. Front row (l to r): Father Walter Waldron, Paul Yelder, Ro Whittington, Lessie Spann, Linda Joyce, Sue Beaton, Ricardo Tavares, Arnaldo Solís, Calucha Campbell, Gus Newport. Back row (l to r): Kyle McKinney, Bob Haas, Anna Brassard, Stephen Hanley, Olivio Teixeira, Ché Madyun, Clayton Turnbull, Julio Henríquez, Della Jones.

Resident Mildred Shelton, Mayor Ray Flynn and State Rep. Gloria Fox (back to camera) at the DSNI neighborhood cleanup, July 1987.

4

PLANNING AN URBAN VILLAGE

While cleaning up Dudley's vacant land through the "Don't Dump On Us" campaign, DSNI began the process of recreating the lots as housing, parks, community centers and businesses. Organizing and planning went hand in hand. In Andrea Nagel's words, DSNI addressed "the issues of today as it was dealing with those of tomorrow."[1]

DSNI members often talked of "flipping planning on its head." Instead of trying to participate in a top-down planning process directed by city government, Dudley residents and agencies would create their own "bottom-up" plan and invite the city to participate. This time, urban renewal would not be "urban removal" because the residents themselves would be the planners.

BOTTOM-UP PLANNING: FORGING A PARTNERSHIP WITH THE CITY

The traditional approach to urban planning calls for the "experts" at City Hall to run the show with strong input from bankers and private developers and lesser input, if any, from community residents. Even a liberal administration which invites neighborhood participation does not want to give up control to low-income residents and community organizations. DSNI won that control.

DSNI had an impressive record to strengthen its position with the city: the ability to unify a cross-section of the neighborhood, grassroots organizing victories and planning funds from respected foundations. Collaboration of any kind would assure the city some degree of influence over a planning process that was clearly going forward with or without it. Over the years, DSNI would forge a new kind of partnership between a community group and city government—a partnership marked not by co-optation of the community group, but by often difficult yet fruitful collaboration between partners with compatible goals but different agendas.

In April 1986, DSNI began discussing Dudley's vacant land with the Public Facilities Department (PFD), the agency that controlled city-owned land and was responsible for most neighborhood-focused development projects in Boston. At the time, PFD owned hundreds of vacant lots in Dudley. Most of the early discussions between DSNI and PFD focused on the need to clean and secure vacant lots. PFD cooperated, through its municipal police force, with DSNI's "Don't Dump On Us" campaign.

When DSNI informed PFD of its intention to hire consultants and create its own plan for development, PFD was uncomfortable at the prospect of losing control, but nevertheless offered to assist. In fact, in an attempt to retain as much control as possible, a PFD official urged DSNI to create a joint planning process in which PFD would share decision making with DSNI. A group less committed to neighborhood empowerment might have jumped at the offer of joint planning with the city. But DSNI saw it as a potentially suffocating partnership on the city's terms. Instead, DSNI stuck to its proposal that PFD cooperate in DSNI's own plan—developed with the help of independent consultants working for DSNI.

In July 1986, PFD Director Lisa Chapnick wrote DSNI that PFD was "committed to working cooperatively with the DSNI and its [planning] consultant." PFD offered to "make available land inventory information and other relevant data to help establish a neighborhood data base"; assign staff to work with DSNI "to review and evaluate existing City policy and process with regard to development in the Dudley Street target area"; and work with DSNI "to explore policy and process changes that will help achieve our common goals of community revitalization that provides both protection and opportunity for existing residents."[2]

"People say 'I'm of the community, I'm for the community and I'm representing the community' all the time," says Chapnick, reflecting on why DSNI won her support. "They very rarely are. They represent an aspect or an issue or a perspective. My experience of DSNI was that it was genuine, that this was really a community effort and that the leadership—both the staff and board leadership—were as committed to the process as they were to the product."

It wasn't the numbers that impressed Chapnick. At that point DSNI had about 400 resident and agency members. "The numbers weren't huge," she says. "Who's kidding who? No, it was the fact that the focus was organizing. The focus was organizing around leadership development, around community development, around...getting that circle bigger and bigger and bigger." She adds, "I always felt like the...number one thing to DSNI was the organization and the organizing and the people, and that out of that would come a shared vision, and out of that vision would come action—and that was the order. [DSNI] was unique in that nobody was setting themselves up as *the* leader or *the* voice or *the* this or *the* that. And [DSNI was] not about to let the city do that either, which was perfectly appropriate because [it was] walking and talking the same game."

It was very clear, observes Chapnick, "that the first thing" DSNI wanted from the city "was respect and equality. That [DSNI was] not, in any way, going to be a junior partner, that it was [DSNI's] neighborhood, it was [DSNI's] vision and [DSNI] had rights. And the fact is that...[DSNI] had earned it."

In June 1986, DSNI had reached agreement with PFD over a moratorium on the disposition of city-owned vacant land. The differing agendas between the city and DSNI were already coming into play. PFD wanted to move the land as quickly as possible to meet Mayor Flynn's commitment to dispose of all city-owned land by the end of his term. DSNI saw this activity as repeating the mistakes of the past. It would allow market forces to drive development and undermine DSNI's efforts to prevent speculation and displacement and implement a coherent community-controlled development plan. With DSNI's planning process about to begin—funded and controlled by the neighborhood, but with the support and assistance of the city—PFD agreed that it made sense to hold off on any more land disposition until the broad blueprint for future development was completed.

GREATER ROXBURY NEIGHBORHOOD AUTHORITY (GRNA)

DSNI's moratorium agreement and evolving partnership contrasted starkly with the city's response to the other major organizing effort around development taking place in Roxbury, the Greater Roxbury Neighborhood Authority (GRNA). While DSNI was focused on rebuilding a neighborhood, GRNA worked on Greater Roxbury as a whole. The two organizations often collaborated, but the city reacted much more negatively to GRNA's efforts at community control—to the detriment of Roxbury citizens.

GRNA was launched in January 1985 with the leadership of former mayoral candidate Mel King and longtime Roxbury activists in movements for Black empowerment, economic justice and community development, including Chuck Turner, Ken Wade, Willie Jones and Bob Terrell. The week before the first GRNA meeting was scheduled to take place, the BRA's Dudley Square Plan (described in Chapter Two) was leaked to the press. When GRNA held its first press conference on February 14—Frederick Douglass Day—it called for a moratorium on the disposition of city-owned land in Roxbury until a "neighborhood authority" was established "to review, monitor and exercise some degree of control over development in the area."[3]

Within the Flynn administration, many viewed GRNA's efforts as little more than a continuation of the 1983 mayoral contest between Ray Flynn and Mel King (actually King played a catalyst role with GRNA; he helped found the organization, but was not significantly involved as it developed). Some of the White activists who joined the Flynn administration operated with an "If you're not for us, you're against us" attitude in their dealings with activists of color and seemed unwilling to take an open-minded approach in understanding the real issues facing the citizens of Roxbury.

GRNA cochair Ken Wade observes, "Flynn basically got less than 5 percent of the Black vote...[He] started out with a problem in terms of how he builds a relationship" with the Black community. Wade says he participated in some meetings to try to "establish a relationship with the so-called progressives that were in the administration—saying, 'In the context of politics in Boston, we're probably on the same side more of the time than we are on the opposite side, so doesn't it make sense to see how we can bridge this Ray Flynn/Mel King schism? Because it is just going to be good for progressive politics to do that.'" They saw politics differently. Wade heard a Flynn adviser say that they "have a coalition government." The coalition includes "the Left, which is them, and Ray [Flynn's] other constituency from his early days in politics, the Right." Most progressive activists of color were outside the "coalition."

GRNA's early organizing culminated in September 1985 at a town meeting of over 400 residents. A 13-member representative body of neighborhood associations, tenants, small merchants, clergy, community development corporations (CDCs) and other constituencies was ratified as the Interim Roxbury Planning Advisory Committee (PAC), pending later elections. After a series of negotiations, the city grudgingly accepted the Interim PAC and agreed to a compromise "statement of principles," among them, adding eight members to the PAC appointed by the mayor and recognizing the PAC as the "public participatory body for the area" which will "set development objectives and criteria." PAC approval would be required for major zoning and planning decisions and requests for proposals on development projects.

Mayor Flynn seemed to have publicly supported the compromise agreement at an October community meeting, but the victory was short-lived. The BRA board of directors, whose formal approval was needed, stalled in bringing the agreement to a vote and then, on May 1, 1986, granted the PAC only "review and comment" advisory power, something already available through the system of community participation set up by Flynn. Many felt that Flynn had reneged on his agreement, since it was believed he could have secured board approval for the negotiated plan if he really wanted it. BRA Director Steve Coyle said he recommended that the board approve the negotiated statement of principles, explaining, "I believe it wouldn't have presented a problem but I respect the board's right to take a position independent of the [BRA] staff and the director." As reported by the *Boston Herald*, a "City Hall source said the abrupt change in tactics may have been the result of concerns by the mayor that giving Roxbury residents a significant voice in the development of their neighborhood would set a precedent for other neighborhoods."[4]

The PAC filed a lawsuit to try to stop the BRA from going ahead with development without a comprehensive redevelopment plan and more community control. It achieved a political victory when most of the mayor's eight PAC appointees supported the suit. The suit was filed as a form of leverage to encourage city concessions and was not followed to its conclusion in court. Negotiations continued between the PAC and the city, and Flynn named the original 13-member PAC plus the 8 mayoral appointees as the official Roxbury Neighborhood Council (RNC), with formal *review* authority over all development in Roxbury. Other neighborhood councils were set up around the city.

"We thought that being institutionalized officially, even without power, was better than being not institutionalized and not having any power," Ken Wade explains. Since Flynn would have appointed an official body anyway, "We figured...our agenda would be far better served by being there and fighting both on the inside—which we did via our official seat and role on the council—but then also, having an advocacy organization—GRNA—that was free to do other kinds of things." Wade says, "To a certain extent...we've won the victory on the principles," for example, the principle of housing affordability.

DSNI and GRNA began organizing to control community development at around the same time. Both made the decision early on to avoid being direct developers or service providers and to concentrate on advocacy and planning. However, there were also important differences between the two organizations. GRNA's target area was much larger geographically and included neighborhoods such as Fort Hill and Dudley Station which were already experiencing large-scale speculation and development pressure. The GRNA leadership was drawn primarily from Roxbury's African American community, in contrast to DSNI's structured guarantee of equal minimum representation from area ethnic groups. Another difference was that DSNI had substantial involvement by area agencies and significant financial support, beginning with the Riley Foundation, while GRNA was never able to develop a solid financial base.

Ken Wade says fundraising was made more difficult because GRNA was competing for limited funds with overlapping organizations. "GRNA found itself going to different meetings with the same people...Do we really need six coalitions to accomplish these three things?...We were in CCCD [the Coalition for Community Control of Development], which was applying for funding. We were in the Washington Street Corridor Coalition, which was applying for funding. We were trying to do this Eviction Free Zone...And some of us also were in the Rainbow Coalition. You show up at the Boston Foundation—it's like, 'Which hat are you all wearing today?'" Comparing GRNA and DSNI, Wade adds, "I think that our basket was too big, but also it was a slightly different basket. [DSNI was] organizing to turn a specific neighborhood around. That was something that a foundation can more easily respond to than the notion of creating a vehicle to advocate for and/or control development."

The lack of sustained funds, says Wade, prevented GRNA from being "able to institutionalize the effort in such a way that it could be long-lasting and sustaining." It's a challenge faced by many groups: As Wade puts it, "You create a groundswell, but then you don't have the resources to sustain it."

Both organizations called for moratoriums on development in their respective areas until comprehensive development plans were created. The city agreed to the moratorium in Dudley, but not to a Roxbury-wide ban, which would have set a much bigger precedent. While GRNA was fighting to attain veto authority over development projects—the ability to *stop* projects that the community did not want—DSNI was able to create a vision for what *should* happen in the Dudley neighborhood. With limited resources and mostly volunteer labor—volunteers who were also busy with the day-to-day agenda of the Roxbury Neighborhood Council—the GRNA planning process was not sustained or comprehensive.

DSNI had a seat on the Interim PAC and was an active participant in internal strategy sessions and meetings with city officials. DSNI also provided small-scale resource support such as photocopying and mailing. In addition, the Riley Foundation, with encouragement from DSNI, made a grant to GRNA to support its operations. Still, their differing approaches raised tensions between them even as DSNI and GRNA collaborated. DSNI knew that to accomplish its agenda it needed support from outside the neighborhood, both within Greater Roxbury and within the city as a whole. At the same time, with an overwhelming work load within the neighborhood, there was little time left for coalition work with other Roxbury and citywide activists. DSNI had chosen an approach that relied on organizing a strong enough organization to maintain control while collaborating with city government. Some GRNA members questioned DSNI's independence and worried about it getting co-opted by the city. Some DSNI members worried that GRNA's approach was too confrontational.

As Wade sums it up, though, DSNI, GRNA and the RNC "were able to accomplish a united front on the broader issues of control over development." DSNI, he says, was able to "continue to pursue its agenda and not allow it[self] to get co-opted and used as leverage against the issues that the GRNA was raising." Over the years, the two groups worked cooperatively in areas such as development, zoning, tenant organizing and campaigns against redlining and for community reinvestment by banks.

The city's cooperation in the DSNI planning process didn't stop DSNI from protesting intolerable neighborhood conditions such as the trash transfer stations discussed in Chapter Three. Organizing continued to drive DSNI.

CHOOSING CONSULTANTS

Before hiring planning consultants in 1986, DSNI sought advice on how to conduct the process of creating a comprehensive development plan. No one on the board or staff had ever undertaken a plan of such magnitude. Indeed, all of the experts DSNI called in Boston and around the country said that a community-based plan of such magnitude had never been done before. Tunney Lee, chair of the Urban Studies Program at MIT and former commissioner of the Massachusetts Department of Capital Planning and Operations, volunteered to assist DSNI in the process of hiring consultants (he had earlier assisted La Alianza Hispana in preparing *From the Ground Up*).

DSNI completed its Request for Proposals (RFP) for hiring planning consultants in July. It raised $123,000 to pay for the consultants, $100,000 of which came from the Riley Foundation and $20,000 from the Boston-based Hyams Trust. Riley's grant was significant not only for its size, but because it provided further evidence of the trustees' willingness to be open and flexible in their relationship with DSNI. Before DSNI, they had reacted negatively to funding planning projects which, they believed, would lead only to reports gathering dust on the shelf.

DSNI's RFP made clear that the plan would not be an academic exercise: "This plan will not be shelved upon completion; residents and agencies in the neighborhood will be mobilized to advocate for the plan's adoption by the City of Boston and the City's financial community."

The RFP required a comprehensive plan with four components: planning, housing, economic development and social services. It called on the prospective consultant to be creative in identifying strategies and resources. Resident control was emphasized: "The planning process required by this contract will in many ways be a unique one. Neighborhood participation in the process is a prerequisite to an acceptable plan....The plan must directly reflect the priorities of the residents and organizations in the neighborhood." Consensus-building would be a crucial component of the planning process.

DSNI hosted a bidders' conference in September 1986, attended by over 25 planning consultants, where DSNI staff and board members explained the planning objectives and PFD staff assured the consultants of the city's commitment. DSNI also informed them of an unusual condition: The consultants would not receive final payment unless there was consensus in the neighborhood around the plan. The bidders, primarily from Boston and Cambridge, ranged from small, local housing consultants to multimillion-dollar general consulting firms with international contracts. DSNI's broad planning agenda proved to be a real challenge. Most firms had expertise in some areas, but not others. Six full proposals were submitted. The DSNI board formed a consultant selection committee of six board members—three residents and three agency representatives—plus Medoff and planning expert Tunney Lee as nonvoting members.

Two firms, both owned by people of color, stood out. They took very different approaches. Stull and Lee (no relation to Tunney), a Boston-based firm with extensive experience in local planning and urban architecture, submitted a proposal showcasing their record in quality physical design. Their plan would provide a detailed visual of development, but the proposal was weak on the community participation needed to make sure the plan truly reflected neighborhood ideas and consensus.[5]

DAC International, a firm from Washington, D.C., spelled out their inclusive consulting philosophy at the beginning of their proposal:

> The principles of planning for lower-income people and their communities are the same as those on behalf of the rich. Technicians are to be hired to serve the goals and objectives set by their employers and not the other way around.
>
> When it comes to low-income residents, however, the rules tend to be reversed. "The experts" seem intent on confusing their community clients with complex terms and coded jargon with the principal message of "let the professionals handle it, because only they understand the process." DAC believes the challenge of this assignment is to assure that the Dudley Street community will both understand the development process and make informed choices as to priorities and goals.
>
> In our view, community participation is a means to an end. It is the vehicle for community residents to become informed decision makers with the staying power and resources to move from decision-making to implementation.[6]

DAC was committed to a comprehensive organizing strategy to assure maximum resident participation in the planning. The DSNI selection committee felt that DAC was more likely to provide a plan with the necessary follow through to assure implementation. In addition, for a slightly lower cost, DAC assigned 30 percent more total hours to the project. Still, the selection committee had a difficult time deciding between the two finalists. Stull and Lee's strengths (physical design, presentation, locally based) and weaknesses (poor community participation strategy and process management, too design-focused) were reverse images of DAC's. The choice before DSNI was reminiscent of the hiring of the first executive director: One consulting candidate was the choice of the agencies, a safer, well known candidate. The other stressed organizing, came from out of town and was a riskier choice.

Selection committee members debated whether it was necessary to hire a local firm. DAC had been working with the Massachusetts Bay Transportation Authority for the past year setting up small businesses owned by people of color along the new Southwest Corridor public transit line and had conveniently opened an office right in Dudley Station, thus giving it some local ties. But Stull and Lee was the locally based firm, and they had the backing of agency representatives who knew their work and thought hiring locally would lessen opposition to the DSNI plan. Stull and Lee was also closely aligned with minority developers in Roxbury, many of whom had ties with some of the agency representatives on DSNI's board.

DAC was ultimately chosen at the urging of residents on the selection committee concerned with maximizing community participation. Shirley Carrington, then director of the Roxbury Multi-Service Center (RMSC), supported Stull and Lee. "I knew them and I liked their presentation...I just thought I could work with them and I thought they knew, really knew, this area better." DAC's hiring didn't stop Carrington from playing an enthusiastic role in the planning process. "You lose some and you win some," she says. "I wasn't going to allow that to hamper my continuing work on the project."

Resident committee member Tubal Padilla saw the consultant selection process as evidence that residents were gaining more power within DSNI. "We wanted someone from the outside," he asserts. An outsider wouldn't have ties strengthening the agencies' hand on the board and would be less likely to have preconceived notions about how to redevelop Dudley. Although there was resident/agency tension, Padilla says there wasn't "animosity." Over time, more trust developed among residents and agency representatives as people got to know each other better.

PLANNING BEGINS

As planning began in January 1987, two lots on Dudley Street were sold for over $20 per square foot, comparable to prices in the more affluent neighborhoods of the South End and the Fenway. Only a couple of years earlier, land prices, if you could find a buyer, were in the $2-$3 per square foot range. When the sale was reported during a Planning Committee meeting, one member joked that he didn't know whether to picket the speculators who had just spent so much money or laugh at them for throwing their money down the drain. The rising speculation strengthened the determination of DSNI members to keep Dudley from becoming "another South End."

DSNI announced the hiring of DAC and the commencement of the nine-month planning process in a press conference at the burned-out intersection of Winthrop and Dennis Streets. On a cold January morning under sunny skies, DSNI members were joined by PFD Director Lisa Chapnick as well as the principals of DAC and Roxbury Neighborhood Council representative Ken Wade. DSNI board members declared that over the next nine months the Dudley Street neighborhood would take control of its future and create a unified community vision of what that future would look like. DAC Vice President Stephen Plumer underscored DSNI's commitment to building on community assets. "We can't just concentrate on the absence of resources," he maintained. "We must look at the resources that are already there and build on them."[7] Chapnick pledged full city support to DSNI's efforts.

DAC International provided a diverse consulting team. Project manager Stephen Plumer, a former university dean who had designed the Institute for Law and Justice for the Antioch School of Law, had over 20 years of organizing and development experience, including Native American economic development projects. DAC Technical Director David Nesbitt, an African American, spoke both Spanish and Portuguese and had over 15 years of major development experience; he formerly had been director of Community Services and Facilities for the Rouse Company, known for, among other things, their development of the planned community of Columbia, Maryland. Other team members included DAC Vice President Carole Smith, an expert in entrepreneurship and human services development, and John Houston, who specialized in economic development and organizational development (Houston's sister, pop star Whitney Houston, later married singer Bobby Brown who hails from Orchard Park). DAC also employed Carla Alonso, a graduate of the MIT School of Urban Planning and a Puerto Rican activist in Boston, as its full-time local coordinator for the project. Some graduate student interns from local universities were employed in data gathering.

DAC held an all-day retreat with the DSNI board and staff to clarify roles and expectations, review the board's vision for the future and identify neighborhood assets and development opportunities and constraints. Board members highlighted several neighborhood assets: location close to downtown, ethnic diversity, neighborhood cohesiveness and the development potential of the abundant vacant land. The board's vision of the future Dudley Street neighborhood included low density, mixed-income housing with owner and renter occupancy, backyards and open space; a mix of retail stores and light industry with significant local ownership; and expanded community services with particular emphasis on the youth and elderly.[8]

DSNI's Planning Committee was responsible for overall management and guidance while Peter Medoff assumed day-to-day coordination with the consultant team. The Planning Committee met every other week with DAC consultants to review activities and improve the process. Because the Planning Committee also had broad development responsibility, it established several subcommittees to deal with such issues as the official rezoning of Roxbury, Dudley development proposals from private developers and financing opportunities. For example, the committee decided to pursue land acquisition financing from Consumers United Insurance Company (CUIC), a worker-owned company with a track record of investing in community projects, whose president was an old friend of DAC's Steve Plumer. DSNI secured a commitment for a $1 million line of credit from CUIC at favorable rates. Unfortunately, several years later, CUIC had to back out due to its own financial constraints.

The Planning Committee was made up of residents who then had little technical background in development, such as Tubal Padilla, Gail Latimore and Della Jones, and experienced development professionals such as Melvyn Colón, Paul Yelder and Bob Haas, who all worked as nonprofit developers. The residents worked hard to learn the technical aspects of development and did not hesitate to challenge the professionals. Tubal Padilla says that on the issues he cared about, he was "as influential as I could have been if I were" on the staff of a development agency. Partly because of his experience with the DSNI planning process, Padilla decided to leave the State Office of Children and pursue a degree and career in planning. His experience with DSNI's mobilization of people around environmental issues such as illegal dumps encouraged him to focus on urban environmental policy.

In the early months of planning, DAC focused on data gathering while DSNI organized resident planning committees. Organizing residents to participate in a long-range planning effort that wouldn't pay off for many years was far more difficult than mobilizing residents around immediate issues such as dump sites and abandoned cars. Residents were informed about the planning process through door-knocking, mailings, flyers, newspaper ads and articles, radio announcements and community meetings.

At a community-wide meeting attended by 150 DSNI members, DAC consultants began a long-term education process to encourage members to think about the neighborhood in new ways. In one particularly effective exchange, the consultants graphically showed how a low-income neighborhood of 15,000 people, with a per capita annual income of $4,000, actually translated into a local economy of $60 million dollars. The message: The Dudley Street neighborhood may be poor, and it may have lots of problems, but it also has enormous assets and resources that have never been tapped. DSNI members were clearly receptive.

DSNI organizers circulated sign-up sheets for resident committees to work with DAC in housing, economic development, human services and land use/planning. Over 120 residents signed up for the committees, which were chaired by board members. DSNI's capacity to keep people informed and involved was stretched to the limit as its two staff organizers juggled the planning process with organizing around the "bread and butter" issues that had built the organization in the first place. Usually, resident committee meetings would combine planning issues with more immediate organizing issues. The lines distinguishing the committees also become blurred as residents found it unworkable to talk only about housing, for example, and not discuss land use, employment and service issues. After a while, the lines were erased and the agendas of each committee included all areas of the plan.

"DAC planners came to residents with more questions than answers," observes Andrea Nagel. "Residents were active participants of the planning process, rather than passive reviewers of options already decided for them."[9]

DAC consultants trained DSNI staff to act as facilitators of focus group discussions where residents were encouraged to "story-tell," illustrating their concerns and suggested solutions with real stories from their own experience. For example, rather than simply stating, "We need a supermarket," residents described a typical shopping expedition outside the neighborhood—lugging bags back on irregular buses. Some members recounted the days of plentiful shops, a stark contrast to the efforts contemporary residents had to make to find a supermarket, pharmacy, bank, department store and so on. "We were able to…find a way of having folks in the neighborhood talk about the neighborhood in their own terms," says Plumer. "It was a really good buy-in strategy and it gave us some very useful information."

In addition to gathering information from residents, DAC compiled an extensive library of background resources and put together a detailed portrait of the neighborhood covering local businesses, consumer preferences, traffic patterns, real estate activity, housing conditions, human services programs, public and private investment, etc. The Boston Redevelopment Authority was a vital source of maps, statistical data and demographic reports. DAC interns conducted a block-by-block "windshield survey" of the neighborhood and created land-use maps of each block.

Perhaps the most disappointing element of this phase of the planning process was the lack of cooperation from many human services providers. DAC prepared an exhaustive survey requesting nonprofit agencies to provide all kinds of information, from program descriptions and case loads to agency budgets and staffing patterns. The survey was introduced to agencies at a meeting of executive directors held at the Dudley branch of the Boston Public Library. Of the 51 agencies identified as potentially serving the residents of Dudley—most located outside the neighborhood—about half attended the orientation session facilitated by DSNI board members Luis Prado and Shirley Carrington, directors of La Alianza Hispana and Roxbury Multi-Service Center, and Steve Plumer and Carole Smith from DAC. Agencies were asked to assign staff to complete the lengthy survey so that a comprehensive picture of the nonprofit economy could be drawn. DAC hoped to begin some collaborative economic development initiatives even before the plan was completed—for example, pooling the purchasing power of the nonprofits to support new neighborhood businesses selling such items as office and custodial supplies.

In designing the survey, DAC underestimated how overworked and understaffed the agencies were and how unwilling they were to share information, especially of a financial nature, though DAC had pledged confidentiality. Despite follow-up calls and offers of assistance, only 16 surveys were returned; some of the respondents were also interviewed.

RMSC Director Shirley Carrington was deeply involved in the planning process. Like the residents, she devoted many Saturdays and evenings, often bringing along her son. "I just pushed beyond the call of duty," she recalls. "I had that commitment...It was one of the first and only opportunities I saw where community people were really in charge." Carrington led the effort to involve social service agencies. She says the survey "was a very microscopic look inside...I remember them saying, 'It's too long. It's too nosy. It's digging too much into our personal business about our budget.'"

Carrington tried to encourage them. "Well, what's the big deal? If you don't have, you don't have. Share it. Tell somebody you don't have—perhaps somebody will give you something." She had more success getting women to respond than men. They were more willing to share information and to take the time to fill out the survey.

La Alianza Hispana Director Luis Prado insists the problem was not unwillingness to share information, but simply the survey's length. He thought it would require much too much of an agency's time to complete, including La Alianza.

Reflecting on why involving many agencies proved so difficult, Plumer says, "I think we were probably not as political as we might have been. Had we been more subtle in the process, perhaps there would have been a greater buy-in." Still, he doubts that would have made a difference, because agencies "tend to be more accountable to the funder than to the neighborhood, and that is an implicit weakness in the system."

The inadequate agency response limited the usefulness of the plan's human services component and exacerbated tensions between residents and social service agencies in the Dudley area. As we shall see, DSNI was able to make more progress on agency collaboration and human services development in subsequent years.

COMMUNITY DESIGN

DSNI's annual meeting and board election were scheduled for April 8, 1987, in the middle of the planning process. To lessen the load on the organization and maintain momentum, the board briefly considered postponing elections until after the plan was completed, but decided that it was important not to do anything that might give the appearance of less than complete inclusiveness and fairness. Though a significant amount of time was spent training new board members and immersing them in the planning process, the elections injected new energy into the planning process and into the organization as a whole, by bringing fresh ideas and new skills onto the board.

By May, the planning process was in full swing. If DSNI's community meetings reminded people of a mini-United Nations, the office began looking like a Rand McNally store with maps of the neighborhood hanging everywhere. DAC was ready to add a more visual component to the planning process. Since design was the weakest part of DAC's expertise, they sought out assistance. Reflecting DSNI's ongoing spirit of coalition-building, DAC collaborated with the firm that had lost out to them for the contract, Stull and Lee. The Stull and Lee team of two staff and five architecture students organized a successful series of design workshops, called "charettes."

At the charettes, designers and architects began to sketch out the kind of neighborhood the residents were describing in words. The June charettes—two evenings and one all-day Saturday—were held over a one-week period at the Orchard Park community center. While most DSNI events were held at the large, centrally located St. Patrick's Church, there was an ongoing concern about involving more tenants from the Orchard Park public housing development, which remained largely isolated from the neighborhood even though it was only a few blocks from St. Patrick's. The DSNI board decided to hold the charettes at Orchard Park and provide transportation there for all those who wanted it. Former Orchard Park Tenants Association President Sarah Flint says that the charettes made a greater number of Orchard Park "residents more aware of what DSNI was doing" and enabled them to "meet other neighbors outside of Orchard Park who lived on the surrounding streets." Orchard Park residents identified the old Dearborn School located in their area as a resource for the development of better Dudley services.

Stull and Lee put together a slide presentation for the evening charettes, showing a wide variety of planned communities in Boston and elsewhere. After the slide show, the well attended gatherings broke down into small groups to discuss design questions with the architects. On newsprint lining the walls, the architects began drawing pictures reflecting residents' ideas and concerns about housing, open space, playgrounds, convenient shopping and other issues. Common concerns included how to design the community to be as safe as possible; how to make the housing roomy enough for families and still affordable for Dudley residents; and how to provide enough new commercial space without taking away from efforts to revitalize the larger shopping districts, Dudley Station and Uphams Corner, located just outside the neighborhood. The architects then took the preliminary drawings and developed several design solutions to the concerns that were raised.

The architects returned to Orchard Park with detailed drawings for the Saturday meeting, attended by about 100 DSNI members. Several themes were discussed that would become cornerstones of the final plan. The most significant idea was the creation of an urban village.

URBAN VILLAGE

Dudley's revitalization would center around a diverse, economically viable and neighborly urban village. The urban village would combine housing, shopping, open space and a multi-use community center. Before DSNI, the Dudley Street area was seen as being between some other places—Dudley Station, Uphams Corner and Grove Hall— and not a place of its own. The urban village would give Dudley a center and strengthen an identity unique to the neighborhood with all of its diverse cultural traditions.

The urban village concept was also a design solution to the concern of Dudley residents about safety. In her groundbreaking book on city planning, Jane Jacobs encouraged mixed-use neighborhoods and pointed to the need for "eyes on the street" for a neighborhood to feel safe.[10] A village center with shops, open space and housing built all around it would enhance the security of Dudley residents with "eyes on the street."

Residents attending the final charette were pleased with the urban village concept. There was further discussion about issues such as density, cost of housing and home ownership versus rental. These discussions underscored the commitment that Dudley residents would not be displaced by development and helped crystallize an image of the "new Dudley" in people's minds.

For longtime Dudley residents, the new Dudley would be in some ways like a multicultural version of the old. Board member Margarita Sturniolo, who has lived in the neighborhood since 1921, remarks, "We would like to see it as it was in the old days, with all the shopping. We had a shopping center in Uphams Corner, one down at the [Dudley Station] terminal, one down on Blue Hill Avenue. And people were not afraid to go to the dances down at Dudley Station. And from the dances they would go across the street to Waldorf's or the Atlantic or one of those restaurants there, 2 or 3 o'clock in the morning. Nobody bothered you, you know? You could walk home."

Gail Latimore's family moved to Mt. Pleasant Avenue in Dudley in 1965. She too remembers Dudley Station as "the hub" when she was young. "That's where you go. You hang out 'down Dudley.' You go shopping. You never had to walk out of your community to get what you needed...We would say, 'We're going down Dudley.'" That was "a big thing." Latimore also has childhood memories of the old drugstore at Mt. Pleasant and Dudley Streets. "There used to be a drugstore with a soda fountain. With a soda fountain!...Go down there with a quarter and get an ice cream soda."

Sturniolo has seen the neighborhood go from majority White to majority people of color. "Everybody gets along," she insists. "We are all here for one purpose, just to get a better neighborhood. We don't care if you are Black, or green, or Irish or Jewish or what you are. You be good to us and we will be good to you. You help me and I will help you." Asked if she is hopeful about the neighborhood changing, Sturniolo has a simple response: "Live in hope, die in despair."

"Not everybody lives to see a neighborhood destroyed and rebuilt from the same address," DSNI member Dorothy Rankin wrote in the organization's newsletter. "I might be that lucky." A participant in the Land Use and Housing Committees, Rankin observed, "Whether these sessions become [just] another exercise in the stockpile of other plans depends upon you and me."[11]

COMPLETING THE PLAN

DAC delivered a draft of the comprehensive plan in late July 1987. The DSNI board and resident planning committees spent several weeks revising it. The most contentious issue highlighted the agency/resident tensions that were evident throughout the planning process. Agency representatives on the board were uneasy about strategies calling for greater accountability by Dudley agencies to their clients. The draft was critical of the agencies' tendency to be more responsive to the demands of funders than to the needs of the community. The lack of involvement by many agencies in the planning process contributed to the tension.

La Alianza Hispana Director Luis Prado asserts there "was a prejudice against services" in the planning process. He says that the DAC plan expressed "the need to focus on the human resources in the community and to find a way of investing in that. The problem was that in human services we are not getting financial resources from the community. We bring them from the outside and we try to invest them in the community. But the wording of the whole [DAC] thing was like the program participants were paying for services or something like that—that it was going to be sort of a closed system here. In that sense, residents had to have more input in the definition of programs and things like that. In philosophical principle I agree. In practice it doesn't work like that." Prado says, "DAC was really for whatever reason disappointed with the local organizations. Maybe they wanted more from us, more work, but…we don't have the time. We didn't have the energy to do it."

Resident board members advocated a strong strategy for agency accountability, but they compromised with agency representatives on a softer position to move a unified plan forward. Still, the final plan clearly identified resident frustration with the agencies, stating, "Given the agencies' need for survival and the competitive character of the grantsmanship process, they frequently respond to the demands of the funding sources rather than the needs of the community. This process diminishes the role of community residents in defining need."[12]

After more revisions the plan was ratified in a neighborhood meeting on September 23. By the time that the 120 or so residents had gathered at St. Patrick's, ratification was a foregone conclusion. Almost everyone in attendance had been involved in the planning and draft review process. When the vote was taken, the plan was approved unanimously—with one abstention—and a huge cheer went up from the crowd. Later, DSNI held two community meetings in different sections of the neighborhood to present the plan to residents who had not yet participated in the planning process, but whose support and involvement in the plan's implementation would be crucial.

THE MASTER PLAN FOR DUDLEY REVITALIZATION

The vision guiding *The Dudley Street Neighborhood Initiative Revitalization Plan: A Comprehensive Community Controlled Strategy* is an urban village, a "new Dudley" promising not just quality affordable housing, but quality of life. Dudley would have a vibrant cultural, commercial and residential community. At the heart of the neighborhood (the intersection of Dudley Street and Blue Hill Avenue) would be a town common, "a place for meeting, strolling, sitting, watching and living" with a park, retail shops and community center.[13] As explained in the plan, the village concept "should foster human growth, where people have choice and opportunity."

Development without displacement is a central goal of the plan. Housing would be both affordable and high-quality. As Ché Madyun puts it, "Why should affordable mean some old two by four box that somebody can just throw up? Why can't affordable mean something that you can be proud of?"

The plan was based on three principles articulated in the earlier community meetings: neighborhood control, critical mass and tandem strategy. Neighborhood control means that the implementation of the development plan would be carried out by an entity controlled by residents. Critical mass is "the process of aggregating sufficient square footage of new and/or rehabilitated space to affect the existing market or create a market of its own." A tandem strategy is "the simultaneous development of new construction and rehab activity in a coordinated manner."[14]

The $135 million five-year plan focused on DSNI's core, which contains over 22 million square feet of land, or over 507 acres. Over one-fifth (107 acres) of the land was vacant land or abandoned buildings at that time. Over one-third of the 1,300 vacant lots were owned by the city of Boston, Boston Redevelopment Authority, the state of Massachusetts and the U.S. Department of Housing and Urban Development. Another one-third of the lots were tax delinquent.

To meet critical mass, the plan recommended between 800 and 1,000 units of new construction and a rehabilitation program of over 1,000 units. It recommended a mix ranging from one- and two-family homes and town houses to mid-rise apartment buildings. To meet the goal of affordability, it targeted most of the projected units for households with incomes of $10,000 to $20,000 (1987 figures).

Over time, the details would change, but not the guiding principles. The plan presented 13 basic strategies:

- *Development.* Creation of a new entity or DSNI subsidiary to plan, finance, market and manage development projects, counsel residents in acquiring housing and negotiate land acquisition.

- *Financing.* Pursuit of a variety of private and public financing including government subsidies, collateral provided by pension funds or insurance companies, and a mortgage pool with private and public lenders. Establishment of a Land Trust for land acquisition to maintain affordability. Alternative forms of ownership such as cooperatives, condominiums, sweat equity and shared equity.

- *Anti-Displacement Measures.* Housing counseling to provide residents with information and assistance in rental, sales and qualification for financing. Subsidized rental housing. Community action and legislation targeting speculative real estate brokers and developers.

- *Marketing Research Approach.* Focus groups of 8 to 15 people to determine community priorities. This approach differs from the conventional needs assessment survey by expanding the power of who defines the questions and seeing the participant not just as a potential client of services provided by others, but as a consumer, opinion leader or expert.

- *Community Review.* Provide increased local control of human service program priorities and resource allocations. Stimulate collaboration among service providers.

- *The Force.* The objective is to introduce a new source of pride, dignity, energy and self-help effort that would support existing efforts and mobilize untapped resources. A cadre of Dudley residents would serve as volunteers, communicators and role models in fighting crime and drug and alcohol abuse and encouraging job development and other projects.

- *Strengthening Racial, Ethnic and Cultural Identity and Diversity.* Provide assistance to the Cape Verdean community to develop human services programs. Encourage agency collaboration around neighborhood diversity.

- *Child Care.* Establish a central Neighborhood Registry for providers and recipients. Determine growth capacity among existing providers. Advocate for additional child care services and youth programs.

- *Recreation and Athletics.* Establish a resident planning committee for recreation and athletics. Develop and submit a master plan to the city Department of Parks and Recreation.

- *Orchard Park Planning Process.* To address the unique needs of the Orchard Park Housing Development, DSNI should provide assistance to the Orchard Park Tenants Association to fund and develop a comprehensive plan.

- *Employment and Training Advocacy.* Do a neighborhood inventory of individual employment needs, aspirations and skills, identify support services required and tap existing training and employment services.

- *Earning/Learning Project.* Work with public and private agencies to develop a comprehensive program of individual training, providing child care, stipends, bilingual instruction and other support services.

- *A Neighborhood-Based Business Development and Training Unit.* Work cooperatively with government and private agencies, including business schools, to provide entrepreneurial training and support for local residents interested in starting or expanding their own business or being employed by new or existing local businesses.

Of all the 13 strategies, most of which resonate in DSNI programs, economic development would move most slowly. The plan proposed a neighborhood retail center to anchor the urban village. The retail center could include such needed enterprises as a supermarket, drugstore, bank, hardware store, bicycle/sports store and restaurants. DAC estimated a potential gross market of over $20 million based on income levels for the core area; local businesses could be expected to capture about 60 percent of those dollars depending on the mix of stores, pricing, marketing practices, appearance and environment. The plan recommended light industrial and manufacturing enterprises in harmony with the surrounding neighborhood. Given that auto-related businesses accounted for over 40 percent of the existing retail square footage in the neighborhood, the plan suggested exploring the feasibility of an auto park. The plan also recommended neighborhood-based construction enterprises to participate in the redevelopment projects; assistance to existing local businesses in addressing the impact of the redevelopment project and possibly pursuing relocation to the new retail center or modernization and expansion of existing facilities; and development of community-based enterprises to provide goods and services for local agencies and residents such as office supply, printing, transportation, equipment and furniture, landscaping, etc. The plan also suggested building on neighborhood cultural diversity by exploring the feasibility of an International Market/Bazaar and Eateries which could attract both tourism and an expanded out-of-neighborhood clientele.

There was widespread satisfaction among DSNI members with the overall planning process. Planning Committee member Tubal Padilla felt that DAC could have done more technical capacity building among residents. As he put it, "There were not whole sessions devoted to, 'Let's learn before we talk.' It was more, 'Let's talk while we learn.'" Still, he says, "It was an exemplary process in terms of involving people. I think the plan reflected...people's aspirations and concerns. An example of that is the question of 'The Force'...I think that is probably the only comprehensive plan anywhere that has such a thing...To me, that reflected that the people understood there was a need for the organization to be really an organizer, to be an advocate, to deal with the not-so-concrete." DSNI never formed "The Force" as envisioned in the plan, but organizing remained the force that powered DSNI and, as seen later, DSNI launched a campaign called Dudley PRIDE to strengthen community pride, activism, safety, environmental health and government responsiveness.

DAC's Steve Plumer thinks that the planning process worked because as a planner, "you have to have the belief that folks in the neighborhood have enough understanding, skills and knowledge to really make decisions for themselves, so you don't...try to con them into going in a certain direction. I think folks know when you are trying to do that."

CELEBRATION AND CITY SUPPORT

The DSNI board decided to release the plan during DSNI's annual multicultural festival that October. It seemed the ideal setting to highlight the strong unity of the Dudley neighborhood. The multicultural festival is a "community builder," explains Sue Beaton, a longtime DSNI board member who, until becoming DSNI deputy director in 1992, was the development director of Project Hope—a shelter for homeless families on Magnolia Street that works effectively to assist guests to move to permanent housing.

The festival is "a multiethnic celebration," says Beaton. "It's breaking down walls. It's learning to respect the rituals and the values of [other cultures]...It's believing that we each can bring something to the event that will make it richer. It's one more time where we're saying that this is not a homogeneous community. We have our differences, but they...can enrich us rather than divide us."

Before the festival, DSNI approached PFD Director Lisa Chapnick with the idea of having the mayor attend and publicly endorse the plan. DSNI realized that the mayor would see risks as well as opportunities in an endorsement. While PFD had assisted the planning process, it was clearly not the plan the city would have developed if it had been in charge. Yet the city recognized DSNI, which then had 800 members, as the representative voice of Dudley. With momentum growing in the neighborhood, DSNI's plan was an attractive vehicle for the mayor to climb aboard. While the plan called for massive redevelopment controlled by residents, it was more a guide than a blueprint, allowing the city to support the larger concept without being locked into any detailed commitments.

The festival was originally scheduled for early October, but as the time approached without any commitment from the mayor to attend, the board decided to postpone it until October 25. At that point, the plan would be released, with or without the mayor's endorsement. After frequent conversations with city officials, the mayor's office finally informed DSNI that Flynn would speak at the press conference during the festival and announce his support.

Festival day was sunny and inviting. Local music and dance groups performed on a stage erected on the playground of Emerson Elementary School on Dudley Street. Residents cooked food and local merchants and organizations set up information tables around the playground. Kids enjoyed a variety of recreational activities. The press conference was timed to go off at the height of the festival, when several hundred people were present.

Mayor Flynn announced that the city was adopting the DSNI master plan as its own. As he explained it years later, "If you want to build a solid foundation for an organization, or a house, you're better off [starting] from the basement up...And the foundation of this whole effort is really people power." Government, said Flynn shortly before leaving office, should be on the side of people trying to improve their neighborhoods, not "telling people in neighborhoods what they should do or what they can't achieve."

At the press conference, DSNI board member Cynthia Lopes-Jefferson summed up the goals of the plan "to rebuild the spirit of this community as well as to develop the neighborhood...We are pleased with the help we have gotten so far, and the future assistance promised to us. But the residents of this neighborhood will be leading the way."

DSNI President Ché Madyun voiced the concerns and hopes of many when she declared, "We will not become another South End. We intend to fight every step of the way to assure that this neighborhood remains a community that is diverse and affordable. We warn speculators...You are not welcome here. At the same time, those developers who want to come in and produce housing we can afford and create jobs that go to this community, we welcome you and look forward to a rejuvenated neighborhood in the years to come."[15]

The event was covered by four television stations, the two major daily newspapers and several community newspapers and radio stations—all producing positive stories on DSNI's ambitious plan to revitalize the neighborhood.

"These are not social workers coming in telling the group what to do and then leaving the neighborhood at 5 o'clock," the mayor's outgoing liaison for Roxbury, Harold Hughey, told the *Boston Globe*. "They know exactly what their needs are—they live there. With these people, it'll be hard for anybody to step on this community again."[16]

DSNI had successfully flipped the traditionally top-down development planning process on its head. It had created a new bottom-up, participatory, comprehensive planning process. And it had organized a neighborhood with sufficient strength to win unprecedented city government support for the *residents'* vision of a revitalized Dudley.

Lisa Chapnick and Clayton Turnbull at the 1993 DSNI open house.

Ché Madyun.

(l to r): Gertrudes Fidalgo, Peter Medoff, Ro Whittington, Ché Madyun and Gus Newport at the 1993 DSNI open house.

CONTROLLING THE LAND THROUGH EMINENT DOMAIN

DSNI members had much to show for the three years since their first community meeting. They had curtailed the trashing of the neighborhood, put Dudley on the city's political map and created a comprehensive plan for redevelopment. Now, to implement the plan, DSNI needed both the political will to control development and the wallet to finance it. DSNI had raised the stakes for residents, city government and would-be developers. It had to show it wasn't bluffing.

EXPANDING STAFF AND OUTSIDE SUPPORT

Even before the master plan was complete, the DSNI board began readying the organization for the complex implementation process. The 1988 budget restructured and expanded the staff of four by adding three new positions: directors of organizing, development and human services. To carry out its ambitious expansion plan DSNI enlisted the support of two important new funders: the Boston Foundation, the city's largest foundation, which over time became DSNI's second-biggest funder after the Riley Foundation, and the Charles Stuart Mott Foundation, the second major national foundation to fund DSNI (the Catholic Church's Campaign for Human Development had awarded DSNI an earlier grant).

DSNI's Planning Committee was renamed the Development Committee. To maintain momentum while searching for a development director, the Development Committee decided to hire consultants: The Community Builders (then known as Greater Boston Community Development) was widely recognized as one of the most successful affordable housing consultants in Massachusetts, having been involved in the development of thousands of new units.

DSNI also located a law firm specializing in real estate to provide it with extensive pro bono legal assistance to implement the development plan.* Rackemann, Sawyer & Brewster, one of Boston's oldest and most respected firms, especially in the area of real estate law, had just finished reorganizing their pro bono program and were seeking new nonpaying clients when DSNI requested assistance. Rackemann, Sawyer & Brewster partner Stephen Anderson was impressed with DSNI's organizing and planning experience and was also familiar with the Riley Foundation from his position as chair of the board of Morgan Memorial Goodwill Industries.

Rackemann, Sawyer & Brewster partner Henry Thayer has been heavily involved with DSNI. Thayer says the firm might not have taken DSNI as a pro bono client if the firm had foreseen the magnitude of the venture, "but we are in it, and we are in it to stay, and frankly the dozen or so lawyers in this 50-lawyer law firm that have been involved feel good about it." As to whether there is any grumbling in the firm over the hundreds of thousands of dollars of in-kind contributions to DSNI, Thayer jokes, "Well, we all wring our hands and say, 'Oh mercy!' and then go right ahead and do it." He says, "It is fun dealing with [DSNI] people...and frankly, you get a sense of meaning something to a group of people." Thayer observes, "You have the feeling that when this all comes to fruition, and this area of the city that looks like postwar Dresden is finally built up, you can look at that and say, 'I was a part of that. I was a part of that change.'"

---

* Powers & Hall, the law firm where Riley trustees are partners, continued to serve as DSNI's pro bono general corporate counsel; another firm, Goulston & Storrs, came aboard later, also pro bono.

Besides their legal expertise, Rackemann, Sawyer & Brewster provided DSNI with added cachet in downtown circles. "All of a sudden," says Thayer, "the resources of a fairly well known downtown Boston real estate firm have now been marshaled to work on and support this project. I can remember talking with someone in the city Tax Title Division. He said, 'Oh yes, this Dudley thing. This is not going anywhere.' I said to this individual, 'Excuse me, X, but I am working for them.' This person was astonished and there were no more murmurings about, 'Oh this Dudley neighborhood thing isn't going anywhere.'"

CRITICAL MASS THROUGH EMINENT DOMAIN

Bolstered by additional staff, funding and legal and technical support, DSNI focused on the challenge of turning the neighborhood's huge amount of vacant land from wasteland to community wealth. Dudley's vacant land is particularly concentrated in the Triangle, a 64-acre area in the heart of the neighborhood (see map at front of book), which is home to about 2,000 people. Decades of disinvestment, arson and demolition left half the Triangle's land vacant. Approximately 15 acres of vacant land were owned by the city of Boston in 1988 and 15 acres were privately owned. Of the 181 privately owned vacant lots, 101 were in tax title—with municipal liens placed against them for back taxes and interest—or currently under petition for tax foreclosure.[1]

On a freezing day in February, Peter Medoff and The Community Builders' director of development, Peter Munkenbeck, took a long tour of the Triangle. Munkenbeck had passed through the Triangle many times before while driving down Blue Hill Avenue. He used to think to himself, "Either we better build some housing down there, or we better buy some tractors." Medoff and Munkenbeck began mapping out the vacant land, using different color markers to distinguish privately owned land from city-owned land.

Munkenbeck recalls looking at their map and seeing a jigsaw puzzle. "You couldn't get a coherent chunk of city-owned property. You couldn't say, 'Gee, if we just [develop] what the city owns, the rest will follow.' Because the city [land] was hopelessly rent, by little, private holdings" scattered all over. Though most of the private holdings were tax delinquent, foreclosing on them one by one would be a complicated and time-consuming process.

There would be no way to meet the plan's goal of neighborhood control and critical mass by combining city-owned land with piecemeal development of private lots, many of them too tiny to develop individually. That would repeat the mistakes of the old "in-fill" strategy of building scattered-site housing without community-controlled comprehensive redevelopment.

Munkenbeck raised the idea of using eminent domain as a way to assemble large tracts of vacant land for development. "We had to invent an eminent domain process and a Redevelopment process with a capital R," Munkenbeck says, "that was as radical as the stuff they did in the sixties with the West End and Scully Square and the South End, but as radically different from that as it could possibly be in its meticulous regard for the tatters of fabric that still were on the ground."

Eminent domain is "the power of the sovereign [the state] to take property for public use without the owner's consent upon making just compensation."[2] The "sovereign" may delegate its eminent domain authority—according to legislation varying by state—to government agencies and private entities such as utilities, railroads and urban development corporations.

When DSNI first considered the eminent domain option, it was not aware that such authority could possibly be delegated to a neighborhood-based nonprofit organization. DSNI's first request to Rackemann, Sawyer & Brewster was to research the issue of eminent domain and provide a summary of the circumstances that would allow eminent domain to take place. DSNI's assumption was that all of the possible circumstances would entail the exercising of eminent domain authority by city agencies. DSNI assumed that by organizing the neighborhood and generating sufficient public support, it would be able to exert a form of "moral site control" over the eminent domain area by being strong enough to pressure the city to support DSNI's development plan.

Rackemann, Sawyer & Brewster's March 1988 memo concluded that "two entities may acquire property in Boston by eminent domain for the purpose of developing low and moderate income housing": the Boston Redevelopment Authority (BRA) and "an urban redevelopment corporation authorized by the BRA to undertake a Chapter 121A project." It was the first time that DSNI staff and members had ever heard of Chapter 121A of the Massachusetts State Statutes.

Could DSNI's plan qualify as a project under Chapter 121A? DSNI staff and board members immediately embraced that option and began the journey that would lead DSNI to become the first community group in the nation to win the right of eminent domain. Not only would eminent domain make possible DSNI's development agenda, but it would also provide long-term land control, through ownership, that could survive changes in city policies and provide DSNI with leverage in dealing with future administrations.

A Chapter 121A "project" is defined as "any undertaking consisting of the construction in a blighted open, decadent or substandard area of decent, safe and sanitary residential, commercial, industrial, institutional, recreational or governmental buildings and such appurtenant or incidental facilities as shall be in the public interest, and the operation and maintenance of such buildings and facilities after construction." A project may include the acquisition, assembly and clearance of land, buildings or structures. To obtain eminent domain authority under Chapter 121A, DSNI would have to form an urban redevelopment corporation and secure the approval of both the BRA board and the mayor.[3]

Knowing that eminent domain was legally possible, DSNI staff and board members pondered two difficult questions: How could DSNI ever get the city to give up that kind of authority to a low-income community group? How could DSNI convince the Dudley neighborhood that eminent domain was a good means to a good end—gaining control of future development? It certainly wasn't obvious.

DEVELOPMENT WITHOUT DISPLACEMENT

The history of eminent domain in Boston and elsewhere had given it a deservedly bad reputation. As discussed previously, Bostonians had witnessed the destruction of the entire West End neighborhood under eminent domain to make way for luxury high-rises. Many Dudley residents were displaced during the South End's gentrified redevelopment.

Dudley residents' first reactions to eminent domain were almost always negative: "Why would we *want* something like that in our neighborhood?" DSNI's challenge was to educate the neighborhood that eminent domain is simply a tool, and it can be put to positive or negative purposes depending on who is using it and how they are using it. In the hands of an organized neighborhood, the power of eminent domain could be used to benefit Dudley residents, not displace them.

DSNI's eminent domain project would differ from previous ones in a crucial respect: eminent domain would cover vacant land, not land with structures on it. No one would be displaced from their homes or businesses. Moreover, it differentiated the one out of three landowners who lived in the neighborhood from the rest who lived outside. Of the 131 individual owners of the 181 privately owned vacant parcels in the Triangle, at least 81 lived outside Roxbury or Dorchester and many of them could not be located.[4] DSNI would work with resident landowners who wanted to build housing on their vacant land or use it for gardens, for example. DSNI wanted resident landowners to be part of the neighborhood consensus supporting eminent domain, a consensus that had to be strong in the face of potential opposition from absentee landowners.

Father Walter Waldron of St. Patrick's Church recalls negative reactions in the Catholic archdiocese when eminent domain was first proposed. Church leaders, he says, worried that DSNI might be "setting up a power base for itself to control a portion of the city," putting power into the hands of DSNI leaders, not the larger community. Waldron also acknowledges that the Catholic Church may have had a more personal concern as a large property owner: "The Church hasn't survived 2,000 years because it doesn't have self-interest. That was obviously the concern, particularly with this empty property across the street" from St. Patrick's, where Roxbury Community College used to be. Waldron assured the diocese that DSNI did not intend to take church property, that eminent domain "was worth the risk because of what was at stake in keeping this community whole over the next 50 years" and that DSNI had already proven itself to be an effective and honest organization. St. Patrick's Church provided DSNI with a letter supporting its application for eminent domain.

Sue Beaton, then a member of the Development Committee, was one of many DSNI members who had had a negative personal experience with eminent domain. She was in grade school when friends of hers lost their Somerville homes to make way for an extension to highway I-93. Beaton remembers as a child, saying, "Someone could come in and actually take your home and put in a highway? I didn't ask for this. They didn't ask for this. It just...got delivered in the name of progress?"

While she came to see that eminent domain made sense for Dudley, Beaton—usually an optimist—doubted that DSNI could succeed, "because my only experience...was that you either had to be very rich to pull it off, or you had to be a government entity that could build a case that they were doing it in the public interest. We're a poor community. And we're supposed to build a case that we're doing this in the public interest? Who's going to listen?...Land to me is power. Whoever controls it has a lot to say about the political process [and] has a lot to say about what the neighborhood looks like."

CONVINCING THE CITY: KEYS TO THE VAULT

DSNI members knew that in asking the city for eminent domain authority they were asking a lot. As one DSNI supporter put it, "Getting the Boston Redevelopment Authority to hand over their power of eminent domain would be a lot like asking the banker for the keys to the vault. Why would they do it?" Why would the mayor endorse it?

Chapter 121A, enacted in 1946 for the purpose of promoting housing development in "blighted" areas, was amended numerous times and used for over 300 development projects around the state, most of them producing housing. Rarely, though, had Chapter 121A included delegation of eminent domain authority and never to a community organization.

The primary use of 121A has been to provide tax incentives to developers. Urban redevelopment corporations are exempt from real estate property taxes for a period of 15 years (and an additional 25 years in the case of government subsidized or financed low- or moderate-income housing projects). Instead they pay lower, more stable excise taxes. In 1960, Chapter 121A was amended so that it also promoted commercial development in "blighted" areas. This allowed its use in the development of the Prudential Center, a massive commercial, residential and open space complex utilizing a former railroad yard and exhibition hall in Boston's Back Bay. The Prudential Center, reports the BRA, "was the first office tower, the first major private investment in the 'New Boston' era, and the first use of Chapter 121A...for a commercial project." Indeed, "when construction started, it was the largest commercial complex in the world." The 1960 act amending Chapter 121A also included a rider that abolished the Boston City Planning Board and shifted its functions to the BRA, then headed by Ed Logue. That "opened the door for Mayor Collins' '90-Million Dollar Development Program for Boston.'"[5]

DSNI's pro bono law firm, Rackemann, Sawyer & Brewster, had done the land title work for the Prudential project. Since Massachusetts had passed a sweeping property tax rollback in 1979, Proposition $2\frac{1}{2}$, the formulas under 121A had become less attractive. DSNI was bringing the first request for 121A designation in ten years. And its bold bid for community eminent domain authority would shock the BRA board.

To win the support of the BRA board and Mayor Flynn, DSNI began working on its formal Chapter 121A application and informally testing the waters around City Hall. DSNI got an early boost when Peter Medoff ran into BRA Director Stephen Coyle at the March 1988 opening of Casa Esperanza in the Dudley neighborhood. Casa Esperanza Director Ricardo Quiroga was an early supporter of DSNI, and the facility was Greater Boston's only bilingual treatment residence for recovering Latino alcoholics. Steve Coyle, now the chief executive officer of the AFL-CIO Housing and Building Investment Trusts, was a controversial figure in the city of Boston. He was lauded by many as an intelligent visionary. He was also criticized as arrogant and unresponsive to views different than his own. One thing on which everyone could agree was that Steve Coyle was not a typical bureaucrat. He was somebody who had enough confidence and vision to look beyond the usual bureaucratic boundaries.

At the Casa Esperanza opening Coyle asked Medoff how things were going in Dudley, and Medoff decided to stick his toe in the water to see what the temperature was like for eminent domain. Medoff said that things were going okay except that DSNI was facing the enormous challenge of figuring out how to assemble the vacant privately owned land in the area. Land assembly, Medoff told Coyle, without volunteering DSNI's interest in eminent domain, appeared to be the biggest hurdle to any significant development in the neighborhood.

Coyle immediately suggested that DSNI form a separate corporation and apply to the BRA for eminent domain authority under Chapter 121A. Medoff couldn't believe it. Not only would DSNI's eminent domain efforts not be rejected out of hand, but Coyle had brought the idea up himself. While DSNI knew that it would need Mayor Flynn's support and that the BRA board was no rubber stamp for Coyle, his support provided early legitimacy and helped convince DSNI that the idea wasn't a pipe dream.

DSNI had a political strategy to build support within the Flynn administration with the ultimate goal of getting the mayor to publicly support eminent domain before the application was brought before the BRA board. DSNI assumed that it could not have only one or two advocates in the administration, but needed as broad a base of support as possible. Indeed, one of DSNI's strategic principles is that the more people who are invested in the DSNI process—inside and outside the organization—the stronger the process will be and the greater its likelihood of success.

DSNI's strategy targeted top officials in the BRA, PFD and Flynn's key staff. Coyle was the first supporter. DSNI also had strong advocates in Tony Williams, the BRA's deputy director for Neighborhood Planning, and Andrea D'Amato, a planner in the Neighborhood Planning Division. DSNI's application was D'Amato's first big assignment at the BRA. She laughingly recalls Williams saying, "Look, I've got a project for you. It's slightly controversial."

There are people in the BRA, says D'Amato, who "don't believe that residents can plan their futures—they just don't have the expertise." She and others believed differently: "From my encounters with the residents involved in DSNI, I think they have a lot of skills and expertise and approach the project in a very professional manner, often more than city officials. Their commitment is very heartfelt...I was convinced that it was a project that was driven by the neighborhood."

Why did Steve Coyle support eminent domain for DSNI? The more cynical interpretation around city government was, as one insider who didn't share this view recalls, "Because it was easy for him. It got rid of all of this land. It got rid of responsibility. He could look like a hero, and he's sort of dumping the problem in the lap of the community...giving it to them to sink or swim." D'Amato says that, on the contrary, Coyle was "committed to the project" as a priority and gave her and Williams a clear mandate "to take this project and make it work."

DSNI's next step was to win the support of PFD staff and Director Lisa Chapnick. Reaction was mixed when DSNI presented its proposal to PFD staff. Rebecca Black, assistant director of Planning and Policy, explains that within PFD there were two basic approaches: The planning people said, "If you build little parcels you will never get anything done. It doesn't make any sense to build until you have pulled all of the pieces together." The development people "just wanted to build, build, build," arguing, "If you don't do something now, it will never happen." PFD staff worried that DSNI's proposal would undermine Flynn's Project 747 to dispose of all city-owned land by the end of his term in 1991. As far as DSNI could tell, the prevailing PFD staff opinion—reflecting PFD's usual emphasis on production over community process—was that DSNI's eminent domain scheme would be a slow boat to nowhere. Later, Lisa Chapnick recalled that she was hearing from staff, "This is great." And she was saying, "This is risky."

From past experience with city government, DSNI knew the importance of going to the top and asked to meet directly with Chapnick. Among the DSNI board and staff members who met with Chapnick in her office on March 31, 1988 were Medoff, Ché Madyun, Paul Yelder and Melvyn Colón. The night before, Medoff decided to add a little humor to DSNI's presentation to break the tension expected in the meeting. Chapnick had a reputation for being intimidating, but she also had a great sense of humor. Among the materials DSNI prepared for the meeting with Chapnick was a map of the Triangle. One of the concerns expressed by PFD staff was that the Triangle area being proposed for redevelopment was far too large. Chapter 121A had never been used before on that grand a scale, not even for projects like the Prudential Center. Perhaps, some PFD staffers suggested, it made more sense to focus on one or two blocks rather than the 64-acre Triangle. With these concerns in mind, Medoff rolled up a map of the world inside the map of the Triangle.

The next day, Medoff began the presentation by unrolling the map of the world and announcing, "Here is the area that DSNI proposes taking by eminent domain." There was a tense moment of silence until Chapnick laughed heartily and everybody joined in.

DSNI made several points in the meeting. First, by granting eminent domain authority, the city would help control speculation and gentrification and prevent the displacement of Dudley residents. Second, it would also facilitate far more development in the area than would otherwise be possible using only scattered city-owned parcels. Third, if all could agree that assembling the private land was necessary to facilitate development as well as control speculation, then everyone had to acknowledge that given the history of eminent domain in Boston, it would never be politically possible for the BRA to use its own eminent domain authority to acquire the land. In fact, the only politically feasible way to assemble the private land was by delegating eminent domain authority to a local community group with the neighborhood support and expertise to assemble the necessary land for large-scale development.

For Chapnick, the eminent domain meeting was extraordinary. "There was a lot of stuff that people said that was, in my humble opinion, ridiculous," she recalls. "But the sincerity and honesty—I bought it. I just bought the people sitting in that room. I've done that probably two other times at PFD where somebody came into my office with this ridiculous kind of 'Take this leap' and I did. Now, that's probably one out of a hundred opportunities that I had and it's probably one out of five hundred that the institution had on a yearly basis." Most proposals didn't make it through the hierarchy to Chapnick. In this case, she decided after the DSNI group walked out, "Let's just do it."

"From my perspective," explains Chapnick, DSNI was "asking the city to delegate its role to a large extent—its financial role, its property role, its legal role...Because it was your neighborhood and could you not, in fact, be in charge of your own destiny? And ultimately, the answer was, yes—that government had failed."

"Part of what made it appealing," says Chapnick, "was the fact that this was a group of people who had come together with a thoughtful, reasonable, potentially doable plan that would create critical mass where there was emptiness. I mean, there would be no way to develop 30 acres brick by brick, inch by inch. So, part of what gave [DSNI] that legitimacy was the vision itself...And while you could look at this and say, 'You've got to be kidding me. Affordable housing, a town common, social services—and apple pie is dietetic!' Nevertheless [these were] the key components and did take up a lot of land."

Despite the well known rivalry between PFD and the BRA, Chapnick and Coyle respected each other. "Steve Coyle bought in early and hard," reflects Chapnick, "and that had a tremendous influence on both the mayor and on me. I think he bought in hard because he is the quintessential risk taker and because he is a visionary...I'm much more conservative...I like to have my ducks in line and my house in order." DSNI's eminent domain proposal "played to each institution's strength," says Chapnick. "You had the city planner and visionary giving you a jump start and you had the city community development agency sweating the details...It just wasn't the traditional kind of jump ball. It was much more like a handoff."

With the BRA and PFD directors on board, support for the proposal began to grow. "I think the combination of [Coyle] and I supporting it was a knockout blow for anybody who opposed it," says Chapnick, "because at the time, Stephen and I almost didn't agree on anything, including on what day it was...And here was someone who was known to be very conservative, cautious—me—agreeing with someone who was known to be very devil-may-care."

DUDLEY NEIGHBORS, INC.

"Someday people are going to be very proud to live on Dudley Street," Ché Madyun told a crowd of about 230 people at DSNI's May 1988 annual meeting. The *Boston Globe* editorialized, "The enthusiasm and sense of achievement displayed at the meeting demonstrate that after decades of decline, hope has returned to Dudley Street."[6]

Beginning in June, DSNI held four community meetings on eminent domain with residents. They were held at different locations throughout the neighborhood: St. Patrick's Church, Orchard Park Community Center, Roxbury Multi-Service Center and St. Paul's Church. It was at the St. Paul's meeting that Clayton Turnbull, a dynamic African American resident active in city politics, who had not been involved previously with DSNI, began to play an important role.

Clayton Turnbull is a local businessman and homeowner who has lived in Dudley since 1966. When DSNI organizer Adalberto Teixeira told him about the plans for eminent domain and asked him to get involved, Turnbull's first reaction was, "Wait a minute! There's problems with this thing. You're talking about taking land." Turnbull says his "concern was the people who lived here. Remember, gentrification's head was raised high in those days, and rightfully so. I and everybody else was skeptical about who was behind this...Who is DSNI? Who is the Riley Foundation? Eminent domain is a strong instrument. Wow, is this the new South End that everybody is always worried about?"

Like others who were worried or skeptical about DSNI before becoming involved, Turnbull jumped in. "Either you stay outside and criticize a process or you join it to make changes," he says. At the St. Paul's meeting, attended by about 30 neighbors, Turnbull stood up and forcefully explained why he had come around to supporting the eminent domain campaign and why he felt others should support it as well. Turnbull's speech led to a spirited discussion about who owned land in the area and what that land was being used for. DSNI representatives explained that the intention was to use eminent domain authority to remove land from speculators who were holding it simply for the purpose of making a future profit at the expense of Dudley residents. Turnbull went on to become one of DSNI's resident leaders and, in 1989, he was elected vice president of the organization.

In August 1988, DSNI formed Dudley Neighbors, Incorporated (DNI), the urban redevelopment corporation required under Chapter 121A. DNI is a nonprofit community land trust that will acquire and own land and oversee the development of affordable housing, community facilities, open space and small business on vacant land in the Triangle. Chuck Collins of the Institute for Community Economics provided technical assistance in setting up the DNI land trust. Later—in April 1989—the firm of Goulston and Storrs, where attorney David Abromowitz is an expert in land trusts, became the third law firm to provide DSNI with ongoing pro bono legal assistance.

DNI's board of directors was designed to include representation from groups and individuals whose support was needed for Chapter 121A approval, while at the same time maintaining majority control within the hands of the DSNI board and neighborhood residents. The DNI board is composed of six DSNI representatives (including at least the DSNI president, one tenant, one nonprofit agency and one local business; the DSNI president and at least three others must be neighborhood residents); two neighborhood residents appointed respectively by the Roxbury Neighborhood Council and the district city councilor; one mayoral appointee; and two nonvoting members appointed by the district's state senator and state representative.

In setting up DNI and carrying out the overall eminent domain campaign, DSNI tried to turn potential critics into supporters. City Councilor Bruce Bolling, for example, ended up backing the proposal, but his support was not taken for granted. Bolling has very strong ties to minority developers and his brother, Royal Bolling Jr., a former state representative, was then the staffperson for the Minority Developers Association (MDA). DSNI thought that MDA members would probably oppose eminent domain authority as a threat to their turf as private developers.

The MDA's members were mostly African American developers, some of whom lived in Roxbury, many of whom did not. The MDA was founded in 1985, in part to oppose the kind of continuing financial and other discrimination that has largely restricted minority developers to doing housing and small commercial projects in minority communities.[7] MDA members established themselves with city officials as the primary developers of housing on city-owned land in Roxbury and saw themselves as competitors with nonprofit developers. The MDA also regularly battled Roxbury activists. While city officials often saw channeling land and development projects to minority developers as the same thing as helping communities of color, Roxbury activists saw it differently: A few minority developers might be making money, but the benefits to the community as a whole were minimal. MDA members worried that if DSNI, which was not beholden to minority developers, was to have control over the disposition of the largest collection of vacant land in Roxbury, MDA access to development opportunities would be limited. At the same time, there was some recognition among the minority developers that the eminent domain process could be the key to major development in the area, leading to expanded opportunities for everyone. DSNI sent a written request to the MDA in July asking for a meeting to explain its plans. At that point the developers did not take the proposal seriously and, after a meeting was scheduled for July 29, the MDA canceled it and never agreed to reschedule.

TOWN COMMON

While organizing around eminent domain, DSNI took a big step toward creating the town common called for in the master plan developed with DAC. Riley Foundation Administrator Newell Flather once again proved to be a door opener. Over dinner one night early in 1988, Flather shared the DSNI story with James Gutensohn, commissioner of the Massachusetts Department of Environmental Management (DEM). Gutensohn quickly saw a way for DEM to play a role through its "City and Town Commons" program, which was established to "preserve or create commons or squares in areas of outstanding historic, cultural or scenic significance, and attract investment to the area."[8] Town commons or "village greens" have historically served as the physical and spiritual center of New England communities. Gutensohn suggested that DSNI apply for a grant to make the Dudley town common a reality.

There were two large hurdles. First, no inner city neighborhood had ever received one of these grants. Second, only one grant would be given in a particular town or city. The Boston Common, the city's central downtown park, had been funded previously and was applying again with the backing of the powerful State Senate President William Bulger. DSNI turned to its partner, the Public Facilities Department, to sponsor its proposal. PFD Director Lisa Chapnick asked the city commissioner of Parks and Recreation to withdraw the application for Boston Common in favor of the DSNI proposal. The Parks and Recreation Department would welcome the competition, she was told, but would not withdraw.

With the help of PFD landscape architect Geeta Pradhan, DSNI developed its proposal for a town common on two separate pieces of land at the neighborhood's main intersection at Dudley Street and Blue Hill Avenue. The proposal stressed the symbolic impact of "the transition from its present blighted appearance to one of a green, inviting place of gathering" with gardens, recreational and open space. It would be a beautiful gateway to Dudley's planned urban village.

DSNI broke new ground by winning a DEM award of $1 million for the town common. Massachusetts Secretary of Environmental Affairs Jamie Hoyte and DEM Commissioner Gutensohn scheduled a press conference with DSNI on the town common site to announce the grant award—the first ever to an inner city project. On September 22, DSNI members, Riley Foundation representatives and government officials gathered at the corner of Blue Hill Avenue and Dudley Street to announce the $1 million grant. The city of Boston committed $500,000 in additional resources and capital improvements for the site. The town common support was a major boost to DSNI's plans to revitalize the neighborhood. It was big news—except the media largely ignored it.

"The odds were so stacked against us," says Lisa Chapnick. Yet when "we won a competition that historically had gone to major parks" like Boston Common, "it was the story that nobody covered," she says, still angry over the lack of media coverage. The next day's *Boston Herald* gave it only a "News/In Brief" mention. In the *Boston Globe* there were stories about assaults and drug busts in Roxbury. The *Globe* has covered other Dudley successes, but that time the paper provided the all too typical media treatment of poor communities—all bad news, no good.

The town common award had great meaning for DSNI members. It brought them closer to realizing the dream of an urban village from the nightmare of vacant lots.

THE MAYOR

By September 1988, the Dudley neighborhood was organized behind eminent domain, support was lined up within the Flynn administration and DSNI had submitted a solid application to the BRA board. What DSNI needed now was Mayor Flynn's public support.

Lisa Chapnick observes that DSNI was "asking for something so fundamentally different and new to government that virtually no one could possibly do that other than the person who ultimately really did it, which was the mayor. I mean, don't underestimate his role in this because there was a controversy within the administration itself. There were some people at the department head level who were very supportive and there were some who were violently opposed."

Chapnick says that the opponents argued, "How can you give away the power of eminent domain! Not only that, but you're going to give away your own rights to your [city-owned] land...How can you do this! This is irresponsible! This is tax dollars, this is foreclosed land...This is precedent, this is unheard of. It's too risky. It's too big. They have no track record, they haven't produced a popsicle stand. Who are these people?"

DSNI had lined up the support of the BRA and PFD directors and top Flynn aides such as Policy Director Neil Sullivan and Don Gillis, director of the Office of Neighborhood Services. Chapnick says Flynn did not need much convincing. "It was astounding. It was just something he believed in," recalls Chapnick. "The mayor usually on major things has a very thoughtful, inclusive kind of process and has lots of discussion [with] lots of people." This time, says Chapnick, "it was an extremely short discussion—one of the shortest I've ever seen in my life—with the mayor who said, 'Do it!'...He was so emphatic that the ones who were opposed dropped out because there was no doubt where he stood."

Flynn explains his support for eminent domain and other DSNI efforts this way: "It was clear to me that there was only one place the city government should be, and that's on their side—not creating barriers for them *not* to be able to do something, but giving them the power so they could do something for themselves...There were so many people who felt—particularly influential people—who thought that eminent domain...was crazy...I saw an opportunity for the neighborhoods to really take control, to have power, to make decisions that affect their neighborhood and their life. And I think that's what really was the key—having confidence in the people, having confidence in the neighborhoods. I just felt that these people were just so committed, so determined, so dedicated, that we should...be on their team, rather than being outside of that process."

Flynn says that eminent domain "was a risk—make no mistake about it from the standpoint of politics—because if this didn't prevail, if it didn't meet with a level of success, it would have been me as the mayor being held responsible for yet another misguided social policy...The question obviously I had to resolve on behalf of the entire city of Boston and its fiduciary interests: Were these people able to make it happen?" Flynn decided the risk was worth taking because of

DSNI's organizing track record, technical capacity and bottom-up "spirit and pride."

Flynn endorsed eminent domain in a September 28, 1988 letter to DSNI: "I am writing in support of a historic proposal...The authority vested in a 121-A corporation—to take and own land—represents an unprecedented opportunity in this city to control the destiny of your community. In fact I believe it is unparalleled anywhere in the country. I am pleased and excited to endorse this effort and to lend the support of my administration to its implementation." Flynn concluded, "Your group has shown the capacity, wisdom, and vision to handle this task, and I am pleased to be able to support your application to the BRA Board." DSNI included Flynn's letter with their application and he sent a similar letter to the BRA board on November 10.[9] When it came to supporting DSNI's eminent domain proposal, Flynn put his campaign promises about empowering the neighborhoods into practice.

Some people linked the Flynn administration's support of DSNI's eminent domain to city opposition to the movement to have Greater Roxbury secede from Boston and reincorporate as a separate city named Mandela—after South African liberation leader Nelson Mandela. A 1986 nonbinding referendum calling for reincorporation had been soundly defeated and the 1988 referendum calling for a feasibility study on the issue would also be defeated. The Mandela referendum's leadership and primary support came from within the African American community. The organizers of the Greater Roxbury Incorporation Project believed that the citizens of Roxbury would do better economically if they created their own city with a government that didn't discriminate against them. Some Mandela organizers claimed that DSNI's eminent domain application was nothing more than a way to sabotage the reincorporation process and provide Flynn with a bone to throw Roxbury.

Greater Roxbury Incorporation Project Director Andrew Jones was quoted in Greater Roxbury's major weekly newspaper, the *Bay State Banner*, shortly before the BRA hearings on DSNI's eminent domain: "This is the twilight zone. It's getting bizarre," said Jones. "It's a purely political move and it's tied to incorporation. It makes no sense at all for any city government to give that power to a private agency. The people in this community have to watch themselves because the city is trying to head off the biggest takeover of all, of 12.5 square miles of Boston, Mandela."[10] Though Jones' opposition to eminent domain was not shared by most of those supporting Mandela, there were others, such as the Roxbury Neighborhood Council's Chuck Turner, who supported DSNI's eminent domain plan, but were worried about the city's motivation in supporting it.

Many Mandela referendum supporters did not actually want Roxbury to secede, but thought passage of the nonbinding referendum would place greater pressure on the Flynn administration to support more community control over development and a fairer distribution of city resources. The Greater Roxbury Neighborhood Authority's Ken Wade explains that GRNA decided to support the referendum "only as a tactical matter. We were not sold on the notion that the major strategy for empowerment should be the creation of a separate city for, principally, people of color. We thought, as a tactical matter, it helped to surface the disparity in terms of service delivery. It helped to provide an organizing tool to get people talking, meeting and in motion around something. If nothing else, our perspective in the GRNA was that you would have to have this study that would reveal how the city is shortchanging that community." But, as GRNA Cochair Bob Terrell explains, "It doesn't make sense to have a separate city that's just as underdeveloped as the neighborhood already is underdeveloped…The shift in the geopolitical definition wouldn't solve our underlying economic problems."

The DSNI board voted not to take a position on the referendum. Board members could be found on both sides. The Mandela issue never came up in DSNI's discussions with city officials. City officials say they never linked Mandela and DSNI in their own deliberations about eminent domain. "I don't think [Mandela] had anything to do with it," says Chapnick. "The mayor doesn't like to be boxed," and, as the city saw it, Mandela wasn't going anywhere anyway.

BRA planner Andrea D'Amato maintains that "Mandela was much more of an issue outside the [BRA] than it ever was internally…The BRA or PFD commitment, to the best of my understanding, was never a response to Mandela. It was never a way of satisfying Mandela in a different way…It was just a weird twist of timing."

"TAKE A STAND, OWN THE LAND"

DSNI came up with a slogan to capture the powerful spirit of the eminent domain campaign: "Take a Stand, Own the Land." People displayed it proudly on buttons and bumper stickers. Throughout the organizing campaign, DSNI tried to avoid premature publicity about eminent domain outside the neighborhood. There was fear that if the effort broke publicly before all the pieces were in place—before there was enough support within the neighborhood and city government— early opposition would doom it. DSNI's strategy was to have enough support lined up so that when most people first heard that DSNI was going after eminent domain authority, it would come across as a done deal. Finally, it was time to go public in a big way.

DSNI organized a rally and press conference to take place on one of the vacant lots subject to eminent domain in the Triangle. It was a vacant lot on the devastated corner of Dudley and Dennis Streets. DSNI wanted the BRA board and the public to see a large crowd of residents and supporters taking a stand on the land, reflecting the hope and determination of the neighborhood.

The event took place on a sunny Saturday afternoon, October 1, 1988. About 200 residents turned out, many displaying buttons, balloons, signs and bumper stickers with the slogan, "Take a Stand, Own the Land." They signed petitions supporting DSNI's application to the BRA. Looking back on the eminent domain campaign, Clayton Turnbull says, "I think what excited me the most was the rally...where we had the residents with all their street signs converging on this land and laughing and joking and talking about everything else that was going on. That gave me a community sense...These people had a hope, they had a dream and it was enough for them to come out on that day...and say, 'We're going to go for it!'"

Sue Beaton came with a group of homeless women and children in transitional housing at Project Hope on Magnolia Street. "I remember the day," she says. "We had a great time standing on the dirt with all the dust flying in our face." They proudly held their sign, "Magnolia Street supports land control." Beaton says that the links between "the homelessness, the land and the housing started making more sense to the women here."

Speakers addressed the crowd from a flatbed truck. Among them were DSNI board members; former DSNI President Nelson Merced, then campaigning to become Massachusetts' first Latino state representative;* City Councilors Bruce Bolling and Rosaria Salerno; and Ken Wade, chair of the Roxbury Neighborhood Council. Speaking as a

---

* Merced became the first state representative from a new predominantly Black and Latino district, including Dudley, created in 1988 after a redistricting struggle.

resident who had lived in the neighborhood for 22 years, Clayton Turnbull declared, "We have paid the price...We remember fire...We saw violence come to our communities." Now, "It's about progress."

"When DSNI began about four years ago, many people thought ours was a pipe dream," Ché Madyun told the crowd. "But now the neighborhood is empowered; we have a shared vision of the future; and what we're announcing today will assure that we are around to enjoy that future...Residents of the neighborhood who own land will be invited to join with us. Many already have. We will work with them to help develop their property, or buy from them if they want to sell. Because the neighborhood itself will have this authority, not an outside entity, we will work with our neighbors, not against them."

Mayor Flynn told the cheering crowd that he was fully backing the effort. "What we're doing here today is sending a very, very clear and powerful message all across the country," he said. "And that is that city government ought to be the best friend of neighborhoods."[11]

Press coverage of the event was excellent. All the major local television stations and several radio stations covered the story that night, and the *Globe* and the *Herald* ran significant pieces in the next day's papers. A few days later, the *Boston Globe* editorialized, "The way to shape a neighborhood's destiny is to control the land...This time, [Chapter] 121a will be at the service of poor people struggling to determine their future."[12]

There was also negative fallout from the event. Just as DSNI had planned, many people were hearing about the eminent domain proposal for the first time—and they were hearing that it was virtually a done deal. Others who DSNI had informed, but who never took the proposal seriously, suddenly realized that it had high-level support. DSNI began receiving calls from politicians, developers and neighborhood landowners with all kinds of questions and concerns. One absentee landowner called DSNI members communists. Another called to say that DSNI was a bunch of thieves.

More importantly, though, the rally generated a lot of new spirit in the neighborhood. There was a sense of victory leading to the BRA hearing. Dudley residents were poised to do something that no one else had done before—and they knew it.

BRA HEARING

DSNI's hearing before the BRA board was scheduled for October 13. This would be the first time that DSNI made its case directly to the board. During the two weeks between the rally and the hearing, DSNI focused on neighborhood organizing to bring large numbers of people out for the hearing. In addition, DSNI continued political organizing to strengthen support among city officials and politicians.

DSNI arranged for a bus to help transport people from Dudley to downtown. The hearing was scheduled for 2:30 P.M. in the BRA boardroom on the ninth floor of City Hall. DSNI organizers did special outreach to the elderly, knowing they were most likely to be able to take time in the middle of the day, and arranged lunch at the DSNI office for everyone going to the hearing.

About 75 Dudley residents and 20 other DSNI supporters packed the BRA boardroom. Other people were present for the non-DSNI-related items on the BRA agenda that afternoon. The press was out in force, including several television crews. "It felt great to see that room filled to overflowing," says Sue Beaton. "It felt great to see kids and old people." Everybody had on their yellow "Take a Stand, Own the Land" buttons. The politicians taking a stand for the DSNI proposal at the hearing included Nelson Merced and City Councilors Bruce Bolling, Rosaria Salerno, Charles Yancey and David Scondras.

PFD Director Lisa Chapnick represented Mayor Flynn. She told the board that the DSNI proposal was "a once in a lifetime chance to turn a tremendous problem into a tremendous opportunity."

For its own presentation, DSNI put together a cross section of staff, consultants and board members, including Ché Madyun, Peter Medoff, board member Sol Angel Rodriguez of Nuestra Comunidad Development Corporation who had served as DSNI development director in 1989, Peter Munkenbeck from The Community Builders and Harold Carroll from Rackemann, Sawyer & Brewster. Having Carroll as part of the team was an important political step. Besides being a partner at the law firm, Carroll was also the former corporation counsel for the city of Boston—the city's chief lawyer during the reign of most members of the BRA board.

Though DSNI was supported by BRA Director Steve Coyle, the majority of the BRA board was not inclined to view the eminent domain request favorably. They felt that DSNI was a ragtag community group from Roxbury that had no professional standing within the development community and no business asking the city for this major power. Several board members opened their eyes wide when Carroll joined the DSNI members making their way to the front row. Carroll's presence on the team helped establish DSNI's credibility before the board.

Two people opposed the application when the floor was opened to the public. DSNI members and BRA staff had expected more opposition. The most dramatic moment of the hearing came during the testimony of Shirley Clark, an absentee landowner living in New York City. Clark owned three lots along Dudley Street, which she acknowledged her husband had bought "for speculative purposes" with the hope that they would "be his pension." She launched into an impassioned speech, declaring, "I think it's the most frightening experience I've ever had. We buy a piece of property, and somebody's going to take it for housing. For anything. I bought it. You have no right to move in there...We all know that you need low-income housing...I could use middle-income housing too. But I don't expect to take somebody else's piece of property that they purchased to do it...It's outrageous." Meanwhile, DSNI staff looked up Clark's name on the landowners list and discovered that her parcels weren't even within the eminent domain boundaries. She had been notified about the process along with other owners whose land abutted the eminent domain area. The matter ended less dramatically when the BRA board cleared up the misunderstanding.

The more significant opposition came from the Minority Developers Association. In addition to DSNI's efforts to gain MDA support, BRA planner Andrea D'Amato and staffperson Laval Wilson Jr. met with MDA representatives before the BRA hearing to try to alleviate their concerns. As D'Amato recalls, the MDA was told, "What do we have to do to convince you that this is okay? Or what do we have to do to change what we're doing so that you feel better?...We want you to endorse the project. We want you to be part of the process." Ultimately, MDA concern boiled down to their fears about not winning bids. D'Amato told them, "I don't know about you getting the bids, but minority developers in the neighborhood will be involved in the project. That is a commitment that is part of the organizational structure of the Dudley Street Neighborhood Initiative." D'Amato was surprised when the MDA spoke in opposition at the hearing. "I felt like their opposition was unfounded at that time because after all the discussions we had, I felt that they understood what the true goals of the project were...I had...the idea that they were in agreement, that they felt that this could be a project they could be involved in, that the politics within the neighborhood would be open toward them."

When Albert Gentry, a resident of the Jamaica Plain neighborhood, spoke on behalf of the MDA at the hearing, his testimony focused not on opposition to the 121A process, but to a supposed lack of opportunity for MDA participation. Wrongly claiming that the MDA had first heard of DSNI's plans only a few days earlier, Gentry testified, "I think the crime at this point is that there has not been an invitation to groups such as the Minority Developers Association, or some of the private citizens who might have opposition into the process." In response, DSNI produced copies of the July letter to the MDA requesting a meeting.

Gentry also claimed that on the DNI board, "There is no representation, as it is currently proposed, for minority business representation." He said, "It's important that minority people in the community own the housing, but...who will be the contractors, the architects, the managers, the construction workers and the financial consultants? Who will end up taking money home at the end of the rainbow?"[13] He questioned the project's commitment to minority hiring and economic development beyond housing. In particular, the MDA was concerned about DSNI's consultants, The Community Builders, a largely White organization that had competed for city-owned development sites and, the MDA argued, had demonstrated a poor record in minority hiring on their projects.

To DSNI members, these pleas from the MDA rang hollow. Here was a community group, most of whose members were people of color from the neighborhood, being lectured by private developers from outside the neighborhood, many of whom did not have good track records in building affordable housing or hiring workers of color. Still, DSNI representatives, led by Clayton Turnbull, met several times with MDA members after the hearing to iron out an agreement. The MDA wanted DSNI to guarantee compliance with the Boston jobs ordinance requiring 30 percent minority participation for all construction contracts and professional and technical services related to the development projects. DSNI members decided to demonstrate their own commitment to hiring people of color by agreeing to a minimum of 30 percent, but including in their eminent domain agreement with the BRA a stated goal of attaining a 50 percent minority participation rate. As Turnbull puts it, "Their ceiling became our basement."

Turnbull knew many of the MDA members and spoke to them about DSNI's plans, including then MDA President Richard Taylor, who Governor William Weld later appointed secretary of transportation. Turnbull says that they were put off by the participation of The Community Builders and they had an arrogance about themselves as "the leadership link downtown to money." Turnbull and other DSNI members tried to assure the MDA that "if we, the community, were not able to assemble this project and make sure that minority developers were involved and minority vendors were involved, then we're really in bad shape. If they can't trust us with that responsibility—they were trusting the community, not the city of Boston—then we've got major problems. I think they heard that."

After the hearing, before the BRA reached its decision, MDA President Richard Taylor appeared on the television program *Say Brother*, one of Boston's leading news shows focused on the Black community. The show was devoted to DSNI's eminent domain proposal, and Taylor appeared with BRA Deputy Director for Neighborhood Planning Tony Williams and Roxbury Neighborhood Council President Ken Wade. The hosts apparently expected Taylor and Wade to be critical of the project. Both said they supported it. Taylor commented, "I think the blight, the deterioration and just the physical condition of that section of the city—for years—weighs heavily in favor of eminent domain proceedings. No one can say that they did not have an opportunity to build housing who currently owns the land. No one can say they had not had a right to sell the land prior to this point in the free and open market."[14]

In the two-week interim between the hearing and the BRA decision, negotiations intensified between DSNI and PFD over a memorandum of understanding for the disposition of the private and public land in the Triangle. A Joint Disposition Committee (JDC) was created, made up of four representatives each from DSNI and PFD. It turned an informal collaboration into a contractual partnership. The JDC would combine the 15 city-owned acres and the 15 acres to be acquired by DSNI/DNI under eminent domain, and be responsible for disposing of the 30 total acres.

The partnership benefited both sides. It gave the city some controls over the land acquired through eminent domain. And it gave DSNI controls over the city-owned land. DSNI and PFD negotiated the timetable for land disposition. The city wanted a timetable that met the mayor's commitment to quickly dispose of all city-owned land (Project

747) by the end of his term in 1991, while DSNI's timetable was one of cautious planned physical development in concert with the other aspects of the comprehensive master plan. They agreed to stipulate that all public land would be disposed of by the end of 1991. The JDC chose a phased disposition schedule that focused first on those areas with large concentrations of city-owned land.

DSNI did not see the timetable as set in stone; the main task at hand was reaching agreement before the BRA vote. Three years was a long time, and anything could happen to change the details before 1991. As we'll see in Chapter Six, the details did change significantly.

THE DRAMA OF THE BRA DECISION

The day of decision by the BRA board was filled with unexpected high drama. Following the hearing and negotiations with PFD and the BRA to resolve outstanding issues, all signs pointed to a favorable decision. On November 10, the day of the BRA board meeting, Mayor Flynn called DSNI and asked that representatives come early to City Hall for a meeting in his office. Up to that point, DSNI members and staff had never discussed eminent domain directly with the mayor. Everyone assumed the meeting would be largely a photo opportunity, providing Flynn and DSNI with good publicity. Medoff and DSNI board members, including Paul Yelder, Ché Madyun, Clayton Turnbull and Sue Beaton, went to the mayor's office for a 2:30 P.M. meeting. The BRA board was supposed to meet a half hour later. It was supposed to be a done deal. It was not.

The DSNI group was ushered into the mayor's inner office. It was a more private office—with a couch, Flynn's desk, some bookshelves—than the one DSNI members had visited during the trash transfer station campaign. Lisa Chapnick was there along with the mayor's official photographer. The DSNI members filled up the couch space and Flynn came in and squeezed his way among them. Chapnick was standing behind the couch and began to lean against one of the shelves that lined the wall. All of a sudden, there was a thud as Chapnick knocked over a picture. It turned out to be an inscribed picture of the mayor with Pope John Paul. Flynn quipped, "Lisa, you wouldn't have done that if that was a picture of me with a rabbi." Everybody laughed. They were all in high spirits. DSNI and the city were about to make history.

The mayor told DSNI how important he thought the decision would be. DSNI members told Flynn how much they appreciated his support and how they felt that a new day was dawning for the Dudley neighborhood. Suddenly, one of Flynn's aides came running into the office and asked the mayor to step outside. When the mayor came back he informed the group that there were some problems with the BRA board. They were apparently balking at approving DSNI's application.

It was now past the 3:00 P.M. starting time for the board meeting, but the board was holed up in a room with Steve Coyle, Neil Sullivan and other mayoral advisers. Flynn was incensed. DSNI representatives were sitting in his office, celebrating the anticipated approval of the application. Many other DSNI residents and supporters were waiting in the BRA boardroom for the meeting to start. TV cameras and print media were there, poised to record the historic event. And the mayor was being told that the appointed board was going to say no.

Flynn informed the DSNI group that he had called the board members down from their offices on the ninth floor to meet directly with him. He suggested that the DSNI contingent step outside the office to avoid the fireworks. Chapnick decided it was best if she left with them. As Chapnick and the DSNI group walked out of Flynn's office they passed the BRA board members filing in. It looked like a scene right out of the book *Make Way for Ducklings.* Coyle was in front leading the five BRA board members, who walked in single file with gloomy expressions on their faces. As the two groups passed each other, DSNI board member Paul Yelder immediately turned around and joined in line behind the BRA board, mimicking their stride and expressions. As Yelder started to go through the door, he smiled at Flynn, quickly turned around and walked back out as the door was shut.

For the next hour, the DSNI group sat in the outer office along with Chapnick and listened to muffled shouts coming from inside. At one point, Flynn opened the door and stuck his head out. His face was bright red. "Get me Connolly!" he yelled, referring to John Connolly, his chief development adviser and an opponent of DSNI's application. Flynn returned to his office, where more commotion ensued.

Meanwhile, upstairs in the BRA boardroom, the crowd was overflowing into the corridors and growing increasingly impatient. Along with reporters and DSNI supporters, there was a large group of union workers from the building trades waiting to speak in favor of a different project before the board. Unaware of the drama unfolding on the fifth floor, the audience chanted, "We want the board."

Downstairs, the door finally opened to the mayor's office and the board members walked out, as they had walked in, single file, gloomy expressions. They avoided eye contact with the waiting DSNI members. Coyle brought up the rear. He flashed a smile and a thumbs up as he walked with the board out of Flynn's office, heading toward the ninth floor.

After a quick goodbye to the mayor, who appeared shaken but victorious, the DSNI crew made their way to the BRA boardroom. Chapnick had seen enough and returned to her office. By the time the board meeting was called to order it was nearly 5 P.M.—almost two hours late. The room was bursting with people and anticipation. Several mayoral advisers were pacing outside. Television cameras were everywhere. Reporters with fast-approaching deadlines were frantically trying to find out what had been going on and surrounded the DSNI members who had been in Flynn's office.

When the BRA meeting finally started, DSNI's eminent domain application was taken out from the middle of the agenda and placed at the top, further annoying those who had come for other issues. Director Coyle led off by summarizing the application, describing the negotiations between BRA staff and DSNI, and recommending board approval. The board's discussion was brief. It was actually more of a lecture to DSNI.

"I don't know why in the world you want to take this undertaking," said board member Clarence "Jeep" Jones, the only Black member. "You will have to walk very softly and you have to take into consideration that people will be offended." Michael Donlan, who opposed the project, urged DSNI to "reach out for help, because a lot of people want your success." And Chairman Farrell, reportedly the staunchest opponent on the board, admonished the DSNI representatives seated up front, "You could set the development process in Roxbury back 25 years if there's a disaster."[15]

The vote was called, and it was over very quickly. All five board members voted yes. It was obvious that most would have preferred to vote no. When the decision was made, the crowd of DSNI supporters let out a collective cheer. It was a very exciting, very energizing moment. They had achieved a goal many once considered unreachable.

Rumors immediately began to circulate that Chairman Farrell had so angered the mayor that he would soon be replaced. Two months later, the mayor announced the resignations of Farrell and another BRA board member.

DSNI was told that during the heated meeting preceding the vote on eminent domain, what most enraged Flynn was when Farrell said he was appalled the mayor would consider giving such authority to a group of "foreigners," referring to Dudley's Cape Verdean and Latino residents. And many, Farrell added, didn't even speak English.

Flynn—who often pointed with pride to his Irish working-class parents—recalls how he felt at the time. "It wasn't so much of a personal anger at any individual," but anger at government arrogance. "Sometimes there is this elitist attitude that only the professional planners know how to get anything done...I've seen professional planners screw up more things than you could shake a stick at, and I've seen a lot of projects that have been unsuccessful because they were jammed down people's throats in the neighborhoods. This is a very different kind of a project. This is bottom-up. This starts with spirit and pride in the neighborhood—people of very diverse backgrounds. I mean, if this project didn't even succeed, and all we ever accomplished was getting a lot of diverse good people...working together and getting to know each other, and young people, kids in the neighborhoods, coming together planning their neighborhood—if that's all that was ever achieved, this would be a monumental success, because we've already done something that is the biggest challenge in America today, and that is bringing people together, particularly people of different backgrounds and ethnicities. You could walk into the Dudley Street area and you would think you're walking through the United Nations. There's just people who are of all walks of life, and it's just extraordinary...long-term residents who were there when James Michael Curley was the mayor of Boston, and then we have people who just arrived from Cape Verde, and everything in between." Dudley, says Flynn, "really represents not only the greatest of Boston in its diversity, but I think it's the future of America as well."

PRECEDENT?

"There's nothing new about community residents unifying to influence the thrust of development in their neighborhoods," the article in *Banker & Tradesman* began. "What is very new, however, is a community-based group that doesn't have just the ability to influence development but the authority to control it as well."[16]

Government officials knew they were setting a local and national precedent by granting eminent domain to DSNI. The city did not want the door opened too widely. Andrea D'Amato acknowledges the concern over precedent within the BRA: "One of our motivating concerns in writing and structuring the 121A...was how do we write this so not every person and their sibling will be coming in here saying, 'I want this.'"

While BRA staff were willing to look at requests by other community groups with comparable cases, they didn't expect to really find any. As the BRA decision on DSNI put it, "The severe problems and unusual land configuration in the project area call for the use of 121A Authority for the purposes of housing development. The area is distinguished in a number of ways: by the unusual concentration of publicly held land, privately owned vacant land, land in tax foreclosure, land held by absentee owners, and in contrast, the absence of parcels suitable for housing development...The strong local momentum of the Dudley Street Neighborhood Initiative and the use of 121A provisions can be combined to accelerate an efficient land assembly process so critical to housing development in the area."[17]

On the record, city officials emphasized Dudley's distinctive patchwork of vacant land and DSNI's demonstrated planning and organizing ability and strong community base to explain their support of eminent domain. Off the record, some officials acknowledged that eminent domain would not go forward, whatever the circumstances, where there were stronger institutional players to challenge it, such as in Boston's Fenway and Chinatown neighborhoods, where hospitals, universities and large businesses owned much of the land. PFD's Rebecca Black remembers the Fenway case coming up and people pointing, among other things, to Dudley's "low property values compared to the Fenway" and its much higher concentration of vacant land, to argue that "it was not replicable."

Some community development activists who supported DSNI's eminent domain also wondered if the city might try to use the precedent in a devious way: "I think at least in the GRNA," says Ken Wade, "we saw—based on who the people in DSNI were—it as a positive thing because it was an expression of community control." They worried, however, about a potential downside: "Did the city have a bigger agenda—that they were hoping to use this granting of eminent domain authority to DSNI to do some other things in other places? You can envision them...creating community organizations to essentially do eminent domain that you know that the city couldn't do itself—the city going out and taking people's property à la the West End and what happened in the South End." During the rest of the Flynn administration, the eminent domain precedent was never put to the test. While several community-based organizations considered the eminent domain option, none decided to pursue it. And the city never tried to use the DSNI precedent to initiate eminent domain elsewhere.

"To a certain extent," Wade observes, "it's always hard for activists to size up the [city's] motivation. I think the best you can do is really see if it provides an opportunity for you to accomplish your agenda and you try to take advantage of it…The long and short of it was that [DSNI] had done enough of what it needed to do to demonstrate it was real."

Flynn explains eminent domain and the larger city partnership with DSNI this way: "Any time you can get a neighborhood organization to work closely and cooperatively with city government, that's a real win-win situation. It's a win for the city, and it's certainly a win for the neighborhood. Usually you read about division and alienation…City Hall versus the people kind of attitude…In this case, it's City Hall and the neighborhood working together…That's not only great policy, it's also great politics."

DSNI also believed eminent domain was a "win-win" outcome. "Win-win" did not mean that the city and DSNI shared each other's full agendas. They did not. DSNI felt confident enough in its community strength that eminent domain—and its larger partnership with the city—would result not in co-optation, but greater community control over Dudley's destiny.

6

LAND AND HOUSING DEVELOPMENT: THE TRIANGLE AND BEYOND

DSNI kicked off 1989 with a "New Office, New Director, New Power, New Year" Party. DSNI members had successfully organized the Dudley neighborhood into a dynamic political force and created a unified vision and plan for neighborhood renewal. They had broken new ground for community groups nationally by winning eminent domain authority over a major portion of vacant land. Now they were ready to transform that land into new homes and common space, beginning with the Dudley Triangle.

DSNI was undergoing a major transition in its staff of eight. Organizer Adalberto Teixeira left in November 1988 to become the mayor's liaison to Roxbury and the Cape Verdean community. Teixeira recruited Gertrudes Fidalgo to succeed him. Fidalgo jokes that she was just an art student, but got the job because she loves to meet new people. Teixeira knew her as a dynamic activist in the Cape Verdean community and DSNI thought she would make a great organizer for the neighborhood as a whole. Her family is very involved with DSNI, including her sister Maria-Goreth Fidalgo, a longtime board member who cochaired the Human Development Committee, and her brothers Jorge and Jose, local businessmen who have served on the board at different times.

In November 1988, DSNI also hired Ros Everdell as the new organizing director. Everdell, a White woman with a masters in community economic development, had many years of organizing experience in New York and Boston around economic justice, food and hunger, welfare rights and women's issues. Before joining DSNI she staffed the Boston Rainbow Coalition and was the Northeast regional coordinator for the Jesse Jackson Campaign for President.

DSNI also changed executive directors. Peter Medoff had informed the board of his intention to step down as DSNI director by early 1989. For one thing, as DSNI's reputation grew, Medoff became more uncomfortable with having the spotlight on a White man from outside the neighborhood leading the staff of an organization dedicated to community self-determination. Also, Medoff was an organizer at heart, but the director's role had become increasingly administrative as DSNI's staff and budget expanded. And, after three years of marathon work weeks, Medoff was simply tired.

Over 50 people applied for the executive director position. The winning candidate was the former mayor of Berkeley, California, Eugene "Gus" Newport. From 1979 to 1986, Newport was mayor of a city well known for progressive public policies. Under his tenure, Berkeley became the first U.S. city to divest from South Africa and establish itself as a sanctuary for Central American refugees. Newport had chaired the U.S. Conference of Mayors Advisory Subcommittee on Employment and Education. He was experienced in creating affordable housing and using eminent domain authority to implement economic development. Newport had spent his first year out of office in Boston as a senior fellow at the University of Massachusetts Trotter Institute for the Study of Black Culture. As an African American social justice activist with international stature and an economic development specialist, Newport was the unanimous choice of the DSNI board. He joined the staff in December 1988. To make the transition smoother, Medoff remained on as a consultant into the spring, focusing primarily on development.

Prior to being hired by DSNI, Newport had interviewed for a position at the Public Facilities Department. He laughingly recalls that "the final question was, 'Will you do or carry out whatever the mayor's policy is, even if you think it's [wrong]?' I said, 'No, buddy, no!'" As director of DSNI, Newport's good-humored forthrightness won over many government and business leaders who knew only of the radical reputation which preceded him to Boston.

FINANCING THE LAND: FORD FOUNDATION LOAN

It's common to hear insiders refer to eminent domain as "taking" land, a shorthand phrase inviting the misinterpretation that land would be taken without compensation to landowners. DSNI Vice President Clayton Turnbull cringes when anyone uses "taking the land" shorthand. "I'm against that language," he says, "and I constantly remind staff and board members, we're not 'taking the land.' If I come in and take something from your house, I'm not buying it, I'm taking it. Even if you don't want that thing, the fact that I'm taking it raises your eyebrows...There's a huge difference between taking land and paying $2 million for it."

DSNI estimated it would need $2-3 million in order to purchase all the privately owned vacant land in the Triangle at fair market value. This estimate turned out to be high, as the city foreclosed on more property—increasing the city share of the vacant land to about 60 percent—and the real estate market crashed along with the Massachusetts economy. The city would sell its vacant land to DSNI's community land trust, Dudley Neighbors, Inc., for the nominal fee of $1. For the private land, DSNI had the $1 million commitment of credit from Consumers United Insurance Company, which was used to help secure eminent domain authority. But even before CUIC backed out in August 1990, DSNI knew it would need additional financing.

In spring 1988, as the eminent domain campaign got underway, Medoff visited Nancy Andrews, an old friend and classmate at the Columbia University School of Urban Planning. Andrews was then a program related investment officer at the Ford Foundation, one of the nation's largest foundations and a major supporter of community development efforts—Ford President Franklin Thomas formerly headed the Bedford-Stuyvesant Restoration Corporation, considered the first CDC in the country. Andrews oversaw a sizable portfolio of program related investments in which Ford loaned large sums of money at very favorable rates to community development projects. These loans were targeted to large-scale programs, such as housing and development loan pools, which were at least citywide and, often, national in scope.

Ford had never made a large loan to a neighborhood group, much less one that had yet to develop a single unit of housing.

Medoff flew down to New York on April 1—April Fool's Day—to make his pitch to Andrews. Andrews liked what she heard. "The thing that really stuck out in my mind and seemed very exciting about the Dudley Street project," recalls Andrews, "was the notion of comprehensiveness [and] of using a citizen participation resident empowerment approach to develop concrete steps and goals for action." Andrews explains that before meeting with Medoff, she "had been trying to figure out how to move the debate and discussion" around development "beyond bricks and mortar and more toward the people side of the equation." She appreciated DSNI's holistic approach to development, where housing is a component of a "total fabric" and "not a goal in and of itself."

With the assistance of its consultant, The Community Builders (TCB), who already had a relationship with Ford, DSNI sent a concept paper and preliminary request for funds to Ford in May. In a later letter providing advice about submitting a formal proposal, Andrews warned DSNI "to expect numerous rounds of questions and review."[1] In December, shortly after obtaining eminent domain authority, DSNI sent Ford a proposal requesting a program related investment (PRI) of $2 million for a term of ten years, divided into two five-year phases of development. Phase One envisioned the purchase of all privately owned vacant land in the Triangle, to be combined with city-owned land, resulting in the construction of 500 units of housing over five years ending in mid-1994. The loan would be rolled over into a second five-year phase entailing the purchase of additional land adjacent to the Triangle and the construction of an additional 500 units of housing in the larger Dudley area.

In early 1989, Andrews met with Mayor Flynn, who assured her of the city's financial and political commitment to the project. "I needed to know that there was really access" at the highest level, Andrews explains. Development projects "never happen when they are supposed to happen. They always take three times as long...and that is no exaggeration. At times, people that you make deals with in the city today are not there tomorrow. So you need clout at the highest level [to] push middle people or lower-level people into action." Andrews says Flynn "gave me all of the warm comfortable feelings that one could possibly have that this was high on his agenda and something he really wanted to see go forward."

The Ford Foundation approved a $2 million PRI, in principle, to DSNI in October 1989. Andrews' division had "made the case for funding it on the basis of the innovativeness of the project," Andrews explains. "That innovativeness rested on two legs. One was the comprehensive nature of the strategy and the resident participation component of the strategy, and the second leg was the innovativeness of the right of...eminent domain." Although Ford's draft letter of approval stated that "such approval is conditioned upon the preparation and execution of definitive Loan Documents satisfactory to the Foundation and its counsel," DSNI anticipated quick progress. One year after obtaining the power of eminent domain, it appeared that the financing necessary to purchase the vacant land would soon be in DSNI's hands. However, the "numerous rounds of questions and review"—and delays—were just beginning.

Because of DSNI's change in executive directors and the difficulty in finding a development director with the right combination of technical expertise and conceptual vision, a lot of work on the Ford PRI went to TCB. That changed when David Rockwell became DSNI's development director in February 1990. Rockwell had worked previously as a real estate developer, city planner and banker, specializing in construction and mortgage loans. In June, DSNI board member Paul Yelder, who had been working on the Ford loan in his capacity as DSNI treasurer, became the director of Dudley Neighbors, Inc. and deputy director of DSNI. Yelder previously worked for the Roxbury Multi-Service Center and the city's Economic Development and Industrial Corporation. TCB's role, for which DSNI was accumulating heavy bills, phased out in 1990 as DSNI relied on staff, board members and its pro bono law firms.

With TCB leaving the picture, the Ford loan approval process became even more complicated. Nancy Andrews says that "a great deal of my comfort on the risk side of the project rested in believing that [TCB] was...going to be a critical and a powerful part of the implementation. When that in fact reversed itself, and they were not, I got real nervous. At one point I said to Gus [Newport], 'You've got a CDC here [DNI] that has never done one house ever. It's done nothing, and you're telling me that in the first project you are going to do 460 units or whatever.' I said the Ford Foundation does not make PRIs to organizations that have no track record. We would never have done that."

Even as DSNI adopted a more phased approach and addressed Ford's concerns over lack of a housing track record by building more safeguards into the plans, Newport says, "We hammered and hammered that our track record was the foundation of people working together to develop a master plan" and rebuild the neighborhood for the long run.

TRIANGLE BUILD-OUT PLAN

While pursuing the Ford loan and beginning the legal process to implement eminent domain, DSNI completed a build-out plan for the Triangle. As its architectural planning consultant, DSNI chose Comunitas, a local firm whose principal architect is Antonio DiMambro. "Of the firms that we interviewed," DNI Director Paul Yelder explains that DiMambro "possessed the stronger sort of advocacy gift—somebody who would...not only articulate the community views or visions, but also stand up in defense of that vision if challenged by the city or anyone else."

Comunitas prepared a series of maps and drawings presenting different types of housing options. An all-day community planning meeting was held at the Shirley-Eustis House on Saturday, May 13, 1989, attended by 60 people. A follow-up evening meeting attended by 125 people took place at St. Patrick's Church. Residents looked at the Triangle block by block and determined the type of housing, community centers, open space, playgrounds, commercial space, parking and other amenities appropriate for each site of vacant land.

Yelder credits the planning process for avoiding the kind of "planner speak" that turns off community participation—using terms like "parcel" when referring to lots of land, for example. "I've got a parcel I got from UPS," he jokes. "I didn't think I lived on one of these rascals." The goal is to keep involving more people in development, not becoming "so immersed that you just assume that everybody thinks of community land trusts and lease expiration terms and...limited equity formulas." Speaking for himself as well as others, Yelder sees making the development process understandable and accessible to all residents as one of DSNI's biggest ongoing challenges.

Yelder says "it was really helpful to have" DiMambro as the architectural consultant. DiMambro "could relate to people directly...and really get to the meat of 'What do you want this stuff to look like, where do you want it, and how close do you want people living together?'" DiMambro comments, "The most important thing I felt that came out of those discussions was the need for community and the need for privacy at the same time."[2]

During the community planning process, residents strongly called for lower-density housing and more tot lots where neighborhood children could play safely, community facilities, day care, open space, off-street parking and other amenities. The original Triangle goal of 500 units of housing was reduced to 364 units, mostly town house-style homes with yards. This was later reduced to 296 units as some sites were found physically unsuitable for housing upon closer inspection and other lots were dropped to avoid disputes with owners in the eminent domain process.

Besides housing, the Triangle build-out plan included new commercial space on Dudley Street and Blue Hill Avenue; a town common at the tip of the Triangle; numerous tot lots; and two community centers to meet the recreational, cultural and social service needs of the neighborhood. DSNI's Triangle redevelopment would be complemented by a city-funded capital improvements project, reconstructing major sections of Dudley Street and Blue Hill Avenue. At DSNI's behest, the city declared the Triangle a "special study area" in which zoning codes could be established independently from the larger process of rezoning Roxbury. DSNI was backed by the Roxbury Neighborhood Council, which was working with the city on Roxbury's rezoning.

On June 21, 1989, the Triangle build-out plan was ratified by members attending the DSNI annual meeting. By then, DSNI's voting membership had grown to over 700 residents, agencies and businesses plus over 200 nonvoting members who lived outside the neighborhood's boundaries.

City officials wanted DSNI to take the community centers out of the build-out plan. "People were afraid of the bill," says Rebecca Black, former PFD assistant director of Planning and Policy. "I don't think it was so much opposition to the concept."

Gus Newport says, "We turned around and said we can't provide the total community needs unless we have all of these elements in place. We're not saying that you are going to have to pay for them, but we are saying they are going to be there."

As discussed earlier, DSNI and PFD had established a Joint Disposition Committee (JDC) with equal responsibility for choosing developers to build on all the vacant land in the Triangle. The partnership with PFD was often difficult. DSNI staffers joke that the partners have been through marriage, separation, divorce and remarriage. In May 1989, city officials threatened to dissolve the partnership because they wanted to push the housing production process much quicker than DSNI did. "Who ever would have thought a community group would be the thing that would slow down the bureaucracy?" comments DSNI Deputy Director Sue Beaton. The city argued, recalls Yelder, that housing and other subsidies "might not be there in the future and we've got the time clock ticking on this project." DSNI argued back that it would not sacrifice the community consensus process to speed up production.

Rebecca Black says PFD staff were getting very nervous because it appeared DSNI's slower timing would jeopardize Mayor Flynn's deadline of disposing of the city's vacant land by the end of 1991. In Black's words, PFD staff felt, "We had gone into this under a certain bottom-line understanding, and that had been betrayed. I think it freaked people out."

Yelder understood that PFD had an edict from the mayor to fill the vacant land: "They didn't get an edict to go out and...rebuild communities. They got an edict to go out and rebuild housing." Newport says, "I think after a while we made them understand [that] we understand their bottom line." But, he adds, "During those conversations I think some cold water got boiled."

PFD Director Lisa Chapnick says, "There was a healthy tension sometimes, that was not healthy when communication lines broke down, but ultimately, we could resolve it. I felt like we could resolve [DSNI's] mission and our mission...I think [DSNI] felt pushed. We felt pushed back. I think it ended up being a 50/50 thing. But if [DSNI] had reneged on that, [it] would have been a memory because a deal is a deal. And that's what [DSNI] expected from us, too."

The Triangle build-out plan has four phases designed to assure a step-by-step process of land acquisition, financing, construction, marketing and sales. The phasing allows a wider group of developers to participate and avoids overloading the housing market in a weakened economy. In August 1989, the JDC issued its first request for qualifications (RFQ) from developers for the Triangle's first phase of about 100 units of housing on two separate, adjoining sites. In a cover letter to prospective developers, Newport and Chapnick wrote, "Working together in a unique partnership, PFD and DSNI have endorsed a comprehensive plan which will turn around a neighborhood...DSNI created the vision, organized the community, and marshaled financial and political support to make this plan a reality. PFD has committed major staff and funding resources, and fifteen acres of land to make this effort a success."[3]

A community meeting attended by over 100 residents was held in December to review proposals by developers. Afterward, the JDC designated two developers for the two Phase One sites: a for-profit partnership and the local nonprofit CDC, Nuestra Comunidad Development Corporation. In 1990, with continued community input, the JDC moved quickly to designate eight developers for Phases Two and Three, which consists of a mix of housing on smaller "buildable lots" and large sites. Flynn's mandate had been met—all the city-owned land was designated for development.

Operating as a redevelopment authority for the neighborhood, it was DSNI's responsibility to assist the developers in securing financing for the housing. By 1990, the "Massachusetts Miracle" of a booming economy had become the "Massachusetts Mirage." Republican William Weld was elected governor and cut the state budget deficit by slashing public spending at a time of rising unemployment and poverty. Cutbacks in the state's nationally recognized housing programs made Dudley Triangle construction and mortgage financing much more difficult.

The development of housing, community facilities and capital improvements in the Triangle are supported by a range of public and private sources including federal, state and city low-income housing tax credits, rental subsidies, block grants and other housing supports. Working with PFD, DSNI applied for a Nehemiah Housing Opportunity Program grant from the Department of Housing and Urban Development. The Nehemiah Program was established by the congressional Housing and Community Development Act of 1987 to promote low-cost home ownership. DSNI's $2.3 million grant, made in October 1990, was the only one in New England and the third largest of the 21 grants given out nationally. The grant provides $15,000 no-interest second mortgages for low- and moderate-income first-time homebuyers.

The $1 million town common grant, awarded to DSNI in 1988, had not been delivered by the Massachusetts Department of Environmental Management, and there was fear that with the change in administrations and the state fiscal crisis, DSNI would never see the grant. Persistent work by DSNI and PFD finally paid off in 1992 when the state authorized a grant of $700,000 for the town common, which would be combined with $500,000 from the city for a total of $1.2 million. As PFD landscape architect Geeta Pradhan told a DSNI community meeting in November 1992, "The State had decided they weren't going to fund these projects anymore. This is now the only project of its sort being funded—and only because of DSNI's community and lobbying."

CLOSING IN ON THE LAND AND THE LOAN

By the time DSNI and the Ford Foundation closed on the $2 million loan in March 1992, the original three-year period of eminent domain authority had already expired. DSNI had to ask the BRA for an extension before a single vacant lot changed hands.[4] The BRA's Andrea D'Amato and Tony Williams believed that the original time frame of securing the land and beginning development in three years had been unrealistic. "We just thought three years was way too short to do development," says D'Amato. "That was still when the economy was good."

The BRA board granted an extension in 1991, giving DSNI until November 1994 to exercise eminent domain. Gus Newport recalls that after DSNI made its case for the extension, a BRA board member said, "'You all have done much more than the city ever did.' Even though there's no build-out, the foundation is in place. There is a master plan and it is zoned."

Still, many DSNI members were growing impatient waiting for building to begin. Organizer Gertrudes Fidalgo says residents frequently asked, "'What's going on? Why isn't there any housing?' We tell them how long it takes to get one little thing done…[much less] something such as a Ford Foundation loan, which is not a little thing. Or how long it takes to [convince] the city, 'That is not what we want. This is really what we want.'…Six months later, you're going through that same process."

Father Walter Waldron recalls that when DSNI began, people doubted it could really get housing built. "Nowadays, I think that people accept that, and their only question is: 'Why isn't it being done next week if it's going to be done?' It's kind of crazy, but it's that whole change of attitude from 'It never can happen' to 'We want it tomorrow' because it can be done."

Not surprisingly, there are conflicting views as to why the Ford loan took over three years to close and what impact that had on the development process. TCB's Peter Munkenbeck did not see the timing as extraordinary. He says it took more than two years to conclude their two Ford PRIs and they had "none of the complexity or overriding complications of a community-driven grassroots process." Gus Newport emphasizes, "This is the first time [Ford has] gone directly to a community group and given a PRI." They wanted to make sure the limb they were going out on was a strong one.

Nancy Andrews, who was promoted to the position of deputy director of Ford's Office of Program and Managed Investment during the loan negotiations, believes that even under the best of circumstances the process would have been lengthy. She says the loan was slowed by such factors as the loss of CUIC as a financing partner, DSNI staff changes and the phasing out of The Community Builders. "On top of that," says Andrews, "the economics of the project changed considerably" from "a gentrifying environment" to a weak economy and housing market. "The question wasn't how do we protect the land from future appreciation, but are we going to pay too much for the land? And can we get people to buy these units? Will the subsidy be enough to induce people?" The land would be loan collateral, she says, but "in this particular case the land that is being acquired, while it has an appraised value, it is really questionable whether you could in fact sell it. It is also really questionable if one would want to try to do that. I mean, would the Ford Foundation really want to go after land in the middle of Roxbury and take it away from people? Probably not."

Andrews says, "It is probably safe to say that the folks at [DSNI] did not feel as acutely the risk that we felt." She says the DSNI deal was so large, complicated and unconventional that "it is the longest, most expensive closing we have ever done at the Ford Foundation." She adds, "At the time that we did it," the $2 million PRI "was one of the largest actions we had ever done."

Many DSNI staff and board members take a more critical view of Ford's role in the long delay before closing the loan and of the burdensome steps required to withdraw loan funds for land purchases. In the words of Kelley Brown, who became DSNI development director when David Rockwell left in January 1991 to become a Shawmut Bank vice president focusing on community reinvestment, "Far and away the biggest issue was Ford's reluctance to basically make the fundamental business decision, continuing for months on end to try and come up with teeny-weeny ways within the scope of the loan agreement to mitigate their risk in the loan."

Henry Thayer, the Rackemann, Sawyer & Brewster lawyer responsible for researching the land titles, believes that even if the Ford loan had closed quickly, the development process would still have been lengthy. "It took time just to examine all of these titles," he says. "Someone who comes along later will benefit from our experience. Probably they can do it somewhat quicker—but just the magnitude of all of these lots to keep track of, and all of these respondents...A lot of time was lost trying to find people. There was one parcel that was taken for taxes in 1936. The owner of the equity of redemption [the right to pay off the taxes]...died and left relatives all over New England and back in Ireland. We started running those people down, and some we are never going to be able to find. Some went to Rhode Island and I hired...a disbarred lawyer [to find them]...He uncovered [that]...one of the heirs of this fellow had been murdered, which accounted for his disappearance."

Thayer found it "interesting to follow the sociology of the neighborhood" through the title searches. It's a sociology of disinvestment, as seen in Chapter One. "You go from Irish, Italian and Jewish neighborhoods," says Thayer. "Then you begin to get Hispanic names and names you sometimes associate with African Americans...You can see the changes. Then you can see the mortgage foreclosures. In some cases we have old mortgages the bank didn't even bother to foreclose and the bank has gone out of business. And thank heavens we have eminent domain. Otherwise, we would never get marketable title...The [Veterans Administration] holds a few mortgages and they are not going to give us a discharge because they can't find their file. So you run into that kind of bureaucracy."

"When you start getting demolition liens and tax takings," Thayer observes, "then you know a neighborhood is in terrible peril. They began in the sixties. We might have foreclosures in the fifties, but there was usually someone to buy the foreclosure sale, a new individual." That changed. "There would be a fire or something. All of a sudden, there is a demo lien...Things started coming down in an accelerating way, I would say, from about the mid-sixties on."

After the title searches came what Thayer calls "the slow grinding mill at the court system." DSNI filed its case with the Massachusetts Superior Court in July 1990. It's not uncommon for motions to "get lost, or they don't get acted on by the judge," says Thayer. The DSNI case was complicated. "The judge to whom it was assigned was simply horrified when he discovered that he had in effect something like 50 eminent domain cases, all wrapped up in one docket number, because there are about 50 owners." DSNI was hesitant to try to push the courts to move faster until the Ford loan for buying the land was in hand. The Superior Court did not issue its summary decision confirming DNI's authority to acquire land through eminent domain until February 1992.

$2 MILLION

When it came time to finally close the Ford loan in March 1992, DSNI decided to wait until later in the year to celebrate it publicly. Gus Newport explains that they didn't "want to raise the flag" while they were still negotiating other aspects of the development process. The Ford PRI provides $2 million at 1 percent interest for nine years. As Nancy Andrews notes, "not even the Federal Reserve lends at 1 percent. We tend to, wherever possible, create favorable outcomes for the group in the financing terms. For instance, with Dudley Street we wanted to make sure that any arbitrage earnings that might occur on the $2 million dollars [the spread between the interest DNI earns through investing that portion of the Ford money not expended and the interest due Ford], which we could have held and used to offset our risk—we released those in order to support their operations." The loan will be repaid in installments from the proceeds of the ground lease payments by developers to whom DNI grants development rights. It is secured by mortgages on the private and city-owned land under DNI's domain in the Triangle.

Newport describes the emotional scene of the Ford closing. "It was a rather jovial, spirited" occasion, he says. "There were these little conversations going on in different corners of the place...As the meeting finally started I said, 'Well, now that we've done our work so well...Nancy, why don't you make the check for $5 million!'"

"Then the people from State Street Bank came in," Newport continues. "Three of them to handle the [$2 million] account. They started making jokes, 'Well, our planes are waiting on the runway and we're going down to the islands.'"

"Finally when everything had been signed and Ché got the check, she picked it up and said, 'Better stay in one place!' As if to say, 'Is this check any good?'" While he delights in the jokes, Newport chokes up in completing the story, thinking of the community effort which brought DSNI to that point. "It gets me," he says. "I don't think anybody ever really believed it was going to happen, even though we all persevered."

The public celebration took place at DSNI's annual meeting on June 24, 1992, which was attended by officials from PFD and other city departments. Before the meeting, DSNI staff and board members had discussed how to reinforce the residents' sense of ownership of the Ford loan. They decided to prepare a huge blowup of the check and invite everyone to come up and endorse it at the meeting, symbolizing how the community, and not the organization itself, was the beneficiary. It was the largest investment Ford had made in Massachusetts. Spirits were high as DSNI members walked up to the podium at St. Patrick's and signed the check.

Behind the check were large poster boards with a time line of DSNI's history, highlighting significant events. The time line, which was displayed after the meeting in DSNI's window, didn't erase members' growing impatience with the seemingly endless housing development process, but it reminded them of what they had accomplished so far.

COMMUNITY LAND TRUST: PRESERVING THE AFFORDABILITY OF QUALITY HOUSING

All the land acquired through eminent domain, as well as all city land folded into the project, will be owned by the community land trust, Dudley Neighbors, Inc., in perpetuity. Developers and homeowners will receive long-term ground leases for the land. In other words, even as new buildings are built, bought and sold, the community will always own the land underneath those buildings through the land trust. Each homeowner will be a voting member of the community land trust and help determine its policies.

The community land trust was a confusing concept to most people. Many wondered if people would really be owning their own home if they didn't own the land—yes, they would. They worried that the land trust could interfere in their privacy or force them out if disagreements arose—no, it could not. So DSNI, with the help of a nonprofit organization specializing in land trusts, the Institute for Community Economics, created an informational road show. Four meetings to familiarize people with the land trust—all facilitated by DSNI Development Committee members—were held throughout the neighborhood in April and May 1990. Among the goals of the road show were to foster a clear sense of community ownership of the land trust; receive community input on the ground lease; and create a land trust leadership base—a group of community individuals with extensive knowledge of the land trust and the ground lease.[5] As DSNI was familiarizing more residents with the land trust, the *Boston Globe* informed more readers about Dudley disinvestment and DSNI's approach to community development with a cover story in the paper's magazine.[6]

The community land trust is designed to ensure affordable housing for first and future generations of buyers. All the housing will be mixed-income, with a majority of units priced for those with low and moderate incomes. To preserve future affordability, the ground lease restricts the price at which owners can sell their units to an approximately 5 percent per year increase or the rate of inflation, whichever is less. Exceptions will be made to compensate owners for home improvements they made.

In designing the homes, DSNI had two central goals: affordability and quality. DSNI made clear to developers and city officials that there would be no cutting corners, producing the kind of cheap, ugly, quickly dilapidated "affordable" housing that plagues poor neighborhoods. In Gus Newport's words, the bottom line for developers should be: "I would not want to build anything except that which I would want to live in myself." He says, "We want quality, and the way to make sure that it is affordable is to find sufficient subsidy to write it down to the level of the people we are trying to serve."

DNI Director Paul Yelder observes, "The ultimate dilemma of community development is how do you improve a neighborhood, but still make it accessible, make it affordable? Just the way market economics works, any improvement is going to be reflected—even if you are trying to control the prices—it is still going to be reflected in enhancing the neighborhood and thereby enhancing the [property] values there." In an uncontrolled real estate market, rising values mean rising costs for homebuyers and tenants, and the displacement of low-income residents. Three ways by which DSNI ensured that residents, and not the market, would drive development are the participatory community planning process, eminent domain and the Community Land Trust.

Yelder explains that residents have to be informed, involved in and prepared for new opportunities. They have to be decision makers in weighing the pros and cons of development options, asserting, "If it's not going to be accessible, then forget it. We've got more work to do." Residents, says Yelder, are less likely to accept the kind of reasoning a third party might to cut corners in quality, make something less affordable or abandon the project with the attitude, "Either this or nothing." As Yelder puts it, "Nothing in some cases still gives you a chance to do something better." He reiterates that DSNI is "building a community and not just building housing."

In December 1990, to take one example, Newport wrote Pat McGuigan, PFD's director of Neighborhood Development, reminding him that the city's estimates of who could afford Phase One housing, given available subsidies, were unacceptable (the estimates were incomes of no less than $29,000 for single-family homes and $22,000 for cooperative housing for those without Section 8 subsidized rental vouchers). "Diligent efforts by both of our organizations toward accomplishing this critical goal of affordability," wrote Newport, "will be the mark of an effective community/city partnership. We have exhibited sensitivity toward the City's designation goals, and now look for the same sensitivity from you on our affordability goals."[7]

DSNI blended quality and affordability in the plans for its new homes, which are also designed to be energy efficient. First to be built would be 38 single-family, semi-attached town houses with three or four bedrooms, one-and-a-half bathrooms and unfinished basement space for future expansion of living area. Constructed along Dennis and Winthrop Streets, they also have porches, good-sized backyards and off-street parking for two cars. The homes are targeted to families with incomes in the range of $18,000 and higher. Qualified buyers for these units have access to heavily subsidized first and second mortgages bringing monthly housing costs (mortgage, taxes, insurance and ground lease fees) down to $495-$800. Homebuyers will also be able to benefit from the tax deduction for mortgage interest payments.

The second group of 45 homes would be even more affordable limited-equity co-ops in which families buy shares in a cooperative with little downpayment and low monthly costs. To be constructed by Nuestra Comunidad Development Corporation and the Boston Metropolitan Housing Partnership, these duplexes, three-family buildings and town houses will have two, three or four bedrooms; they will also have basements, yards and off-street parking. The co-ops will be affordable to households with incomes of $15,000, perhaps even lower.

DSNI organizers began the "Dudley List" in mid-1990, asking people to sign up if they were interested in new housing opportunities. To make sure as many residents as possible were reached, DSNI made a special arrangement to use a subsection of the city's resident list encompassing Dudley. Each person received information about the

Dudley List along with the DSNI newsletter. By 1992, the Dudley List had over 400 names, including people from outside the neighborhood.

The composition of the Dudley List underscores the need for a range of affordable housing opportunities and economic development. DSNI organizers Ros Everdell and Gertrudes Fidalgo point out that most of those on the list are tenants—some of them doubled up in homes owned by family members. Most of those on the list have incomes under $20,000, have dependents and need two to four bedrooms. Many people want private home ownership, but they don't have the income to support it. However low the mortgage, the additional cost of property taxes, insurance, utilities and repairs is beyond the reach of many people. For them the best options may be cooperatives and rental housing. Many people on the Dudley List indicated their desire for affordable, quality rentals.

BEYOND THE TRIANGLE: TENANT ORGANIZING, CO-OPS AND ORCHARD PARK REDEVELOPMENT

Ros Everdell emphasizes that while "the Triangle is seen as everybody's victory, it doesn't meet everybody's needs." The Triangle build-out plan must be seen as part of a larger program to address the needs of current and future homeowners and tenants.

In December 1991, the Dudley neighborhood celebrated the opening of the eight-unit Magnolia Cooperative Housing, developed by Project Hope with the support of DSNI on land donated by the city. The cooperative was designed to be affordable to families with incomes of $10,000 to $25,000. The owners of the eight units invested up to 300 hours of "sweat equity," and they self-manage the cooperative. Among the very proud co-op owners is Ché Madyun.

In 1990, DSNI and GRNA collaborated on an intensive tenant campaign to improve the Cottage Brook Apartments. A majority of the tenants are Latinos. DSNI and GRNA, which were among a handful of groups to wrestle temporary funding from the city for tenant organizing, decided to combine their $5,000 grants to hire a tenant organizer who would be based half-time in each organization. The organizer did tenant education focusing on ending housing code violations at the Cottage Brook Apartments. With 147 units in 50 buildings scattered over seven different streets—mostly outside the Triangle—Cottage Brook is the biggest privately owned complex with publicly subsidized apartments in the neighborhood. It was known for its large apartments—and terrible conditions.

Everdell explains, "The city Inspectional Services Department was pressed to hold a mass inspection to expose the whole picture of code violations. Tenants came forward together to challenge management to fix the violations. The repairs that were done were poor, patchwork. So, the tenants pushed for a change in ownership." The Dorchester Bay Economic Development Corporation, a CDC represented on the DSNI board, responded. In January 1993, Dorchester Bay replaced Larry Smith, the former president of the Minority Developers Association, as the owner of the Cottage Brook Apartments and began extensive renovations. DSNI has continued to assist Cottage Brook tenants, many of whom are DSNI members. Dorchester Bay also developed the highly affordable 38-unit Alexander-Magnolia Co-ops.

Another important part of Dudley's rebuilding is the rehabilitation of the Orchard Park public housing development, led by the Orchard Park Tenants Association, a member of the DSNI board. Orchard Park is the poorest part of the Dudley neighborhood. Longtime city neglect left apartments in disrepair, with a host of problems from constant leaks to peeling lead paint and abandoned buildings. The Dearborn School, located in the development, was closed in 1981. So was a public gym. Half the Orchard Park residents are children under 17.

When Orchard Park was built during wartime in 1942, the first few Black military families were segregated into one section. Like the larger Dudley neighborhood, as Orchard Park went from predominantly White to increasingly Black and Latino, city services disappeared. "They were just zip," says former Tenants Association Chair Sarah Flint, who first moved to Orchard Park as a child in 1963. "That is one of the reasons I got involved. I finally got so fed up with the conditions—living in public housing and being treated like second-class citizens…There is no sense in complaining if you are not going to try to do anything constructively to change it." Flint, who worked in community outreach for Lena Park Community Development Corporation, was chair of the Orchard Park Tenants Association from 1984 to 1987; she then became executive director of the citywide public housing tenants organization and, later, PFD project manager for homeless families.

Flint had another, deeper motivation for getting involved in tenant organizing in 1984. "I had lost a son. I was a real, real angry person. I am saying, something has got to change…I had been living there all that time, and I did not know about [the] tenant organization. I got involved really around violence." Tenants from Orchard Park and other Boston Housing Authority (BHA) developments met with the police commissioner and other officials to demand that they increase "public safety in public housing." They got some response, but not enough.

As Flint recalls it, "We really started organizing" in 1985 after hearing about the BRA Dudley Square Plan, which marked Orchard Park for "urban renewal" as condominiums. Besides that, says Flint, "We heard rumors that they were going to turn the Dearborn School into a prison." It turned out there were no plans for a prison, but the city was using the school building for police training. "They were actually doing exercises with guns," says Flint, "in the heart of the development. It was like, there are no residents around."

Orchard Park tenants fought back against disinvestment, crime and violence. The Orchard Park Tenants Association negotiated with the BHA to convert a residential building into a community center, with a small youth center and health clinic run by Roxbury Comprehensive, and it is working with PFD to renovate the abandoned gym into a recreation facility. With support from the Riley Foundation, Hyams Foundation, Boston Foundation and others, Orchard Park tenants are pursuing a project to redevelop the abandoned old Dearborn School and annex into a multiservice center with health, youth, adult education and other programs (in coordination with other Dudley community center projects, as discussed in Chapter Seven). The tenants won agreement from the BHA for a multimillion-dollar five-year renovation program, using HUD funding, which was scheduled to begin in 1993. But the plans stalled under new BHA leadership. Orchard Park tenants and their supporters have had to re-fight some old battles to get the renovation program back on track.

Nancy Green, acting executive director of the Tenants Association, says of the Orchard Park leadership, "It's like an extended family. The residents are not planning to leave here. What they want is to leave a legacy for the children."[8] DSNI is also working to strengthen the involvement of Orchard Park tenants in the larger neighborhood rebuilding activities.

HOMEBUYERS AND BANKS

In 1992, DSNI began free classes and counseling for prospective homeowners. The homebuyer training, led by Herbert Riggs, covers how to finance downpayments, research and clear up any inaccuracies or problems with credit histories, and apply and qualify for mortgages. Ros Everdell notes that not all those qualified to buy a home will live in the Triangle housing. "Some will be ready to buy before the DSNI housing is ready, or want to live elsewhere," she says. "This is all part of empowering the community—putting information in people's hands so they can make their own decisions."

The importance of DSNI's assistance in qualifying homeowners for mortgages was underscored when the Federal Reserve Bank of Boston released its 1992 report on racial disparities in mortgage lending. The powerful study took into account a full array of financial and employment variables used by lenders, including credit histories, loan-to-value ratios, income-to-debt burdens, etc. It found that even after controlling for all these variables, Black and Latino mortgage applicants in the Boston metropolitan area were about 60 percent more likely to be turned down than whites. "In fact," the report states, "high-income minorities in Boston were more likely to be turned down than low-income whites."

The Boston Federal Reserve report showed that most mortgage applicants, of any race, do not have perfect credentials, and lenders have considerable discretion over how to judge compensating factors in weighing income-to-debt ratios, past credit problems and other factors. "The results of this study suggest that for the same imperfections whites seem to enjoy a general presumption of creditworthiness that black and Hispanic applicants do not, and that lenders seem to be more willing to overlook flaws for white applicants than for minority applicants."[9]

In 1989, DSNI founded the Community Investment Coalition (CIC) with GRNA, Local 26 of the Hotel and Restaurant Workers Union and the Massachusetts Affordable Housing Alliance Home Buyers Union. The CIC worked to end banking discrimination and improve services in the long redlined neighborhoods of Roxbury, Dorchester and Mattapan. It held public meetings and actions, such as a peaceful demonstration at the Bank of Boston during which six people were arrested for trespassing (the charges were later dropped). In January 1990, after extensive negotiations between CIC representatives and executives from area banks, a ten-year community reinvestment plan was announced. As then DSNI board member Ro Whittington put it, the bankers finally realized that "our money is the same color as theirs."[10] The plan included provisions to open new bank branches, finance affordable housing, provide mortgages to first-time, low-income homebuyers and finance economic development. The banks, however, lagged badly in implementing it.

Before David Rockwell left DSNI to return to banking, he wrote in a December 1990 letter to the Development Committee, "You can be assured that, as a banker involved with his institution's community investment responsibilities, I will take what I have learned at DSNI with me. I have a new understanding of the needs of the city's neighborhoods of color, and of the justifiable anger felt by those living there."

Unfortunately, while individuals like Rockwell are working to improve the situation, the banks have still not made the necessary institutional effort to end discriminatory practices. Gus Newport says part of the problem is that what is agreed to by bank executives, "the people we are sitting at the table with, does not get moved into the institution itself." Commitment at the top must be followed up by changed everyday behavior at all levels.

Everdell describes the refinancing saga of Peter and Maria "Uia" Teixeira, a Cape Verdean couple who own and live in the building where DSNI is housed. The Teixeiras began trying to refinance their high-interest mortgage before the CIC-banking agreement and kept trying afterwards. "We followed through with them for two years," recalls Everdell. "Uia pursued it aggressively, calling every bank in the city and others outside. We tried to provide the names of key people from each of those banks who were saying they would follow through on the CIC agreement. It took two years...[even though] they own their building. They co-own Davey's Market, one of the most successful neighborhood businesses. They both work. Uia is a good example of someone...refusing to take no for an answer. But the only reason they got refinanced was because of David Rockwell having been [at DSNI] and then being at Shawmut Bank and knowing them and seeing what happened with the campaign here...For me the problem remains: The banks have not changed the way they operate for the person in the street."

Rockwell says, "It's just about access to capital. All I did was call [someone at Shawmut] and said, 'Meet with them.' That is all I did. I didn't even stay for the meeting." Rockwell says that although banks are improving, it's still the case that bankers "know what's going on in the suburban markets and in the various other markets all over the country, but you mention the word Roxbury to a banker and they go crazy. They can't even think about it. All they think about is people getting shot. How can you possibly make any rational decisions about doing business if that's your first concept?"

Rockwell adds, "You know, one of the things I spend a lot of time doing is just helping people understand urban economics. The people, the board members and the residents of [the Dudley] neighborhood know more about urban economics than a lot of people coming out of Harvard and MIT, because they've just seen it happen. All it is is facts. Some of them are hard facts, but it's just facts. You've got to strip away the fear and the mythology and all this stuff and just look at what's really going on. Then you can start being confidently involved as a financial partner and you can make a loan to a [Dudley resident or businessperson] because you can really understand what their business commitments are, and their skills and their weaknesses and everything."

"All the community wants is access to capital," says Rockwell, "in the same way everybody else has had access to capital. That's all it is. Nobody wants charity...They want to be able to walk into the bank and have somebody sit down and talk to them about their business plans...What we've tried to do is take the mythology out of community investment activity and just look at it as a business, and do the absolutely best job we can of building good assets by working with the best people—whether they are for-profit or nonprofit—who are doing development, but also never forgetting to look at neighborhood impact."

Gareth Saunders became the Dudley area's new City Council representative in 1993. Before that he was chair of the Roxbury Neighborhood Council, treasurer of DNI and a neighborhood banking officer with Bay Banks. Saunders, too, thinks the banking situation is "getting better, but it still has a way to go as far as lending practices. I think the best solution to that is for the banks...to make sure that you have people who are sensitive to what's going on in the various communities, so it's not just a perception from what a friend told you, what you read in the newspaper, or saw on TV. You have to get out there and see what the people in the neighborhoods are doing. You know, walk the neighborhood, locate branches in the neighborhood, so you get a feel of the community. Once fears are taken away, I think that's when there's going to be...more progress around lending in communities of color." Saunders says that people are needed "who are representative of the communities that the bank is providing service to. You need to have them in some of the decision-making positions."

Ros Everdell is pleased that DSNI was able to gain bank support for the Triangle redevelopment. But, she says, it will not be acceptable if banks are "very focused on the new housing and homebuyers, but just as unresponsive as they've ever been to people in existing housing or businesses." In 1993, DSNI Homebuyer Counselor Herbert Riggs began developing a project to counsel residents in how to finance and carry out rehab of their existing homes or other neighborhood properties. The project would also benefit local hardware and building supply businesses.

In 1992, the CIC, renamed the Community Investment and Economic Development Coalition, launched a new effort to hold the banks accountable, including demands for compensation for those discriminated against in the past and a comprehensive program for future community investment. Community action, combined with toughened local and federal enforcement of the long ignored Community Reinvestment Act and fair lending laws, has begun producing more results in Boston and elsewhere. If communities like Dudley are to rebuild successfully, they must have fair access to private and public financing.

Sophia McCarthy and young residents at the 1992 DSNI neighborhood cleanup.

Celebrating the first graduation from DSNI homebuyer classes.

7

HOLISTIC DEVELOPMENT: HUMAN, ECONOMIC, ENVIRONMENTAL

DSNI has always defined its development mission as more than "bricks and mortar." After winning eminent domain, DSNI adopted the slogan "Building Houses and People Too" to highlight its holistic approach to human, economic and physical community development. "I believed in that motto from Jump Street," says Ché Madyun. "You can build all the doggone houses, condominiums, whatever you want. But if you're not trying to touch people's lives and help them improve their lives—you're just putting up bricks and mortar."

Low-income people and communities, like middle- and upper-income people and communities, have a mix of strengths and weaknesses, needs and capacities. But poor communities are uniquely portrayed as the negative sum of their needs and "risks." DSNI rejects that approach.

All people and communities need services. In higher-income communities, people needing doctors or psychologists, lawyers or drug treatment, tutors or child care, can afford pricey private practitioners and avoid the stigma that often accompanies public social services. In lower-income communities they cannot. This problem is especially bad in the United States because, though long the world's wealthiest nation, it lags behind other industrialized democracies in assuring basic human needs—health care being today's best known example. Here, though unemployment is high and wages increasingly low, public social services are commonly stingy, humiliating and punitive. Here, while income inequality is widening and the "safety net" shredded, prisons and other "corrections spending" make up the fastest growing part of state budgets.[1]

One out of four children is born into poverty in the United States—according to the official measure.[2] The top 1 percent of U.S. families have a combined financial net worth greater than that of the entire bottom 90 percent. Income inequality has grown so much that the top 4 percent of Americans earn more in wages and salaries than the entire bottom half—in 1959, by contrast, the top 4 percent earned as much as the bottom 35 percent.[3]

A comparison among industrialized democracies showed that U.S. income is the most unevenly distributed and found "that the child poverty rate in the U.S., after taxes and benefits are considered, was more than twice that in Canada and four times the average child poverty rate in the other nations in the study. It also showed that the poverty rate just among white children in the U.S. was higher than the poverty rate among *all* children in all other countries in the study except Australia. In short, the private economy in the United States generates more relative poverty among children than the private economies of many other western, industrialized nations—and the U.S. then does far less than the other nations to address this problem."[4] (Italics in original.)

As a consequence of unconscionable poverty and governmental neglect, more children die before their first birthday in the United States, per capita, than in 20 other countries. The death rate of Black babies in the United States ranks 35th, tied with the infant mortality ranking of Bulgaria and Chile and behind such nations as Jamaica, Sri Lanka, Poland, Cuba and Kuwait. In the United States, Black babies are more than twice as likely to die before their first birthday as White babies, and their life expectancy is seven years less.[5] Even as it works to implement community redevelopment and promote better government policies, DSNI is trying to ensure that poverty does not mean a life of limits for Dudley children.

The DSNI approach assumes that low-income communities have extensive resources—from multilingual residents, local businesspeople and family day care providers to underemployed people, underutilized land and school facilities, and children with dreams and talents to share. People who live and work in Dudley are proud that the neighborhood is rich in diversity and perseverance.

In the words of DSNI's 1993 *Framework for a Human Development Agenda*: "Our community has a gold mine of natural assets and resources...They take many forms: human, institutional and physical. Our community rebuilding strategy must be anchored in the power and strength of our people and our neighborhood....We know the process of rebuilding and reknitting our community back together is *as* important as the goal itself." Among "our richest resources is our young people....As adults we must assure them of the gifts they hold and of the gifts they are."[6]

HUMAN DEVELOPMENT

DSNI's human development mission is to advance community-wide strategies to achieve the goals of increasing resident participation and control over circumstances affecting their physical, spiritual and mental well-being; foster coordinated, resident-driven, capacity-building human services; and influence government policymaking.

Najwa Abdul-Tawwab, who chaired DSNI's first Human Development Committee—originally called the Human Services Committee—has lived in the Dudley area since 1974. She taught in the Sister Clara Muhammad School, an alternative school in the neighborhood run by the Masjid Al-Quran Mosque, and was a substitute teacher in the Boston Public Schools. In 1986, Abdul-Tawwab became a full-time public school teacher, teaching first and second grade. She first became involved with DSNI indirectly: Her husband Qasim was the one who encouraged Ché Madyun to attend the first DSNI community meeting, and Abdul-Tawwab facilitated Madyun's involvement by baby-sitting for her children.

As Abdul-Tawwab became involved more directly in the organization, she was impressed by DSNI's efforts "to get residents to realize, no matter what level or background they were on, that we all had to become invested in some general community concerns, and that we really didn't live in isolation. And whatever I could do to help my neighbor's situation become better would in fact help me—and vice versa."

Madyun says, "Service doesn't mean handout. It doesn't mean 'I'm giving to you.'" It means helping people "to improve themselves at whatever level they're at. I mean, it could be this person may only need to read, whereas this person over here may just need care for their mother who's getting old." DSNI is about "helping everyone have access to everything."

Azalech "Azi" Teklamariam became DSNI's first human services director in July 1988. She is an Ethiopian who directed one of the largest and most successful neighborhood self-empowerment efforts in the capital city, Addis Ababa, before seeking political asylum in the United States with her husband. Teklamariam brought a deep commitment to organizing local residents to take control over human services. She began meeting with local human service agencies to improve and initiate programs in a variety of areas including employment and training, senior citizens, child care and youth.

DSNI's Human Development Committee held its first meeting in October 1988 and began new efforts to coordinate and strengthen the work of human service agencies in the Dudley area, increase agency accountability to neighborhood residents and develop a comprehensive plan for human services. In March 1989, DSNI hosted a meeting of human service agencies at the Morgan Memorial facilities across the street from Orchard Park—where earlier efforts had led to greater access. Many agencies were represented by their executive directors. They discussed the problem of mistrust due to competition among agencies for scarce funding and the need for a united approach to the human and physical development of the community.

DSNI's human development work was set back when, in June 1989, Teklamariam left the DSNI staff to return to Ethiopia. The position remained vacant for a year as DSNI searched for someone blending social service experience, an organizer's mind-set and multicultural sensitivity. Najwa Abdul-Tawwab explains why the search took so long: "We had a hard time hearing what we needed to hear from all of the people that came out. A lot of people had wonderful résumés. But we needed someone whose scope was broad enough...to be able to understand cultural backgrounds and differences...A job description really didn't adequately describe what we were looking for."

Without a director, work in human development lagged behind implementation of DSNI's physical development agenda. Human development was also harder to define and measure. Abdul-Tawwab reflects, "You can say, a house is a house. You can see it—the foundation being laid, the structure...That's really concrete and it's measurable...a beginning and an ending. But [with] human development—I would [sometimes wonder], what are we ever really accomplishing? What goals do we have that are measurable and are obtainable?...You're talking about people and development of character and addressing their human needs that you can't just pour into a glass or a bottle and put a lid on it...You need money to do the building and you need money to help build the people up."

Abdul-Tawwab also observes that the human development area is more sensitive and private: "People don't mind telling you, 'I need a house and I want it to be improved.' When we start talking about, 'Well, my children are having problems in school' or...things like that, that's real touchy and folks don't want to just open up on that level...[It] takes a lot of tact and skill" to work in human development.

Without a human development director, Organizing Director Ros Everdell and Najwa Abdul-Tawwab undertook initiatives with committee members such as Maria-Goreth Fidalgo, a Dudley resident and social worker at Brigham and Women's Hospital; Arnaldo Solís, then a Dudley resident on the staff of La Alianza Hispana; and WAITT House Director Stephen Hanley. DSNI began a series of focus groups to fill in the portrait of Dudley's strengths and weaknesses in the area of human development. From January to May 1990, a Field Project Team of five graduate students from the Tufts University Department of Urban and Environmental Policy provided assistance.[7] DSNI held three focus groups in April and May with human service agencies, parents and youth.

Abdul-Tawwab says that during the focus groups two questions "kept being asked: 'What can the community do for you?' [and] 'What can you give back to the community?'" While participants discussed many issues, the focus groups centered on challenges facing youth and on possible uses for the community centers planned in the Dudley Triangle. Following the focus groups, a major component of human development work was the Dudley Young Architects and Planners Program discussed in Chapter Eight.

Members of the Human Development Committee were insistent from the start that the human development assessment and planning process involve residents as partners rather than subjects, focus on neighborhood resources as well as needs, and be action-oriented. DSNI moved forward quickly in a variety of areas and received a great boost when former organizer Andrea Nagel rejoined the staff as human development director in June 1990.

The Human Development Committee formed a Child Care Committee to address the issue of affordable preschool and school-age child care in the neighborhood. It held its first meeting with parents and family- and agency-based child care providers in July 1990. The Child Care Committee supported the Mason Elementary School in creating an after-school program. It also launched the DSNI Family Day Care Providers Network, a group of providers from the greater Dudley area who do licensed child care in a home setting. The Family Day Care Providers Network publishes a Child Care Directory; holds an annual Child Care Fair for parents; and organizes around such issues as state child care funding, resource and curriculum development, and insurance and tax issues for professional family providers. Their philosophy draws on the African proverb, "It takes a village to raise a child."

The Human Development Committee also formed a Scholarship Fund Committee to assist young people and adults in pursuing higher education or vocational training. It evolved into the "Dollars for Scholars of the Dudley Street Neighborhood," a nonprofit fund run by a community board. Dollars for Scholars has focused on the eighth grade at the local Dearborn Middle School to encourage kids to graduate and go on to higher education.

In fall 1993, following the recommendation of the Human Development Committee, the DSNI board designated education as the area within human development where DSNI would focus its planning and organizing activity for the next few years. The Human Development Committee targeted education after asking the question: "What is the most important thing to offer people in human development?" By education, DSNI means multicultural, intergenerational education—from preschool to adult education, from the home to the classroom, from the street to the community center. The Human Development Committee is creating an education master plan, which will spell out short- and long-term strategies.

Jenny Cintrón and Jacqui Cairo Williams, two Human Development Committee leaders, explain their commitment to working on an education agenda by saying they are doing it for their children and grandchildren. Cintrón, a Latina parent, who became a Dudley resident when she bought one of the Project Hope co-ops, is president of the Parents' Advisory Council for her school zone. She believes strongly that parents must not leave their children's education and development up to School Department officials. Williams, an African American and longtime Dudley resident who is raising her granddaughter, joined the

DSNI board in 1993. She says, "No one downtown has ever taken a lot of interest and it's going to be up to us to make the difference. I'm involved in my church and have always made it a priority to be involved in my community. That's why I joined DSNI. DSNI is serious about making things better."

AGENCY COLLABORATIVE

Beginning in 1990, the Human Development Committee undertook a Community Resource Inventory of all social services available to residents in the Dudley area—services that become both more strained and essential in a time of severe government cutbacks. With a clear inventory of existing services and their funding sources, DSNI can better identify service and funding gaps and formulate policy recommendations and action plans.

DSNI reinitiated meetings with area agencies in July 1990 to coordinate services and develop a human services plan. Participants began discussing ways to institutionalize a community "agency collaborative." However, many agencies, especially the larger ones, showed the same reluctance to share financial and other information as they had during 1987 when DSNI developed the comprehensive revitalization plan for the neighborhood.

The Agency Collaborative was formally launched in December 1990 as a vehicle to coordinate and strengthen human services in the Dudley area and influence policymaking at the local and state levels. In the beginning, the Agency Collaborative alternated monthly meeting sites among the participating agencies to increase familiarity with each other's programs and facilities. Active members of the DSNI-facilitated collaborative have included:

- Bird Street Community Center: recreation, after-school child care, substance abuse prevention, tutoring, ESL-English as a second language

- Children's Services of Roxbury: child abuse counseling, private adoption placement and support, etc.

- City Year: youth community service corps

- Dudley Branch Library: books, art displays, after-school programming, community meeting space

- First, Inc.: residential drug treatment facility, comprehensive services including education, job training and placement

- Gang Peace: youth development, diverse programs including computer training and collaborative studio project with Berklee College of Music
- Greater Boston Legal Services: immigration, housing, etc.
- Greater Roxbury Neighborhood Authority: tenant advocacy, antiredlining organizing, community control issues
- Networking for Life: pregnancy counseling, prenatal and postnatal care, parenting skills
- Nuestra Comunidad Development Corporation: housing and economic development
- Orchard Park Tenants Association: tenant organizing, Orchard Park redevelopment
- Project Hope: transitional shelter for families, co-op housing
- Roxbury Boys and Girls Club: community center, recreation, education, etc.
- Roxbury Defenders: public defenders for youth, counseling, job preparation
- Roxbury Multi-Service Center: career counseling, youth employment, emergency food, housing advocacy, rape crisis center, Department of Social Services contracts
- Roxbury YMCA: recreation, education, after-school programs, etc.
- Roxbury YouthWorks: rehabilitation, employment training and advocacy for juvenile offenders
- Strand Theatre: expanding access to arts and culture, Teen Players and other youth programs
- Uphams Corner Neighborhood Health Center: multilingual primary health facility, WIC, home health care program, HIV/AIDS prevention
- Urban League: civil rights advocacy, mentoring and other education programs
- Veterans Benefits Clearinghouse: advocacy, counseling, developing single-room occupancy housing units, etc.
- WAITT House: adult education, high school equivalency
- YouthBuild: construction trade training for out-of-school youth

Human Development Director Andrea Nagel says that the smaller agencies are the most consistent participants. They "show the most interest...They embrace the idea of a community planning and priority setting process for human services. They struggle with the question of *how* to do it." The larger agencies generally do not. "They continue to do what they have always done—provide *for* their 'clients.'"

Arnaldo Solís, who has served on the DSNI board and both the Human Development and Development Committees, is deputy director of Children's Services of Roxbury and former director of Counseling and Social Services at La Alianza Hispana. He helped Azi Teklamariam plan the initial meeting to promote agency collaboration. Solís explains that some agency directors have resisted DSNI's concept of an agency collaborative because they have fundamentally different views of community empowerment. To these agency directors, "Community empowerment means [to] identify leadership within the community to provide the guidelines as to how the community can support itself, but for those leaders to pretty much run it because the people don't really know what they want—they're not as politically astute, or not sophisticated enough. They need somebody that has [more] knowledge and [skills to] guide them. And as long as the leadership is from the community—it's community empowerment."

To DSNI, explains Solís, community empowerment means "the people themselves are learning these skills...so that they can take ownership of whatever changes need to be done within the community." Some agency leaders were in conflict with that, he says, "because it downplayed their importance within the community and before the eyes of other folks...It's also a threat, because if you give the community residents that kind of power, it means then that you are open to criticism by these same people if you're not rendering the type of services that you have identified as needs within the community, or that the community itself identified as needs. And I don't think agencies are all too receptive to that."

Solís also points to the problem of agencies responding to the priorities of their funding sources rather than the priorities of the community. DSNI board member Steve Hanley, the director of WAITT House, elaborates on the impact of "unhealthy competition" for scarce funding: "Agencies and organizations fighting against each other need to be working together...Many agencies have not been fully committed to making that change...Agencies will not say...'We're not going to collaborate,' but there is sometimes an indifference or an apathy there."

Hanley says that funders may claim to encourage collaboration, but actually undermine community consensus. "We have many funding sources, private or public, saying, 'Collaborate, collaborate,'" he observes. "But much time and energy is spent, and sometimes [funder criteria is] not suitable for the community." Agencies and residents may agree on priorities and projects that "do not come to fruition because...funding sources...have a different agenda. They may say, 'Collaborate.' But under whose terms?"

"The DSNI Agency Collaborative has been unique," says Hanley. "We've been meeting because we're seeing for the future—not what we can receive right now in our request for proposals."

Through the Agency Collaborative, DSNI is promoting a coordinated, comprehensive, resident-driven human service model, like that used in Dudley's physical planning. The Agency Collaborative is guided by the following principles of a community capacity-building strategy:

> 1. Decentralized community-based (versus funder-driven) planning and service delivery.

> 2. Comprehensive, family approach in which a responsive delivery system provides services and supports as an integrated package intended to address the needs of the entire family and, by extension, the neighborhood.

> 3. Preventive intervention, in which program initiatives are responsive to existing needs and emerging trends, and services are understood as an investment in the human capital of the neighborhood, not only the maintenance of an individual.

> 4. Allocation of resources based on needs consistent with the concept of identifying service and funding priorities at the point of delivery.[8]

In November 1992, DSNI organized a focused planning process among agencies developing new community facilities in the Dudley area. Participants were motivated by the question, "What can we do together that we cannot do alone?" Participants in the Community Facilities Planning Group include: DSNI, which is developing a community center on two sites as part of the Triangle build-out plan; Orchard Park Tenants Association, which is developing a multiservice center and gym; Bird Street Community Center, which wants a facility to expand its educational and recreational youth programs; a team—composed of the Masjid Al-Quran Mosque, Dorchester Bay Economic Development Corporation, Bird Street Community Center and Project Hope—working to redevelop the Sister Clara Muhammad School (closed in 1990) as a community educational center; and another team—composed of Nuestra Comunidad Development Corporation, the Cape Verdean Association of New England, Roxbury YMCA, Escuelita Agueybana Child Development Center and the Mt. Pleasant

Neighborhood Association—working to redevelop the Cape Verdean Community House (closed in 1989) as a multiservice facility.

The Community Facilities Planning Group agreed to collaborate on defining priorities for new and expanded community facilities and carry out joint fundraising. They agreed on the importance of providing young people with passes that would allow them to enter *all* the new centers. They also decided to work together to maximize access to existing facilities inside and outside the neighborhood while the new community facilities are being planned and built. In 1993, the Roxbury YMCA—located just outside the DSNI neighborhood boundary—responded with a concerted effort to involve Dudley youth in its after-school, recreational and educational programs as well as its summer camp. The YMCA hired a bilingual youth development specialist—with funding from the Riley Foundation—to strengthen links with the Dudley neighborhood and reach out to Latino and Cape Verdean youth.

DUDLEY PRIDE

In fall 1991, DSNI launched Dudley PRIDE—People and Resources Investing in Dudley's Environment. Two community meetings were held to develop the goals, priorities and initial actions of Dudley PRIDE. The goals are to organize residents block by block to work together to enhance the neighborhood; raise the level of self-esteem, self-respect and community pride; project a positive image about the neighborhood; increase public safety; and heighten city responsiveness around health, safety and environmental issues. Dudley PRIDE promotes the idea that "everyone can make a difference" in improving their physical and community environment. DSNI is producing a periodic Dudley PRIDE newsletter in three languages.

"Dudley PRIDE can be the best thing DSNI ever pursued," asserts Clayton Turnbull. "Dudley PRIDE is where you say, 'Okay, let us look within ourselves and compete within ourselves and be our own best neighbors and be wholesome'...It's not going to be a funder or a grant that makes us sweep the front of our street...City sweepers are great, but do we wait until they come to sweep? No. Do we get to know who lives next door? Yes...If someone asked me what I would want to do, building pride [in] urban America...should be the number-one thing...If you have pride, you want to go to school. If you have pride, you respect your mother and father. It doesn't cost anything for pride, that's the thing about it. We don't have to go and get funding for it. All you've got to [have] is hope and a belief."

As DSNI's winter 1992-93 newsletter put it, "When we listen to the radio, read the papers or watch TV, we are constantly told that our neighborhood and the people who live here are bad. We are told we do nothing to make our lives better. But we know otherwise. Yes, there is crime and there are people who cause harm, like any other community. But unlike other communities, these same media outlets rarely talk about what is good, great and courageous about us. Imagine if we heard as much about what is good in our community, about who we are and what we are trying to do. That's why we have Dudley PRIDE—a campaign to make the streets clean, the gardens grow, the streets safe. This is a campaign to develop our economic base, to push government for our fair share...Be part of Dudley PRIDE, show 'em what we got!"

Dudley PRIDE builds on the "Don't Dump On Us" campaign. Dumping in the neighborhood has been reduced, but not eliminated. Indeed, since the vacant lots are blocked off, trucks sometimes dump illegally on the streets or sidewalks. Organizer Gertrudes Fidalgo says, "It's not as bad as it used to be [when] we would drive around...and find so many places that are trashed out and so many [abandoned] cars. It's not as bad, but it's still a problem" requiring DSNI's time and attention.

DSNI was successful in getting the city to more regularly remove abandoned cars and support the neighborhood cleanups, which since 1990 have been held twice yearly. DSNI enlisted the Bank of Boston to purchase public trash barrels, which the city placed along Dudley Street and empties on a regular basis. As part of deepening budget cuts, however, the city diminished its support for neighborhood cleanups. DSNI has had to re-fight past battles and is organizing residents to push the city to be as committed to preventing and cleaning up trash in low-income neighborhoods like Dudley as it is in wealthier ones.

"I don't envy them," Najwa Abdul-Tawwab says about other neighborhoods accustomed to getting better city services. "But I really feel bad for my community—that we're missing out on so many of those things that...we are entitled to." She says people have to be "advocates for one another to make sure that the government, the city, is giving us the same things as folks are getting elsewhere. When my children were much younger they would ask, 'Why aren't there trash cans on our street, Mommy?'...There were no trash cans around. There were no flower barrels to beautify the street. And now—seven, eight years later—these things are just coming about."

In September 1992, DSNI received the city's 1992 Best Kept Neighborhood Civic Award. But awards are no substitute for city services. The volunteer labor of Dudley residents should not be expected to substitute for municipal services other neighborhoods take for granted. DSNI is working to improve government response to immediate problems and enhance ongoing government services. If necessary, DSNI remains ready to take the kind of direct action used during the earlier "Don't Dump On Us" campaign.

NEIGHBORHOOD GREENING

Ros Everdell observes, "Much of DSNI's work over the past seven years has been environmental, but only recently has it been identified that way." Dudley PRIDE's environmental and health efforts are wide-ranging.

The Dudley neighborhood is one of Boston's "hot spots" for lead poisoning. Nearly every street has at least one confirmed case of lead poisoning of children from old paint and contaminated soil and water. DSNI is sponsoring a major lead poisoning prevention campaign, including door-to-door community education, with interns from the Environmental Careers Organization and City Year youth corps and donated materials from the City Health and Hospitals Department. An initial survey of over 400 residents identified 80 people interested in volunteering with the campaign. To ensure that gardens and play areas are not poisoned by lead, DSNI is working to have soil tested and is pursuing soil replacement where necessary and possible.

"Environmental racism"—the disproportionate exposure to environmental hazards among people and communities of color—has been associated with lead poisoning in children, the location of municipal landfills and incinerators and the distribution of air pollution and toxic waste. As the United Church of Christ's Commission for Racial Justice reported, race, even more than poverty, predicted the exposure of communities to toxic wastes.[9]

As of September 1993, the Dudley neighborhood had 60 hazardous waste sites on the state Department of Environmental Protection (DEP) list—including the site formerly used by AFL Disposal trash transfer station. Most of the sites, which generally come to DEP's attention when property changes hands, are active commercial sites in areas zoned for industrial use. They are mostly contaminated with petroleum, which, though containing carcinogens, is not a state priority for cleanup. Every year, new sites are added to the state list, and environmental activists assume that Dudley, with its hundreds of vacant lots, has more hazardous waste yet to be exposed.

DSNI is part of a broad coalition effort to oppose the building of an environmentally hazardous asphalt plant in the neighborhood. The coalition has brought together a wide range of people opposing the plant—"doctors from City Hospital, meat cutters from Newmarket, residents from Roxbury, South Boston and the South End."[10] DSNI is also leading a campaign to discourage the dumping of oil and other toxic materials into neighborhood storm drains. With the support of the Massachusetts Water Resource Administration, DSNI youth volunteers painted the drains with a stencil showing a fish and the message, in three languages, "Don't Dump: Drains to Boston Harbor." DSNI is also supporting public and private recycling efforts.

Dudley PRIDE's neighborhood greening programs support community gardens, landscaping and the planting of trees provided by the City Parks and Recreation Department. Boston Urban Gardeners, the Boston Natural Areas Fund and the Massachusetts Horticultural Society all work with DSNI to nurture community gardens. A new neighborhood garden celebrated its first harvest in summer 1992.

The Dacia-Woodcliff Community Garden was a four-year organizing effort led by Alex Johnson, a DSNI board member, a vice president of Mass. Senior Action Council and president of the Cardinal Medeiros Manor (CMM) Resident Council. CMM has 55 units of housing for the elderly and physically challenged at the intersection of Woodcliff and Dacia Streets. Before 1987, when CMM was built on land owned by the Archdiocese of Boston, all four corners of that intersection were vacant; the controversial Dacia housing was erected in 1989.

Ros Everdell explains that "the CMM 'newcomers' first organized around getting a bus stop near their building and having the sidewalks repaired, but their biggest project was to turn a large weed-strewn vacant lot into a garden." As Alex Johnson puts it, "It was plain determination. I wanted to see something other than a junk pile over there."[11]

The CMM garden found a home when the city gave the land to the Boston Natural Areas Fund. "And what a garden it is," exclaims Everdell. "There are 44 plots and huge old trees provide shade for a seating area. Two raised garden beds were specially designed for elderly who can garden standing up without bending over and a third bed allows those in wheelchairs to come right up under a tray and garden from their chairs. The elderly who are at home during the day provide security for the area. The garden has built a stronger sense of community across different generations and between CMM residents, Dacia residents and longtime homeowners and tenants."

The Massachusetts Horticultural Society and the Boston Natural Areas Fund started the "Green Team" with DSNI in 1992 to hire youth from the neighborhood to supervise and staff two landscaping crews. Throughout the summer they worked in the four community gardens, assisted elderly with yard work and worked on street beautification. The program was so successful that it was expanded the following year. Many neighborhood youths had worked previously as "Red Shirts" in the mayor's youth campaign, doing the tedious and exhausting job of cleaning up vacant lots throughout the summer—known as weed whacking for its primary activity. The "Green Team" provides greater diversity of work, skill development and leadership development. Casimiro Barros, the Green Team's first supervisor, was so committed that he came back home from college to supervise the program for a second summer.

In summer 1993, Drumlin Farm, an organic farm owned by the Massachusetts Audubon Society, developed a continuing project with DSNI combining community service, youth employment and food production. Tony Alves, Yaqana Madyun and other teenagers from Dudley, other parts of Roxbury and Dorchester, and the suburbs worked together growing vegetables and flowers and distributing them to food pantries, soup kitchens and homeless shelters.

DSNI is also working with UrbanArts to bring more public art into the neighborhood and bring the work of Dudley artists out to the larger Boston community. UrbanArts and DSNI plan to collaborate on landscaping, murals and other beautification projects. UrbanArts also has a Youth Works/Art Works program that employs youth in arts-related jobs and provides public forums for the arts. In 1993, the Human Development Committee worked with UrbanArts youth to plan a "greenway" linking the two community center sites along the path of an old brook.

TRANSITION

During summer 1992, two longtime DSNI board members, Rogelio Whittington and Sue Beaton, joined the staff as executive director and deputy director/development director, respectively. Beaton brought her hands-on experience as the developer of housing for Project Hope and as a DSNI Development Committee member, a masters degree in community economic development and her deep spiritual faith and commitment to justice. "I have grown in my appre-ciation of what land means in terms of stewardship," she reflects. "I think I see this as—if I can use my own language—as much of a spiritual journey in a sense of trying to reclaim some basic truths about the jubilee* and redistribution of the land. The whole sense that we are walking this earth, but it's not ours—we're only sojourners."

People have been "so disconnected from themselves because we've been so discounted for so long," says Beaton. "I think there has to be a sense of stewardship that says, 'If I think I'm garbage, my outer world is going to be garbage. If I think that I'm something, then maybe I'll be a better caretaker of what has been entrusted.' I mean all of that agenda is far more important to me than building a house."

Gus Newport, who had served as DSNI executive director since December 1988, stepped down because of family responsibilities. He moved back to California in 1992 in order to be with his daughter while she finished high school. He commuted regularly to Boston while DSNI completed its search for a new executive director.

Newport recalls many people asking, "How did somebody who has been a mayor come to work for this little community group?" They can't understand it, he says, because "a lot of them don't enjoy themselves. I find that out more and more—especially about the bankers and people downtown. When you get to the point where you can talk one-on-one with these people they don't feel good about themselves...It's a shame! I mean, to try and climb that professional ladder removes you so much from just being a person."

At DSNI, Newport found a sense of family. "How many situations have you ever worked in where people can work together and feel good about one another?...I think everybody is looking for that sense of family. Very few understand how [simple] it should be, and how it

---

* The jubilee has many religious and secular meanings, including: a year of restoration of land to rightful owners, leaving land fallow to rejuvenate and emancipation of slaves (ancient Hebrew); a year of repentance and piety (Catholic); special 25th or 50th anniversary; season of celebration; and a religious song, usually referring to a time of future happiness (African American).

is all about respecting differences and everything else, and being able to work together, and just understand that we are all human beings."

At the June 1992 annual meeting, Newport told the members that having served as DSNI's executive director "has been far and away the best professional experience that I have had in my lifetime." He is continuing to work with DSNI as coordinator of its support group, Friends of DSNI, which is dedicated to raising funds for major development projects and increasing the national visibility of DSNI's innovative approach to rebuilding the inner city.

Rogelio "Ro" Whittington succeeded Newport as executive director. Whittington was previously treasurer on the DSNI board and an accountant specializing in serving nonprofit agencies and small businesses. He is the first resident and first Latino to serve as DSNI's director.

Whittington and his family immigrated to Brooklyn, New York from Panama in 1960—both his Caribbean grandfathers had immigrated to Panama to work on the canal. Whittington's family had lived in the Canal Zone, then under U.S. rule, and he attended U.S. schools there. In the early 1950s, he had his first experience with urban renewal when the U.S. military displaced canal workers and their families to build its own housing. In 1965, Whittington moved to Boston where he attended college. From 1971 to 1976, he was director of the South End Neighborhood Action Program (SNAP), where he had worked previously as an accountant. There, he became involved in the community struggle to control urban renewal in the South End.

Clayton Turnbull says that when it came to choosing a new DSNI director, Whittington's position as a resident board member was "significant, but not the reason why he got the job...I didn't see any resident preference. Maybe we should have had it, but we didn't have it." However, having a local resident as director, says Turnbull, is "true empowerment...Maybe Ro Whittington one day can be a success story to other people who used to live here, who have gone off and made it scholastically or professionally, to come back and live here. It's a proud place to live!"

MOVING ON ECONOMIC DEVELOPMENT

Since DSNI began, economic development has lagged behind human development and, especially, housing and other physical development. DSNI Director Ro Whittington worries that if DSNI does not close the gap, Dudley residents may be vulnerable to displacement.

He sees a lot of similarities between the way the South End was perceived by the public before and the way Roxbury is perceived today—as an area high in crime, drug dealers and absentee landlords. Because of Dudley's proximity to downtown, it remains a possible target of speculators seeing opportunities in a housing market that has bottomed out and DSNI's multimillion-dollar redevelopment project.

Among the likely targets of speculators, says Whittington, are poor elderly residents ready to retire. "Somebody comes with an attractive offer to buy your house and it's very difficult to refuse that" if the income is needed for retirement, he says. "The only thing they have is the house. That house is a pension plan. To some extent, we might be able to stop big movements, but I don't think we're going to stop individual people [from selling]. And you don't want to do that." Whittington believes DSNI should monitor neighborhood housing transactions and try "to match individuals [who] want to purchase houses to individuals who want to sell houses"—cutting would-be real estate speculators out of the process.

"If people want to come into this community and help to build it up," says Whittington, "I don't care what ethnic group they're coming from, we're going to support that. But we're not going to support people who come to make money off of housing."

Whittington worries that without concerted economic development, "It's conceivable that we could build this housing and people around here still not have jobs." He is working to "fast track" economic development to catch up with the housing plans. "We've got to boost people's income as a strategy towards affording housing," he says.

In past years, DSNI has worked to place Dudley residents in private and public sector jobs in the neighborhood and outside—e.g., youth summer jobs programs, Jet-a-Way's recycling facility, Pizzano Woodworking—but the efforts were not part of a comprehensive economic development strategy. In 1988, DSNI organized the Dudley Neighbors Business Alliance, which worked for a short time to increase safety and access to capital and strengthen Dudley businesses. The alliance had limited resources and results. DSNI began focusing more attention on economic development in fall 1991, launching the first in a series of community economic development strategy sessions.

"ECONOMIC$ WITH PEOPLE IN MIND"

At a May 1992 community economic development strategy session residents were asked to create their own vision of what economic development means to them and the community. They outlined these objectives: Build on local resources and assets—such as residents' skills, vacant land and buildings, small businesses, existing and proposed housing, convenience to downtown; increase retail services; break down barriers to attracting financial investment; identify and take advantage of development opportunities; raise the median income of the community; provide Dudley residents access to existing private and public jobs (e.g., major public works construction, medical facilities, colleges, malls, industrial parks) in the Boston metropolitan area; and develop an economic plan for the future.

In the winter 1992-93 newsletter, DSNI underscored the importance of building on neighborhood assets by encouraging residents to help DSNI compile a list of resident skills: "Are you a carpenter, plumber or electrician? Do you take care of children? Are your hobbies photography, or cooking or sewing? Whatever your skills or expertise or interests, we want you to sign up with our new skills bank. By compiling a list of residents' skills, we will have a ready bank of people to fill jobs as they open....REMEMBER: Everyone has skills! You are the most important asset!"

DSNI's Economic Development Committee—then called a task force—began meeting regularly in November 1992. Following up on the objectives outlined at the May 1992 community meeting, task force members decided to organize an economic summit for residents with the theme: "Economic$ with People in Mind." Over 300 people attended the April 22, 1993 summit at Roxbury Community College, including Dudley residents and businesspeople, government officials, large Boston-area employers, labor organizers, lenders, small business developers and community service organizations. This successful summit was geared to immediate concerns, as indicated by the three workshops: Starting a Business, Finding Job Skills and Jobs Now.

Ro Whittington told participants, this summit is about "getting you connected. It's not just a jobs fair. It's a truth fair—about the myths and realities of economics." One of the truths voiced in the summit's open speakout was that people of color are not getting fair access to the contracts and jobs in the massive Central Artery highway and Third Harbor Tunnel construction projects paid for by tax dollars.

A later report by the University of Massachusetts Trotter Institute analyzing state contracts with businesses owned by people of color showed a large gap between policy commitments and actual practices. Instead of meeting the goal of awarding 10 percent of its construction contracts and buying 5 percent of its goods from businesses owned by people of color, the state awarded just 1.7 percent of construction contracts and bought 1.5 percent of goods from those firms.[12] Businesses owned by people of color continue to be disinvested in the city and state. A city survey of 150 firms owned by people of color found that 64 percent had trouble obtaining financing for ongoing operations and 59 percent reported that expansion financing was virtually nonexistent.[13]

Following the April 1993 summit, DSNI concentrated on three areas:

> *Direct Advocacy*, meeting with developers and city officials to try and secure jobs for residents in current large city projects, such as the South Bay Center Mall and the Central Artery Tunnel Project.

> *General Brokering*, providing information about job training and job opportunities to residents, helping residents get prepared for existing job training and small business programs, and providing information and referrals to companies interested in hiring residents.

> *Concrete Planning*, developing a long range plan and goals for local economic development 5, 10, and 15 years from now.[14]

As in the areas of housing and human development, DSNI's economic development work combines immediate projects with long-range planning and goals. For example, DSNI is exploring the feasibility of developing new enterprises at the block-long old furniture factory across from the DSNI office. DSNI also wants to reestablish the Dudley Neighbors Business Alliance as a much stronger organization. DSNI's own redevelopment project is one source of jobs. The jobs policy for construction of DSNI's housing, established with the PFD, uses the Boston Residents' Jobs Policy—which calls for 50 percent Boston residents, 30 percent minorities and 10 percent women on city-sponsored construction projects—as a minimum goal. DSNI set a higher construction target goal of 50 percent people of color and 20 percent women.

At an October 1993 DSNI board retreat on economic development, participants stressed the need for strong involvement by young people. While developing a longer-run strategy, DSNI has increased its efforts to facilitate youth employment and is developing plans with YouthBuild to rehab housing in the neighborhood.

Looking to the future, DSNI stresses that a resident-driven economic development strategy must be comprehensive and visionary. Several key themes are guiding DSNI's evolving approach to economic development:

> Neighborhood Economic Development is a complex process which involves nearly all aspects of personal and community life, and is deeply influenced by regional, national and international forces.
>
> A community group like DSNI must see economic renewal as a long-term process which will require a whole range of efforts and a sustained, focused strategy. No one project, program or organization will turn the local economy around.
>
> There is one inescapable fact. The incomes of those who live in the neighborhood must rise for the neighborhood to experience greater economic vitality. The key to economic renewal for the neighborhood is ultimately—neighborhood residents who have greater access to a wide range of opportunity (education, jobs, small businesses) both within and outside of the neighborhood, and who see the wisdom of spending their time, energy and money locally.[15]

DSNI's goals of increasing resident income and realizing economic renewal challenge the discriminatory investment and hiring practices that continue undermining Dudley residents and businesses. They challenge intensifying trends toward shrinking wages and constantly threatened livelihoods. DSNI's visionary urban village is meant to be an enduring legacy for residents' children and future generations. DSNI knows, as stated above, that "Neighborhood Economic Development is...deeply influenced by regional, national and international forces." Below, we look at key economic forces affecting Dudley now and into the future.

ECONOMICS WITHOUT PEOPLE IN MIND

Before DSNI's economic summit, the Dudley area was hit with the news that Digital Equipment Corporation (DEC) and Stride Rite shoe corporation would be shutting down their Roxbury operations (in 1981, Stride Rite had moved its headquarters from Roxbury to Cambridge). DSNI members were among the 340 employees to lose their jobs in the two plant closures. As a city document noted, "The DEC and Stride Rite facilities accounted for fully 17% of the manufacturing jobs in Roxbury.

Not only will the job loss exacerbate the already staggering proportions of unemployment in Roxbury, but the ripple effect of the closings throughout the neighborhood pose a severe threat to its viability. Local merchants will lose between 5%-10% of their business and over 500 men, women, and children in Roxbury will loose their principal source of income as a result of these two plant closings."[16]

Digital was located in the Crosstown Industrial Park, founded in 1980 with the promise of jobs for the inner city, and nurtured with government support. Mayor Flynn was among those protesting the shutdowns, accusing Digital of "an unwarranted disinvestment in a city which has invested millions of dollars in the company's success," citing bond financing, tax incentives, free rent and other subsidies. "In the final analysis, the company got what they could get from the city and from the neighborhood and then decided to get out."[17]

As explained by DSNI economic development staffer Marcia Szymanski, the Digital and Stride Rite plant closures highlighted the fallacy of the traditional "enterprise zones" approach—discussed further in Chapter Nine—and the need to develop enduring, mutually beneficial partnerships with the private sector. They also underlined the need to explore community ownership and reinvestment structures such as lending pools and credit unions. As Clayton Turnbull told people at the DSNI summit, money is a tool that can be used in many ways: "You don't have to be 18 to vote with the dollar."

In Szymanski's words, the shutdowns underscored the need for DSNI to factor disinvestment strategies into the planning process and "ensure we do not recreate the next Digital/Stride Rite as we look to bring business to the neighborhood." Let's explore Stride Rite more closely, for a better understanding of corporate strategies.

The Stride Rite Corporation is a cofounder of Businesses for Social Responsibility and long renowned for its day care facilities and philanthropy—such as Harvard scholarships for inner city students doing community service. Still, it has, reports the *Wall Street Journal,* "prospered partly by closing 15 factories, mostly in the Northeast and several in depressed areas," the Roxbury plant among them, "and moving most of its production to various low-cost Asian countries." There, "Stride Rite continues its quest for labor bargains. In recent years, it has switched from factories in South Korea as pay rose there to lower-wage Indonesia and China." A Stride Rite director says, "It has become sort of Holy Grail for us." In China, skilled workers "earn $100 to $150 a month, working 50 to 65 hours a week. Unskilled workers—packers and sorters—get $50 to $70 a month."

Stride Rite shifted its U.S. distribution facilities from Roxbury and New Bedford, Massachusetts to Kentucky. "It was a difficult decision," says Chairman Ervin Shames. "Our hearts said, 'Stay,' but our heads said, 'Move.'" According to the *Wall Street Journal*, "Kentucky won mainly because of a $24 million tax break over 10 years, vs a $3 million offer from Massachusetts. Lower wage rates also played a role." The United Food and Commercial Workers Union represented the workers in Massachusetts. After being built nonunion, the Kentucky plant will open nonunion.

While researching the Stride Rite story, reporter Joseph Pereira called DSNI, and the staff arranged for him to meet some Stride Rite workers, including Cape Verdean DSNI member Miguel Brandão. At age 46, Brandão had worked for Stride Rite for 11 years when the shutdown was announced. "Among the many lessons learned from the closings, one has struck especially close to home for Mr. Brandão in Roxbury. A 70-year-old Irish immigrant, who rented a room from him, died recently, leaving behind a 32-year-old mentally disabled son. 'I don't have the heart to ask him to leave,' he says...'If I did, I would be doing to him what my company is doing to me.'"[18] The son remains in Brandão's home.

UNDERSTANDING ECONOMIC TRENDS THAT UNDERMINE COMMUNITY DEVELOPMENT

Miguel Brandão and the other Stride Rite and Digital workers lost their jobs to corporate decisions over which they had no control. To win unprecedented control over land and housing development, DSNI has had to be informed, united, bold and creative. The struggle for community control over economic development will require no less.

Today's corporate strategies maximize the ability of corporations to rapidly invest *and disinvest* regardless of the impact on workers or communities—whether in Massachusetts, Puerto Rico or Ireland, California, Mexico or China. Corporations are aggressively automating and "downsizing" their workforces and shifting operations among states and countries in a continual search for greater public subsidies and higher private profits, lower taxes, less regulation (e.g., health and safety, environmental) and cheaper labor.[19] "Cheap" does not mean low-skill.

Corporations are already switching to lower-paid, high-skilled industrial and service sector employees such as computer programmers and engineers. As a *Business Week* cover story on Mexico and the North American Free Trade Agreement (NAFTA) put it, Mexican workers are "smart, motivated, cheap." The U.S. minimum wage comes out to a measly $34 a day. In Mexico it's much worse, $30 a week. U.S. minimum wages have declined by about a third since the 1970s, after adjusting for inflation. Mexican minimum wages lost two-thirds of their purchasing power between 1982 and 1991.[20]

The oft-heard scapegoating stereotype of deadbeat poor people masks the growing reality of dead-end jobs and disposable workers. Living standards are falling for younger generations despite the fact that many households have two wage earners, have fewer children and are better educated than their parents. The inflation-adjusted median income for families with children headed by persons younger than 30 plunged 32 percent between 1973 and 1990. For Black families with children headed by persons under 30, median income was cut in half.

Forty percent of all children in families headed by someone younger than 30 were *officially* living in poverty in 1990—up from 20 percent in 1973—including one out of four children in White young families and one out of five children in young married-couple families.[21]

The average inflation-adjusted earnings of nonsupervisory workers crashed 19 percent between 1973 and 1990—that's a loss of nearly one dollar in every five.[22] The average chief executive officer (CEO) of a large corporation, meanwhile, now measures yearly pay in the millions, counting salary, bonuses, stock options and dividends. Look at the widening worker-executive pay gap: The average CEO "earned" as much as 41 factory workers in 1960, 42 factory workers in 1980, 104 factory workers in 1991 and *157 factory workers* in 1992. By contrast, Japan's average CEO earns less than 32 factory workers.[23]

For more and more Americans, a job is not a ticket out of poverty, but into the ranks of the working poor. The official poverty rate for working families with children jumped one-third between 1979 and 1990. The shrinking middle class is misled into thinking those below them on the economic ladder are pulling them down, when in reality those on the top rungs of the ladder are rising at the expense of those below.[24]

It shouldn't be surprising that Black and Latino families—whether one-parent or two-parent families—have higher poverty rates than White families since the wages and job opportunities of people of color reflect educational and employment discrimination. Since single mothers of color experience both race and gender discrimination, their families are the most impoverished.[25]

Over half of Dudley's children live in households headed by women, and over half of those families live below the official poverty line. Instead of rooting out discrimination and implementing the kind of family supports common in numerous countries, many policy makers are busily blaming women for their disproportionate poverty.[26]

The fact that many female-headed households are poorer because women are generally paid less than men is taken as a given in much poverty policy discussion, as if pay equity were a pipe dream not even worth mentioning. A 1977 government study found that if working women were paid what similarly qualified men earn, the number of poor families would decrease by half.[27] A 1991 government study found that "many single mothers will remain near or below the poverty line even if they work at full-time jobs. Problems they are likely to face include low earnings; vulnerability to layoffs and other work interruptions; lack of important fringe benefits such as paid sick leave and health insurance; and relatively high expenses for child care."[28]

In the words of a comprehensive study commissioned by the Boston Foundation, after food, housing and taxes, child care is the biggest expense for working parents of all incomes. "For moderate-income families, child care costs can swamp dreams of going back to school, home ownership, or saving for college. For the working poor and for low-income families, subsidized child care can be the key to staying off welfare, to getting an education, a better job, and housing." State-funded child care subsidies are in short supply and the federal tax deduction for child care expenses is capped at an absurdly low amount. Boston's child care costs are among the highest in the nation: the average annual costs in a licensed child care center were $10,000 for infants, $9,000 for toddlers and $7,500 for preschoolers in 1991. And it's not because child care providers are paid well. Nationally, the average wages of teachers and assistants at child care centers, nearly all women, ranged from $5 to $8.85 an hour; people who take care of zoo animals make an average $2,500 more a year than child care teachers.[29]

"Good jobs at good wages" are becoming harder to find and keep. Between 1979 and 1990, the proportion of full-time, year-round workers paid low wages (below $12,195 in 1990) increased by half—to nearly one in every five full-time workers overall, one out of four women workers, one out of four Black workers and nearly one out of three Latino workers. Among young full-time workers (ages 18-24), the percent earning low wages nearly doubled from 23 percent in 1979 to over 43 percent in 1990. Among young women workers, nearly half earn low wages.[30] Two out of three workers who earn minimum wage are women. Full-time work at minimum wage ($4.25 an hour) earns below the official poverty line for a family of two.

The entry-level wage for high school graduates fell 22 percent between 1979 and 1991, a reflection of "the shift toward lower-paying industries, the lower value of the minimum wage, less unionization" and other trends. College graduates do better, but they too are feeling the wage rollback. Entry-level wages for college graduates fell slightly overall (-0.2 percent) between 1979 and 1991, but Black college graduates lost over 3 percent and Latino college graduates lost nearly 15 percent.[31] According to a 1992 Labor Department study, 30 percent of each new class of college "graduates between now and 2005 will march straight into the ranks of the jobless or the underemployed."[32]

What about all those supposedly high-paid jobs in high-tech industries? The occupations with high growth rates are not the same occupations creating the largest number of jobs. As a congressional report sums it up, "Those who look at occupational employment growth rates have concluded that faster-growing occupations generally require higher levels of education or training" and are generally higher paid. As projected for the years 1990-2005, the ten *fastest growing occupations by growth rate* are, in descending order: home health aides, paralegals, systems analysts and computer scientists, personal and home care aides, physical therapists, medical assistants, operations research analysts, human services workers, radiologic technologists and technicians, and medical secretaries. "In contrast, 8 of the 10 occupations projected to experience the largest absolute increase in employment...typically require high school graduation or less education" and are generally low paid. The ten *occupations producing the most new jobs* are: retail salespersons, registered nurses, cashiers, general office clerks, truck drivers, general managers and top executives, janitors and cleaners, nursing aides/orderlies/and attendants, food counter/fountain/and related workers, waiters and waitresses.[33]

The jobs of today and tomorrow not only pay less than the fast disappearing unionized jobs—with mass layoffs and union-busting, only 11 percent of private sector jobs are now unionized. They are much more precarious. Corporations are dividing their employees into a shrinking core of full-time employees and a second-class pool of "contingent workers"—some of them fired and then hired or "leased" back at a large discount by the same companies.[34]

This is "the age of the contingent or temporary worker, of the consultant and subcontractor, of the just-in-time work force—fluid, flexible, disposable," writes Lance Morrow in *Time* magazine. "Companies are portable, workers are throwaway."[35] Contingent workers— temporary employees, contract workers, "leased" employees and part-time workers, many of whom want permanent full-time work— made up a third of the U.S. workforce in 1993, up significantly from one-fourth in 1988.

Contingent workers are expected to *outnumber* permanent full-time employees by the end of the decade. In 1992, the average weekly income of full-time workers was $445, while it was $259 for temporary workers and $132 for part-time workers. "'You can't identify any industry that could be the engine for growth in the future for high-wage jobs,' says Anthony Ferrara, head of the US Bureau of Labor Statistics in New England...'Two of the fastest-growing jobs today are contract jobs for janitors and cleaners, and security and night watchmen. But they are $5- and $6-an-hour jobs.'"[36]

Contingent workers are also more vulnerable to discrimination, harassment, and health and safety violations and penalized by current labor law, unemployment and Social Security programs. As *Time* summed it up:

> Long-term commitments of all kinds are anathema to the modern corporation. For the growing ranks of contingent workers, that means no more pensions, health insurance or paid vacations. No more promises or promotions or costly training programs. No more lawsuits for wrongful termination or other such hassles for the boss....Being a short-timer can mean doing hazardous work without essential training, or putting up with sexual and racial harassment. Placement officers report client requests for "blond bombshells" or people without accents. Says an agency counselor: "One client called and asked us not to send any black people, and we didn't. We do whatever the clients want, whether it's right or not."[37]

How do workers increasingly forced to migrate from job to job, at low and inconsistent wage rates, without paid vacation, much less a pension, care for themselves and their families, own a home, pay for college, save for retirement, build a future?

What about workers without jobs? The official unemployment rate averaged 4.5 percent in the 1950s, 4.7 percent in the 1960s, 6.2 percent in the 1970s and 7.3 percent in the 1980s—not counting workers so discouraged by a fruitless job search that they stopped actively looking.[38] The 1990s began with another official recession followed by a so-called "jobless recovery." That's like declaring recovery for a patient resuscitated into a coma. Black unemployment is more than double the White rate; the Latino rate is almost double the White rate. The proportion of Black men ages 25-34 who were either unemployed or earned below the official poverty line rose from nearly 37 percent in 1979 to over 45 percent in 1989.[39]

The Labor Department acknowledged in late 1993 that the government has been substantially underestimating unemployment, especially among women. As more women worked outside the home, government interviewers continued to begin their survey this way: When men responded the interviewer typically asked, "What were you doing most of last week, working or something else?" Women were typically asked whether they were "keeping house or something else." If they answered keeping house, the interviewer didn't bother to find out if they were laid off or looking for work, so even if they were, the government counted them as homemakers, not unemployed members of the workforce. When the government tried to correct the unemployment rate for the 12 months through August 1993 it was 7.6 percent, not 7.1 percent.[40] That's still only a partial unemployment picture.

The National Urban League's Hidden Unemployment Index measures the officially counted unemployed plus discouraged workers and involuntarily part-time workers, a growing category in the changing workforce. The overall 1991 hidden unemployment rate was, at 13 percent, almost twice the official rate. For Black men and women—"last hired, first fired"—the hidden 1991 unemployment rate was a Great Depression-level 23 percent. At Digital, for example, Blacks made up under 7 percent of the workforce in 1990 and bore 11 percent of the layoffs by 1991. At BankAmerica, Blacks were under 8 percent of the workforce and bore 28 percent of the job losses.

Black teenagers had a hidden unemployment rate of 57 percent in 1991 (36 percent officially) and White teenagers had a hidden rate of 30 percent (16 percent officially). Roxbury's *official* unemployment rate was an estimated 22 percent in early 1993.[41] The hidden unemployment rate is much higher.

To make matters worse, many unemployed workers receive no unemployment benefits.[42] Low-wage workers, disproportionately women and people of color, are less likely than others to qualify for unemployment benefits—they may not meet work time or earnings requirements. And, when they do qualify, their temporary payments are only a fraction of their meager wages.

"Studies in several states have found that a substantial proportion of new AFDC (Aid to Families with Dependent Children) families are headed by individuals who have recently lost their jobs," reports the Washington-based Center on Budget and Policy Priorities. "For unemployed people who do not have children, little or no cash assistance may be available if they fail to receive unemployment benefits. Many states and localities lack any general assistance program or else limit such a program to people who are elderly or have disabilities."[43] In other words, there is no safety net for many people thrown out of work. Studies have found that the extent of homelessness in urban areas is directly related to the availability—or lack—of general assistance benefits. Massachusetts ranked second behind Michigan in the "depth and breadth of the cuts" instituted by states in low-income programs in 1991, including general assistance and housing.[44]

In the Dudley neighborhood, 40 percent of children ages 14 and under lived in a household with an adult receiving AFDC, Federal Supplemental Security Income (SSI) or other public assistance income in 1989. AFDC benefits have been chopped repeatedly as if, once you have too little money, it doesn't matter how little you have. Between 1970 and 1992, AFDC benefits plunged 43 percent nationally, adjusting for inflation. When food stamps are added to AFDC, the combined median benefit is still only 72 percent of the poverty line, which is supposed to be the minimum needed for subsistence according to the government—the actual minimum is higher. The downward benefits trend continues.[45] Less than one out of four AFDC families lives in public housing or receive any rent subsidies.[46]

About 38 percent of families receiving AFDC are White (the same percentage as in 1973), 39 percent are Black (a lower percentage than 1973), 17 percent are Latino, 3 percent are Asian and 1 percent are Native American. In Massachusetts, 54 percent of families are White, 16 percent Black, 24 percent Latino and 3 percent Asian. There are disproportionately more people of color on welfare because disproportionately more people of color are poor and unemployed, and they have disproportionately less access to other government income support programs such as Unemployment Insurance and Workers Compensation. Contrary to the stereotype, "the typical recipient is a short-term user."[47] In the name of reform, politicians—Massachusetts

Governor Weld among them—have substituted fighting welfare for fighting poverty. One result: nationally, the number of AFDC child recipients as a percent of children in poverty fell from 81 percent in 1973 to 60 percent in 1991.[48]

Budget cutters pretend that AFDC is a major drain on public money—in 1991, AFDC actually accounted for less than 1 percent of federal outlays, and states spent 2 percent of their revenues on AFDC. Politicians and the media sow the seeds of hatred with scapegoating stereotypes—discussed further in Chapter Eight—of corrupt and lazy "welfare queens." When California cut its AFDC payment for a mother and two children in 1991—which was already $2,645 below the official annual poverty line—Governor Pete Wilson said it meant "one less six-pack per week."[49]

Today's welfare system minimizes help and maximizes humiliation. When Barbara Sobel, then head of the New York City Human Resources Administration, posed as a welfare applicant to experience the system firsthand, she was misdirected, mistreated and so "depersonalized," she says, "I ceased to be." She remained on welfare, with a mandatory part-time job as a clerk in a city office, despite repeated pleas for full-time work, and learned that most recipients desperately want jobs.[50]

Rosemary Bray, a former editor of the *New York Times Book Review* who was on welfare as a child, writes, "The demonization of the welfare mother allows for denial about the depth and intransigence of racism" and reinforcement of the patriarchal notion "that women and children without a man are fundamentally damaged goods."[51] It allows those benefiting from rising economic inequality to blame the system's failures in producing sufficient jobs and income on supposed personal failures such as deficient "work ethic."

The widespread pretense that leaving welfare through "workfare" means leaving poverty and necessarily benefits children undermines efforts to make work fair and supportive of all families with adequate jobs, wages, child care, health care, training, unemployment insurance, paid family leave (the unpaid family leave finally enacted in 1993 does not even cover most workers) and so on. An Ohio study found that a woman on maternity leave is ten times more likely to lose her job than one on medical leave for other reasons.[52] Forty percent of AFDC families have a child under three years of age. In a discriminatory, dangerous move to expand day care for AFDC recipients on the cheap, many states are exempting child care providers from health and safety regulations or loosening them for care under the so-called Family Support Act.[53]

As Rosemary Bray observes, "The writers and scholars and politicians who wax most rhapsodic about the need to replace welfare with work make their harsh judgments from the comfortable and supportive environs of offices and libraries and think tanks. If they need to go to the bathroom midsentence, there is no one timing their absence. If they take longer than a half-hour for lunch, there is no one waiting to dock their pay. If their baby sitter gets sick, there is no risk of someone having taken their place at work by the next morning. Yet these are conditions that low-wage women routinely face."[54]

The Clinton administration's stated goal of assuring that no one working full time lives below the poverty line—by raising the Earned Income Tax Credit and, eventually, raising the minimum wage—is a step forward, but it does not address these realities: The poverty line is set well below actual sufficiency in basic necessities, full-time jobs are becoming scarcer and many parents with young children cannot work full-time inside the home *and* full-time outside it.

Former DSNI Director Gus Newport observes, "The banks fail, but Congress bails them out with our tax dollars...If the poor fail, there is no lobbyist there with [the] capacity to bail them out." Every hour during the 1991-92 fiscal year, the federal government spent $33.7 million on the military, $8.7 million on the savings and loan bailout, $2.9 million on education and $1.8 million on children's health.[55]

The cycle of unequal opportunity has been reinforced by tax cuts rewarding wealthy people and corporations and ballooning the national debt. According to Robert Reich, now U.S. secretary of labor, "Were the tax code as progressive as it was even as late as 1977," the top 10 percent of income earners "would have paid approximately $93 billion more in taxes" than they paid in 1989.[56] How much is $93 billion? About the same amount as the combined 1989 government budget for all these programs for low-income persons: AFDC ($19.7 billion); Supplemental Security Income, SSI ($15.8 billion); food benefits, including food stamps, the school lunch program, WIC—supplemental nutrition program for pregnant and nursing Women, Infants and Children—($22 billion); housing benefits, including low-rent public housing, lower-income housing assistance, etc. ($15.9 billion); jobs and employment training ($3.9 billion); education aid, including Head Start, college loans, etc. ($13 billion); and General Assistance ($2.8 billion).[57]

Lower-income Americans pay for the debt with cutbacks and less-talked-about tax hikes. Payroll taxes, which are regressive because they tax the poor proportionately more than the rich, are up; the Social Security payroll tax increased 30 percent between 1978 and 1990. Up also are regressive state and local sales, excise and property taxes. After Clinton's tax reforms, the top personal income tax bracket still "remains well below the average top rate, 47%, charged by the 86 countries with an income tax." Moreover, the tax increase for "the wealthiest 1% of the population, whose average incomes are $800,000, will average only $53,600. This does not come close to taking back the $160,000 per family these wealthiest taxpayers will save this year alone from the supply-side tax giveaways instituted during the 1980s."[58] Making things still worse, Massachusetts and other state and local governments are rushing to expand lotteries, video poker and other government-promoted gambling to raise revenues, again disproportionately from the poor, which they should be raising from a fair tax system.[59]

Robert Reich has warned of the "secession of the successful." He wrote that the wealthy top fifth of Americans "is quietly seceding from the rest of the nation." They have withdrawn "their dollars from the support of public spaces and institutions shared by all and dedicated the savings to their own private services"—from schools to security guards to walled-off residential communities.[60]

DSNI knows that the path of separate and unequal is neither just nor sustainable. DSNI knows there is a better way: the way of hope—and not fear; building successful communities and nations that are greater than the sum of their parts—and not torn apart; mutual cooperation for mutual progress and security. The neighborly way.

DECLARATION OF COMMUNITY RIGHTS

Dudley residents inspire themselves, and others, with their shared vision of the future. That vision lights the way as Dudley residents not only resist destructive economic and social policies, but implement community-building alternatives. In the summer of 1993, DSNI's vision was crystallized again in a "Declaration of Community Rights." The declaration, produced by the Human Development Committee, highlights fundamental DSNI objectives in all areas of community development.

Najwa Abdul-Tawwab, a full-time school teacher, lessened her involvement in DSNI for a couple of years to devote more time to her four growing children. She was thrilled to see the Declaration of Community Rights. She recalls how the Human Development Committee had long struggled to find the "words that would express what everybody was concerned about: the young, the old, the child care, the housing, the safety..." Abdul-Tawwab says their attempts "never really hit the spot." But reading the declaration, she says, "I smiled and I said, 'Yes, that's it!' It was like a [very long] labor and then, finally, the delivery!"

The declaration is even more than a bill of human, economic and other community rights. It is a proud declaration of interdependence.

DSNI'S DECLARATION OF COMMUNITY RIGHTS

We—the youth, adults, seniors of African, Latin American, Caribbean, Native American, Asian and European ancestry—are the Dudley community. Nine years ago, we were Boston's dumping ground and forgotten neighborhood. Today, we are on the rise! We are reclaiming our dignity, rebuilding housing and reknitting the fabric of our communities. Tomorrow, we realize our vision of a vibrant, culturally diverse neighborhood, where everyone is valued for their talents and contributions to the larger community. We, the residents of the Dudley area, dedicate and declare ourselves to the following:

1. We have the right to shape the *development of all plans, programs and policies* likely to affect the quality of our lives as neighborhood residents.

2. We have the right to quality, affordable *health care* that is both accessible to all neighborhood residents and culturally sensitive.

3. We have the right to control the *development* of neighborhood land in ways which insure adequate *open space* for parks, gardens, tot lots and a range of recreational uses.

4. We have the right to live in a hazard-free *environment* that promotes the health and safety of our families.

5. We have the right to celebrate the vibrant cultural diversity of the neighborhood through all *artistic forms of expression.*

6. We have the right to *education and training* that will encourage our children, youth, adults and elders to meet their maximum potentials.

7. We have the right to a share in the *jobs* and prosperity created by economic development initiatives in metro-Boston generally, and in our neighborhood specifically.

8. We have the right to quality and affordable *housing* in the neighborhood as both tenants and homeowners.

9. We have the right to quality and affordable *child care* responsive to the distinct needs of the child and family as well as available in a home or center-based setting.

10. We have the right to safe and accessible *public transportation* serving the neighborhood.

11. We have the right to enjoy quality *goods and services,* made available through an active, neighborhood-based commercial district.

12. We have the right to enjoy full *spiritual and religious* life in appropriate places of worship.

13. We have the right to *safety and security* in our homes and in our neighborhoods.

8

THE POWER OF YOUTH

It is common for members and staff to use the word "family" in describing DSNI—a friendly, diverse, extended family where people cooperate and genuinely care about one another. Children and teenagers, a third of the Dudley population, are very much a part of the DSNI family.

Neighborhood kids drop by the DSNI office after school and during the summer to talk with staff, play computer games and help out with leafleting and other DSNI activities. Teenagers run their own Youth Committee and serve on the DSNI board. The office walls are alive with youth poems and drawings. People have said DSNI partly resembles a child care center. It definitely cares about kids.

Jason Webb is one of the regular volunteers. He started going to DSNI's neighborhood cleanups while still in elementary school. His father renovated the DSNI office at 513 Dudley Street and Jason says proudly, "I was around and I know almost everything to know about the building." When he was 11, Jason built a cardboard computer, complete with cardboard disks, and made his own little corner of office space. Jason describes DSNI as "a place where I can meet my friends and I can help out the community at the same time." His younger sisters also participate.

When asked at age 13 if DSNI makes him feel differently about what he wants to do when he's older, Jason responded, "I'm going to come here first to get a job, because they already said, 'Well, we're going to keep a little spot for you, Jason.'" He wants to be a DSNI organizer.

At the 1993 DSNI annual meeting, Director Ro Whittington gave a warm and witty introduction to the yet-unannounced winner of DSNI's first Community Service Award. Whittington praised the awardee as a youth role model and future leader and called out his many attributes—from being responsible to being funny. Jason Webb won the award. He got a loving, standing ovation as he shyly accepted his award and he shook many hands walking back up the aisle of the St. Patrick's chapel to his seat.

RISKY STEREOTYPES

Jason Webb doesn't fit common stereotypes about inner city youth—nor do most children and teenagers in Dudley and inner city neighborhoods elsewhere. They don't fit the stereotypes, but the stereotypes affect them.

The stereotypical images of youth from the inner city "urban jungle" are teenage welfare mothers, savage gang members and wannabes. They are further stigmatized as drug dealers and users who reject "mainstream values" about school and the "work ethic." In shorthand stereotype, boys mean danger, girls mean welfare, they all mean drugs. They are all suspect.[1] It would be just as absurd and offensive to stereotype Italian kids as mobsters or mobster wannabes.

Carline Dorcena, cochair of the DSNI Youth Committee, attends Monsignor Ryan Memorial High School in Dorchester. Her parents are Haitian immigrants. She has experienced being stereotyped as a girl from Roxbury and as a Haitian. Carline elaborates the different stereotypes for girls and boys. Boys, she says, are stereotyped as "gangbangers, as in gang members and drug dealers. The big gold chains, the fresh sneakers." Girls are stereotyped as "being on welfare and...getting pregnant" and "walking around in Spandex and saying, 'Yo! What's up!' Mostly, they see us as illiterate—like we can't articulate. We cannot express ourselves in a positive way, that we always have to be negative, or that we're 'easy.'

"It's not true. Most of my friends from around here, from this community, are...positive people. There are some people who I would say are kind of falling through the cracks and, I mean, society had a big part in that."

Carline says, "I get crazy reactions when people find out I'm Haitian, which I think is sad. You have the Irish who came over here—they had to struggle. The Italians, the African Americans—everybody had to struggle." Carline describes one kid's reaction after he inquired about her ethnicity. "I told him I was Haitian. Automatically, an expression lit up in his face and I said, 'Why are you looking at me that way? What's the matter?' Then he made some kind of reference to Voodoo. Hello! You should be aware here."

A nationwide 1990 survey by the National Opinion Research Center at the University of Chicago—in which most respondents were White—found an abundance of racist stereotypes: 78 percent of the non-Black respondents said Blacks are more likely than Whites to "prefer to live off welfare" and less likely to "prefer to be self-supporting." In addition, 62 percent said Blacks are more likely to be lazy; 56 percent said Blacks are violence-prone; and 53 percent said Blacks are less intelligent. Among non-Latino respondents, 74 percent said Hispanics are more likely to prefer to live off welfare; 56 percent said they are more lazy; 50 percent thought them more violence-prone; and 55 percent said Hispanics are less intelligent.[2]

Stereotypes can influence perception of even unambiguous events. In one study, "subjects were shown pictures of a white man holding a razor during an argument with a black man. When the pictures were described to others, the white subjects recalled the black man as wielding the razor!"[3]

Riley Foundation Trustee Bob Holmes speaks up when he hears people saying things like, "'Oh, all this violence that's down in Roxbury and Dorchester—the place is just getting worse' and all that. Then I will put my two bits in and say, 'You know, you can't attribute a lot of gang mentality...to the rest of the people who live in the area. There are a lot of people who are trying to do a lot of positive things.'" When asked what kind of response he gets, Holmes says, "Oh, usually disbelief."

Stereotypes reinforce the supposed behavioral explanations of persistent poverty which provide cover for economies that persistently impoverish many people. Boston's Irish immigrants were portrayed as having a culture of poverty and violence a century before Oscar Lewis famously applied the term "culture of poverty" to Mexicans, Puerto Ricans and African Americans. After 1845, "the Irish were the largest components of the state poorhouse population and a great majority of all paupers."[4] The "famine Irish" were economically exploited and socially stereotyped as immoral, drunkards and criminals—hence the term "Paddy wagon" for police wagon. Alcoholism was once recorded in the Massachusetts registry as a cause of death for Irish immigrants, not for Protestant Anglo-Saxons.

In the late nineteenth and early twentieth centuries, large numbers of Italians, Greeks, Russian Jews and others came to Boston. Again, they were labeled as "dangerous and undesirable elements" and "inferior."[5] But as White immigrants and especially their children were assimilated, racism against African Americans—who, unlike Whites, were systematically, violently enslaved and segregated—remained virulent. The U.S. Constitution once defined Black slaves as worth three-fifths of a human being. Today, Black per capita income is three-fifths of Whites. That's an economic measure of racism. The Latino-White ratio is similar.[6]

Historically, "women have been viewed as the breeders of poverty, criminality and other social problems," observes Mimi Abramovitz, professor of Social Policy at the Hunter College School of Social Work. "From the 'tenement classes' of the mid-1800s and the 'dangerous classes' of the 1880s, to Social Darwinism and eugenics, to Freudian theories of motherhood, to Moynihan's 'Black matriarchy' and today's 'underclass,' society blames women for the failed policies of business and the state."[7] Liberals and conservatives alike accuse single mothers, especially Black single mothers, of putting their children and all society at risk.[8]

In many ways, the wholesale labeling of children of single mothers, and inner city children generally, as "at risk" has become a stigmatizing code word for "illegitimate"—which also means contrary to law, rules and logic. In the past, "The bodies of black women became political terrain on which some proponents of white [and male] supremacy mounted their campaigns," observes Ricki Solinger in her historical study of single motherhood and race, and "the black illegitimate baby became the child white politicians and taxpayers loved to hate."[9] So it goes today.

The stigmatizing of children of single mothers is "very destructive," says Nancy Green, acting executive director of the Orchard Park Tenants Association, which has many single mothers. "It [fits] the same pattern of saying, 'Because your skin is different, because your culture is different, you are less of a human being.'"

Stigma is accompanied by prejudiced expectations and unfair treatment. For example, "teachers shown a videotape of a child engaging in a variety of actions consistently rate the child much more negatively on a wide range of dimensions when they are told that he or she comes from a divorced family than when they believe the child to come from an intact home."[10]

In a lengthy 1993 series of front-page stories, the *New York Times* profiled the "Children of the Shadows" living "in neighborhoods defined by hopeless girls with babies and angry boys with guns."[11] In the stereotype world, the exceptions make the rule—the stereotypical inner city female is an intergenerational "welfare mother" who had the first of her many children as a young teenager. The typical welfare recipient has one child and, as seen in the previous chapter, "is a short-term user" of welfare. In the "Replacing Welfare with Work" chapter of the Democratic Leadership Council's blueprint for the Clinton presidency, the only age reference is to the "15-year-old welfare mother with a new baby." In reality, less than 1 percent of mothers receiving AFDC are 15 or younger and only 4 percent are 18 or younger.[12] The "babies having babies" stereotype of welfare feeds the welfare backlash and undermines much-needed efforts to actually help young teenage mothers complete school, pursue higher education, secure decent child care and get a job with a living wage in these increasingly difficult economic times.

Contrary to image, most daughters in families who received welfare do not become welfare recipients as adults. The myth of an intergenerational Black matriarchy of "welfare queens" is particularly disgusting since Black women were enslaved workers for over two centuries and have always had a high labor force participation rate and, because of racism and sexism, a disproportionate share of low wages and poverty.[13]

The stereotype world of poor people of color is defined by the worst stereotypes of the highest-rise, lowest-income projects of Chicago and New York and of the Los Angeles "hoods" with the heaviest gang activity—and the heaviest police repression and entertainment industry interest. But even in Los Angeles, most young people of color are not "gangstas."[14]

DSNI Organizer Gertrudes Fidalgo, who was raised in Dudley and has nieces and nephews growing up there now, says the stereotyping of inner city kids as gang members has gotten so bad, "People say, 'Look at those gang members' when they see any group of Black kids standing together outside a store or wherever. They don't even have to know each other...It's see a group of Black kids, 'They're a gang.'"

Fidalgo tells how the stereotypes affect a DSNI Youth Committee member who is involved in varied youth activities through which he meets kids from the suburbs. He told Fidalgo that he commonly gets two kinds of reactions from suburban kids when he says that he's from Roxbury: They're suddenly afraid of him and don't want to be near him. Or, they want to fight him because they believe Roxbury kids think they're tough and they want to put him in his place. He's not looking for a fight. He walks away.

Jason Webb, whose heritage is both White and Cape Verdean, has a ready response when people put down Roxbury and stereotype the kids as drug-dealing gang members. "Mostly I say, 'Well, I'm from Roxbury and there's nothing wrong with me.' Mostly kids that say that...have never even been in Roxbury or Dorchester...They don't know what's going on."

Illicit drug dealing is often associated with poor communities like Dudley, but many of the dealers and buyers come from outside the neighborhood. To take an earlier example, members of the Lepardo family were involved in drug dealing as well as using Dudley for their illegal trash transfer station. The commander of the Boston Police Department's Drug Control Unit observes, "We've arrested people from every town in the metropolitan area for buying drugs in the city. The majority are fully-employed white males in their 30's."[15]

In April 1993, DSNI representatives attended one of the *Boston Globe's* "get to know the *Globe*" sessions with community organizations. Organizing Director Ros Everdell asked *Globe* columnist Alan Lupo if he "would be interested in doing a column around the fact that the head of the drug unit describes the majority of people who buy drugs in the city as White men, fully employed, from the suburbs." Everdell told him that such a column would be valuable because it would credibly contradict stereotypes that feed the negative image of Roxbury. Lupo followed up the conversation with the op-ed piece excerpted below:

> You can dump on city neighborhoods all you like, suburbanites, but banal as it seems, it does take two to tango.
>
> There is proof in the numbers, which come from the office of Boston Police Deputy Superintendent James Wood, the man in charge of the Drug Control Unit since 1986...
>
> For years cops were making arrests at a house on Talbot Avenue in Dorchester. And for years the dealing continued. Then the cops scooped up the buyers in September and again in October of 1991. Of 69 arrested, 51 were white males, 8 were white females and most were

suburbanites. By arresting customers, Wood says, police were finally able to shut down the operation...

"People have the wrong idea of a drug customer," says Wood. "They think it's a black guy with a needle hanging out of his arm. Totally wrong."...

The customers, fellow suburbanites, are our neighbors.[16]

Black kids are not more likely to use drugs than White kids, but they're much more likely to be stigmatized and jailed for it. In May 1992, then Health and Human Services Secretary Louis Sullivan "announced a national media campaign aimed at dispelling misconceptions about alcohol and other drug use among African-American youth and at reinforcing the strengths and positive activities among these youths." Sullivan said, "Our studies show that contrary to many misconceptions, these youngsters are less likely to use alcohol and other drugs than are kids from other ethnic groups."[17]

The misconceptions continue in large part because the biased "War on Drugs" is sweeping up more and more people of color in a racist dragnet while ignoring or treating more leniently the much larger number of White dealers and users. More than three out of four drug users are White (not of Hispanic origin).[18] But Blacks are much more likely to be arrested and convicted for drug offenses—most drug arrests are for possession—and receive much harsher sentences.[19] The American Bar Association (ABA) found that between 1986 and 1991, drug arrests skyrocketed by 78 percent for juveniles of color, while *decreasing* by a third for other juveniles.[20] A *USA Today* special report found that nationally, in 1991, Blacks were four times more likely than Whites to be arrested on drug charges; in Boston they were five times more likely.

> In every part of the country—from densely packed urban neighborhoods to sprawling new suburbs, amid racial turmoil and racial calm—blacks are arrested at rates sometimes wildly disproportionate to those of whites...
>
> Tens of thousands of arrests—mostly in the inner-city—resulted from dragnets with paramilitary names. Operation Pressure Point in New York City. Operation Thunderbolt in Memphis. Operation Hammer in Los Angeles...
>
> [Police officials] say Blacks are arrested more frequently because drug use often is easier to spot in the Black community, with dealing on urban street corners...rather than behind closed doors.
>
> And, the police officials say, it's cheaper to target in the black community.
>
> "We don't have whites on corners selling drugs...They're in houses and offices," says police chief John Dale of Albany, N.Y., where blacks

are eight times as likely as whites to be arrested for drugs..."We're locking up kids who are scrambling for crumbs, not the people who make big money."[21]

Notwithstanding the fact that many of the easily spotted street corner buyers are White, as well as many "big money" traffickers and money launderers, one doesn't have to be dealing or buying on street corners to feel the racial bias of the "War on Drugs." A study in the *New England Journal of Medicine* found that drug and alcohol rates were slightly higher for pregnant White women than pregnant Black women, but Black women were about ten times more likely to be reported to authorities by private doctors and public health clinics—under a mandatory reporting law. Poor women were also more likely to be reported.[22]

Former Director of National Drug Control Policy Bob Martínez has acknowledged the misleading impression left by account after account of Blacks being arrested. It is "one of the big tragedies in the whole news coverage of the drug war...You will never know it by virtue of the way that the drug war is covered, by virtue of the way that police engage in sweeps, and that's wrong, because I'm telling you that when kids come out of sometimes difficult conditions and remain drug-free, are not abusing alcohol, are not using tobacco, somebody's doing some kind of a job in that neighborhood, and that does not get out."[23]

WHOSE "CULTURE OF VIOLENCE"?

In the stereotype world, violence is largely the product of "gunsanddrugs" and gangs. That's a dangerous falsehood.[24] The United States has had the industrial world's highest homicide rates for some 150 years. The 1986 homicide rate for young White males in the United States was twice as high as the rate for all young men in other industrialized nations.[25] In reality, the heavily advertised legal drug alcohol is the drug most linked to violence and death. Alcohol is associated with more homicides nationally than illicit drugs, and almost the same number of people are killed annually by drunk drivers as are murdered; drunk drivers are overwhelmingly White males.[26] For women of all races and backgrounds, the greatest threat of violent injury and death comes from so-called "domestic violence" by past or present boyfriends or spouses, which "is the leading cause of injury to women and accounts for more visits to hospital emergency departments than car crashes, muggings, and rapes combined."[27] Making matters worse,

"The criminal justice system is directing more of its attention to drug offenses and less to violent crime."[28] And that attention is focused much more on punishment than treatment and prevention.

Like alcohol Prohibition earlier, today's drug prohibition means profit for modern Al Capones and criminal enterprises who will use violence to control their market. Overall homicide rates reached their highest peak for this century in the early 1930s, coinciding with Prohibition *and* the Great Depression. To avoid the harsh mandatory sentences of the contemporary "War on Drugs," adults have pulled more youth into drug dealing, who in turn pull in their peers. And the deepening economic depression experienced by youth of color greatly intensifies the pull of the underground economy.

Between 1987 and 1991, approximately 31 people died by homicide in the Dudley core area—out of 481 for Boston—of whom 14 were ages 15-24 and 1 was under 15.[29] Nationally, homicide is now the second-largest killer of young people of all races, ages 15-24. Accidents, mostly motor vehicle, are first; suicide is third. For Black young people, homicide leads accidents and suicides. For Whites, accidents and suicide lead homicide. Public health specialists believe that the many fatal auto "accidents" caused by drunk and reckless driving have more in common with homicide and suicide than commonly thought.[30] In 1990, young Black males were nearly 11 times more likely to be murdered by gunfire than their White counterparts. The gap in their overall death rates from accidents and violence was much lower, though still large at 2 to 1; that's about the same ratio as in 1970. Black men and women have historically had higher homicide rates and today's horrific rates have past precedent.[31] Research has shown "that when socioeconomic status is taken into consideration, racial differences in homicide mortality rates all but disappear."[32]

Increasingly deadly weapons designed for hunting people are produced for profit by major manufacturers and proudly defended by the National Rifle Association. In many places, you can legally possess firearms before you can legally drink, and it's easier to buy a gun than to register to vote. Half the homes in the country contain firearms, and guns in the home greatly increase the risk of murder and suicide for family members and close acquaintances.[33] As far as gun manufacturers are concerned, children are just another consumer market. One advertisement encouraged parents to consider buying guns for children as young as ten:

Age is not the major yardstick. Some youngsters are ready to start at 10, others at 14. The only real measures are those of maturity and individual responsibility. Does your youngster follow directions well? Is he conscientious and reliable? Would you send him to the grocery store with a list and a $20 bill? If the answers to these questions or similar ones are "yes" then the answer can also be "yes" when your child asks for his first gun.[34]

The FBI reports an escalation of juvenile violence "evident in all races, social classes, and lifestyles." In Little Rock, Arkansas, one of many small cities where youth violence is rising, "one of the most violent gangs is composed of white middle-class children."[35] Instead of nonviolent conflict resolution, children are widely taught, through popular wars and media "entertainment," that violence is the way to deal with problems—at a time when military-style weapons have become commonplace.

"In the media world, brutality is portrayed as ordinary and amusing" and often merged with sex, observes Dr. Deborah Prothrow-Stith, former Massachusetts commissioner of Public Health. She says, "In the same spirit as President Reagan when he urged the Libyans to 'make my day,' by attacking, the violent hero cannot wait for the opportunity to, in the words of...President Bush, 'kick ass'" in Iraq.[36] Between 1982 and 1988—a period when children's TV was deregulated and networks defended programs like *G.I. Joe* as "educational"— television time devoted to war cartoons jumped from 90 minutes to 27 hours a week. By age 18, the average American child will have seen 40,000 murders on television. Violent "superhero" shows are created expressly to sell toys to children. Virtual reality video games are bringing even more graphic and participatory "virtual" violence. The strong consensus of private and government research is that on-screen violence contributes to off-screen violence.[37]

James Alan Fox, dean of the College of Criminal Justice at Northeastern University, observes, "It is well known that positive reinforcement for pro-social behavior will always outperform negative reinforcement for anti-social behavior. And, besides, it is far cheaper to hire elementary school teachers and pay them wages commensurate with the importance of their jobs than it is to build more prisons and hire more corrections officers. Unfortunately, for some of our leaders, there remains a more immediate political payoff in advocating a return to the three R's of retribution, retaliation and revenge."[38]

Lost in the system of immediate political payoffs are the thousands of infants and children killed yearly by poverty-related hunger and disease. In the words of the Children's Defense Fund, every day in the

United States, "9 children are murdered, 13 children die from guns, 27 children—a classroom—die from poverty...101 babies die before their first birthday."[39] Both economic and physical forms of violence are intolerable. Racist perceptions of the problems undercut the solutions.

PRIDE AND PREJUDICE

Too often, poverty and prejudice limit the life expectancies and expectations of inner city children of color. When they start school, children of color are commonly expected to fail. They begin as "excited and hungry to learn" as White kids, writes Deborah Prothrow-Stith.[40] They are often starved of school resources and positive reinforcement in an "educational" system characterized by "savage inequalities."[41]

Prothrow-Stith summarizes an Illinois study where "66 student teachers were told to teach a math concept to four pupils—two white and two black. All of the pupils were of equal, average intelligence. The student teachers were told that in each set of four, one white and one black student was intellectually gifted, the others were labelled as average. The student teachers were monitored through a one-way mirror to see how they reinforced their students' efforts. The 'superior' white pupils received two positive reinforcements for every negative one. The 'average' white students received one positive reinforcement for every negative reinforcement. The average black student received one positive reinforcement for every 1.5 negative reinforcements, while the 'superior' black students received one positive response for every 3.5 negative ones." While "superior" intelligence was nurtured in the White students by the young student teachers, it was discouraged in the Black "superior" students.

Prothrow-Stith observes, "Social scientists and educators have proven time and again that children tend to perform academically as they are expected to perform. By and large, children who are expected by their parents and their teachers to work hard and achieve, do just that...Children who are labelled as 'C' students, tend to do 'C' work." The negative reinforcement given many children of color in school is part of a process that social psychologist Jeff Howard calls "spirit murder."[42]

In a school system rigged in favor of the already-privileged, some kids are tracked for success, others for failure. They are tracked by school, within school and within the classroom. "American children in general—and black children in particular—are rated, sorted, and boxed like so many potatoes moving down a conveyer belt," observes Jeff

Howard. "There is the 'gifted and talented' or advanced placement track for those few (exceedingly few when it comes to black children) considered highly intelligent. There are the regular programs for those of more modest endowment, and the vocational or special education classes for those considered 'slow.' Only children in the gifted programs can expect the kind of education that will give them access to the challenges and rewards of the 21st century. Placement in vocational or special education programs is tantamount to a sentence of economic marginality at best." Howard points out, "Black students make up 16 percent of public school students, yet make up almost 40 percent of those placed in special education or classified as mentally retarded or disabled. They are even more severely underrepresented in the upper end of the placement hierarchy."[43]

Jeannie Oakes, author of *Keeping Track: How Schools Structure Inequality*, found that youngsters of color "were consistently assigned to lower tracks even when they had higher test scores than white youngsters who were placed in the highest tracks."[44]

For DSNI member Najwa Abdul-Tawwab, who teaches first and second graders in the Boston Public Schools, teaching academic skills and a can-do spirit of self-esteem go together. Abdul-Tawwab has been honored for her teaching by the city, and in 1993 she was a finalist for Massachusetts Teacher of the Year and won a "Terrific Teachers Making A Difference" award, recognizing teachers nationally for their ability to foster self-esteem in students.

As a teacher and as an African American parent of three girls and a boy, Abdul-Tawwab knows all about the dangers of stereotyping kids into failure. "Before they've even completed kindergarten," she exclaims, children are labeled "at risk." They are bombarded with negative expectations. "I hate that terminology, 'at risk,'" she says. "We cannot have such a depressing attitude!" She stresses, "Kindergarten through twelfth grade, adult educators [have a responsibility] to work with and show [youngsters] how to move from point A to B," and so on, and empower children to overcome problems, not compound them.

Abdul-Tawwab has "sat on the other side of the table as a parent" and confronted teachers who were shortchanging her children. She recalls a parent/teacher conference about her twin daughters, Faridah and Fatimah, then in an eighth grade honors class. The child of the parent seeing the teacher before Abdul-Tawwab had gotten a B. "The teacher gave the parent about six ways in which that youngster could bring her grade up from a B to an A. When it was my turn—and my children had gotten Ds—I said, 'I would really like to know how I can help my children improve.'" The teacher responded, "'Well, don't worry about it. They did the best that they could.' Well, I was livid."

Abdul-Tawwab immediately went to the headmaster, who looked into the matter. He found that the children who had done poorly, including her own, had all had the same teacher the previous year and had not been given "the proper foundation to move on." The headmaster set "up an emergency tutorial...until school ended, to bring the children up to the level at which they needed to be in order to be competitive with the other students."

Abdul-Tawwab tells another parent/teacher conference story. When Fatimah was a senior, "she had all the documentation of why she should have gotten a B+" instead of a C in biology. "Another young lady sitting in front of me with her mom had gotten a C...All she said was, 'I really tried and don't you think that you could do a little bit better by me?' The biology teacher said, 'Okay, I'll change your grade to an A- so you can get on the honor roll.'" Both the teacher and the other child happened to be White. "The child is just wonderful. It's nothing against the child," says Abdul-Tawwab. "I fault the teacher," who, she says, has since changed for the better. When it was Abdul-Tawwab's turn, the teacher insisted Fatimah was mistaken. Abdul-Tawwab said, "'Well, if there is a mistake, I want you to show it to me. Show me your record book'...Well, he couldn't pull out a grade sheet or a record at all. He took a napkin and he started writing down three tests—90, 90, 85—and he just doodled...When he finished, he said, 'This is what she got.' I took the napkin and snatched it out of his hand" and took it to the headmistress. "It didn't make any sense for a high school teacher not to have information in front of him—or any teacher for that matter...The headmistress...could see that I was really upset. There were just two issues: one, in terms of how I felt that I had been treated because I was a parent of color and then, secondly, the fact that this teacher had no documentation of what my child had been doing." After the headmistress reviewed Fatimah's grades with the teacher, who was able to do a computer printout, the grade was changed to the B+ Fatimah had said she had earned all along.

Abdul-Tawwab's twin daughters, now in college, graduated from a top high school in the Boston Public School system. "I tell you, I probably had to fight at that school as much as if they were at a non-exam school in this city," she says. She worries that "most parents might not know how to do that...Teachers can start whipping out all these terminologies." Parents may "just get frustrated and say, 'Hey, well that's the way it is.'"

Abdul-Tawwab is among the DSNI members working to help parents and young people "speak up for what you believe is right" and hold educators accountable. As discussed in Chapter Seven, in fall 1993 the DSNI board designated education—intergenerational and multicultural—as the new priority for human development work.

Nationally, despite continued discrimination in school resources and expectations, Blacks have almost closed the once wide gap with Whites on high school graduation rates and narrowed it for those with at least four years of college, though there the artificial gap remains wide.[45] Skyrocketing tuition and educational cutbacks are undermining progress at a time when a college degree is increasingly essential for jobs providing adequate income. According to a congressionally mandated commission, "In the 1980s, the cost of attending a private college or university soared 146 percent—a higher rate than medical, home, food and car costs." But between 1980 and 1990, federal financial aid rose only 47 percent, says the Independent College Association. In Massachusetts, state public higher education funding was slashed by a third between 1988 and 1991.[46]

Biased attitudes and behaviors abound in employment as well as education. In 1992, the Massachusetts Commission Against Discrimination (MCAD) became the first state-sponsored program in the country to use testers to assess employment discrimination. As reported in the *Boston Globe*, "Although they were strangers, Quinn O'Brien and Darryl Vance had much in common. Both were handsome, articulate undergraduates with ambition. Vance had his eye on medical school; O'Brien was prelaw." They were among six students trained as MCAD employment testers. The Canadian O'Brien, who is White, was a junior at Boston College. Vance, who is Black, was a junior at Northeastern University. Vance was given better educational and employment credentials for the testing. O'Brien received many job offers while Vance's offers were scarcer and for less money and fewer benefits.[47]

The Urban Institute documented in a 1991 study, using carefully matched and trained pairs of White and Black young men applying for entry-level jobs, that discrimination against Black job seekers is "entrenched and widespread." An earlier study documented discrimination against Latinos.[48] The official unemployment rate for Black male teenagers ages 16-19 was 42 percent in 1992, compared with 18 percent for Whites and 28 percent for Latinos; the rate for Black men ages 20-24 was nearly 25 percent, compared with 10 percent for Whites and nearly 14 percent for Latinos. The official unemployment rate for Black female teenagers was over 37 percent in 1992 compared with under 16 percent for Whites and 26 percent for Latinas; the rate for Black women 20-24 years old was 23 percent, compared with 8 percent for Whites and over 12 percent for Latinas.[49] Remember, the official rate counts people who are unemployed and actively seeking work, not those so discouraged they have stopped looking or taken part-time jobs because that's all they could find.

On top of discrimination comes insult. It's common for people of color to get none of the credit when they succeed—portrayed as undeserving beneficiaries of affirmative action and "reverse discrimination"—and all of the blame when they fail. A study of the views of young people, ages 15-24, found that 49 percent of Whites believe that it is more likely that "qualified whites lose out on scholarships, jobs, and promotions because minorities get special preferences" than that "qualified minorities are denied scholarships, jobs, and promotions because of racial prejudice." Only 34 percent believed that minorities are more likely to lose out. Many Whites voiced racist stereotypes.[50]

For centuries there were virtual quotas of zero for people of color in top universities, higher-paid industries and government. There is still, without stigma, de facto affirmative action for college alumni offspring who don't otherwise meet college "standards" despite their more privileged childhoods. A *Boston Globe* article on so-called "legacy admissions" noted that the acceptance rate for children of Harvard alumni was more than double the rate for all applicants, class of 1992. "Far from being more qualified, or even equally qualified, the average admitted legacy at Harvard between 1981 and 1988 was significantly *less* qualified than the average nonlegacy."[51]

The top rungs of corporate America remain almost exclusively White and male. A national survey of senior executives found that in the 1980s, Blacks increased their minuscule share of top corporate positions from 0.2 to 0.6 percent; Latinos from 0.1 to 0.4 percent; and women from 0.5 to 3.0 percent.[52] The false charge of "reverse discrimination" provides scapegoats, rather than solutions, for the economic distress being felt by more Americans of all races.

PART OF THE SOLUTION

Imagine regular news coverage of the many children and adults, like those in DSNI, working hard to succeed and remove the walls and ceilings set by prejudice. When Youth Committee Cochair Carline Dorcena is stereotyped by suburban kids, at youth conventions for example, she sometimes responds this way: "I'll look at them and say, 'What's the matter? Why are you looking at me that way?' They'll say whatever, and I'll say, 'Aren't we putting up stereotypes here? Aren't we building up our walls?'...I run into it a lot. The way I deal with it is to hopefully talk to the person and say, 'What's up with these kinds of stereotypes?' By them seeing me, they could see that mostly it's not true. If that's what they choose to believe, that's what they choose to believe. But again, that shouldn't hold me back."

Young people working with DSNI don't minimize the problems they and their community face. They see them, however, as problems to overcome, not problems to be overwhelmed by. The children and teenagers of the Dudley Street Neighborhood Initiative are very much a part of the solution.

In March 1991, DSNI held a focus group of kids, ages 12 to 14, to discuss neighborhood problems and their ideas for solutions. There were six girls and one boy, mostly of Cape Verdean origin. Here's their list of solutions, ranging from playful to deadly serious:

□ gyms
□ parks
□ playgrounds
□ community centers
□ advice on drugs, etc.
□ tutoring center
□ pregnancy advice center
□ more welfare centers
□ jobs centers
□ day care
□ zoo (also for dogs, rats and cockroaches, they joked)
□ build trees
□ amusement park
□ more DSNI
□ more public phones
□ more security cameras

□ place for meetings
□ more schools
□ more computers
□ more apartments
□ more money
□ build a good college in the neighborhood like Harvard
□ place you can focus your career
□ more festivals
□ more pencils
□ more school trips
□ more health clinics
□ help lines
□ place to go after school
□ place to talk with adults about your problems

□ place to get kids jobs
□ get superstars to visit our neighborhood
□ homeless shelters
□ movie theater
□ too much violence in movies
□ educational counseling
□ place you stop the violence
□ learn more safety about AIDS
□ more jobs
□ someone to talk to if feeling depressed
□ stable for cows, burros and horses.

After the focus group, some of the girls began volunteering with DSNI after school.

Over the years, children and teenagers have played an increasingly active role in shaping DSNI's agenda. From the beginning, neighborhood kids hung out in the office, seeking constructive activity and advice from staff members. During her tenure as human services director in 1988-89, Azi Teklamariam began meeting with neighborhood youth, involving them in the Human Development Committee and working with local agencies to develop new and improved programs for children and teenagers. Teklamariam worked with a group of about 20 youth, ages 8-19, who met to discuss issues of concern. They "indicated that most of the agency providers never include the youth, the beneficiaries, in their program planning process." Among their suggestions were neighborhood summer day camps where parents and grandparents could be involved in the programs and where older youth could work.[53] They began organizing activities such as ice-skating, swimming and art museum visits.*

In her report to the DSNI board for July-August 1990, Ros Everdell wrote of the neighborhood cleanup that "Seventy-five young people came and twenty showed up 2 hours before we were to start!" Three weeks after the cleanup, youth were the backbone of DSNI's contingent in a march up Blue Hill Avenue during the National Night Out Against Crime. DSNI also involved youth and parents in the Latino Youth AIDS Education Project of the Hispanic Office of Planning and Evaluation (HOPE), a social service agency serving Roxbury and Jamaica Plain.

Everdell concluded her report by underscoring the challenge of finding "ongoing way[s] to involve the young people in the revitalization effort." DSNI took a great step forward with an innovative project called Dudley's Young Architects and Planners.

DUDLEY'S YOUNG ARCHITECTS AND PLANNERS

In her foreword to a report on Dudley's Young Architects and Planners, DSNI President Ché Madyun writes, "The Dudley's Young Architects and Planners Project integrates DSNI's commitment to com-

---

* Teklamariam returned to DSNI briefly in January-August 1991 to serve as youth coordinator. Her primary work was to develop a project in which ten local youth learned video skills and produced six videos later aired on cable television.

munity control with the search for an outlet for the transformative power of youth. At a time when national concern about violence by and against young people produces curfews, increased jail sentences, and fear of the youngsters who are our future, Dudley's Young Architects and Planners Project...is based on the dreams and creativity of youngsters too often written off by others as worthless."[54]

The catalyst for Dudley's Young Architects and Planners was a May 1990 youth focus group where DSNI's proposed community center was the central topic of discussion. The kids' enthusiasm was apparent as the 12 who were invited brought along friends and relatives, bringing the total to 26 kids, ages 9 to 15. Right from the start they envisioned the community center as combining recreation and culture with educational and employment activities. Their wish list included: basketball, baseball, ballet, swimming, karate, music, art and language classes, after-school tutoring, college and career counseling, theater, a library, computer center, a youth-run ice-cream parlor and a day care center where youth could work. They came up with a comprehensive list of rules to ensure community center safety. The rules included, "No fighting, no drugs and no weapons" and no clothing identifiable as gang colors. The kids were also concerned about countering common misconceptions of the neighborhood by outsiders who "think we're all like pigs" and police who "mistake you for gang members."

At one point, the kids were asked what jobs they wanted when they were older. "Hands went up immediately, and a diverse list was generated, including a pediatrician, three security guards, a day-care teacher, two lawyers, numerous basketball stars, two engineers, a singer, a rapper, an actress, an artist, and a lifeguard."[55]

Sue Beaton, then a DSNI board member and now deputy director, was one of the focus group facilitators. She was very moved listening to the kids talk "about wanting structure in their lives, wanting to feel safe, wanting help with homework, wanting books that could help them do that, wanting people that could help them understand the books." They talked about "the swimming pool, the basketball court, and all that...but then they got to some pretty basic stuff of wanting security guards."

"I think kids are beginning to form their own communities of goodness," Beaton observes. "They want to be good. It's our responsibility to help them remain good. That's what they want. And they've put that out there. Now what do we as adults do to [help them]?"

The day after the focus group, several kids asked DSNI staff when the next meeting would take place. Shortly before, local architect Gail Sullivan had approached DSNI about working pro bono because she wanted to do architectural work as part of a community process and appreciated DSNI's dynamic blend of development and organizing. Her timing was perfect for a project with youth.

Ros Everdell recalls, "We had a lot of young people around the office, particularly during the summer, looking for things to do, wanting to be involved, expressing such eagerness, participating in cleanups and other activities. It was a wealth of good energy coming from the kids. At the same time, we were overwhelmed because we could not get anything done in the office." DSNI wanted to do more to address the immediate needs of young people for activities and strengthen their long-term involvement in the community rebuilding process.

As Everdell puts it, "The young people in the neighborhood are really the ones who are going to live this revitalization much more than the adults who are currently planning it...If you do all this work to assure that adults feel that this is their neighborhood and their effort, how do we know that the next generation is going to feel the same way?" To be successful, says Everdell, DSNI has to ensure that "from one generation to another you have a sense that 'This is my community, I can make a difference and we have power.'"

The DSNI staff talked a lot informally with the kids in the office about the neighborhood and what changes they wanted to see. The community center focus group was a turning point toward greater action. In a series of focus groups, also involving adult residents and agencies, the youth group "was the most successful," says Everdell. "They couldn't stop talking." From that point on, she says, DSNI decided to make a more organizational commitment to youth "so that their voices are institutionalized." Dudley's Young Architects and Planners Project was the crucial next step.

"I don't know what Ros and Gus [Newport] were thinking initially," says Gail Sullivan. "But it had sounded to me as though we were talking about me working with 10 or 12 kids! Surprise, surprise!"

"Well, 75 kids have said that they're interested," Everdell told Sullivan. Sullivan knew she would need a lot of help and worked with Everdell and Human Development Director Andrea Nagel to pull together a core group of ten volunteer architects and urban planners who could facilitate teams of youth. They made sure that the adults would be as multiracial a group as the kids.

The project ended up with 45 young people, many of whom had participated in the earlier focus group. At the suggestion of older youth, the project was organized into a preteen group (ages 10-12), two teen groups (ages 13-15) and an older teen group (ages 16-20). For three months, each group met with its team facilitators for two hours one evening a week at Defenders of the Faith Church; the teen and older teen groups continued for another month to build the final models. As for the preteens, Sullivan says they "would have come every single night, every Saturday and every Sunday."

Even before the project started in early September 1990, some kids began going to the Dudley Library, taking out books on model-making and drawing sketches for the community centers. All the groups followed a general curriculum guide prepared by Sullivan and updated each week with group facilitators. In the first phase of the project, the groups brainstormed about activities and designs and interviewed family members and neighbors of all ages about what they wanted to see in the centers. Participants learned basic skills such as how to use surveyor's tape to lay out different site and building components; they made individual measuring sticks to use in designing and drawing to scale.

Sullivan says several of the kids "couldn't add three plus six when we started doing the measuring...They had to count with their fingers...Some of them had creative and unique systems for figuring out square footage. They found a way to make the math work for them...We really challenged the kids a lot around math in particular because of all the measuring, because they had to understand square footage of areas and working in scale, which a lot of adults have a hard time dealing with. I think that their...math comprehension and their appreciation for math's usefulness has increased."

The participants went in two large groups to the sites, where they discussed physical features, including solar orientation, topography and trees. Sullivan says, "We discussed the best location for the building entrances and we laid out some of the rooms on the sites with bamboo poles and surveyor's tape to give them a sense of the size of the rooms they wanted and where they would best be located. We had a great time and good discussions. We had a whole big debate about whether to save the existing trees or plant new ones."

Later, recalls Sullivan, Nolando Jones, then 15 years old, "came to me with this little index card, and he had drawn out an entire building floor plan saving the trees, creating a small courtyard with a day care center that sort of wrapped around the courtyard...He didn't know any of the [technical] words for the things that he had drawn, yet his design sense was so incredible. He very shyly brought me over this little index card—4 x 6. 'See, I saved the trees!'"

Nolando—whose mother was active in DSNI's Family Day Care Providers Network—also raised the issue of accessibility for the disabled before Sullivan or any other facilitator brought it up. "He had done this drawing, and started talking about needing an elevator for people with wheelchairs...Nolando raised the whole issue, and then the group got into a discussion. Everybody was very familiar with the issue of wheelchair accessibility and very interested in it." They then broadened the discussion to include how the design could best accommodate people who were deaf or blind or elderly.

Dudley's Young Architects and Planners took a field trip to MIT in Cambridge to examine the student center and recreational center which had many of the elements the kids wanted in their community centers. Sullivan recalls they were interested in everything from balconies and elevators, to video game rooms, to asking about particular light fixtures they wanted to use. The field trip also prompted discussion about college and careers. Kids began talking excitedly about wanting to go to MIT, wanting to know if it was expensive. The project facilitators later connected a few of the youth with professionals in particular fields of interest like architecture and medicine.

The design phase began with projects to encourage participants to individually develop their own vision of the community center, based on the list of activity spaces they had collectively chosen to be included. Using templates representing each room in scale, they cut the rooms out of colored paper and made floor plans to present to their team members. Then each teen and older teen group reached consensus on their designs and built community center models out of model-making board, balsa wood and other materials. The preteen group worked less formally, individually and in small groups, to prepare models for particular parts of the community center.

The young people were encouraged to dream—for themselves, their sisters and brothers, their parents and grandparents, their community. "We didn't set any limitations," says Sullivan. "We never said you can only spend so much money, or you will only have so much space. We didn't introduce zoning and other regulations such as parking requirements. We basically allowed them to add anything to the list that they wanted to add. They weren't having to compete—'Either you get

a gym or you get a pool, but you can't have both.' Well, there were
some limits. They couldn't fit the full-sized baseball diamond they
wanted on site."

DESIGNS AND DREAMS

Dudley's Young Architects and Planners publicly presented their
community center drawings and models at DSNI events in February
and April 1991. Their community center models include a gym, weight
room, indoor track, swimming pool, video game room, computer room,
media and arts room, library and study space, exhibit space, day care
centers, outdoor courtyard play space, classroom and workshop space,
office and meeting space for community organizations, cafeterias, elder
day programs and landscaped gardens. The Young Architects and
Planners made clear that they had designed their models with everybody in the neighborhood in mind.

Nolando Jones captured the spirit of the project when he said at
one of the presentations, "We don't want you to think we just thought
about ourselves."

José Hernández, then 12 years old, wrote a rap song for the April
event with the help of DNI Director Paul Yelder. Everyone had a good
laugh when the kids insisted that then DSNI Director Gus Newport take
the mike and the performance was captured on videotape. Yelder
dubbed them Heavy G and the Young APs.

COMMUNITY CENTER RAP

One day, I was walking down the street
Things were looking bad all around my feet

So I said this ain't right, what I see
We need a new Center for the Community

I called up the dudes and said we have to fix this mess
Let's make a community center that's totally fresh

We worked so hard making models with Gail
Had to plan everything from the screws and the nails

So we are here tonight everybody from the Crew
To show you the models and the pictures we drew

We're not finished and we will be around
Until this community center's in the ground

Najwa Abdul-Tawwab's children all participated in Dudley's Young Architects and Planners. She recalls how the project was usually the next day's dinner discussion. "They would talk about the importance of being involved at this young an age in deciding what their community would be like...They would look with a different eye as they traveled through the city...to see what kind of resources were available elsewhere."

Abdul-Tawwab says that in school her daughter Faridah, who is now in college pursuing her interest in engineering, "got mixed signals from her teachers about what girls can or can't do." Not in Dudley's Young Architects and Planners. "I felt that they were really learning something from" the project, says Abdul-Tawwab. "I would give it an A+."

Gevel Marrero, who had taken drafting classes before joining the project at age 17, planned to attend the University of Massachusetts, Lowell, on a football scholarship. With the encouragement of project facilitators, Gevel decided to enroll at Wentworth Institute of Technology in 1991 to study architecture. He quickly won a city design competition.

Six months after the project ended, one of the preteens greeted a DSNI staff member, "Do you remember me? I'm one of the architects." Nagel and Sullivan wrote in their report on the project, "Dudley's young people refuse to accept as their inheritance disinvestment, neglect, and despair."[56]

"I've been out to the [community center] site almost every day...trying to visualize what it's going to look like," says Jason Webb. "The community centers can be around when my kids are little...and they'll have places to go."

RECLAIMING A PARK

In 1991, DSNI launched a project to reclaim Mary Hannon Park—the only park on Dudley Street—as a safe community space, especially for kids. Mary Hannon Park was the most visible focus of drug dealing in the neighborhood and parents were afraid to let their children play there. "People were so sick and tired of negative activities there," says Ros Everdell, "that some were ready to fence it off. Instead of permanently denying the community this public resource, residents decided to make it a public resource for the community."

The cornerstone of DSNI's campaign to reclaim Mary Hannon Park was the Community Summerfest, a campaign of cultural pride, healthy recreation and positive activities. The Summerfest slogan was "Unite the Community, Celebrate our Diversity."

DSNI held planning sessions from January to June 1991 with residents and agencies and established four committees: safety, media, recreation and culture. To directly address safety issues in the park and the larger neighborhood, DSNI demanded better policing with community involvement and, after much effort, got a written commitment at headquarters level that the police would provide support to the community activities at the park. DSNI Organizer Ricardo Mayol, a minister who joined DSNI's staff in October 1990, worked with churches, such as Defenders of the Faith Church, and parishioners who are former drug addicts and alcoholics to create a "street ministry." They talked with dealers and addicts at the park to offer them assistance in getting out of drug dealing or off drugs and told them of the Summerfest plans to use the park for kids.

By the time Summerfest began, there had been enough publicity and advance work done that the drug activity had moved out of the park. Drug dealing continues on nearby blocks, but the park has remained a well-used community space and is especially safe and lively in the summer. Ricardo Mayol left DSNI in August 1991 to accept a long-awaited church position abroad and, unfortunately, the short-lived "street ministry" was not institutionalized. In Boston as elsewhere, demand for drug treatment far outstrips resources and capacity—especially hurting people who cannot afford private treatment.[57] Andrea Nagel stresses that not only are there extremely long waits to get into treatment at area facilities such as Casa Esperanza and First, Inc., but, "like with addiction to cigarettes, people often have to try more than once to quit. And a variety of treatment approaches are needed because what's effective for some people may not work for others, and vice versa." DSNI hopes that filling in vacant lots with homes, businesses, community facilities and cared-for common green space will lessen the opportunity for drug dealing, and that new jobs, education and other programs will lessen the economic motivation. Meanwhile, DSNI members and agencies continue working to improve safety throughout Dudley and provide positive reinforcement for youth.

Community Summerfest included a nine-week youth recreation program; three cultural affirmation weeks (Cape Verdean, Latin American, African American); and a Neighborhood Multicultural Festival for

the September grand finale. About 200 children and teenagers participated in Summerfest recreation activities at the park, which has
basketball courts, a baseball field and playground. Counselors, including eight paid teen counselors from the neighborhood, also took the
kids swimming and on other field trips. The summer camp was
coordinated by DSNI staff, board member Julio Henríquez and two high
school seniors, with assistance from the Bird Street Community Center,
the Roxbury Boys and Girls Club and Action for Boston Community
Development. The city Parks and Recreation Department supplied
equipment. Former Celtics basketball star M.L. Carr participated—
through the Bank of Boston community relations program—in the
Celebration for Youth culminating the summer camp program.

Because the Summerfest demonstrated so dramatically the need
for more youth programs, DSNI looked to area agencies to make it an
ongoing part of their activities. The Bird Street Community Center took
up the challenge and began running an annual Mary Hannon Park
Summer Youth Program. In 1992, over 400 children and teenagers were
involved in the summer camp, baseball camp, basketball league and
arts and crafts programs. Because of the DSNI and Bird Street activities,
many voices came together to advocate for park improvements, and
the Parks and Recreation Department responded with renovations the
following year.

Julio Henríquez was formerly director of Community Relations
and Information for the Boston School Department and runs a track
team called the Boston Flyers for boys and girls from Roxbury,
Dorchester and Mattapan. He knows kids are looking for attention and
wants to help them get positive attention on the track, in school and
elsewhere. He maintains, "Kids do look to adults for leadership and
when they don't get it they assume the adults are not interested. Many
of the people I hear complaining about the violence are doing nothing
to contribute to a solution. If you're not part of the solution then you're
part of the problem."[58]

A YOUTH LEADER'S STORY

John Barros, who entered Dartmouth College in 1992, was the
first youth to serve on the DSNI board and the founding cochair of
DSNI's Youth Committee. John's parents had emigrated from Cape
Verde to Boston before he was born. He first got involved with DSNI
as a child through the neighborhood cleanups. Later, he began helping

around the office and staff members encouraged him to apply his artistic talent to illustrating DSNI materials. Gertrudes Fidalgo is John's aunt. He says that she and Ros Everdell encouraged him and other kids to take on more leadership. Fidalgo's attitude, he says, wasn't "'Let's organize something and call the kids in on it.' Gertrudes would be, 'Let the kids organize it.'"

John worries that many adults, even in the Dudley community, have absorbed the widespread negative images of youth of color—exaggerating gang involvement, for example—and have internalized negative images about themselves. He thinks DSNI's Youth Committee "has changed people's perception of youths, especially [people who] are involved with DSNI...but as far as the [larger] community, it has a long way to go."

The kids, says John, think "'Hold on! We're not that bad! That is not actually what is happening.' [The kids] are fighting a lot of battles they shouldn't be fighting." And many kids aren't even "fighting them because it seems hopeless." There are "a lot of battles out there," John explains. "First you have the battle of trying to survive daily. Then you have the battle of trying to go to school in the city of Boston...School is so bad that even the guidance counselors tell all of my friends, 'Maybe you should go to Roxbury Community College' or 'Maybe you should think of a trade.'" They aren't encouraged to set their sights higher.

John went to St. Patrick's grade school in Roxbury and then to the predominantly White Boston College (B.C.) High School. "I wasn't a bad student at St. Patrick's. I did pretty good work, but I wasn't so much above those other kids that they could not go to B.C. High." John says his eighth grade teacher encouraged him to go to B.C. High. "I guess she said I had potential. She...wanted to put me in the right environment, because she also knew that going through the Boston Public School system probably was not the best thing for me."

When he first got to B.C. High School, John recalls, "I was getting C's and C+'s and everybody was going, 'Oh that's great! You're really doing a good job here.'...What they were [really] saying was, 'For a kid in the inner city this is great!'" John saw that this wasn't the expectation for the White kids in his classes.

John says, "Sometimes I would be categorized as the 'good Negro.' You know. 'He's a good Black kid.'...The kids [who knew] the Black kids at my school would say, 'These are good Black kids, but the other kids in the inner city are real bad. You know, we watch TV, and they kill and stuff like that. We have Black friends, but they're exceptions.'"

The expectation was that "a 'good Negro' would pull a C+ unless he was a genius."

John could have coasted through high school getting C's, but that's not what he or his parents wanted. "My mother would always talk. Even if I got an A, she's nagging…'You are not doing enough reading…You're going out too much.' I don't know. I just set high goals. I think that is the key—to set high goals for yourself…It took me a long time to realize that, so I didn't do as well as I should have in high school. I did all right in my last two years—actually earlier than that. But I should have went in there with the right attitude, the right goals in mind. It really should not have been, 'Well, John, maybe you can make it there.' That is the attitude of most of the youth here. It's like to get over day by day. It is a daily struggle to just get over and live the next day."

John remembers the last quarter of his freshman year as a turning point. He did well enough to be recognized "at an honors award banquet. They called me up for fourth quarter. I was like, 'Wow, Barros!'" He was further motivated when some fellow students questioned his achievement. "When you do good in tests and kids are saying, 'Did you cheat?'…you set out to prove [yourself]."

John says some of the White students "would write in the newspaper that Black kids were there for affirmative action reasons. They would write in the bathrooms, 'Niggers don't belong here. Go back.'…They would say things like, 'My friend, he had good grades, and he didn't get in'—not even knowing our grades, not even knowing what our transcripts even looked like."

By the time John graduated high school, he had been elected to the Student Council, had served as president of the Inter-Racial Awareness Council, had participated in the Community Council and Students Against Drinking and Driving, and had played on the football and basketball teams. He had been chosen as a student representative in the school's hiring of a diversity coordinator and had been involved in recruiting inner city kids to the high school. He also had served as a youth group leader at the combined teen program of St. Patrick's Church and three other Catholic parishes.

John is pained thinking about some kids who went to St. Patrick's with him who should have kept doing well, but drowned in the Boston Public Schools. Asked what he would say to city officials and those who blame the kids more than the school system for their failures, John asserts, "I'm putting the school system in total blame. I'm taking all the blame off the kids. I am saying the school system really…stinks. It's a day care center, where you can put the kids there in the morning. Maybe they won't get in trouble...Then when they graduate you can catch them on a little offense and keep them in jail or something because they are not going anywhere. And they *are not* going anywhere. You've got to look at it. A four-year degree from college is not getting you a job these days. What is a high school degree going to do for you? It's going to do nothing. That is like putting the kid through a four-year wasted high school, and knowingly doing so...I don't think the thing is to send the kids out of [the Boston school system] because you end up sending kids to environments where they are told that they cannot do better, so a lot of kids fall into that trap and they don't do better actually. That is not the solution, going outside of the Boston school system." The solution, he believes, is to improve the public schools.

John was helping other DSNI members and staff with setting up the 1991 DSNI annual meeting and board election when people saw that there weren't enough candidates for the three Cape Verdean seats. "They were saying, 'John, why don't you run?' I thought they were joking." They were serious, telling him, 'It would be great having a youth on the board.'" John agreed. "When I got to the annual meeting, there were a lot of people there. There were some cameras and some lights...I ran under a Cape Verdean seat, but my pitch was more [as] a youth."

John told DSNI members, "'You are going to make a lot of decisions that affect the youth without the youth. You are trying to change the community and you only have half of the community to help you.'...Then I kind of made the promise that I would have more youths there at the next meeting. And there were more youths there, thank God." He had kept his first campaign promise.

The summer he was elected to the board, John worked in the Community Summerfest as a camp counselor and supervisor. The kids, he recalls, "were really excited that there was something in the neighborhood for them to do, actually in the neighborhood...You know, you really get to talk to some of those kids one on one—the young kids. There were some kids that were having some real adult problems...So you would kind of act like a big brother actually, because that is what they were really looking for."

During the Summerfest, youth counselors met weekly to evaluate the project and formed an informal youth committee. John was the oldest counselor. Later, with support from Fidalgo and Everdell, he recruited more older kids and an official DSNI Youth Committee was institutionalized.

Youth Committee members decided to name their group Nubian Roots. Cochair Carline Dorcena recalls, "We didn't just want to be 'DSNI Youth Committee.' It's kind of dull." Committee members thought of lots of different names. One, Carline recalls, was "Crossroads, because of the ethnic groups crossing. We picked Nubian Roots because when you look at it, whether you're Hispanic, whether you're Caucasian, whether you're Irish or Italian or you're Haitian or you're Cape Verdean—it all comes down to Nubian Roots." John explains that by combining the name of Nubia—an ancient African kingdom along the Nile River in what is now Egypt and Sudan—with the term "roots," it would highlight how all people, of all races, "came from the same root." Carline adds, "Either you have Nubian roots or it could be like a personality or an attitude you present—like being proud of yourself…You've got to be proud of yourself so other people could look at you with respect…If they don't respect you, at least *you* know you're doing something positive."

At the June 1992 DSNI annual meeting, Ro Whittington brought John up to the front to thank him for his contributions before he was to leave for college in the fall. John asked all the young people in the room to stand up so the adults could see how many were participating in DSNI.

Earlier, in an article for the St. Patrick's Church newsletter, John wrote: "Contrary to Mass Media portrayal and crime statistics, I believe that the Roxbury and Dorchester area is a great place to live. There are so many good people as residents, doing wonderful things to help their community. I've lived in Roxbury for 17 years, born at Boston City Hospital, and I don't plan on leaving." He wrote of his plans to go to college, concluding: "I am choosing higher education in order to continue on the road I'm on and to be in a better position to provide services which will help my community, parish and family. I hope to make it possible for people in this area to have the same opportunities, advice and assistance that I've had. If my dream and the dream of my friends come true we may help others in the next century to accept the challenges that they will face as a community and overcome them."[59]

"GUILTY OF BEING BLACK"

In May 1992, John Barros almost became a police statistic instead of a college student. John, his brother Casimiro (Caz), who had supervised DSNI's Green Teams, their friend Adilson, who was also on the DSNI Youth Committee, and some other Cape Verdean friends and relatives from the Dudley area—all of them high school or college students and/or job holders—had gone to their friend João's apartment, where they played cards. João* lives in a nearby Boston neighborhood which is predominantly White. It was a weekend night. As John, Caz and Adilson were leaving the apartment to go home after midnight they saw a police car in front of their friend Bob's car. Bob had doubleparked after giving some friends a ride to João's.

As Caz and Adilson went back inside to tell Bob to move his car, John talked to the police officer. The officer was just there about the doubleparked car. No neighbors had complained; there wasn't any loud music or other noise coming from João's. John tells what happened: "I let the cop know that Bob, the owner of the car, was coming out to move it. The cop said, 'He better hurry up and move it.' Then he looked at me and asked if I lived there. I said no. The cop asked where I was from and I said 'Roxbury.' The cop then lifted the cover of his book of tickets where he had already made a ticket for Bob's car. At this time Bob had already reached the car and started to unlock the door. The cop asked Bob where he was from. Bob said 'Dorchester,' and the cop threw the ticket on Bob's windshield and said, 'I want all of you guys to get out of here and go back to where you came from.'

"Then he asked Bob for his license and registration and started yelling, 'Get out of here and go back to where you came from.' After the cop repeated this several times one of the guys ["Miguel"] asked the cop if everyone could go back inside and everything would be all right. Then the cop dragged him out to the street and called backup while he tried to handcuff him."

Miguel remembers saying, "'All right officer, I'll get my friends inside so there will be no problem.' That's when he just grabbed me by my jacket and hit me against the car a few times and shoved me across the sidewalk onto the street. While doing this he said, 'Oh, so

---

* João, Miguel and Tony are pseudonyms. The neighborhood is purposefully left unidentified.

you want to go in' and [said] that he was arresting me. Then I asked, 'What for, what did I do?' The cop threw me on the car and told me to put my hands on the car. I didn't put my hands on the car because I didn't do anything. I told him repeatedly, 'You can't take me in for nothing.' Then another cop came and took me by [the] right arm and twisted it all the way around to my back. I could see my fist over my back. I yelled and said, 'You are going to break my arm,' and the cop said, 'So stop resisting.' They handcuffed me with my right arm twisted behind my back and put on the handcuffs so tight that they cut my wrists. They threw me into the police car and went inside João's apartment. The officer [who] put me in the car came back and ripped the chain off my neck and threw it down my shirt and said, 'Here, this belongs to you.' I said, 'That belongs to my two-year-old son,' and he said he didn't care."

Another friend, "Tony," went outside. Tony "heard Miguel telling the officer he was going inside to call everyone to leave and there was no need for the officer to keep screaming. The officer grabbed him, and Miguel kept asking the cop why he was being arrested. The cop did not even answer, and I told the cop he couldn't do that. The cop continued to shove Miguel around and I got upset and said to Miguel, 'Chill out Miguel, you don't know how easy it is for them to kill you.' After saying this I started heading inside because the cop had asked us to go inside."

Tony turned to see "four to five cops coming straight towards me. I continued to walk into the house and the police officers tried to grab me and I said, 'You can't arrest me, I'm in my friend's property,' but they still kept on charging towards me. Then Adilson tried to get me into the apartment, when one of the cops hit Adilson with a flashlight and repeatedly swung a flashlight at my head. They hit me repeatedly until my friend pulled me all the way into the apartment. João told the police officers that they cannot come into his apartment and arrest anyone. The police officers then tried to grab me [and] ripped my shirt. Then I just let them grab me and they were still hitting me, while I clearly repeated, 'I am not resisting arrest,' but they continued to shove me around. They put me in a head lock and started choking me and I kept saying I was not resisting arrest so there was no need for violence, but they still did not stop. Finally, they brought me outside and handcuffed me. I then told the police officer that the handcuffs were on too tight and he stopped me and made the handcuffs tighter. He then threw me into the paddy wagon without reading my rights."

John Barros saw the cops rush into the apartment. "The police officers hit Tony and Adilson over the head, both of whom were in the hallway of the apartment. Adilson hit the floor after the third hit to his head. Then Tony and Adilson managed to get back into the apartment. The glass on the front door broke when an officer hit it trying to hit Adilson. When the police officers got into the apartment they shoved everyone who was in their way of getting to Tony. One officer said to Tony, 'Your ass is coming with us,' and then grabbed Casimiro, who was already trying to get out of the way, and threw him into another room while saying, 'Get the fuck out of the way.' They dragged Tony out of the apartment hitting him, tore his shirt, and at one point had him in a chokehold."

Police officers, recalls João, "rushed into the apartment with no warning, dragging Tony from the apartment. Tony kept saying, 'I am not resisting an arrest' and the officer had him in a head lock and kept beating him with a long black object that looked like a flashlight. Tony got hit several times on the head as he kept repeating he was not resisting arrest."

João says, "I asked for a warrant. The officer told me, 'You've been watching too much TV, you fucking spick!' He also said, 'You've said enough, you damn 'Rican.' Then he grabbed me and I screamed because I have back pain. He handcuffed me in the hallway. The officer did not read my rights. First they said they were arresting me for disorderly behavior and later at the station they changed it to 'keeper of a disorderly house.' I was searched several times. In the station an officer asked, 'Why were you arrested?' and I asked, 'What do you call it when an officer rushes into your home and arrests you?'"

After the arrests, says John, "the officers started to make everyone leave the apartment. We had no choice, it was either leave or else get arrested." They all left.

Miguel says, "My rights were never read to me, and they never told me why I was being arrested until I got to the station. I was so confused about what the officers did to me because I just wanted to bring my friends into the apartment. I was in a state of shock and scared. Nothing like this has ever happened to me before."

Tony recalls, "After arriving at the police station I was searched several times. I told them that my rights were not read to [me] at the time of the arrest, and [the sergeant] said they don't have to. I also told him that the officers ripped off my shirt. The sergeant said that I did that myself."

Tony says that officers who were at the station, and not at the scene, "were very surprised when I told them I had never been arrested before. An officer then asked me if I was arrested by any other name and I said no. Then the officer said, 'I'm going to search for your records and when I find them you are going to be in big trouble.'"

Tony was taken downtown to be fingerprinted in the continuing search for a record that didn't exist. He was bailed out by friends in the morning; they had been able to bail out João and Miguel earlier.

The other young men think Tony got singled out for the harshest treatment because he has the darkest complexion and was the largest youth there, and the police saw only their stereotypes when they looked at him. Tony remembers a cop saying later in court that he was "intimidating." Tony ended up with a sore back and bruises on his head. After getting out of jail he went to a health clinic for treatment.

Tony had never been arrested before, although, he says, "I've been harassed before—like every other week. Cops stopping you, even in front of your own house. Saying, 'Go home. Get off the street. Get out of here.'"

For John Barros, it was his first time getting harassed by the police. "It was the first time for me actually being in it…I was the first one to try to talk to the cop—to see his reaction and everything…I have seen cops actually get nasty with kids, but I wasn't actually in it…I mean, I heard a lot of stories and things, but to really say, wow, I was there, and that's me, and that made no sense whatsoever…If I were to tell you exactly how it went on people would kind of doubt it. They would say I just added a little salt to it, seasoned it up, you know.

"To actually see my friends get hit right in front of me and stuff was kind of rough. A lot of people question the rappers [but they are] just trying to show the frustration of the youths in the streets…You know that N.W.A. song 'Fuck the police! 911 is a joke.'" John explains, "It gets really scary when you have to worry about gangs, and then you have to worry about cops. Then you are like caught in the corner. That's rough."

Caz's first reaction was to call 911 for help. But who do you call when it's the police beating you up?

John had a lot going through his mind as the incident unfolded. "Like I am going to go in for nothing. There goes Dartmouth, there goes everything, forget it. I've got a record…I might have a bruise, or a broken bone or something. My mother is going to pick me up at the station. I will never have a clean record again. I will be another 'nigger' with a bad record. Of course, I will go to jail. [I won't be able to] defend things like saying, 'Oh yes, we are good youths.'...It would all go down the toilet—everything on that one night. Everything would just go down the toilet.

"Every time I would have to file an application for a job or school, whatever, there would be that one essay that I would have to write as to why I got arrested...'Oh, you're Black? Of course you got arrested.'

On Monday some of the young men came by DSNI to tell the staff what happened. They hadn't all been arrested, but they had all been affected. They were upset, thinking their lives were going to be ruined over nothing—over what should have been a simple parking ticket.

Some wanted to file police harassment complaints. Others were so despondent they didn't want to do anything. John recalls them feeling, "'You can't beat the system.' The cop actually laughed at us when we told them what we were going to do" about challenging the harassment. The officer had good reason to laugh since the Police Department routinely rejects citizen complaints. As the St. Clair Commission on the Boston Police Department reported later to Mayor Flynn, "It appears that the Department seldom, if ever, believes allegations of police misconduct by Boston's citizens."[60]

As she listened to the young men tell their stories, Ros Everdell thought, "These are the choir boys this happened to! We need to take a stand here and now." DSNI staff knew they needed to offer more than empathy. They sure didn't want the young men to end up with criminal records for the unstated "crime" of doubleparking in a predominantly White neighborhood.

DSNI staff called Riley Trustee Bob Holmes to get his recommendation for a good criminal lawyer who might take the cases pro bono. His contacts led them to the firm of Goodwin, Proctor and Hoar. DSNI's concern and help with finding a lawyer made the kids more optimistic, especially those who thought they could do nothing to beat a system stacked against them.

Tony was very upset before DSNI became involved. He had already decided not to use the court-appointed lawyer when he saw him hanging out with the cops and thought he was too friendly with them. Tony doesn't know what he would have done since he couldn't afford a private lawyer. With DSNI helping, he says, "everything was rolling" and he felt better.

In the end, João was charged with being the keeper of a disorderly house. The charge was dropped in court. Miguel was charged with being a disorderly person and received probation. Tony was charged with disorderly conduct, assault and battery on a police officer and malicious destruction of property (the glass door). His charges were continued without a finding while he did six months' probation. They all believe it would have been much worse without a good lawyer.

That fall, John Barros went to Dartmouth College. Tony, Caz and Adilson transferred from Roxbury Community College as planned and continued their education at a private out-of-state university. Miguel, a husband and father, worked full time.

Until the probation period was over, Tony and Miguel worried that the police would seek them out for arrest, giving them permanent records, if not jail time. Tony had a bad scare when a warrant was issued for his arrest for allegedly failing to check in with his probation officer. Tony had called the officer from college and left messages on his answering machine without hearing back. He had the phone bills to show he had called, and his lawyer was able to clear the warrant.[61]

After their probation periods expired, Tony and Miguel were no longer part of the "criminal justice" system. Without the support of DSNI and a good defense attorney, three more Dudley young men might now have permanent police records.

GIVE THE KID A RECORD

John Barros responded quickly when asked if he felt any different now about the oft-cited statistic that one out of four Black men in their twenties is either in jail or prison, on parole or probation: "I understand why they are in jail or on probation. I truly do." When Tony was booked, the police officer asked, "Where are your other records?" He doesn't understand, says John, "why the kid doesn't have any other record. I thought, okay, your mission is to get every Black kid on the street a record...Once you have a record it makes that wall so much bigger. Once you have that record, forget it. Are the cops trying to help you or what are they trying to do? Once you have that record it makes life a lot harder."

The United States imprisons Black males at a rate almost five times higher than South Africa. The United States now has the world's highest overall imprisonment rate.[62] The federal prison population is over half Black and Latino. The state prison population is 35 percent non-Hispanic White, 46 percent Black and 17 percent Latino. The racially biased "War on Drugs" discussed earlier is partly responsible.[63]

It was a study by the Washington-based Sentencing Project that found that in the United States on an average day in 1989 one out of four Black men in their twenties was in prison or jail, on probation or on parole; the comparable figure for Latino males was one in ten and for White males, one in sixteen. Women's rates were much lower, but the racial disproportions were parallel.[64] Other studies found that on an average day in 1991, 42 percent of Black males aged 18-35 living in Washington, D.C. and 56 percent of those living in Baltimore were either in jail or prison, on probation or parole, out on bond awaiting disposition of criminal charges or being sought on an arrest warrant. The great majority of arrests were not for violent crimes. If present policies continue, some three out of four Black males in the nation's capital will be arrested and imprisoned at least once between the ages of 18 and 35.[65]

A couple of weeks before the Dudley young men were roughed up and arrested, the *Boston Globe* ran an article titled, "GUILTY...of being black: Black men say success doesn't save them from being suspected, harassed and detained." The article, which came on the heels of the Los Angeles Rodney King case, began, "They are among Boston's most accomplished citizens. They each have a story to tell about being viewed suspiciously by salespeople, bank clerks or police...The incidents are frighteningly common." For example, Boston Celtics basketball player Dee Brown was forced to the pavement by suburban police with drawn guns who mistook him for a bank robber; never mind that he didn't fit the description and was simply looking through mail with his fiancee outside the Wellesley post office. Ron Homer, chairman of the Boston Bank of Commerce, says he "has been mistaken for a waiter and a doorman and has had trouble cashing checks." Homer, who lives in the wealthy, predominantly White suburb of Lexington, hesitates to shop in neighboring suburbs where suspicious shopkeepers don't know him. Harvard Law School Professor Charles Ogletree says he has "encounters with police almost annually, and they never cease to amaze me. They frequently happen when I am out of uniform—that is, not wearing my suit and tie. They are as innocuous as being pulled over because my car looks suspicious, or being stopped and frisked because I fit the description of someone who is wanted by police."

Ogletree "worries about his son, who dresses in the 'standard uniform of most young black males: high-top sneakers, blue jeans, a baseball cap...It scares the hell out of me when I think that there is little I can do to ensure his safety, because the police don't see him as a person. They see him as a statistic, one they equate with crime.'"[66]

In spring 1989, the Boston Police Department formalized a "search on sight," "stop and frisk" policy against Black and Latino youths ostensibly directed at gang members. A September 1989 Suffolk Superior Court ruling found that the announcement of the policy by Deputy Superintendent William Celester, commander of Area B, which includes Dudley, "was, in effect, a proclamation of martial law in Roxbury for a narrow class of people, young blacks, suspected of membership in a gang or perceived by the police to be in the company of someone thought to be a member." Justice Cortland Mathers said, "I have taken and credit testimony from blacks in the Egleston Square area that they, as individuals and in groups, are forced to open their mouths, placed spread eagle against walls, required to drop their trousers in public places and subjected to underclothing examinations. Deputy Celester stated to a reporter for the *Boston Herald* that his policy has resulted in 'hundreds of searches but few arrests.' The Court finds a tacit understanding exists in the Boston Police Department that constitutionally impermissible searches will not only be countenanced but applauded in the Roxbury area."[67]

Some of the public police strip searches occurred in Dudley. As a report by the Massachusetts State Attorney General's office noted, "A minister reported that in July 1989 while driving down Dudley Street in Roxbury, he observed about 15 male teenagers lined up spread-eagled against a wall, with two plainclothes police officers searching them. One officer was standing near the corner of Dudley Street and Howard Avenue, holding a gun in the air. The other was going down the line frisking each youth in turn, emptying their pockets, then making them drop their pants and undershorts. After about 15 minutes there were 15 bare bottoms displayed on the street. In some instances the officer spread open the person's buttocks. No one was arrested and after the search was completed the officers drove away."[68]

Police misconduct reached new heights in October 1989 when a White furrier from the Boston suburbs named Charles Stuart killed his pregnant wife Carol after a birthing class in the racially mixed Mission Hill neighborhood. He blamed the crime on a Black male assailant, setting off a racist police and media dragnet for the inner city destroyer of the "Camelot couple" from the suburbs. The dragnet yielded a suspect sharing the same first name with Willie Horton, the 1988 presidential election's Black symbol of White fear, and the frame-up didn't end until Charles Stuart committed suicide when his brother finally went to authorities in January 1990. Glen Pierce of Northeastern University's Center of Applied Science calculated that the likelihood of a White woman in Massachusetts being shot to death by a Black man she did not know is one in four million—the same risk she runs of being hit by lightning. Pierce "believes that consciously or unconsciously, reporters used the deaths of Carol Stuart and her unborn child to increase ratings and boost sales...He believes that by misrepresenting the crime problem, reporters are frightening the electorate and driving them to the right," making White voters with exaggerated fears more punitive in their politics and blind to the reality that poor communities and poor people of color are most often the victims of crime.[69]

The State Attorney General's report on the Stuart case and the overall "search on sight" policy concluded that police officers had "engaged in improper, and unconstitutional, conduct." It found the practice of public strip searches "so demeaning and invasive of fundamental precepts of privacy that it can only be condemned in the strongest terms." The report stated, "The communities hardest hit by crime must not be forced to accept the harassment of their young people as the price for aggressive law enforcement. Many of those very same young people are the key to reversing the disturbing trends toward violence. It is hardly an object lesson in respect for the law and for the police to be searched for no other reason than that you are young, black and wearing a baseball cap."[70] Despite the critical reports and court rulings, police discipline has been virtually nonexistent.

The pattern of racial persecution under the guise of prosecution is a national one. Former Los Angeles Police Department Chief Daryl Gates acknowledged, "I think people believe that the only strategy we have is to put a lot of police officers on the street and harass people and make arrests for inconsequential things. Well, that's part of the strategy, no question about it."[71] A study of California, Michigan and Texas found that controlling "for relevant variables influential in sentencing...blacks and Hispanics were more likely to be sentenced to prison, with longer sentences, and less likely to be accorded probation than white felony offenders."[72] Other studies have found that people of color experience overcharges at arrest and disproportionately high bail even for minor offenses, and "detainees are more likely to be indicted, convicted, and sentenced more harshly than released defendants."[73] A hard search for a job becomes an even harder one after you have a criminal record on your life résumé.

A 1990 Department of Justice report observed, "The fact that the legal order not only countenanced but sustained slavery, segregation, and discrimination for most of our Nation's history—and the fact that the police were bound to uphold that order—set a pattern for police behavior and attitudes toward minority communities that has persisted until the present day. That pattern includes the idea that minorities have fewer civil rights, that the task of the police is to keep them under control, and that the police have little responsibility for protecting them from crime within their communities."[74]

In an editorial shortly after the Los Angeles riots, the *New York Times* quoted a 1990 report by the Correctional Association of New York and the New York State Coalition for Criminal Justice: "It is no accident that our correctional facilities are filled with African-American and Latino youths out of all proportion...Prisons are now the last stop along a continuum of injustice for these youths that literally starts before birth." The *Times* observes, "It costs about $25,000 a year to keep a kid in prison [not counting the enormous cost of prison construction]. That's more than the Job Corps, or college." The *Times* concludes, "There's nothing inherently criminal in young black men of the 1990's any more than there was in young immigrant men of the 1890's. What is criminal is to write them off, fearfully, blind to the knowledge that thousands can be saved, from lives of crime and for lives of dignity."[75]

DSNI activist Najwa Abdul-Tawwab asserts, "A lot of people are afraid to stop and talk to teenagers. But we can't afford that attitude. Too many of the boys—12, 13 and 14 years old—walk around with their hands in their hip pockets, as if they have no destiny. We're the ones who have to tell them they have a destiny."[76]

DSNI wants to ensure that all kids have fair opportunities to succeed and that second chances aren't just a privilege of the more affluent. DSNI knows that the neighborhood's destiny will greatly reflect its children's destinies. It will reflect their opportunities—and disadvantages. Their successes—and failures. Their dreams—and nightmares. DSNI is about seeing kids as the future, not the enemy.

"UNITED WE STAND, DIVIDED WE FALL"

On a sunny September day in 1993, DSNI had something special to celebrate at its annual multicultural community festival—a beautiful mural created by the Youth Committee on the side of Davey's market on Dudley Street. The mural's theme is "Unity Through Diversity." It was designed principally by John Barros using images brainstormed in Youth Committee sessions, coordinated by Adilson Cardoso and painted by many youths with the help of a professional artist.

There are many familiar faces in the mural, among them neighborhood elders Sophia McCarthy and Mildred Daniels, Ché Madyun performing dance, Youth Committee members and younger neighborhood children. There's a tribute to the late Celtics basketball captain Reggie Lewis, a hero for his support of inner city youth. There's a flourishing tree with "Nubian roots." In front of the mural is a rock garden where people can sit on colorfully painted boulders taken from the site of DSNI's first housing.

The Youth Committee will need to keep rejuvenating itself with new members. Cochair Carline Dorcena has been working to keep the committee strong with younger leaders such as Jason Webb and Patricia Felix. Carline's older sister Linda and brother William were founding Youth Committee members along with John and Caz Barros and other Dudley young people now working or away at college. Many of them assist the Youth Committee's efforts when they can.

Carline has the confidence and charisma of someone older than a high school student. She intends to "apply to Harvard and see if I could get in. If I do, great. If I don't, there's always other institutions. I hopefully want to be something to do with psychology mixed with business. But definitely, whatever I am—be it a lawyer, an educator, a philosopher or a corporate psychologist and international businesswoman—I want to come back to the community."

Carline thinks DSNI has "made a great impact…I think it gives the community a voice—the voice of the community." DSNI, she says, shows "that if you work together you could get things accomplished. 'United we stand, divided we fall.'…You've got to come back and invest in your own community and also communities around. You've got to start at home. You've got to love yourself before you could love someone else. Right? Because that way, you know that you have your positive self-esteem. You know who you are and you respect yourself; therefore, other people could respect you and you could respect other people. That's kind of how our community is. You have to be proud of your community. Like the Dudley PRIDE slogan. You've got to take pride in it, do whatever you can to help renovate it and then when you know how nice your community is—not only externally but internally, like the attitudes and people working together, the leadership quality, the initiatives—that's when you can go out and be like, 'I'm from Dudley and I want to help you.' People could actually look at you and say, 'I respect you because you're from Dudley and I know you're trying to do something.'"

Carline and the other youth activists personify DSNI's can-do spirit of self-esteem without selfishness and mutual progress with mutual respect. Sharing an idea she first heard from Gus Newport, Carline says: "The seed you plant in the first day of spring—it's going to grow and keep on growing." That's how she sees DSNI and the Youth Committee—planting seeds that will "keep on growing."

DSNI Youth Committee founders in front of the mural, August 1993. Front: Adilson Cardoso and Madueno Baptista Jr. Standing (l to r): Alex Gonçalves, Ed Carvalho, Gertrudes Fidalgo (staff), William Dorcena, Jason Webb, Linda Dorcena, Casimiro Barros Jr., Joseph "Nino" Delar, John Barros, Hamilton Rodrigues.
Inset: Carline Dorcena.

Dudley's Young Architects and Planners. Older teen group design presented by Gevel Marrero, front left. Clockwise behind Gevel are Ed Carvalho, Andy Carvalho Jr., Debka Colson (facilitator), Gilda Teixeira, Nate Ruffin and Miguel Fernandes.

Mary Hannon Park Summer Youth Program celebration, July 1992. Across the street from Cottage Brook Apartments.

9

PATHFINDERS

In April 1992, dispossessed Los Angeles burned in rage. Embers of anger and despair flared up the coast in San Francisco, Oakland and Seattle and across the country in Las Vegas and Atlanta. A few weeks earlier, the Dudley community had come together in celebration. L.A. exploded with the crushed dreams of inner city America. Dudley surged with the power and pride of dreams unfolding. As DSNI President Ché Madyun put it in the 1992 DSNI annual report, "Hope is the great ally of organizing."

The riots were a multiracial explosion of rage against past injustice and "a perception of a future already looted."[1] South Central L.A. Congresswoman Maxine Waters told a Senate committee, "The verdict in the Rodney King case...was only the most recent injustice—piled upon many other injustices...I have seen our community continually and systematically ravaged—ravaged by banks who would not lend to us, ravaged by governments which abandoned us or punished us for our poverty, and ravaged by big business who exported our jobs."[2]

Waters quoted Robert Kennedy's words from 1968: "There is another kind of violence in America, slower but just as deadly, destructive as the shot or bomb in the night...This is the violence of institutions; indifference and inaction and slow decay. This is the violence that afflicts the poor, that poisons relations between men and women because their skin is different colors. This is the slow destruction of a child by hunger, and schools without books and homes without heat in the winter." Waters added, "What a tragedy it is that America has still...not learned such an important lesson."[3]

As in South Central Los Angeles, the residents of Dudley have suffered exploitation and exclusion. Their community has been used as a dumping ground for the waste of wealthier neighborhoods and starved of jobs and government services. They saw downtown Boston undergo an economic boom while Dudley continued to go bust. They have borne the burden of redlining while their tax dollars are used to bail out Savings and Loan spendthrifts. They have endured cops with a colonial mentality.

"Riots are the voices of the unheard," said Martin Luther King. Dudley's pathfinders found a way to be heard. The city found a way to listen.

DSNI board member Stephen Hanley remarks, "The people in this community know even when there were good times [in Boston], they were shafted. So while things are bad right now, at least they're on the right track."

On April 3, 1992, over 800 people filled the historic Strand Theatre in Uphams Corner to celebrate DSNI's accomplishments and thank the outgoing executive director, Gus Newport. Youth leader John Barros drew the portrait of Newport that graced the program booklet. Newport's old friend, actor Danny Glover, was the master of ceremonies. Hundreds of Dudley residents were joined by community activists from other neighborhoods, funders, politicians, the mayor and various city officials, businesspeople and others of many different backgrounds committed to seeing Dudley's rebirth.

There was a short video history of Dudley and DSNI—part of a longer film in progress by Leah Mahan and Mark Lipman. The video clip of Gus Newport rapping with kids from Dudley's Young Architects and Planners—Heavy G and the Young APs—brought the house down. Everyone shared a multiethnic meal prepared by Dudley residents and enjoyed performances by local dancers, actors, singers and musicians— among them Ché Madyun, who performed an original solo dance, and DNI Director Paul Yelder in his persona of blues singer Luap Redley. Newell Flather presented Newport with a framed piece of the Riley Foundation's rug, which Newport had frequently trod. It was a symbolic bridge between Dudley's past—the disinvestment represented by the old worn rug at La Alianza Hispana—and the more constructive, contemporary relationship between Dudley and downtown.

REBUILD DUDLEY AND L.A.

When Boston city official Lisa Chapnick was asked if she had thought of DSNI at the time of the L.A. riots, she responded quickly, "I certainly did. I said, 'If there were more DSNIs, L.A. wouldn't have happened.'" Chapnick continues, "I think DSNI is the future of our country. I think the challenge is, how do you replicate it?...How do you find residents who have hope and heart when they should be bitter?" The riot, she says, "was a wake-up call that's long overdue. Of course, it looks like nothing is going to happen with it."

The embers of disrespect, discrimination and disinvestment still smolder in cities around the country. Rebuild L.A., launched after the riots with much fanfare and promises of inclusion and "greenlining," has not delivered in process or product. Rebuild L.A.'s first director, Peter Ueberroth—impresario of the commercialized 1984 Olympics and chairman of the California Council on Competitiveness, which advocated rolling back environmental and land use regulations—represented "corporatism dressed up in the language of cooperation," says Eric Mann, director of the Labor/Community Strategy Center in Los Angeles. Power on the Rebuild L.A. (R.L.A.) board "is firmly in the hands of representatives of Arco, I.B.M., Warner Brothers, Southern California Edison, U.S.C., Disney and the Chamber of Commerce."

In July 1992, says Mann, "Ueberroth cheered when General Motors announced that it would channel $15 million in contracts from its Hughes Aircraft subsidiary to inner-city suppliers. The move, which would generate a few hundred jobs at most, was hyped by R.L.A. as corporate benevolence in action. One month later G.M. shut down the Van Nuys automobile assembly plant, its last in L.A., eliminating 3,000 workers, about two-thirds of whom are Latino and black." At a job training conference sponsored by Toyota and the Urban League in fall 1992, "Ueberroth hailed *minimum*-wage jobs as bringing 'dignity to those who labor in them.' Workers from Justice for Janitors, a campaign of the Service Employees International Union, marched on R.L.A. shortly after to tell him that for hundreds of thousands of Angelenos who already have full-time jobs, the minimum wage means living below the federal poverty line, usually without health insurance or job security."[4]

"'Nothing, nothing at all has been learned from the riots,' says María Elena Durazo, leader of the mostly Latino Hotel and Restaurant Employees Local 11....Since the riots the business community has been pushing the city and the state to roll back environmental, tax, and workers' compensation regulations. 'What it means is that they want to squeeze even more out of a vulnerable work force.' Durazo adds, 'Don't they see they are creating more of the very same conditions that led to the riots?'"[5]

In the words of author Mike Davis, California "Governor Wilson and the state legislature in Sacramento figuratively burned down the city a second time with billions of dollars of school and public-sector cutbacks." Legislators ignored "a report on the state's children that showed youth unemployment and homicide rates soaring in tandem."[6]

In January 1994, on the day the nation celebrates Martin Luther King's birthday, Los Angeles shook and burned from the force of a catastrophic earthquake. Angelenos must now rebuild from riots sparked by repression and economic depression, nature's earthquake and the fires in between. Pacific News Service editor Rubén Martínez contemplated how, in the Latino immigrant *barrios,* the solidarity Angelenos showed each other in responding to the earthquake "is the survival mechanism of daily life." Martínez looked beyond one of the poignant events shown widely on television: the rescue of Salvador Peña, an immigrant from El Salvador, from "the pancaked parking lot of the Northridge Fashion Mall" where he was driving a street sweeper. "An army of hundreds of thousands of Salvador Peñas toils from dusk to dawn in L.A., cleaning office buildings, preparing meals for the white collars. They do so because without work there is no future, and without a future there is no hope."

"Yes, this rescue assured us, good will can guide us through tragedy," Martínez observes. But the economic, racial and ethnic fault lines that divide Angelenos remain.[7] Looking to the future, the question is, will Los Angeles rebuild together—or apart and volatile? That's a question many others around the country can ask of their communities and their nation.

"TOGETHER, WE'LL FIND THE WAY"

While he was directing Rebuild L.A., Peter Ueberroth said that many businesses gutted in the riot were "not of any great, huge value." He said that local activists demanding a faster flow of money should "get out of the way."[8]

In Dudley, residents successfully got "in the way" of both a city redevelopment plan that threatened to displace them and an agency/funder-driven coalition to rebuild the neighborhood. Dudley residents got in the way—and created a new way forward. As DSNI board member Paul Bothwell affirms, "Together, we'll find the way."

Bothwell offers three lessons he finds true to Dudley as it rebuilds and true to his own "re-membering" after the accident described in the Introduction. First, "the heart is far more important than the head. Lots of efforts are head efforts. Lots of things have money and expertise, they have this and that and everything else, but they don't have any heart. Anybody on the street can read that. If there isn't a heart to it, then the head doesn't even matter."

Second, says Bothwell, "being is really more important than doing. What something *is*, is more important even than what it can do. What you are or what I am—what's going on in the nature of heart, spirit, personhood and all that—that, in the end, is all we have. In the end…if we're crippled and broken by accident or anything else, what does that mean? That you're not worth something anymore? There's nothing here anymore? Of course not. Being is far more important than doing." Bothwell adds, "People don't trust DSNI just because it can do something. That's a big factor—because nobody else has been able to do anything. [But] I think people trust DSNI…because of what it is…People see themselves reflected here."

Third, says Bothwell, "doing together, living together is far more important than doing alone. I think that reflects that proverb I gave earlier: 'Together, we'll find the way.' You try to do that alone—we're all so broken, we're all so crippled, we're all so fragile, we're all so partial, and I'm talking about organizations as well as people and communities. You try to do it alone, it's not going to go anywhere."

Bothwell's lessons speak directly to DSNI's essence. The heart is more important than the head: DSNI's efforts are not guided by professional "experts" or leaders with swelled heads. Rather, DSNI is guided by those at the heart of the neighborhood—the residents—who are, in turn, guided by their hearts, hopes, dreams, knowledge and experiences. Being is more important than doing: DSNI emphasizes process before product, knowing that in the long run the products will be more and better if the process is empowering. DSNI's way of being is rooted in diversity and unity, self-esteem and comm*unity* pride. Doing together is more important than doing alone: Dudley residents have shown that together they are powerful visionaries and together they can make their vision and plans for the neighborhood more real every day.

"We work as a team here," says Ché Madyun. "It's not like any one person just does something...It's not me leading anything. It's us working together." Sue Beaton, a longtime board member who became DSNI's deputy director, comments, "We're a humble group, a motley group. No grandstanders, really...That was probably the most refreshing piece of it to me—that there wasn't the political grandstanding and the turf issues that exist all over...[where] people are more into sometimes the ego development than they are into the community development." She remembers "going to [DSNI] meetings and just seeing residents—you know, my next-door neighbor kind of thing—participating and growing in their own belief that maybe if we hang in there together...and learn together...we can maybe make some difference."

"It was good to feel things happen," Madyun says. "The community was getting better and you're meeting new people...People listen to you and hear what you have to say and share ideas. It was wonderful...People worked like a family, you know."

DSNI Human Development Director Andrea Nagel recalls that when she was doing interviews for her masters thesis, the word family "really began to ring in my ears" when people talked about DSNI. "There is a sense that this is a growing relationship and the mistrust has subsided," she says. "It's refreshing," remarks Arnaldo Solís, who has served on DSNI's board and committees. "We sit there and argue sometimes, but yet when we come out—'So how's things?' and 'What are you doing tomorrow?' And we're hugging, and it's nice."

Gus Newport was struck when he first came to Boston by the polarization among people he found there. "DSNI is different," he says. There, "people work in mutual respect. DSNI is like a family and that is its strength. Everybody complemented one another. DSNI created an equal playing field. That's the way society should be built."

DSNI is an extending family. By fall 1993, the membership included over 1,800 voting members (neighborhood residents, agencies, businesses, religious institutions) plus another 2,200 nonvoting supporters from outside DSNI's core and secondary boundaries. Most voting members to date come from the core area where DSNI has done its most sustained organizing.[9] About 130 residents work extensively on DSNI's many committees. Hundreds more residents, young and old, participate regularly in annual meetings, neighborhood cleanups, community meetings, planning workshops, demonstrations, multicultural festivals and other activities. Organizer Gertrudes Fidalgo points out that many DSNI members work two jobs to make a living for themselves and their families. "We do most of our meetings during the night shift," she says. When DSNI does daytime and weekend events, "we see people that we don't see during the nighttime." The membership is still growing steadily.

FROM DUMPING GROUND TO BREAKING GROUND

DSNI rang in the new year 1993 with a party and a press conference. "We have a very, very special announcement," Ché Madyun exalted. "We have finally made it. We worked hard to get to this point. We've had to wait a long time. For those of you who thought that we weren't going to make it, I'm here to tell you, we are here! For those of you who thought, 'Well, maybe we're going to make it,' I want you to know, we are here! Those of you that said, 'They ain't going to make it,' *we are here!*"

After nine years of organizing, envisioning, planning, designing, financing and partnering, DSNI was ready to add a new chapter to its story of community rebirth. Madyun announced that DSNI would soon break ground for the first new homes to be built on the land in the community trust—the land where DSNI had taken a stand.

The groundbreaking is a "symbolic breakthrough," says Sue Beaton. "So many people, situations, processes, bureaucracies, hurdles have been lived through, and somehow it's like a phoenix rising from the ashes...We never gave up...I think we're all proud of ourselves."

DSNI broke ground on the first day of spring 1993. Over 400 people came to make "A Stake in the Neighborhood" at the groundbreaking and at the community brunch that followed. Sunny skies and sunnier smiles warmed people as they mingled amid the burnt-out lots of Dennis Street where snow still lingered from the Blizzard of '93. Balloons made the gathering visible from afar. The youth organizations City Year and YouthBuild constructed a picket fence on the site, where DSNI hung placards thanking people, organizations, foundations, banks and businesses who had made a financial stake in the neighborhood. Gus Newport and Lisa Chapnick, who was then Commissioner of Inspectional Services, helped lead the fundraising effort. DAC planners Stephen Plumer and David Nesbitt came back to share in celebrating the fruition of plans to which they had contributed six years earlier. Among those crowding the event were politicians hoping to succeed Ray Flynn as mayor. President Clinton had just selected Mayor Flynn as the U.S. ambassador to the Vatican. DSNI made sure the would-be mayors knew the importance Dudley residents would place on their attendance. Then City Council President Tom Menino, now mayor of Boston, was there.

A *Boston Globe* article on the event told how Lorraine Smith, a resident for over 40 years who was interested in purchasing one of the new homes, "could only point to her throat to convey her emotions. 'I keep trying to explain to people how I feel,' she said. 'I get this big old lump in here.'" DSNI Director Ro Whittington was quoted in the same article stressing the importance of city financial support for the project and pointing to continued problems in accessing bank financing. "'Because they don't want to live here, they don't think anyone else wants to live here,' Whittington said. 'But we have 400 people on a waiting list.'"[10]

Among those wearing the traditional hard hats and wielding the shovels that day were residents who had helped create the community path to the groundbreaking. There was Alex Johnson, a nurturer of gardens, elderly housing and community spirit. There was Sophia McCarthy, a resident since the 1920s, who always believed that "the squeaky wheel gets the grease." There was Clayton Turnbull, an entrepreneur and longtime resident, who helped make sure that the power of eminent domain would truly serve the community. There was Gino Teixeira, whose Ideal Sub Shop nourishes people living and working in Dudley and who is working with DSNI for community economic development. There was Arnaldo Solís, a longtime voice for human development and agency collaboration. And there was Ché Madyun, who stood up at the very first DSNI community meeting to challenge the facilitators to practice the community control they preached—and helped change the course of Dudley history.

In November 1993, DSNI members, staff and supporters gathered again at the groundbreaking site, this time to cut the ribbon on DSNI's first completed homes and welcome the families who would shortly be moving in. Ché Madyun also took a moment to recognize someone in the crowd who had played a pivotal role in making meaningful the word "neighborhood" in DSNI's name: former DSNI Cochair Fadilah Muhammad.

"A VISION WITH A TASK"

Before the groundbreaking, DSNI asked members, staff and supporters, "What does this groundbreaking mean to you?" and published many of the responses in the program for the event. Sister Margaret Leonard, director of Project Hope, observed, "It is best captured in a favorite quote: 'A vision without a task is but a dream. A task without a vision is a drudgery. But a vision with a task can change the world.' These small sometimes 'mustard seed' revelations speak to this truth: we, a community from diverse races, cultures, traditions, nations, bonded together as brothers and sisters with a mission, can begin to change the world. That is what this means to me!"

The Dudley Street neighborhood has changed in many tangible ways since 1984—though people who view Dudley through their car windows may still "see" it as a poor neighborhood with an abundance of vacant lots. Beginning with the "Don't Dump on Us" campaign, DSNI cleaned up the vacant lots and abandoned cars, closed down illegal trash transfer stations and brought fresh air—literally and figuratively—to the neighborhood. There are new and revitalized neighborhood associations and gardens, a renewed neighborhood park, growing summer camp and strengthened youth programs. There are new stop lights, better mass transit, a human services Agency Collaborative and a scholarship program. There are new and refurbished homes completed by DSNI, Project Hope, Dorchester Bay Economic Development Corporation and Nuestra Comunidad Development Corporation. There is a beautiful mural on Dudley Street celebrating community unity and diversity. Over the next couple years, there will be many more new and rehabilitated houses and apartments, a town common, new playgrounds and a community center where people of all ages will be able to study, play, meet and perform. The Dudley neighborhood has come a long way since Ché Madyun lamented, "Everything was over there, over there, over there. There was nothing ever in here."

Even more significantly, the neighborhood has changed most in intangible ways since 1984. Where there was once despair, there is hope. Where there was once isolation and fragmentation, there is strong neighborhood identity. Where there was once powerlessness, there is community control. Where there was once that "perception of a future already looted," there is a vision and plan of action. There is Dudley pride.

DSNI offers a rich variety of lessons for all those struggling to find the answers to community development and empowerment. DSNI has an enormous amount of work yet to do, many challenges to overcome. DSNI doesn't have all the answers for itself, much less for others. It offers more a process than a model. Indeed, a key lesson from DSNI's experience is that the right model for any community can only emerge from a community process. It cannot and should not be imported or imposed. Still, the DSNI experience raises many issues crucial to neighborhood activists, organizers, funders and policymakers committed to community revitalization.

BUILDING ON NEIGHBORHOOD ASSETS

Community development must begin by recognizing and reinforcing the resources *within* the community. DSNI assumes and demonstrates that people in low-income neighborhoods—like people in all neighborhoods—have solutions as well as problems. Like people of every income level, they have individual and community assets—a mix of skills, talents, knowledge, experience and resources—that are vital elements of the redevelopment process.

As John McKnight, director of the Center for Urban Affairs and Policy Research at Northwestern University, puts it, "No community is built with a focus on deficiencies and needs. Every community, forever in the past and forever in the future, will be built on the capacities and gifts of the people who live there."[11]

Andrea Nagel, who first served DSNI as an organizer and later as Human Development director, underscores the capacity-building approach. DSNI, she says, is continually "exposing, strengthening and building upon the gifts that this neighborhood has—its people, its vacant land, its businesses…The glass is half full to us, you know. We make an effort to look through the positive lens—understanding, not denying the reality, not minimizing or understating what hardships and difficult realities that people face in this neighborhood. But never, ever losing sight of what is often written off and completely overlooked, and that is its people and resources."

Low-income neighborhoods are often viewed as dependent receivers of services and dollars—ignoring the vast resources they export in the form of taxes; underpaid labor; bank savings invested in communities that have not been redlined; exorbitant interest and insurance payments; work and purchases at businesses located outside the neighborhood; volunteering in and donating to nonprofit, religious and civic organizations; and so on.

Government, private foundations and human service agencies often demean low-income residents, viewing them as incapable, culpable, "at risk," dependent clients—clients they treat as second-class citizens or worse. Many policymakers, funders and human service "providers" have fostered atomized communities that no longer recognize their own assets, their own vision, their own power. They are, in McKnight's words, "dominated by systems that have institutionalized degraded visions for devalued people."[12]

Many human service agencies felt threatened by DSNI's resident-controlled agenda. McKnight predicts that this conflict will always arise: "Service systems act on the premise that the professional has the expertise and the client has the problem. The problem solving power of the people in the neighborhoods is unimportant. That professional idea is exactly the opposite of what community organizing attempts to do. The organizer tells the people that they have problem solving abilities and they can change their communities."[13]

DSNI has worked hard to build an Agency Collaborative to strengthen agency accountability to residents, minimize competition, maximize cooperation and improve human development resources and policies. Funders, as emphasized later, can play an important role by encouraging collaboration and respecting the priorities of a resident-driven collaborative process—priorities which may well differ from funders' preconceived ideas.

The community of residents as a whole brings invaluable assets to the redevelopment process. Residents have experienced the history of the neighborhood. They have been the ones to stay and struggle as the neighborhood was being disinvested in, or made a new stake where others would not. Only residents working together can create a self-determined vision of the neighborhood's future. Only residents can foster the political will necessary to make the vision a reality. After years of being disrespected, dismissed and discriminated against, residents may not always realize they have these capacities. Through organizing together, they reveal and reinforce their individual and collective assets.

In the words of DSNI activist Najwa Abdul-Tawwab, what's "key about DSNI is the word 'initiative.' It works to help people initiate."

NURTURING DIVERSITY, UNITY AND NEIGHBORHOOD LEADERSHIP

"Most nonprofits are based in communities, and are not community-based. Those are two different things," says Bill Slotnik, director of the Community Training and Assistance Center (CTAC), which works with DSNI and other groups around the country. Slotnik describes DSNI as "the broadest-based effort in the United States to turn an urban neighborhood around under community control."

The Dudley Street initiative's commitment to community power was put to the test early by neighborhood residents refusing to confuse resident participation with resident control. The initial convenors of DSNI—nonprofit agencies and the Riley Foundation—learned, beginning with the first, heated community meeting, that residents must not only be included in the process; they must be in the forefront of any revitalization effort if it is to succeed. This is a lesson that existing community development initiatives should learn and new initiatives should not have to relearn.

Residents such as Ché Madyun and Fadilah Muhammad, who had objected to DSNI's initial process, reshaped the organization and became leaders. Since then, DSNI has continued to demonstrate openness and inclusion by inviting skeptics and critics into the process. Vice President Clayton Turnbull, for example, was someone who put DSNI's openness and flexibility to the test and found that it was real.

Inclusion must be built into both the structure and the process. DSNI was restructured after its first community meeting to ensure resident control and maximum participation from a diversity of residents, agencies, businesses, religious institutions and others. Residents were given the majority of seats on the elected board. An equal, minimum number of seats—a floor, not a ceiling—are reserved for each of the neighborhood's major ethnic groups. Gus Newport calls that "one of the master strokes...Because that [meant] they were going to collectively focus on the issues, rather than each other."

DSNI emphasizes "unity through diversity." DSNI's diversity is evident in its embrace of people of all races, ethnicities, ages, religions, political views and so on. Members, staff and supporters cross the political spectrum—from conservative to left. There are Muslims and Jews and Catholics and Baptists and Protestant Evangelicals. An elderly Irish American woman named Sophia McCarthy and an elderly African

American woman named Mildred Daniels are prominently featured in the mural created by a multiracial group of teenagers.

DSNI asks, "What can you do for your community?" *and* "What can your community do for you?" In forging consensus, DSNI tries to have everybody's interests placed on the table up front—rather than being hidden and coming out later in a disruptive fashion. DSNI does not ask everyone to subordinate their personal interests to an abstract larger good or settle for lowest common denominator demands. It challenges people to forge consensus by maximizing everybody's stakes, not minimizing them.

Being inclusive can make building consensus more difficult. But it is precisely that consensus that underpins the neighborhood's power. By speaking in one voice—the harmony of many voices—the neighborhood demands that it be listened to.

Though DSNI's bylaws spelled out inclusion, structure does not always ensure substance. True inclusive participation does not just mean large numbers turning out to meetings. As Slotnik says, you can set up a structure that's representative and "still have basically one or two people running the show. There are a lot of organizations who do that. Just having everybody at the table isn't enough." They have to be fully involved. And it's important "to make sure you're always looking to bring more people to the table."

DSNI has always looked to bring new people to the table and develop new leadership. Many of DSNI's leaders were not previously in leadership positions in the community or outside. Many are people whose leadership abilities were first noticed and nurtured within DSNI. Every community has potential leaders yet unknown. No community organization need think of leadership ability as a rare gift. Leadership operates at many levels—formal and informal—and is continually arising and evolving.

DSNI's leadership has changed and grown significantly over the years. While some people have won repeated reelection to the board, there has also been healthy turnover. With a strong commitment to membership education and leadership development, DSNI has been able to benefit from a changing mix of long-term leaders and new leaders. The first two presidents, Nelson Merced and Melvyn Colón, were agency directors who worked, but did not live, in the neighborhood. Resident Ché Madyun has served as president since 1987. Other elected leadership positions—vice president, treasurer, clerk—have changed numerous times; resident Clayton Turnbull has served as vice president since 1989. Some of DSNI's most inspiring activists have never run for the board—choosing to make their contribution as committee leaders, for example. Najwa Abdul-Tawwab, the past chair of the Human Development Committee, is a case in point.

The DSNI staff has experienced significant turnover, with over 30 different employees since 1986, not including numerous interns. Ro Whittington is DSNI's third executive director. How could an organization with that much turnover provide enough continuity? Some staff have been with DSNI for many years, such as Andrea Nagel, Ros Everdell and Gertrudes Fidalgo. Some former staff, such as the past executive directors and former Development Director David Rockwell, provide continued support. The key answer, however, is that, unlike many groups, DSNI has remained a resident-controlled organization. Professional staff are important players in accomplishing DSNI goals, but the staff works closely with and is accountable to the resident-led board and committees.

In recent years, three longtime board members—Paul Yelder, Ro Whittington and Sue Beaton—were hired as senior staff. These transitions helped foster a strong sense of continuity and empowerment within the organization. They also raised a new challenge: how to maintain a clear line between the roles of the board and the staff. As board members, Yelder, Whittington and Beaton were elected leaders, responsible for setting and carrying out DSNI's agenda and acting as spokespeople for the organization. As staff, their role is to advise and implement the agenda set by the board on which they once sat and to which they are now accountable. They have to act assertively in promoting DSNI's agenda to city officials and funders, for example. But board members are DSNI's primary representatives to the Dudley neighborhood and the larger public.

THE IMPORTANCE OF YOUTH

DSNI is an intergenerational organization, embracing youngsters and adults—children, parents and grandparents. Board members range in age from 17 to well over 70. While elders have always played a leadership role in DSNI and young people have long been involved, DSNI has learned to place an increasing emphasis on youth participation and leadership.

Early on, numerous children and teenagers participated in DSNI activities, such as neighborhood cleanups, and an ad hoc youth committee worked with staff to organize youth activities and try to strengthen youth programs in Dudley. Youth leadership, however, was not a priority. Over the years, young people have increasingly become visionaries, architects and planners of DSNI programs and Dudley's future. In 1991, DSNI institutionalized an official Youth Committee and elected its first youth, John Barros, to the board. Carline Dorcena joined the DSNI board in 1993. Youth leaders such as John and Carline, Caz Barros, Jason Webb, Patricia Felix and Adilson Cardoso are truly inspirational.

Youth leadership not only enables DSNI to better serve the needs of young people, it encourages youth to better serve their community. DSNI is one of the all-too-rare places in this divided nation where youth of all races are esteemed, and thus their respect for themselves and their community can grow. It offers young people a chance to develop and exercise leadership skills—the kind of caring, respectful, open-minded leadership so needed in the larger world.

DSNI represents a future with more opportunity for Dudley youth. And the youth represent not only Dudley's future, but the nation's.

ORGANIZE, ORGANIZE, ORGANIZE

Organizing is the renewable energy that powers DSNI's human, economic and physical development. The most important resources of any neighborhood are the people who live there. To maximize that resource, successful community revitalization must have at its core an organizing agenda with the goal of involving all parts of the community in the comprehensive redevelopment of the neighborhood.

For decades, community development has largely meant the delivery of services and the building of structures, not organizing. Some of the War on Poverty's Community Action Programs of the 1960s did involve organizing and, in the words of one historian, "those few communities that stressed nonviolent mobilization and community organizing got more results in terms of institutional reform and better services than those who focused just on services." However, by 1966, most Community Action Programs practiced "traditional client-bureaucratic forms of service provision and accommodation to political and bureaucratic elites"—elites who were opposed to the mobilization and leadership of poor people in their Model Cities.[14]

In 1966, the community development movement took a significant turn when, after touring the Bedford-Stuyvesant neighborhood of

Brooklyn, New York, Senator Robert Kennedy cosponsored federal legislation to amend the Economic Opportunities Act—the core of the War on Poverty—to provide government support for community development corporations. By the late 1980s, several thousand CDCs were operating around the country, responsible for the construction and rehabilitation of well over 100,000 units of housing and hundreds of economic development projects.[15] The problem is that in most neighborhoods where CDCs operate, new buildings go up, but for community residents the old obstacles to essential resources, jobs and services remain.

Most CDCs, like government and business planners, have focused on the product, such as affordable housing, and not the process of making development resident-driven and comprehensive. They are "based in communities," but they are not "community-based."

Community development consultant Bill Traynor—who formerly directed the Coalition for a Better Acre, an unusual CDC discussed below—writes:

> If the primary success story of the past 25 years has been the development of a legitimate, skilled nonprofit sector with the capacity to create and preserve housing, jobs and businesses, the major failure has been the dominance of a narrowly focused—technical—production-related model of community development, which is estranged from strong neighborhood control and which does not impact many of the issues affecting poor neighborhoods.
>
> This model is recreating the same dependent, service delivery/client relationship that has dominated the lives of poor inner-city residents for more than two generations. Often times it acts as little more than a delivery system for projects with a marginal impact on neighborhoods, projects defined by funders and lenders rather than by community residents. The model has confused the building of power with the building of structures.[16]

When unaccompanied by large-scale organizing and inclusive action, physical development is a technical process that excludes. It is a disempowering tool. Community development in the truest sense is only possible when the community is organized to control development. Few CDCs have engaged in this broader approach to community development. Blending the realities of housing development—cost effectiveness, technical expertise and cooperative deal-making—with the requirements of successful organizing—inclusiveness, great independence in thought and action—has proved a daunting challenge for many a neighborhood. Yet it is a challenge that must be met.

In her urban planning masters thesis, Ricanne Hadrian examines two organizations that have successfully combined organizing and development: Coalition for a Better Acre in Lowell, Massachusetts and East Brooklyn Churches in New York. Unlike DSNI, both organizations regularly act as developers. Like DSNI, they found that the product-oriented approach of development can coexist with the process-oriented approach of organizing when organizing is seen as the guiding force that creates the development opportunities. They "have always been clear about their missions; the roles of organizing and housing development are in tandem, with organizing the primary goal."[17]

If community development is to succeed, the organizing agenda must guide the development agenda. It is the organizing activity that excites residents enough to get involved and provides the organization the strength to move its development agenda forward. It is through organizing that residents exercise leadership, achieve immediate goals, forge a comprehensive, long-term vision and translate that vision into reality.

It is through *organizing* that the organization exhibits momentum, rather than inertia. It is through organizing that residents can resist pressure to accommodate their vision to political and bureaucratic elites.

At DSNI, the commitment to organizing was regularly reiterated by the board and staff. Organizing Director Ros Everdell says, "We train everyone in DSNI, all staff and leaders, to see themselves as organizers." As president, Ché Madyun has chosen to avoid immersing herself in development details and focus her attention on organizing and overall organizational priorities. DSNI's staff was structured with the organizing, development and human development directors all on the same level. Far more DSNI members are regularly involved in day-to-day organizing activities than in planning or physical development. Development planning takes place in combination with other organizing. Rarely did DSNI hold a meeting where only long-range planning was discussed; usually immediate issues were also addressed. DSNI's successful campaign to shut down the trash transfer stations, for example, took place in the middle of the process of developing the comprehensive master plan.

In Gus Newport's words, "The foundation and the glue which has held DSNI together is the organizing component."

CREATING VISION AND POLITICAL WILL

Reflecting on the period before DSNI's formation, Paul Bothwell says, "[What] continued to break my heart, as well as mobilize this terrific fire inside me personally and others," was that neighborhood decline "is not something that happens in communities by itself...It's not something that's just sheer chance. It's not because people here are stupid...This is the result of city policy, of other kinds of large-scale things that systematically cripple or dismember a community. Nobody who can do anything about it really cares. Everybody who is here, who really to a great degree can't do anything about it, cares." DSNI's challenge was to translate caring into control.

Creating a vision begins by building up expectations and stoking a constructive "fire inside." As Bill Slotnik puts it, "First, the people have to care about the neighborhood in which they live, and I think that exists in most neighborhoods. Second, they've got to have a feeling that things aren't going to get better unless we get involved. Third, there has to be a sense of confidence that something can come together that will make a difference."

Most bureaucrats, whether in public or private agencies, will advise keeping expectations low. If expectations aren't fulfilled, they claim, people will become disappointed and lose interest in staying involved. This approach fosters dependency and passivity. Higher expectations enable a community to Think Big—the kind of thinking not only needed to create a comprehensive vision, but needed to make it real. By thinking big and acting powerful, a neighborhood can create the political will and attract the attention and resources it needs to translate vision into reality.

"If you want to separate yourself from the traditional, you have to do something nontraditional," city official Lisa Chapnick observes. "If you want to create that flash point, that special moment, that special relationship, you've got to have a component that's unique and big and risky." A bureaucracy doesn't respond well to risky ventures, but good leaders do. And that is why DSNI held to the motto of "going to the top." Time and again, DSNI members learned that when bureaucracy ground to a halt, political leadership could quickly get it moving again. All that was necessary was for the leader to possess the political will. And that political will is created back in the neighborhood.

A unified, visionary community can create political will where there was none before and make government a partner rather than an obstacle or adversary. Comprehensive redevelopment requires significant resources from outside the neighborhood as well as inside it—resources people rightfully deserve, but which are often distributed unfairly.

Government policymakers often point to resource limitations to rationalize why they cannot meet citizen demands. Nonprofit service agencies too often conform, however unhappily, to government's top-down limitations on what is possible. Yet, lack of resources does not limit the most costly policies seen as necessary by those in power—such as the Gulf War and the Savings and Loan bailout. The problem is *not,* as often stated, "having more will than wallet." Rather, lack of political will limits what is possible. Communities must build enough power to make government truly representative and hold politicians and officials accountable.

In a community-controlled planning process, neighborhood residents are organized to provide the vision, define the priorities and plans, and participate in the implementation. As Andrea Nagel emphasizes, residents also have the best understanding of what has *not* worked in their neighborhood.

Professional staff and consultants must see themselves as working for the residents. The notion that creating a successful plan relies more on organizing capacity than on technical skills flies directly against traditional, elitist views of planning. DSNI's choice of a firm like DAC, committed to DSNI's view of comprehensive community revitalization and a resident-driven process, was crucial. DAC differentiated itself from traditional planners in its original proposal: "The principles of planning for lower-income people and their communities are the same as those on behalf of the rich. Technicians are to be hired to serve the goals and objectives set by their employers...When it comes to low-income residents, however, the rules tend to be reversed. 'The experts' seem intent on confusing their community clients with complex terms and coded jargon with the principal message of 'let the professionals handle it, because only they understand the process.'"[18]

Organizing produces the political will necessary for the vision's adoption and successful implementation. While the content of the plan that DSNI created with DAC was technically sound, many technically solid plans are not implemented because they lack the necessary support inside and outside the neighborhood. DSNI successfully built a consensus around development that no politician or government official wanted to challenge. When Mayor Flynn announced his support for the plan, few people believed he had ever read the document. What led politicians and others to support the plan was not so much the details of its contents, but rather, its political power derived from an organizing process that assured inclusion of all segments of the Dudley community.

CONTROLLING THE REAL ESTATE MARKET

While creating a community-controlled redevelopment plan is difficult, carrying it out is even more so. One of the greatest challenges is ensuring that the investment and development interest generated by such a plan does not result in speculation and the displacement of current residents. City government has traditionally seen its role as jump-starting the market by investing public dollars and letting the private sector drive development. The results are isolated projects or speculation and gentrification—not community development.

Some would ask, "What is the alternative? Let a suffering neighborhood continue to suffer?" No, neither disinvestment nor displacement are acceptable. The answer is to find mechanisms to control the market and have the market complement, rather than derail, the resident-controlled redevelopment effort.

DSNI decided to apply for the power of eminent domain, absolute control over 30 acres of land in the heart of the neighborhood. As Gus Newport observes, eminent domain provided residents with "a sense of security. This helps stabilize the lives of people who have...never been able to say, 'This is my area. This is where I'm going to set my tent.'...And expect to be there for the rest of their lives and raise their children there."

For many people, especially outside Dudley, obtaining eminent domain authority is the most important event in DSNI's history. It has a lasting symbolic impact. It spells community power. Lisa Chapnick sees eminent domain as a tool providing exceptional leverage, a tool that separated DSNI from the traditional: "PFD at any given time had anywhere between 250 and 300 projects...worth a billion dollars. DSNI occupied a tremendous amount of staff time, dollars and my time. The fact that I can, years later, talk...about this is" a reflection of DSNI's difference and importance. "When you get the attention of the top— which is the director of BRA, the director of PFD and the mayor—you get a different life and a different sanction than when you are [simply another] project going through a system."

In Bill Slotnik's view, eminent domain "is a real useful form of power to move the Initiative's agenda along," given the amount of vacant land in the neighborhood. "Perceptually, it's very important both within the neighborhood and outside the neighborhood because it was a way of saying, 'This isn't just something we want to do, but now we have the vehicle to be able to do it.'" Without eminent domain, "it would be a much, much slower process—more arduous, a lot costlier—and it would be tougher to turn the whole neighborhood around." Eminent domain, says Slotnik, is also "a superb marketing vehicle." Nationally, he says, "If anybody knows about the Initiative it's...[likely that] what they know about it is [that] it has eminent domain."

Though other communities should consider eminent domain where appropriate, Slotnik emphasizes that "their whole strategy shouldn't be built around that...The pursuit of eminent domain was a tactic in the context of a larger strategy. I suspect that a lot of others hearing about the Initiative would probably feel that it was the strategy itself, and I think that would be an error."

Ultimately, says Slotnik, DSNI's strongest tools are "the concept of the master plan and the action of aggressive community organizing." The very things DSNI "had to have in place to win eminent domain" would still be the keys to its success even without eminent domain.

There are other mechanisms that can be used to control development, avoid speculation and displacement, and preserve affordability. Some neighborhoods, including Dudley, have established community land trusts through which land is held in perpetuity by the community. If a neighborhood is organized well enough, it can maintain "moral site control" over land. That is, no developer can build in the neighborhood without the approval of the local resident-led organization. Speculators are confronted by angry neighbors who hold demonstrations against those who only see profit to be taken out of the community. Government actions such as the imposition of a speculation tax—in which speculators pay a higher tax rate on the appreciation of their investment—and strict zoning codes can also be used to control development activity. Residents can push government to authorize neighborhood councils to exercise a broad range of community control involving comprehensive development planning, zoning, and site and developer designation. The Roxbury Neighborhood Council, for example, was able to win review and advisory power, but not the decision-making authority it first envisioned.

For years, neighborhood activists and conscientious urban planners and government officials have struggled with the question of how to revitalize a community without displacing its residents. DSNI's successful campaign for eminent domain authority was a bold and innovative way of tackling the challenge. The bottom line is that if a neighborhood is to benefit from creating new energy and interest, it must use all the tools available to assure that residents are not overtaken by the power of the real estate market.

COMPREHENSIVE COMMUNITY REVITALIZATION

The Dudley Street Neighborhood Initiative has fostered an alternative, holistic approach to community development. While recognizing the importance of affordable housing and other physical development, DSNI sees that development as part of a much larger, dynamic process of community renewal led by neighborhood residents. In DSNI's view, a revitalized community is neighborly at heart, healthy in body and spirit, and socially, economically and culturally vibrant.

DSNI's successful methodology was to begin with organizing, create the long-term vision for the community and then assure the vision's implementation. Over the years, DSNI's capacity for comprehensive human, economic, physical and environmental development has grown stronger. It has had different priorities at different times— variously combining planning, organizing and implementation and variously addressing immediate and long-term goals. After its formation in 1984, DSNI was restructured in 1985 to reflect resident control and elected its first board. DSNI hired its first staff in early 1986. The 1986 priority was organizing—developing and expanding the membership base and strengthening board leadership; undertaking the "Don't Dump On Us" campaign; strengthening new and existing neighborhood associations; putting on the first multicultural festival; and restoring the commuter rail stop. In 1987, while organizing continued in full force— including the successful campaign to close down the trash transfer stations—DSNI's priorities expanded to include creating the comprehensive master plan for development and having the city adopt it. In 1988, the priorities expanded further to include implementation of the plan—gaining land control through eminent domain and winning a grant for the town common. DSNI also closed two largely vacant streets where dumping was still a terrible problem.

In 1989-90, DSNI emphasized "We Build Houses and People Too," pursuing major human development and organizing efforts such as Dudley's Young Architects and Planners; focus groups; the Agency Collaborative; tenant organizing; developing the Community Land Trust; completing and financing the build-out plan for the Dudley Triangle; choosing housing developers; and cofounding the antiredlining Community Investment Coalition. DSNI's 1991 priorities were reclaiming the local park through Community Summerfest, with its extensive youth programs; forming a Youth Committee; and launching the Dudley PRIDE campaign, stressing community esteem and initiative, public health and safety, and neighborhood greening; as well as strengthening child care and starting the Dudley Housing List.

In 1992, Dudley PRIDE was a continuing priority as DSNI began homebuyer classes to ensure access to the new housing and stepped up planning around economic development—the area that had lagged. The 1993 priorities were the groundbreaking and construction of DSNI's first new homes; economic development, as highlighted by the first economic summit; completing a Human Development Framework and Declaration of Community Rights; community design of the town common; organizing in broad coalition against a hazardous asphalt plant; completing the mural; pursuing joint planning with other agencies around existing and future community facilities; and continuing Dudley PRIDE.

At this writing, DSNI's 1994 priorities are completing an economic development plan and pursuing short- and long-term economic development projects; completing phase one construction in the Triangle and welcoming the new homeowners as members of the Community Land Trust; completing design and starting construction of the town common; finalizing plans and financing DSNI's community center while maximizing use of existing area facilities; carrying forward Dudley PRIDE; launching a major focus on education, from preschool to adult education; and organizing a major event celebrating DSNI's tenth anniversary.

In addition to everything above, the annual meeting, periodic community-wide meetings, neighborhood cleanups and multicultural festivals are major regular events. DSNI staff also respond to immediate resident concerns, whether by connecting residents to the proper public or private agencies (and following up as needed) or becoming directly involved in resolving problems such as specific incidents of illegal dumping, the unwarranted arrest of neighborhood youth or dangerous conditions (e.g., lack of winter heat) in apartments owned by unscrupulous landlords.

As this brief review highlights, DSNI has strengthened its commitment to comprehensive community revitalization.

BUILDING ON SUCCESS

An enormous challenge for any group engaged in comprehensive community redevelopment is how to maintain momentum—how to stay spirited and address pressing issues, old and new, without bogging down under organizational overload. To meet this challenge, groups must first focus on ways to increase capacity and foster new leadership so that fresh energy and vision will constantly be rising forth. Second, groups must become exceptionally disciplined in choosing which issues to engage in given organizational capacity. Success produces increasing demands to do more, and the board and staff must be able to effectively balance new activities with ongoing commitments in a way that keeps the organization moving forward.

As DSNI's organizational capacity grew, so did the demands on that capacity. As CTAC facilitators Bill Traynor and John Vaughn stressed in a memo following up on an October 1993 DSNI board retreat, "even though the organization has more staff and more people in the neighborhood involved than ever before—it has *less discretionary time and capacity* than it has ever had before. Most of DSNI's staff and board time is dedicated to some project or program that has already been committed to." (Italics in original.) They emphasized that "setting clear priorities and making sure that organizational capacity is well spent is more important today than ever before."[19]

Moreover, when choosing how to spend organizational capacity, it is important to remember that running a participatory organization such as DSNI is itself a major organizing project: informing, involving and expanding the membership; servicing and strengthening the board and committees; nurturing new leaders; holding elections; sponsoring major community fundraising events; holding periodic board retreats; and supporting resident leadership in the partnership with the city as well as in DSNI's relations with the larger public, funders, corporations and media.

In promoting Dudley's redevelopment, DSNI leaders decided early on that the organization would not become a developer or human services provider. While it would plan and manage the development process and essentially act as the development authority in the neighborhood, it would not take on the role of developer of specific projects. This decision enabled DSNI to focus its energy on empowering residents to gain control over the development process without having development implementation demands overpower the organization's capacity. It also enabled DSNI to work with member CDCs, rather than competing with them, and gave DSNI added legitimacy to review other development projects in the neighborhood without appearing to have a conflict of interest. And it would allow DSNI to keep playing the important role of objective monitor and community advocate during design and construction.

In 1993, however, DSNI found it necessary to assume the developer's role to keep the first housing on track. The designated private developer kept pushing DSNI to assume more and more financial risk and other responsibility until DSNI was functioning as the actual developer in all but name. The city also required DSNI to act as the conduit for the city loans and grants that would be used to subsidize and finance construction. Another reason DSNI may have been forced into the developer role was that it had not developed a strategy early on to increase the capacity of the local CDCs so that when the private developer did not work out, a CDC, rather than DSNI, could have assumed the task.

DSNI has not needed to act as the developer for the second group of homes, for which Nuestra Comunidad Development Corporation is the developer, and does not expect to have to again in the future. Paul Yelder observes, "As the monitor/advocate, DSNI makes sure the developer isn't cutting corners to save money. As a developer, DSNI is in the position of juggling what's cost-effective with what's desirable. We're still able to balance the roles of monitor/advocate and developer, but it's not as easy as when there is a clear division." At an October 1993 retreat, the DSNI board and staff reiterated the original intent to play the roles of organizer, planner, monitor, enabler and protector of the community interest. The board decided that the organization would try to avoid acting as the developer of future projects—in part by figuring out how to better enable others to effectively fulfill the developer role—but it would do so again if necessary to see the plan through.

DSNI's inability to remain independent from the developer's role greatly challenged its ability to guide itself by its organizing agenda and spirit. At a December 1993 board and staff retreat focused on organizing, participants agreed on the need to reemphasize organizing as the heart of DSNI's mission and rejuvenate DSNI's organizing spirit and capacity.

Resident control over the neighborhood's redevelopment does not mean going it alone. Though a community's own resources must be the foundation upon which all else is developed, outside support and resources play a significant role in the process of building on success. By the early 1990s, foundations and government had invested millions of dollars in DSNI's redevelopment agenda. They had a significant stake in Dudley's revitalization. They were helping to assure its continued success.

DSNI was never afraid to reach out for assistance and found many ready to lend a hand when asked; others volunteered themselves. DSNI has benefited, for example, from extensive pro bono services from three law firms, accountants and architects; support from the Community Training and Assistance Center and Institute for Community Economics; and the assistance of numerous professors, student interns and environmental groups.

DSNI has also received support from former neighborhood residents and their families. Fundraiser Sue Karant says that DSNI has received notes from former Irish American residents, for example, in response to various DSNI mailings. "They've told us they used to live near St. Patrick's Church and they're glad to see what DSNI is doing and support it."

In recent years, DSNI has developed a growing relationship with the local Combined Jewish Philanthropies. Their Community Relations Council is strengthening links between the Jewish community throughout the Greater Boston suburbs and social justice programs in the city of Boston. They are developing urban partnerships with groups such as DSNI, including, for example, business-to-business technical assistance, as well as funding support. Sue Karant says that the Dudley partnership touches people personally: "People often comment that their families used to live in the Dudley neighborhood or tell us about how they used to shop in the stores once lining Blue Hill Avenue and Dudley Street. They're happy to be reconnecting with the neighborhood."

DSNI has often worked in coalition with other Boston neighborhoods and organizations. Many struggles affect more than a single community and require coalition efforts to succeed. DSNI has regularly weighed how much to focus on Dudley alone—a focus that continues to overstretch the organization—and how much to work on larger issues with others such as in the Community Investment Coalition, Roxbury Neighborhood Council, Coalition for Community Control of Development, Washington Street Corridor Coalition and the Coalition Against the Asphalt Plant. Some groups outside Dudley wish DSNI would do more. Some resent that DSNI tapped public and private resources that they were unable to access. Still, DSNI has maintained strong relationships with many groups, has provided support to others when it could and has received frequent support from other groups for its own activities.

COMMUNITY-FOUNDATION PARTNERSHIP

Local and national foundations are rethinking their approach to community development. In the past, community development funding has been piecemeal, CDC-centered—emphasizing production over process—and social service agency-centered—focusing on community deficits while devaluing assets. The foundation community is recognizing that physical development without long-term human and economic development will always bring limited results. A holistic, capacity-building approach is essential. In 1991, Edward Skloot, the executive director of the Surdna Foundation, a major New York City-based foundation focusing on community development, told a group of local development corporations, "If you have good housing but the schools are blighted, the situation will only deteriorate. In short, every piece of neighborhood life must fit into every other. Communities must be seen holistically—comprehensively—in order to create visions and strategies of urban revitalization."[20]

At the end of 1993, the Annie E. Casey Foundation, a national foundation dedicated to improving the lives of children, launched "Rebuilding Communities," a comprehensive multiyear planning and capacity-building initiative focused on communities already engaged in revitalization efforts. DSNI and four other neighborhood organizations from Philadelphia, Washington, D.C., Denver and Detroit were selected for funding.[21]

Five foundations from around the country, including the Riley and Ford Foundations, sponsored a 1992 report by Arlene Eisen on "Comprehensive Neighborhood-Based Community-Empowerment Initiatives" in which foundations play a strong collaborative role. DSNI was one of the 17 efforts profiled; most were still very new. "Community empowerment, in the experience of the initiatives we profile," wrote

Eisen, "is both the process and outcome of *organized* community members gaining control over their lives. This concept is the antithesis of dependency or paternalism."[22] [Italics in original.]

Foundation executives spoke of being informed and "inspired by their new relationship with community residents," reports Eisen. Prudence Brown of the Ford Foundation asserted, "This comprehensive approach contributes to our staff's development. It encourages them to see their own programs in early childhood or housing or economic development, for example, as part of a whole, rather than as isolated strategies."

Funders expressed a strong commitment to community empowerment. Still, only six of the initiatives surveyed have policymaking boards in which "grassroots residents" were the majority. Unlike DSNI, nine of the initiatives have foundation representatives sitting on the policymaking board. Many have relied on social service agencies to drive the process.[23]

Gus Newport observes, "The sad thing is the models that I'm seeing in other places around the country don't necessarily start with a process that brings the community to the table from the beginning. So you've got agency directors or [other] people who develop a plan, and then...invite the community in...Even though they might say [that] more than 50 percent of the seats [are set aside for community residents], well, much of the plan, and the planning process itself, is already determined."

All the foundations surveyed by Eisen "recognize the need for flexibility and patience. Invariably, the process requires more time than anticipated. These funders recognize that the traditional paradigm of annual funding cycles does not apply. They understand that these initiatives are no 'quick fix.'" She adds, "There are risks involved in the process....It is neither cheap, nor easy. Achieving genuine neighborhood-based comprehensive community empowerment is labor intensive....Both the process of building trust in a collaborative relationship between funder and grantee, and the process of neighborhood-based decision making, require more time than traditional grantmaking requires."[24]

In supporting DSNI, the Riley Foundation was one of the first funders in the nation to devote a major portion of its grantmaking to one neighborhood initiative—funding a neighborhood, not a program. In many cities, there are one or two sizable foundations at most. They typically spread their grants around and constrain them with artificial time limits so that impact in any one neighborhood is often negligible and short-lived.

In addition, most foundations are resistant to making planning grants, even when the direct link between planning and programmatic action is clear. For a community to truly redevelop, residents must be given the necessary tools to articulate their vision of the future and implement it. Funders should be far more open to planning grants as part of a larger process of community-controlled development. As noted above, the Casey Foundation's multiyear initiative begins with a planning phase.

The Riley Foundation recognized that resident-controlled revitalization cannot be nickled and dimed. Resident empowerment must be supported with a level of commitment matching the challenge. Decades of disinvestment cannot be reversed in one- to three-year foundation funding cycles. With the promise of patient funding, DSNI could hire staff and effectively organize the community. DSNI also had to contend with the mistaken perception among funders that this was a "Riley initiative" and their participation was neither needed nor wanted. Over time, this perception faded as DSNI and the Riley Foundation encouraged other funders to become involved, for example, through the early Funders Day.

With adequate funding from Riley, the Boston Foundation, the Hyams Foundation and others, DSNI could not only Think Big, it could Think Quality. It didn't Think Cheap when it came to hiring consultants or paying staff salaries or designing homes or community centers or anything else—although it also used pro bono services and public resources where possible. In January 1991, to enhance its financial viability, DSNI hired an experienced fundraising consultant, Sue Karant, who implemented a multifaceted fundraising strategy, including individual donors, direct mail and special events such as the 1992 Strand Theatre celebration and the 1993 "Stake in the Neighborhood" groundbreaking, which both raised tens of thousands of dollars. In 1993, DSNI had a staff of 12, not including interns, and an operating budget of over $840,000, including over $200,000 in pro bono legal and other in-kind services (not including land purchase or construction financing).

The Riley Foundation also understood the value of trusting the grantee. Riley gave DSNI the space to make its own decisions—and to make its own mistakes—while standing ready to assist in any way requested. It was DSNI that defined the relationship with Riley, not the other way around. This is not an easy role for a funder, but one that is imperative for a project to be successful. In 1990, the Riley Foundation and the Boston Foundation established a DSNI monitoring project to provide independent evaluation of organizational progress and finances and make recommendations. These recommendations are properly nonbinding. The monitoring, which includes regular meetings with the DSNI president and staff, is performed by Laura Henze, a Grants Management Associates employee experienced in community development and organizational management. The monitoring project was introduced only after real bonds of trust had been developed between DSNI and foundation personnel.

The trust that developed between Riley staff and trustees—White corporate lawyers—and DSNI staff, board and members—many of them people of color and low-income residents—did not occur without a concerted effort by both sides. In Bill Slotnik's words, Riley told DSNI, "'We care about you. We want to support something that can make a difference here, but we want you to tell us what that is, and we're going to provide resources to help you figure that out.' That would be my definition of an enlightened institution relating to a neighborhood."

In the view of Riley Administrator Newell Flather, Riley personnel took a "hands on" approach to their goal of "bringing the community to the table" and were fortunately able to learn firsthand at the early community meetings that "we needed to change our understanding of 'community' and adjust." Foundations must balance being, in Flather's words, "on hand" enough to support these initiatives, but not so "hands on" that they undermine community empowerment.

Too many foundations have looked to assure success by being active decision makers in the programs of their large grantees. Yet that very involvement undermines the process of community control and successful redevelopment. Flather says, "I think it is useful for other funders interested in initiatives of this kind to look for the kind of staff for whom the idea of listening to community people isn't alien." In his remarks at DSNI's 1993 groundbreaking, he said, "I think it's wonderful for the city of Boston as well as the Dudley community that so many extraordinary friendships have emerged among people who otherwise wouldn't have had a chance to get to know each other."

Flather sums up the change needed in foundation support for community development when he states, "It's a great experience learning the catalytic role rather than the controlling one."[25]

Riley Trustee Bob Holmes is satisfied that DSNI has become "a player in terms of what's happening to the city." He adds, "The personal side of it is that I met a lot of people and learned a lot of things that I never would have had the opportunity to do."

Flather observes, "It's one of the most exciting things that I've been associated with in my lifetime...[one of] that handful of wonderful experiences that, when I ripen, I will know made my life worth living."

Funders can also play an important role by enabling their grantees to best serve their constituencies. Too often, nonprofits are accountable not to residents or "clients," but to the funders upon whom they depend for grants. Foundations often operate in synch with each other's priorities—e.g., favoring environmental causes some years, economic justice other years; favoring education some years, health other years—but out of synch with what a particular neighborhood needs. The frequently shifting, top-down priorities undermine a comprehensive long-term approach and encourage competition rather than cooperation.

Foundations must not limit their definition of signs of success to easily quantifiable outcomes such as number of units built, number of clients served—encouraging production at the expense of process, quantity at the expense of quality. If we are to begin to restructure how community development takes place, then foundations must consciously change their evaluation criteria and let those changes be known to their grantees. They have to reinforce, rather than undermine, the principle of agency accountability to residents, enabling residents to set priorities that may differ from neighborhood to neighborhood.

Foundations can provide much more support than money. Eisen found in her survey that "foundation support is not simply...a question of providing funds. The foundations become catalysts, conveners, facilitators and brokers for the initiatives they support."[26]

Foundations can offer, for example, professional and political connections that are often unavailable to low-income residents. Local nonprofits played an active part in DSNI's birth, in part because a major funder had asked them to participate. Also, Riley's well known involvement in DSNI opened doors within city government before DSNI had built up substantial credibility of its own. Doors were also opened to other foundations. Knowing that a respected foundation had made a long-term commitment helped other foundations to contribute with less risk. Riley also provided increased support not only to DSNI but to other Dudley-based agencies and encouraged larger agencies, such as the Boy Scouts and Morgan Memorial Goodwill, to establish new programming and operations in Dudley. By informally discussing their grant applications with DSNI, Riley was able to ensure that the programs they funded were working in concert with DSNI and offering real benefits to the community.

Eisen also underscores the role of foundations in influencing public policy. Community development "initiatives cannot imply shifting the burden of providing resources onto the community. Foundations that support these initiatives need to leverage funds from other private and, especially, public sources. While all these foundations have developed a belief in the capacity of these neighborhoods, such a belief cannot substitute for...long-term, deep funding support...To raise the necessary public funds, foundations must press for policy changes to make more funds available for neighborhood revitalization."[27]

AVOIDING PREMATURE PARTNERSHIPS

Partnership has become a buzz word in community development. However, in most cases around the country, "public-private partnerships," in which representatives from low-income neighborhoods are asked to sit at the table with government, business and other private sector leaders, have led to little gain for the community and sometimes great harm. Sitting at the table is not the same as exercising community power. Communities that are unorganized, have forged little or no consensus as to what they want to see done, and have not yet identified resources to bring to the table cannot be expected to participate as equal partners with government and private sector leaders bringing traditionally recognized resources and planning capacity—and often elitist assumptions—to the process. The result of this premature partnership is almost always failure.

To forge an effective partnership, the community must be organized well enough to be an equal partner at the table, not a junior partner. It must participate out of strength, so that it can pursue its own agenda and not be suffocated or co-opted by the agendas of others. It must be united, so that community representatives and constituencies cannot be divided and defeated. As DSNI activists emphasize: "United we stand, divided we fall."

The community must be perceived as bringing resources to the table, not necessarily financial, but principally the power to create political will and the vision of how the future should be shaped. The community must be respected by those involved. Their ideas and perspectives must be valued by the participants.

Though Boston city officials claim to have developed partnerships with other neighborhoods based on the DSNI precedent, the results have been mixed at best because no other neighborhood has yet won the community control necessary to make that kind of partnership work.

What if city officials or private sector leaders ask community representatives to sit at the table before the community organizes itself to demand its rightful place? Then community activists should insist that they demonstrate their commitment to true partnership by giving the community time and resources to organize itself and to create a representative community organization if none exists and support the kind of participatory planning process that will produce a comprehensive, unified vision of community revitalization and ensure that public and private resources are best utilized over the long term.

LOCAL COMMUNITY-GOVERNMENT PARTNERSHIP

Over the years, DSNI forged a new kind of partnership between a community group and city government. It is a partnership marked not by co-optation of the community group, but by often difficult, yet fruitful collaboration between partners with compatible goals but different agendas.

DSNI's early organizing was guided by the assumption that the city would respond to a broad-based community group that demanded improved services—and backed up its demands with direct action. Though Ray Flynn had been elected mayor on a "neighborhood first" platform, DSNI did not assume that that would make campaigns like "Don't Dump On Us" less necessary, especially in a neighborhood where people of color were in the majority and had voted heavily for Flynn's 1983 opponent, Mel King. Whatever the political leanings of government, Frederick Douglass' timeless message applies: "Power concedes nothing without a demand."*

When the planning phase began, DSNI's relationship with the city evolved. The organizing leading to the plan, coupled with foundation

---

* Douglass said, "The whole history of the progress of human liberty shows that all concessions yet made to her august claims have been born of earnest struggle. If there is no struggle, there is no progress. Those who profess to favor freedom, and yet deprecate agitation, are men who want crops without plowing up the ground, they want rain without thunder and lightning. They want the ocean without the awful roar of its many waters." Source: John W. Blassingame, *Frederick Douglass: The Clarion Voice* (1976).

support, allowed DSNI to define the terms of the planning process while inviting the city into the bottom-up process. As Lisa Chapnick puts it, it was very clear that DSNI wanted "respect and equality. That [DSNI was] not, in any way, going to be a junior partner, that it was [DSNI's] neighborhood, it was [DSNI's] vision and [DSNI] had rights. And the fact is that...[DSNI] had earned it."

After the plan was completed, DSNI got the city to cede the power of eminent domain and it secured a large loan from the Ford Foundation to buy the land. It was because of its community-based organizing and Think Big vision that DSNI was able to create the political will to get eminent domain and, with eminent domain authority, DSNI had added leverage and independence in its ongoing partnership with the city.

Chapnick says eminent domain was "pragmatic, dramatic and risky...[DSNI] found their own solution...If they had come and just said, 'We want a partnership,' it would have looked and felt, to a large extent, like a lot of other people." Eminent domain speeded the process and "raised the stakes on every level. Number one, it credentialed the group because [DSNI] had already done legal [and financial] research...Then, once [DSNI] got it, everyone was vested." Chapnick adds, DSNI "wanted power, [DSNI] wanted control and [DSNI] also took the responsibility. Big difference. A lot of people want power and money and no responsibility. This group took a lot of responsibility and took it seriously. That's very legitimizing."

DSNI's partnership with the city was not born in trust, but wariness. After decades of disinvestment and discrimination, the residents of Dudley—like poor people and people of color elsewhere—had no reason to trust government. They had no reason to trust Ray Flynn, the candidate who had opposed busing to integrate the schools and defeated Mel King. What they developed over time, however, was a trust in individual government officials that enabled the partnership to grow. "It's taken me years to understand that any city employee or public official has to pay for the sins of the past, which are deep and legitimate," says Chapnick. "I always felt like people didn't trust me for the longest, longest time. It's like, 'But wait a minute. When you call, I answer the phone. When you ask for an answer, I give you an answer. When you want it in writing, I give you...'" Chapnick not only earned trust, but, like Riley personnel, she developed some lasting friendships.

It is important to remember, though, that tensions and conflicts arise among friends, especially when those friends are government officials directing large, traditionally unresponsive bureaucracies. Community organizations cannot rely on friendly officials to safeguard their interests. And those officials can't expect their community partners to allow friendly relationships to hinder, rather than help, resolving problems as they arise.

Most Dudley residents still do not trust government—experiencing the sins of the present as well as the past. In general, the bureaucracy continues to treat people of color, poor people and immigrants who don't arrive speaking English with less respect and responsiveness than those who are White and middle- or upper-class. DSNI's partnership with the city is part of a larger, longer process of making government more responsive to all its citizens.

Through its partnership with DSNI, the city of Boston began to change its view of community development and relations with community groups. Government officials often see community groups as barriers to development—vehicles for stopping projects the city and developers deem desirable. Working with DSNI, the city of Boston began to recognize the value of neighborhood expertise and vision.

Mary Nee, who spent eight years running a settlement house in South Boston, succeeded Lisa Chapnick as PFD director. Nee observes, "DSNI was the project in which people were forced by the community to work comprehensively, to think more than about just the single vacant lot that you could build something on...Clearly there is a tremendous need for affordable housing, but to think beyond just a shelter [to] what constitutes a community and how do you rebuild communities?...On the physical side it's about open space planning and housing and capital infrastructure. But then there's that whole human capital that needs to come together. And if there are not jobs and the communities aren't organized, and if they don't feel safe and feel connected with their neighbors, then communities and neighborhoods will not be revitalized, strong and stable." As Nee put it in her remarks at DSNI's 1993 groundbreaking, "This is a different way of urban planning...The rebuilding of this community is not just real estate...[It's building]...on the community strengths that involve family, that involve youth, recreation, jobs, the churches, every part of what makes community strong."

DSNI leaders and staff were aware that the partnership with the city, and the significant resources the city directed to Dudley, held a danger of co-optation—of acting as a brake on the kind of aggressive organizing needed to make government move. When, in 1987, DSNI members threatened to drop garbage from the illegal dumps on Mayor

Flynn's desk, they had little to lose. But over time, the city of Boston provided major technical, financial and other support to DSNI's redevelopment agenda. How could DSNI organizing remain unfettered by this relationship? This is a dilemma common to community development organizations.

Gertrudes Fidalgo asserts, "I wouldn't hesitate to go dump trash on [the mayor's] desk if that was something that needed to be done." Ros Everdell agrees. What's different, she says, "is that because there is a relationship developed, you have some people you can call now who are supposed to respond. So, before we mobilize direct action, we lean on them."

It is much easier to resist top-down co-optation when the organization is not run in a top-down manner. Gus Newport says that neither he nor his predecessor as DSNI director would "make any decisions without having an okay from the board. What City Hall always tries to do is take an executive director and bring that person into the inner circle" and co-opt that person. But, says Newport, "the board might sometimes speak stronger than we would. I mean, it was the greatest strength that we had." There were many occasions when city officials were surprised to see DSNI board members attending meetings along with the executive director.

Clayton Turnbull asserts that DSNI is not "this little house-boy-type group that [believes], 'The big masters are with us now so we feel good.' We've never had that posture and never will."

Time and experience produced a set of personal relationships among leaders and staff of DSNI and city officials that provided an outlet for addressing the institutional conflicts that regularly arose. "Dudley...[let] us know you can have the fights, you can have your disagreements, you can be perfectly honest about your limits and your pragmatic parameters around money and stuff and still work together," says PFD Deputy Director Deborah Goddard.

Even as the partnership solidified, DSNI never let itself believe that the city shared its full agenda. DSNI always believed that the community-driven agenda was different. It didn't operate on a four-year election cycle. It practiced and envisioned far more grassroots empowerment and community control.

In Turnbull's words, DSNI "never changed its tune. We said we're going up the river and that's where we were going. No matter what they threw at us, if we took a swerve, it was a swerve going upward. We were going up that river."

Reflecting on his administration's relationship with DSNI shortly before leaving office to become ambassador to the Vatican, Ray Flynn emphasized that government must "have confidence in people in the community." Flynn observes, "I know the word 'partnership' has been used many, many times in politics across this country, but the Dudley Street initiative is really partnership, and it begins with community. It begins with people in the community and you bring government along. It doesn't start at City Hall and then in the final analysis—after all the decisions are made—you then have a briefing out in the community. It starts with the planning in the living rooms and the kitchens…[until] you have all the community working together. Then you build the…community center and housing, creating jobs, programs for youth. That's how you build strong, stable urban communities. It's not impossible. It can be done. And the Dudley Street area of Boston is an example, a clear national model of how it can be done."

Flynn believes that Dudley's "extraordinary" progress is significant not only because it is an area of the city "that was really distressed," but because it took place during a period when there were not "a lot of federal dollars around. If we only could get the federal government to come to the table here with neighborhood stability, neighborhood revitalization, jobs and affordable housing, just improving the quality of life. You know, you either pay now or you pay later. I'd rather pay this money up front—stabilizing neighborhoods, stabilizing families, giving kids opportunities."

COMMUNITY-FEDERAL GOVERNMENT PARTNERSHIP

The federal government has a crucial role to play in supporting neighborhood revitalization. Federal funding must be targeted, not just for much-needed affordable housing or human services, but for comprehensive, holistic approaches to community development rooted in neighborhood organizing.

Inner cities have been disinvested since the federal government began pushing suburbanization and then downtown-directed urban renewal, as described in Chapter One. During the 1980s, the federal government made conditions much worse for low-income people and neighborhoods. Housing, jobs programs and other social programs were gutted and the few programs that supported neighborhood organizing disappeared altogether. Federal aid as a portion of cities' budgets was slashed by more than 60 percent in the 1980s.[28] As seen in Chapters Seven and Eight, growing numbers of children and adults were condemned to lasting economic depression whether or not the economy was in recession or "recovery." The federal government subsidized the overbuilding of retail and office space in largely White suburbia. The inner cities and their residents were treated as disposable. The 1992 riots were one result.

The Washington-based Milton S. Eisenhower Foundation was created by members and staff of President Johnson's National Advisory Commission on Civil Disorders, known as the Kerner Commission, and two other presidential commissions from the late 1960s. It was following the 1968 riots that the Kerner Commission issued its famous warning that the United States was becoming "two societies, one black, one white—separate and unequal." Twenty-five years later, the Eisenhower Foundation issued a report concluding: "Overall, in spite of some gains since the 1960s but especially because of the federal disinvestments of the 1980s, the famous prophesy of the Kerner Commission...is more relevant today than in 1968, and more complex, with the emergence of multiracial disparities and growing income segregation."

In the words of the Eisenhower Foundation report, "Federal tax and income policy that helped the rich was accompanied by federal disinvestment policy that hurt the poor....From 1980 to 1990, federal community development block grants to the cities were cut from over $6B [billion] to under $3B." Moreover, "from 1979 to 1990, overall federal outlays on defense skyrocketed from close to $200B per year to nearly $300B per year, while overall federal outlays for education, job training, employment and social services declined from over $50B per year to under $40B per year—an astounding drop of over twenty percent...The huge military increases were financed only in a small way by the domestic cuts. Most was paid for by running up the national debt." The Eisenhower Foundation adds:

> One exception to the federal government's domestic disinvestment was prison building...costing $37B at the federal and state levels over the decade...Because the inmates were disproportionately young, in many ways prison building became the American youth policy of choice over the mid 1980s and early 1990s....[Because they were disproportionately youth of color,] in some ways prison building became part of the nation's civil rights policy. Given that the population in American prisons more than doubled over the decade, while funding for housing for the poor was cut, incredibly, by more than eighty percent from 1978 to 1991 [after

accounting for inflation], and given that the cost of a new prison cell in New York State was about the average cost of a new home purchased in the U.S. nationally, in some ways prison building became the American low-income housing policy of the 1980s.[29]

Just as Reaganite ideologues intended, the federal budget deficit—produced by tax cuts favoring the wealthy and skyrocketing military spending—has been used as a permanent enforcer of cutbacks in social spending generally and inner city reinvestment in particular. In place of a comprehensive approach to community revitalization, the deficit has been used to justify a zero sum game in which most lose competing for scarcer federal dollars. As Howard Leibowitz, then Mayor Flynn's director of Federal Relations, testified to the Boston City Council, "We didn't cause the deficit, but we are paying for it…We have had an increase in the 'robbing Peter to pay Paul' syndrome, in which community health centers are cut to pay for new infant mortality initiatives and public housing programs are cut to increase the number of shelter beds."[30]

There was hope that under the Clinton administration, the federal government would play a significant, positive role in the revitalization of urban neighborhoods. The administration has taken some steps in the right direction—for example, by promoting youth corps initiatives such as City Year and YouthBuild. But Clinton's overall urban agenda is short on funds and bold progressive initiatives, and the administration lacks the political will to carry out its better ideas. Clinton's campaign program to "Rebuild America" was largely sacrificed on the alter of deficit reduction. Domestic investment spending will be stagnant or falling in fiscal year 1994 and beyond, after adjusting for inflation. Behind the headlines about new commitments to Head Start, for example, overall education and training spending has declined.[31] The "robbing Peter to pay Paul" syndrome continues.

The Clinton urban agenda borrows heavily from the Reagan-Bush policy of "enterprise zones." President Reagan described their objective as "utilizing the market to solve urban problems, relying primarily on private sector institutions. The idea is to create a productive, free market environment in economically depressed areas by reducing taxes, regulations and other government burdens on economic activity. The removal of these burdens will create and expand economic activity within the zone areas allowing private sector firms and entrepreneurs to create jobs."[32]

As the Eisenhower Foundation sums it up, "Over the last decade, more than five hundred enterprise zones have been tried in thirty seven states." The evidence shows them "to represent still more failed, trickle-down economics." As the Urban Institute reported, "Extensive evaluations of state enterprise zone programs have found no evidence that incentives have contributed to employment or investment growth in designated areas" and the tax benefits go "to reward businesses for behavior that will not necessarily benefit the poor."[33]

It is also important to understand that revenue lost through "tax incentives" to often-large corporations is sorely missed. As Eric Mann wrote of Los Angeles in 1993, "Enterprise zones, which L.A. has had for five years, have created a total of 837 jobs...The attendant tax breaks, which have contributed to the city's current $180 million budgetary shortfall, were often claimed by companies already operating in the inner city." Many more jobs were lost in the corporate search for even cheaper labor, greater government subsidies and fewer environmental and other regulations at home and abroad.[34]

For DSNI, the closure of the Digital Equipment and Stride Rite plants in Roxbury underscored the bankruptcy of past enterprise zone strategies. The Clinton administration has revamped enterprise zones into a small number of large "empowerment zones," promising a combination of social services and tax breaks to businesses providing jobs, and more numerous "urban enterprise communities," with less government support. The "empowerment zone" program is scheduled to cost the federal government $3.5 billion over five years, much less than the cost of two stealth bombers.

If "empowerment zones" and "urban enterprise communities" are to be more than enterprise zones with new names and rhetoric, government must support enterprising efforts by community organizations like DSNI to create economic development plans and strategies as part of a larger community development process—strategies building on neighborhood assets, not devaluing and undermining them. Government should reinforce organizations like DSNI by providing support for organizing and planning and financing to help them implement comprehensive revitalization plans.

The focal point of the kind of financial and other assistance typically provided corporations through enterprise zones—in the name of benefiting the community—should be the representative community organization, not corporations and government planners. There can be no community "empowerment" without organizing. Without community organizing, planning and long-term control, there will be no "economics with people in mind" and no sustainable, comprehensive community development.

Bill Clinton campaigned on a promise to create 100 new community development banks during his first term. Whatever the merit of that particular approach, the lack of access to capital by inner city residents and businesses is a primary obstacle to economic renewal. Along with strengthening enforcement of the Community Reinvestment Act and other laws requiring banks to practice fair lending in low-income neighborhoods, an infusion of new capital through community-based lending institutions offers great potential. Across the country, there are already many established institutions that Washington can support, including community development banks, credit unions, loan funds and micro-loan funds. They provide important vehicles for maximizing existing capital and attracting new capital into low-income neighborhoods—capital that is invested in those living and working in these neighborhoods, not speculators, corner-cutting developers and others seeking profit at the community's expense.

In sum, to support community development, the federal government must combine flexible support for neighborhood organizing and capacity building with adequate resources for economic development, education, housing, health care, child care and other human needs and aspirations.

New federal priorities are not a matter of wallet, but will. The wallet can be assured by adopting a fair tax system and a defense budget that is not a bloated captive of the military-industrial complex that conservative President Dwight Eisenhower, formerly a top general, warned of decades ago.[35] As the Children's Defense Fund asks, for example, "Do we need a new aircraft carrier which will cost $5 billion in 1995 more than we need after-school and weekend and summer programs for children and youths?"[36] Clinton chose the course of less national security, not more, when he declared in his 1994 State of the Union address, "We must not cut defense further." With sufficient vision and will, the wallet for needed federal commitments can be assured through a just and effective distribution of public money and, ultimately, through a healthier economy and society.

In 1967, Martin Luther King called for a revolution of values in *Where Do We Go From Here: Chaos or Community?* His call is more urgent than ever:

The time has come for us to civilize ourselves by the total, direct and immediate abolition of poverty....

A true revolution of values will soon cause us to question the fairness and justice of many of our past and present policies. We are called to play the good samaritan on life's roadside; but...One day the whole Jericho road must be transformed so that men and women will not be beaten and robbed as they make their journey through life....

A nation that continues year after year to spend more money on military defense than on programs of social uplift is approaching spiritual death.

...There is nothing but a lack of social vision to prevent us from paying an adequate wage to every American citizen whether he be a hospital worker, laundry worker, maid or day laborer. There is nothing except shortsightedness to prevent us from guaranteeing an annual minimum—and *livable*—income for every American family. There is nothing, except a tragic death wish, to prevent us from reordering our priorities, so that the pursuit of peace will take precedence over the pursuit of war. There is nothing to keep us from remolding a recalcitrant status quo with bruised hands until we have fashioned it into a brotherhood.[37]

COMMUNITY

"We're learning how to be a better community together," says DSNI's Sue Beaton. "But whether we look perfect at the end is really not, to me, the issue. It's how many people have participated along the way, who gets the benefits of whatever we can accomplish together, and how do we hang together and not get co-opted in the process of doing whatever we're doing." She adds, "I would like us to be a community of integrity."

Clayton Turnbull observes, "This community, along with Black people in America [generally, have long felt] like they rent their community. They don't feel like they own it even when they own a house...Subconsciously or consciously, they don't feel like they own it." Turnbull points to the L.A. riots: "People say, 'Why do all these people burn down their own communities?' It wasn't their community! They didn't own the stores! They didn't work in them! They didn't own the houses!...So, why do you call it 'your community'? Because you geographically, residentially live there? That's not what 'your community' means."

"DSNI has changed that attitude with the process, with the Community Land Trust and so on," says Turnbull. "People now say...'I own it' [and 'We own it.']...That's why I say to people, 'Urban America has to now set policies for politicians to come in and follow.'" That's what DSNI did, says Turnbull. "We set the policies."

The Dudley community has spent almost a decade renewing their dreams, their lives and their neighborhood. They found a way to forge a united vision of the future and institutionalize resident control. They have had many victories over the years. Yet, they have much more work ahead. Ultimately, what distinguishes the residents of Dudley is not their ability to stop dumping or create a comprehensive redevelopment plan for the neighborhood or get eminent domain or attract millions of dollars in resources into the neighborhood. What distinguishes Dudley residents from many other communities is this: They found a way to dream together and not allow their dreams—to borrow from Langston Hughes—to be deferred, to dry up like a raisin in the sun, or explode. Together, they found a way.

As stated in the preamble to DSNI's Declaration of Community Rights: "We—the youth, adults, seniors of African, Latin American, Caribbean, Native American, Asian and European ancestry—are the Dudley community. Nine years ago, we were Boston's dumping ground and forgotten neighborhood. Today, we are on the rise! We are reclaiming our dignity, rebuilding housing and reknitting the fabric of our communities. Tomorrow, we realize our vision of a vibrant, culturally diverse neighborhood, where everyone is valued for their talents and contributions to the larger community."

Dudley residents have a long way to go, but they have come a long way, and the journey itself has been rewarding. They have learned from others' experiences, and they hope others can learn from theirs. For ultimately, we as a nation must find a way to progress together—with diversity, not divisiveness—lest our children inherit a world even more impoverished and dangerous than today's. A world of chaos, not community. DSNI's local alternative of multiracial, mutual progress and holistic community development is no less relevant nationally. It is an alternative vision in which no one is disposable. Together, we must find a way.

Old view from Winthrop Street, looking across Dennis Street (toward Huckins Street). Site of new DSNI homes.

Two homebuyers cutting the ribbon on DSNI's first new home on Dennis Street, November 1993, joined by DSNI, city, foundation and banking officials.

NOTES

INTRODUCTION

1. All quotes are from author interviews or firsthand knowledge unless noted otherwise. See List of Interviews.
2. See census data in Appendix tables. The official poverty line was established in the 1960s by determining the cost of a minimally adequate diet and multiplying by three, assuming then that the average family spent one-third of its budget on food (specific poverty thresholds are set for different size households). The government has not adjusted the formula to reflect the current cost of food, which is now much lower in relation to housing, health care and other necessities. Instead, it simply takes the previous year's poverty line, based on an increasingly out-of-date formula, and adjusts it for the general inflation rate. In their book on the working poor, John Schwarz and Thomas Volgy show that, based on a stringent economy budget, a family of four needed a 1990 income of about $20,700—or 155 percent of the official 1990 poverty line of $13,359—to buy minimally sufficient food, housing, health care, transportation, clothing and other personal and household items and pay taxes. Patricia Ruggles of the Urban Institute likewise concluded that the 1990 poverty line would have had to rise by over $6,000 to a level of $16,685 for a family of three just to match the original poverty formula. Schwarz and Volgy note that their stringent budget does not cover many things, such as paying for child care or being unable to find low-cost housing. John E. Schwarz and Thomas J. Volgy, *The Forgotten Americans: Thirty Million Working Poor in the Land of Opportunity* (New York: W.W. Norton, 1992), pp. 38-46, 61-62; "Above the Line—But Poor," *The Nation*, February 15, 1993; Patricia Ruggles, *Drawing the Line: Alternative Poverty Measures and their Implications for Public Policy* (Washington, D.C.: Urban Institute Press, 1990), presented in Tim Wise, "Being Poor Isn't Enough," *Dollars & Sense*, September 1990.

    More than one-third of all officially poor families do not get food stamps and three out of four get no government housing assistance of any kind. In 1990, low-income families with children spent one-fourth of their incomes on child care. According to Department of Agriculture estimates, a low-income family of three (mother with two preteen children) needed $309 a month to purchase a nutritionally adequate diet in 1989. The Department of Housing and Urban Development (HUD) estimated that rent and utilities for a modest two-bedroom apartment cost $482 a month. That left $33 for *all* other expenses *if* a family of three had the official 1989 poverty line annual income of $9,885. The average poor family's income falls far below the official poverty line. Children's Defense Fund and Northeastern University's Center for Labor Market Studies, *Vanishing Dreams: The Economic Plight of America's Young Families* (Washington, D.C.: Children's Defense Fund, 1992), p. 22; Clifford M. Johnson, et al., *Child Poverty in America* (Children's Defense Fund, 1991), pp. 13-15, 25; Children's Defense Fund, *The State of America's Children 1992*, p. 19.

HUD considers housing affordable if it costs no more than 30 percent of household income, but such housing is often not available. In a study of 44 major metropolitan areas for 1989, affordable housing was so scarce that four out of five poor renters spent more than 30 percent of their income on housing costs (rent and utilities) and more than one out of two spent at least half their income. More than two out of three poor homeowners spent more than 30 percent, and 43 percent spent more than half their incomes on housing. Two-thirds of poor people are renters, one-third are homeowners, many of them elderly homeowners. Boston has the second highest rents in the nation. In the larger Boston metropolitan area (which, as defined by the U.S. Census Bureau, includes the city of Boston; Essex, Middlesex, Norfolk and Plymouth counties and parts of Bristol and Worcester counties in Massachusetts; and Hillsborough and Rockingham counties in New Hampshire), 86 percent of poor renters spent at least 30 percent and 71 percent spent at least half their income on housing. Virtually all poor homeowners spent at least 30 percent of their income and 81 percent spent at least half their income on housing. Paul A. Leonard and Edward B. Lazere, *A Place To Call Home: The Low Income Housing Crisis In 44 Major Metropolitan Areas* (Washington, D.C.: Center on Budget and Policy Priorities, November 1992), pp. 1, 5-8, "Highlights: Northeastern Metropolitan Areas, Boston."

3. Michael B. Katz, "The Urban 'Underclass' as a Metaphor of Social Transformation," in Katz, ed., *The 'Underclass' Debate: Views From History* (Princeton, NJ: Princeton University Press, 1993), p. 21. Also see Jacqueline Jones, *The Dispossessed: America's Underclasses from the Civil War to the Present* (New York: Basic Books, 1992); Adolph Reed Jr., "The Underclass as Myth and Symbol: The Poverty of Discourse About Poverty," *Radical America* 24:1 (January 1992); Adolph Reed Jr. and Julian Bond, eds., "The Assault on Equality: Race, Rights and the New Orthodoxy," *The Nation* special issue, December 9, 1991.

4. Children's Defense Fund, *Vanishing Dreams*, p. 10.

CHAPTER 1

1. Francis S. Drake, *Town of Roxbury: Its Memorable Persons and Places* (Roxbury: published by the author, 1878); Boston Redevelopment Authority (BRA), Neighborhood Planning Program, *Dorchester Uphams Corner: District Profile and Proposed 1979-1981 Neighborhood Improvement Program*, 1979, p. 6.

2. Howard Zinn, *A People's History of the United States* (New York: Harper Colophon Books, 1980), pp. 47-48. The spelling is modernized.

3. Ibid., pp. 13-17. Also see Richard Drinnon, *Facing West: The Metaphysics of Indian Hating and Empire Building* (New York: Schocken Books, 1990), Chapters 1-5.

4. Oscar Handlin, *Boston's Immigrants: 1790-1880* (Belknap/Harvard University Press, 1991 revised ed.), p. 15.

5. Sam B. Warner Jr., *Streetcar Suburbs: The Process of Growth in Boston, 1870-1900* (New York: Atheneum, 1974, first pub. 1962), p. 40.

6. BRA, Neighborhood Planning Program, *Roxbury: District Profile and Proposed 1979-1981 Neighborhood Improvement Program*, 1979, p. 4.

7. Handlin, *Boston's Immigrants*, pp. 44-48, 52, 261.

8. Warner, *Streetcar Suburbs*, pp. 38-40, 64-66; BRA, *Roxbury: Neighborhood Profile 1988*, p. 1.

9. Warner, *Streetcar Suburbs*, pp. 65-66.

10. BRA, *Roxbury District Profile and Proposed 1979-1981 Neighborhood Improvement Program,* p. 4.

11. Robert C. Hayden, *African-Americans in Boston: More than 350 Years* (Boston: Trustees of the Boston Public Library, 1991), p. 15. Also see Luix Overbea, *Black Bostonia* (Boston 200 Neighborhood History Series, 1976).

12. Handlin, *Boston's Immigrants,* p. 249, citing Oliver Warner, *Abstract of the Census of Massachusetts, 1865.*

13. Robert C. Hayden, "An Historical Overview of Poverty Among Blacks in Boston: 1850-1990," in James Jennings, ed., *Perspectives on Poverty in Boston's Black Community* (The Boston Persistent Poverty Project, The Boston Foundation, February 1992), pp. 5, 7-11.

14. BRA, *Dorchester Uphams Corner: District Profile and Proposed 1979-1981 Neighborhood Improvement Program,* pp. 6-7.

15. Ruth B. Grant, "Pebbles to Ponder: The Story of St. Patrick's Church and Parish in Roxbury," *The Patrician,* special issue on "St. Patrick's Parish: 150 Years (1836-1986)," October 5, 1986, p. 21.

16. Tom Lyons, *The Patrician* special issue, pp. 5-6.

17. Jeffrey Brown, BRA Research Department, *Profile of Boston: 1929-1980* (October 1982), pp. 21, 31.

18. Mel King, *Chain of Change: Struggles for Black Community Development* (Boston: South End Press, 1981), p. 26.

19. Total Studio, MIT, *From the Ground Up: A Strategy for the Dudley Street Neighborhood,* prepared for La Alianza Hispana, Roxbury, 1981, p. 19.

20. Reverend Pio Gottin, O.F.M. Cap., *The Patrician* special issue, pp. 5-6.

21. DSNI staff arrived at this estimate based on knowledge of the neighborhood, census information and conversations with officials from the city and the Cape Verdean consulate. An estimated 37 percent of Dudley residents are non-Cape Verdean Black. Cape Verdean ethnicity is not a census category; Cape Verdeans in Dudley define themselves for the census as Black or "Other" race. The census also asks a survey sample to indicate "language spoken at home," including Portuguese/Portuguese Creole as an option, which in the Dudley area indicates Cape Verdeans; 15 percent chose that option, and it is assumed that others would have answered affirmatively if they did not interpret it to mean that they did not also speak English. It is also assumed that the census undercount of Cape Verdeans is very high. A 1976 BRA survey estimated the Cape Verdean population at 8 percent in a part of the Dudley area bounded by Blue Hill Avenue, Magazine, East Cottage and Columbia Road. Cited in BRA, *Dorchester Uphams Corner District Profile,* p. 8.

22. *Polk's Boston* (R.L. Polk & Co.) 1950, 1960, 1970, 1980. Also see DSNI surveys of Dudley businesses, 1987; Hispanic Office of Planning and Evaluation, *Hispanic Businesses: The Dudley Neighborhood* (Boston: HOPE, May 1982).

23. Gregory D. Squires, "Community Reinvestment: An Emerging Social Movement," in Squires, ed., *From Redlining to Reinvestment: Community Responses to Urban Disinvestment* (Philadelphia: Temple University Press, 1992), p. 5.

24. Cited in Dennis R. Judd, "Segregation Forever?" *The Nation,* December 9, 1991.

25. Ibid.

26. Hillel Levine and Lawrence Harmon, *The Death of An American Jewish Community: A Tragedy of Good Intentions* (New York: Free Press, 1992), p. 70., citing Charles Abrams, *Forbidden Neighbors: A Study of Prejudice in Housing* (New York: Harper and Bros., 1955), p. 230.

27. Judd, "Segregation Forever?"

28. Levine and Harmon, *Death of An American Jewish Community,* p. 167, citing "Building the American City," report of the National Commission on Urban Problems, December 1968, pp. 100-02 (analysis available in Rachel Bratt, *A Homeownership Survey: A Report on the Boston Banks Urban Renewal Group,* Boston Model City Administration, 1972, p. 7).

29. Squires, "Community Reinvestment," p. 6.

30. William W. Goldsmith and Edward J. Blakely, *Separate Societies: Poverty and Inequality in U.S. Cities* (Philadelphia, Temple University Press, 1992), pp. 119-22; U.S. Bureau of the Census, *The Black Population in the United States: March 1991,* Table 3.

31. Richard Lacayo, "This Land is Your Land," *Time,* May 18, 1992, p. 3.

32. The HUD statistic is 59 percent. Penda D. Hair, "Civil Rights," in Citizens Transition Project, Mark Green, ed., *Changing America: Blueprints for the New Administration* (New York: Newmarket Press, 1992), pp. 341-42.

33. Boston's population dropped by 230,000 between 1930 and 1980 while the metropolitan area's population increased by over 400,000 during 1940-1980. The percentage of people of color in Boston's population rose from 2.6 percent in 1930 to 16 percent in 1970 and 26 percent in 1980. The metropolitan area was 6 percent people of color in 1970 and only 9 percent in 1980. Brown, BRA, *Profile of Boston: 1929-1980,* pp. 7, 21, 31, 35.

34. Boston's labor force participation rate for men dropped from 84 percent in 1930 to 68 percent in 1980, below the national average. Women's increasing labor force participation, on the other hand, continued to exceed the national average, rising from one-third of women (age 14 and over) in 1930 to over half of women (16 and over) in 1980. See Brown, BRA, *Profile of Boston: 1929-1980,* pp. 7, 12, 16, 23.

35. Alexander Ganz, BRA, Policy Development and Research Department, *Housing Market Change in Boston's Minority Neighborhoods,* June 30, 1987, "New Horizons for Roxbury."

36. Herbert J. Gans, *The Urban Villagers: Group and Class in the Life of Italian-Americans* (New York: The Free Press, 1962), p. 287, citing Bill Cunningham, "Two Projects to Alter Boston," *Boston Herald,* November 17, 1957.

37. Gans, *The Urban Villagers,* pp. 8-9, 285.

38. The city of Boston had bought the West End land under eminent domain for $7.40 per square foot and then revalued it at $1.40 a square foot for Jerome Rappaport, the lead developer of the West End renewal project and the former chief assistant for Mayor John Hynes—candidate of the business-led "New Boston" coalition. John H. Mollenkopf, *The Contested City* (Princeton, NJ: Princeton University Press, 1983), p. 150. Also see Levine and Harmon, *Death of An American Jewish Community,* pp. 73-74.

39. Mollenkopf, *Contested City,* p. 159.

40. Langley C. Keyes Jr., *The Rehabilitation Planning Game: A Study in the Diversity of Neighborhood* (Cambridge, MA: MIT Press, 1969), pp. 29-30, citing BRA, *1965-1975 General Plan for the City of Boston and the Regional Core,* November 1964, pp. vi-2.

41. Keyes, *The Rehabilitation Planning Game,* p. 30; Mollenkopf, *The Contested City,* p. 175.

42. See Keyes, *The Rehabilitation Planning Game,* Chapter 5 on Washington Park; BRA, *Roxbury District Profile,* 1979, p. 7; BRA, *Boston Population and Housing by Neighborhood Areas, 1980: Demographic Information from the U.S. Bureau of the Census,* September 1983.

43. John King, "Dudley Station: The BRA tries again," *Boston Business Journal: Monthly Real Estate Supplement,* February 1986.

44. BRA, *Roxbury: A Plan to Manage Growth,* Neighborhood Planning & Zoning, The Interim Planning Overlay District, 1987, p. 28.

45. BRA, *South End Neighborhood Profile 1988,* pp. 1-2.

46. Mollenkopf, *The Contested City,* pp. 171-72.

47. Ibid., p. 176.

48. King, *Chain of Change,* pp. 111-13.

49. Ibid., p. 205.

50. Miren Uriarte, "Contra Viento Y Marea (Against All Odds): Latinos Build Community in Boston," in Uriarte, et al., *Latinos in Boston: Confronting Poverty, Building Community,* A Program Paper of the Boston Persistent Poverty Project, the Boston Foundation, March 1992, pp. 15, 21-22.

51. BRA, *South End Neighborhood Profile 1988,* pp. 3-6; Mollenkopf, *The Contested City,* pp. 182, 199.

52. Mollenkopf, *The Contested City,* pp. 165-66. Also see BRA, *Fact Sheets* on urban renewal projects, September 1975.

53. Mollenkopf, *The Contested City,* pp. 209-11.

54. In 1991, about 81 percent of the $37 billion in tax benefits from deductible mortgage interest went to the top 20 percent of households, with incomes above $50,000. See Edward B. Lazere, et al., *A Place to Call Home: The Low Income Housing Crisis Continues* (Washington, D.C.: Center on Budget and Policy Priorities/Low Income Housing Information Service, December 1991), pp. 27, 30-31, 34-35.

55. Jeffrey P. Brown, BRA Research Department, *The Revitalization of Downtown Boston: History, Assessment and Case Studies,* Draft chapter for *Cities Reborn,* a publication of the Urban Land Institute, March 1987, p. 11.

   By 1992, only 5 percent of Boston's jobs were in manufacturing. Their average wage was 9 percent higher than for the service sector. See Economic Development and Industrial Corporation, *Boston's Manufacturing Industries: Protecting Jobs, Incomes, and the City's Economy* (Boston: May 1993), pp. 3-4.

56. Brown, BRA, *The Revitalization of Downtown Boston,* Executive Summary and pp. 8-9, 19-20. Some statistics taken from BRA, *Boston at Mid-Decade: Results of the 1985 Household Survey: Summary Report.*

57. BRA, *Boston at Mid-Decade: Summary Report,* p. 13; *Boston at Mid-Decade: Some Highlights,* February 28, 1989.

58. Jeffrey Brown, BRA Research Department, *Indicators of Minority Participation in Boston's Growing Economy,* Draft, September 1986, Tables 8, 9 and unnumbered pages.

59. Charles Finn, *Mortgage Lending in Boston's Neighborhoods 1981-1987,* study commissioned by the Boston Redevelopment Authority (University of Minnesota: Hubert H. Humphrey Institute of Public Affairs, December 1989), p. 1.

60. BRA, *Dorchester Uphams Corner District Profile,* pp. 7, 9.

61. Levine and Harmon, *Death of An American Jewish Community,* pp. 5-6.

62. Ibid., pp. 6-7, 37, 53-54, 63.

63. Anonymous, "Confessions of a Blockbuster," *Metropolitan Real Estate Journal,* May 1987, cited in Ibid., pp. 2-5.

64. Levine and Harmon, *Death of An American Jewish Community,* pp. 207-08.

65. Ibid., pp. 276-77.

66. Finn, *Mortgage Lending in Boston's Neighborhoods,* pp. 9-10.

67. See Squires, ed., *From Redlining to Reinvestment.*

68. James T. Campen, "The Struggle for Community Investment in Boston: 1989-1991," in Squires, ed., *From Redlining to Reinvestment,* p. 40.

69. Finn, *Mortgage Lending in Boston,* pp. 15-19. Also see Katharine L. Bradbury, Karl E. Case and Constance R. Dunham, "Geographic Patterns of Mortgage Lending in Boston, 1982-87," unofficial study of the Federal Reserve Bank of Boston, August 31, 1989, later published in the Boston Federal Reserve Bank's *New England Economic Review,* September/October 1989; Melvin W. Laprade and Andrea Nagel, *Roxbury—A Community at Risk: An Analysis of the Disparities in Mortgage Lending Patterns,* Greater Roxbury Neighborhood Authority, 1988.

70. Finn, *Mortgage Lending in Boston,* pp. 2-3.

71. Rolf Goetze, BRA, Research Department, *Boston's Changing Housing Patterns: 1970 to 1985,* p. 2.

72. Alicia H. Munnell, et al., *Mortgage Lending in Boston: Interpreting HMDA Data,* Working Paper No. 92-7, Federal Reserve Bank of Boston, October 1992, p. 1. Also see Statement of Ronald A. Homer, Boston Bank of Commerce, Hearing on The Credit Crisis for American Consumers and Small Businesses, before the U.S. House of Representatives Subcommittee on Consumer Credit and Insurance of the Committee on Banking, Finance and Urban Affairs, February 18, 1983.

73. See, for example, *Frontline,* "Your Loan is Denied," WGBH-TV, Boston, June 23, 1992; Peter Dreier, "Pssst...Need a Loan," *Dollars and Sense,* October 1991.

74. Rep. Joseph P. Kennedy II, chairman, House Banking Subcommittee on Consumer Credit and Insurance, Statement at Hearing on Insurance Redlining, February 24, 1993; also see testimony by Rev. Charles Cummings Jr., Treasurer, Washington, D.C. chapter of ACORN, and Professor Gregory D. Squires. Also see Kimberly Blanton, "Nice home, WRONG BLOCK," *Boston Globe,* March 23, 1993, which looked at insurance redlining of Roxbury, Dorchester and Mattapan.

75. Warner, *Streetcar Suburbs,* p. 116.

76. Alexander Ganz, BRA, Policy Development and Research Department, *Housing Market Change in Boston's Minority Neighborhoods,* June 30, 1987, p. 1.

77. City of Boston Arson Prevention Commission, *Report to the Boston Redevelopment Authority on the Status of Arson in Dudley Square,* September 4, 1985, pp. 1-2.

78. BRA, *Dorchester Uphams Corner District Profile,* pp. 10-12, 14.

79. Ibid., pp. 15-16.

80. Boston Fire Department, Field Incident Report, April 21, 1976; Walter Haynes, "Roxbury fire burns 11 houses," *Boston Globe,* April 21, 1976.

81. BRA, *Dorchester Uphams Corner District Profile,* p. 16.

CHAPTER 2

1. *The Dudley Neighborhoods: A Report to the Communities Surrounding RCC,* class project in the Community Organizing Course, Division of Continuing Education, Roxbury Community College, Spring 1981, pp. 5-9.

2. Minutes of the Meeting for Neighborhood Action, Roxbury Community College, May 13, 1991,

3. MIT Total Studio, *From the Ground Up,* Chapter 4.

4. *In Search of Community: A Strategic Planning Conference in Boston's Dudley Street Neighborhood,* conference report, July 1984, pp. 17-18, 28-29.

5. Draft minutes, The Riley Foundation, Trustees' Meeting, April 13, 1984.

6. Newell Flather and Nancy Condit, *The Dudley Initiative: A Review of the Dudley Neighborhood and Consideration of New Directions in Grantmaking for the Riley Foundation,* prepared for the Riley Trustees, July 17, 1984, pp. 6, 10.

7. Ibid., p. 2.

8. The Riley Foundation, Trustees' Meeting minutes, July 18, 1984.

9. Detailed memo on the meeting from Bill Slotnik, CTAC, to the Riley Foundation, September 21, 1984.

10. As of January 1985, regular participants in the Dudley Advisory Group included: Nelson Merced, La Alianza Hispana; Charlotte Kahn, Boston Urban Gardeners; Valerie Gregory and Karen Horton, Cape Verdean Community House; Ricardo Quiroga, Casa Esperanza; Bill Slotnik, Community Training and Assistance Center; Shirley Lewis, Denison House; Lucia David and Cecilia Hunt, Escuelita Agueybana; John Bartholomew, Federated Dorchester Neighborhood Houses; Stephen Johnson, Greater Roxbury Development Corporation; Nate Allen and Shirley Carrington, Lena Park Community Development Corporation; Edward Cooper, National Caucus and Center on Black Aged; Angela Giudice, Neighborhood Arts Center; Melvyn Colón and Arne Abramson, Nuestra Comunidad Development Corporation; Sarah Flint, Orchard Park United Tenants Association (and Lena Park CDC); Mary Ann Crayton, Roxbury Community News; Lou Simon, Roxbury Dental and Medical Group; Shelley Hoon and Ricardo Millett, Roxbury Multi-Service Center; Rick Detwiller, Shirley-Eustis House; Father Walter Waldron, St. Patrick's Church; Ed Grimes, Uphams Corner Health Center; Sister Pauline O'Leary and Mary Rogers, WAITT House; Janet Taylor, Associated Grantmakers of Massachusetts; Riley Foundation trustees Andrew Bailey, Douglas Danner, Robert Holmes and Guy Sturgeon and staff Nancy Condit, Newell Flather and Mary Phillips.

11. Richard J. Margolis, "Will the Patient Live?" *Foundation News,* September/October 1985, p. 37.

12. Dudley Initiative, Plenary Group Meeting, October 15, 1984, minutes prepared by CTAC.

13. Dudley Initiative, Ad Hoc Community-Wide Meeting Committee minutes, December 5, 1984, prepared by CTAC.

14. Alan Lupo, *Boston Globe,* "Change is in the air along Dudley Street," February 17, 1985.

15. BRA Briefing Book, *Dudley Square Plan: A Strategy for Neighborhood Revitalization,* Draft, December 17, 1984, not paginated. For an alternative view of Dudley Station development, contrasting three scenarios (disinvestment, gentrification/displacement and popular power/balanced development), see Mauricio Gastón and Marie Kennedy, *Dudley in 2001: After the El...Center for Whom?,* a project of the Community Service Program, College of Public and Community Service, University of Massachusetts-Boston, prepared for the Roxbury Action Program, January 1985.

16. BRA, *Boston at Mid-Decade: Results of the 1985 Household Survey, II: Income and Poverty,* Table 9, p. 21.

17. Committee for Boston Public Housing, Inc., *Beyond the Safety Net: Families in Boston Housing Authority Developments,* Boston, April 1985.

18. BRA, *Dudley Square Plan.* Also see Gregory W. Perkins, BRA Research Department, *A Profile of Dudley Square: Current Characteristics and Future Development Potential,* October 1984 and John Avault and Deborah Oriola, BRA Research

Department, *Expanding Homeownership Opportunities in Roxbury,* A Working Paper of the Dudley Square Planning Team, Draft revised May 29, 1985.

19. Merced and Johnson quoted in Bob Keough, "Dudley Street Neighborhood Initiative brings community together," *Dorchester Community News,* March 5, 1985.
20. DSNI Community-Wide Meeting, February 23, 1985, St. Patrick's Church, report.
21. Report on the first community-wide meeting, February 25, 1985.
22. The Dudley core population was then estimated at 40 percent Black, 30 percent Latino, 20 percent Cape Verdean and 10 percent White. See Tables 1 and 6 for 1990 figures.
23. Memo to members of DSNI from the Elections Committee, May 1, 1985; Sample ballot and final tallies.
24. DSNI board minutes, June 3, 1985.
25. DSNI board minutes, June 10, 1985.
26. See, for example, King, *Chain of Change,* p. 159.
27. James Green, "The Making of Mel King's Rainbow Coalition: Political Changes in Boston, 1963-1983," in James Jennings and Mel King, eds., *From Access to Power: Black Politics in Boston* (Cambridge, MA: Schenkman Books, 1986), p. 105, citing *Boston Globe,* November 16, 1983. Also see articles by King and others.

CHAPTER 3

1. City of Boston Arson Prevention Commission, *Report to the BRA on the Status of Arson in Dudley Square,* pp. 1-2.
2. Mauricio Gastón and Marie Kennedy, "Blueprint for Tomorrow: The fight for community control in Boston's black and Latino neighborhoods," *Radical America* 20:5 (September/October 1986), p. 15.
3. Quoted in Michael K. Frisby and Sarah Snyder, "Flynn aides had advance word on city arson study," *Boston Globe,* March 14, 1986.
4. Bonnie V. Winston, "Roxbury residents tell city they want dumping to stop," *Boston Globe,* June 19, 1986.
5. See Gary Delgado, *Organizing the Movement: The Roots and Growth of ACORN* (Philadelphia: Temple University Press, 1986), pp. 117-22.
6. DSNI board minutes, August 4, 1986; Planning Committee minutes, August 18, 1986.
7. Uriarte, "Contra Viento Y Marea (Against All Odds)."
8. Riley Foundation annual reports and worksheets of Dudley-related grants.
9. Alexander Reid, "Hub trash causing a stink," *Boston Globe,* July 11, 1987.
10. Elizabeth Neuffer, "Indictments say 26 ran $155m drug ring in Massachusetts," *Boston Globe,* December 18, 1990.
11. DSNI press release, July 24, 1987.
12. Reid, "Hub trash causing a stink."
13. News reports, Channel 56 and Neighborhood Network News.
14. Alexander Reid, "City padlocks two illegal trash stations," *Boston Globe,* July 25, 1987; Channel 4, July 23, 1987; DSNI press release, July 24, 1987.

CHAPTER 4

1. See Andrea Isabel Nagel, *The Dudley Street Neighborhood Initiative: A Case Study in Community-Controlled Planning*, Masters thesis, Massachusetts Institute of Technology (MIT), Department of Urban Studies and Planning, May 1990, p. 76.
2. Letter from Lisa Chapnick, director of the Boston Public Facilities Department, to Peter Medoff, director of DSNI, July 7, 1986.
3. Interim Roxbury Planning Advisory Committee, "Housing Strategy for Roxbury," draft prepared by the GRNA Housing Subcommittee (with assistance from the Roxbury Technical Assistance Project, RTAP, of the College of Public and Community Service, University of Massachusetts, Boston), May 12, 1986, p. 1. Also see Gastón and Kennedy, "Blueprint for Tomorrow," and interviews with Bob Terrell and Chuck Turner in *Radical America* 20:5.
4. Geoffrey Rowan, "City's ruling riles Roxbury," *Boston Herald,* May 2, 1986.
5. Stull and Lee, et al., *Proposal to Develop: A Comprehensive Plan for the Dudley Street Neighborhood,* October 1986.
6. DAC International, *A Proposal to Develop a Comprehensive Plan for the Dudley Street Neighborhood,* October 13, 1986.
7. Quoted in Joanne Ball, "Dudley group seeks own answers," *Boston Globe,* January 27, 1987.
8. DAC International workshop summary, DSNI Board/Staff Orientation Workshop, February 7, 1987.
9. Nagel, *The Dudley Street Neighborhood Initiative,* pp. 73-74.
10. Jacobs, an *Architectural Forum* editor, shook up the planning field without a degree in planning or architecture. See Jane Jacobs, *The Death and Life of Great American Cities* (New York: Vintage Books, 1961). See also Robert Fulford, "When Jane Jacobs Took On the World, *New York Times Book Review,* February 16, 1992.
11. Dorothy Rankin, "The Rebuilding of Roxbury (15 years later)," *DSNI Newsletter,* Summer/Fall, 1987, p. 1.
12. *The Dudley Street Neighborhood Initiative Revitalization Plan: A Comprehensive Community Controlled Strategy,* prepared by DAC International, September 1987, p. 47.
13. Ibid., p. 24.
14. Ibid., p. 23.
15. DSNI press release and statement of Ché Madyun, October 25, 1987.
16. Alexander Reid, "Dudley Street neighbors fight blight with hope," *Boston Globe,* January 30, 1988.

CHAPTER 5

1. *Report and Decision of the Boston Redevelopment Authority Regarding the 121A Application of the Dudley Neighbors, Inc.,* November 10, 1988, p. 7.
2. *Nichols Treatise on Eminent Domain,* 3.1.
3. Memorandum re: DSNI and eminent domain from R.I. Goetz, Rackemann, Sawyer & Brewster, March 14, 1988; *Rules and Regulations, Urban Redevelopment Corporations, Chapter 121A,* Massachusetts General Laws, As Amended by the 1975

Legislature, Division of Economic Development, Executive Office of Communities and Development.

4. Dudley Neighbors, Incorporated, *Chapter 121A Application*, submitted August 19, 1988, p. 10.

5. Brown, BRA, *The Revitalization of Downtown Boston*, pp. 25-27.

6. *Boston Globe* editorial, May 6, 1988.

7. See "Minority Developers: Building an economic base in a different world," interview with L. Duane Jackson, *Boston Globe*, April 12, 1992.

8. "Vacant Lots in Roxbury to be Filled with History and Pride," Department of Environmental Management, *DEM Dimensions*, 1988.

9. Letter from Mayor Raymond Flynn to Ché Madyun and Peter Medoff, DSNI, September 28, 1988; letter from Mayor Flynn to BRA Board, November 10, 1988.

10. Devonua N. Havis, "Dudley Street group aims for eminent domain rights," *Bay State Banner*, October 6, 1988.

11. Patricia Mangan, "'Unique' housing plan praised," *Boston Herald*, October 2, 1988. Also see Gus Martins, "Dudley Street group launches plan to build housing on vacant lots," *Boston Globe*, October 2, 1988.

12. *Boston Globe* editorial, October 6, 1988.

13. Transcript of Boston Redevelopment Authority, "In the matter of Dudley Street Neighbors, Inc.," October 13, 1988.

14. Videotape of *Say Brother*, October 27, 1988.

15. Quoted in Margaret Pantridge, "Roxbury group can take land for housing," *Boston Herald*, November 11, 1988.

16. Ann Handley, "Eminent Domain Award Unique But Empowerment Goal Widely Shared," *Banker & Tradesman*, March 1, 1989.

17. *Report and Decision of the Boston Redevelopment Authority Regarding the 121A Application of the Dudley Neighbors, Inc.*, pp. 3-4.

CHAPTER 6

1. Letter from Nancy Andrews, Ford Foundation, to Peter Medoff, DSNI, October 20, 1988.

2. DiMambro speaking to Neighborhood Network News at the June 21, 1989 DSNI annual meeting.

3. "The Dudley Triangle: Request For Qualifications," August 1, 1989.

4. Dudley Neighbors, Incorporated, *Application to the Boston Redevelopment Authority, To Amend Existing Authorization and Approval of a Project Under Chapter 121A of the General Laws*, March 29, 1991.

5. DSNI, "Facilitators' Handbook for Community Land Trust 'Road Shows,'" 1989.

6. Norman Boucher, "The Death and Life of Dudley: A Lesson in Urban Economics," *Boston Globe Magazine*, April 8, 1990.

7. Letter from Gus Newport, DSNI, to Patrick McGuigan, PFD, December 20, 1990.

8. Quoted in Luz Delgado, "BHA programs fostering new optimism in public housing," *Boston Globe*, December 6, 1992.

9. Munnell, et al., *Mortgage Lending in Boston*, pp. 1, 3. Also see *Frontline*, "Your Loan is Denied."

10. Quoted in Boucher, "The Death and Life of Dudley," p. 54.

CHAPTER 7

1. Campaign For An Effective Crime Policy, *Evaluating Mandatory Minimum Sentences* (Washington, D.C., October 1993), p. 5, citing National Conference of State Legislatures, "State Budget and Tax Actions 1993," *City & State,* August 16, 1993.

2. The official 1992 U.S. child poverty rate was 25 percent for children under age six and 21.9 percent for all children. For White children, it was 16.9 percent; for Latino children, 39.9 percent; and for Black children, 46.6 percent. U.S. Bureau of the Census, *Poverty in the United States: 1992* (1993), pp. viii, x, Tables 3, 5. See our Introduction, fn. 1, for an explanation of how the official measure understates the actual extent of poverty.

3. In 1989, the top 1 percent of families had 37.7 percent of total net worth (assets minus debt); the bottom 90 percent had 29.2 percent. The top fifth had 83.6 percent; the upper middle fifth, 12.3 percent; the middle fifth, 4.9 percent; the lower middle fifth, 0.8 percent; the bottom fifth, minus 1.7 percent. Looking at family income, the top fifth had 55.5 percent; the upper middle fifth, 20.7 percent; the middle fifth, 13.3 percent; the lower middle fifth, 7.6 percent; the bottom fifth, 3.1 percent. Edward N. Wolff, "The Rich Get Increasingly Richer: Latest Data on Household Wealth During the 1980s," *Briefing Paper* (Washington, D.C.: Economic Policy Institute, 1992), p. 6. Income inequality comparison to 1959 from Donald L. Barlett and James B. Steele, *America: What Went Wrong* (Kansas City: Andrews and McMeel, 1992), p. ix.

4. Isaac Shapiro and Robert Greenstein, *Selective Prosperity: Increasing Income Disparities Since 1977* (Center on Budget and Policy Priorities, July 1991), pp. 22-23, citing the Luxembourg Income Study of the United States, Australia, Britain, Canada, Germany, Israel, the Netherlands, Norway, Sweden and Switzerland.

5. Latino infant mortality rates are higher than for non-Hispanic Whites and lower than for Blacks. The Black-White infant mortality gap is growing. Reuters, "Baby deaths for blacks 2.5 times white rate," *Boston Globe,* December 10, 1993; Children's Defense Fund, *Decade of Indifference: Maternal and Child Health Trends* (March 1993 press edition), pp. 7-8, Tables B and C, Table 22; Joseph Tiang-Yau Liu, et al., *The Health of America's Children 1992* (Children's Defense Fund, 1992), pp. 12-13. On Boston, see, for example, Richard A. Knox, "AIDS is top killer for ages 25-44 in Mass.," *Boston Globe,* January 26, 1994; "Birth in the 'Death Zones,'" *Boston Globe,* September 10, 1990; "Compassion's Short Supply," *Boston Globe* editorial, September 21, 1990; City of Boston Department of Health and Hospitals, Office of Health and Vital Statistics in the Institute for Urban Health Policy, Research and Education, *Natality and Infant Mortality Data for Boston Residents,* various years.

6. DSNI Human Development Committee, *A Framework for a Human Development Agenda,* 1993.

7. Ceil Blumenstock, Kim Briscoe, Laura Buxbaum, Paul Elwood and Bryan Vosseler, "Assessing Human Needs: A Report to the Dudley Street Neighborhood Initiative," Department of Urban and Environmental Policy, Tufts University, May 1990.

8. "A Concept Paper of the Dudley Street Neighborhood Initiative Agency Collaborative," Draft 2, December 1992.

9. See Robert D. Bullard, ed., *Confronting Environmental Racism: Voices from the Grassroots* (Boston: South End Press, 1993), p. 21, passim. Also see, for example, PBS/Earthkeeping, "Toxic Racism," January 18, 1993.

10. DSNI board minutes, July 7, 1993.

11. "A garden grows in Dorchester-Roxbury plot," *Boston Globe,* January 31, 1993.

12. Meg Vaillancourt, "State vows to help minority-owned businesses," *Boston Globe,* October 30, 1993.

13. Diane E. Lewis, "Rebuild Roxbury," *Boston Globe,* March 30, 1993, citing survey by the city Economic Development Industrial Corporation.

14. "'Economics With People In Mind': A Report on DSNI's Economic Summit," *DSNI Economic News,* August 1993.

15. DSNI Economic Development Committee, "Economics With People In Mind: A Summary of DSNI's Approach to Economic Development," 1993.

16. Draft PFD document related to DSNI furniture factory project.

17. Frederic M. Biddle and Josh Hyatt, "City, state at odds on Stride Rite plan," *Boston Globe,* December 19, 1992.

18. Joseph Pereira, "Split Personality: Social Responsibility and Need for Low Cost Clash at Stride Rite," *Wall Street Journal,* May 28, 1993. Also see Tolle Graham, "Plant Closings in Boston," *The Labor Page* (City Life, Boston), March/April 1993.

19. See Holly Sklar, "Disposable Workers," *Z Magazine,* January 1994; *Trilateralism: The Trilateral Commission and Elite Planning for World Management* (Boston: South End Press, 1980); "Brave New World Order," in Cynthia Peters, ed., *Collateral Damage: The New World Order at Home and Abroad* (Boston: South End Press, 1992); "Imagine a Country," in Paula S. Rothenberg, ed., *Race, Class and Gender in the United States: An Integrated Study,* 3rd edition (New York: St. Martin's Press, forthcoming 1994).

20. "The Mexican Worker: Smart, Motivated, Cheap," *Business Week,* April 19, 1993. Mexican minimum wage figures from Resource Center (Albuquerque), "Industry on the Run," *Resource Center Bulletin,* Fall 1993, p. 4.

21. In 1973, young families with children needed 26 percent of their median income to pay the mortgage, property tax, insurance and maintenance costs of their typical new home. By 1990, the same house would have consumed 48 percent of their median income. Not surprisingly, the percentage of young family homeowners fell from 47 percent in 1980 to 32 percent in 1991. Young family income and poverty data from Children's Defense Fund, *Vanishing Dreams,* pp. 2-3, 10-17, 23, tables in Appendix.

22. "Spiraling down: The fall of real wages," *Dollars & Sense,* April 1992.

23. "Executive Pay: It Doesn't Add Up," editorial, and "Executive Pay: The Party Ain't Over Yet," *Business Week,* April 26, 1993; "What, Me Overpaid? CEOs Fight Back," *Business Week,* May 4, 1992.

24. Between 1977 and 1989, average after-tax, inflation-adjusted income fell by over 10 percent for the lowest fifth of families, 10 percent for the second fifth and over 5 percent for the third fifth, while the top fifth gained over 28 percent. Incomes at the very top of the pyramid skyrocketed: The top 5 percent gained nearly 53 percent and the top 1 percent gained over 102 percent. During that period, notes *Business Week,* "the U.S. economy grew at a rate that would have lifted everybody's real income by 10% if the gains had been distributed evenly." The top fifth of families had pretax incomes of $61,490 and above in 1990; the top 5 percent, $102,358 and above. Income data from U.S. House of Representatives, Committee on Ways and Means, Subcommittee on Human Resources, *Background Material on Family Income and Benefit Changes* (December 19, 1991), p. 68. Quote from "Who'll Get the Lion's Share of Wealth in the '90s? The Lions," *Business Week,* June 8, 1992, p. 86.

25. The official 1992 poverty rates were 39.1 percent for White single mothers, 19.3 percent for White single fathers; 57.2 percent for Black single mothers, 33.3 percent for Black fathers; and 57.4 and 37.1 percent respectively for Latinos. U.S. Bureau of the Census, *Poverty in the United States: 1992,* Table 4.

26. See Holly Sklar, "The Upperclass and Mothers N the Hood," *Z Magazine*, March 1993. The proportion of households headed by women has been rising in all regions of the world. In the United States today, most single mothers are separated or divorced. A report by the U.S. General Accounting Office (GAO) observes that the typical women behind the rise in never-married mothers in the 1980s "differed from the stereotype: They were not unemployed teenaged dropouts but rather working women aged 25 to 44 who had completed high school." The percent of total births to teenage mothers was less in 1990 than in 1980. A portion of the growth in "single parents" is also explained by the rise in unmarried couples living together. The U.S. government does not assure pay equity or affordable child care or provide the social welfare supports common in Western Europe. France, Britain, Denmark and Sweden have similar or much higher proportions of births to unmarried women without U.S. proportions of poverty. GAO, *Poverty Trends, 1980-88: Changes in Family Composition and Income Sources Among the Poor* (September 1992), pp. 4, 35-38, 40-43, 53; U.S. Bureau of the Census, *Statistical Abstract of the United States 1993*, Table 102; U.S. House of Representatives, Committee on Ways and Means, *1993 Green Book: Overview of Entitlement Programs* (July 7, 1993), pp. 1116, 1138-46; House Committee on Ways and Means, *1992 Green Book*, pp. 1077, 1288-1300; United Nations Children's Fund (UNICEF), *The Progress of Nations* (New York: 1993), pp. 13, 41, 43.

27. Karin Stallard, Barbara Ehrenreich and Holly Sklar, *Poverty in the American Dream: Women and Children First* (Boston: South End Press, 1983), p. 9, citing Patricia C. Sexton, *Women and Work*, R. and D. Monograph No. 46, U.S. Department of Labor, Employment and Training Administration (1977).

28. GAO, *Mother-Only Families: Low Earnings Will Keep Many Children in Poverty* (April 1991), pp. 3, 6. Also see Heidi Hartmann, et al., "Raising Wages: The Family Issue of the 90's," *Equal Means*, Winter 1991.

29. The Boston Foundation Carol R. Goldberg Seminar on Child Care, *Embracing Our Future: A Child Care Action Agenda* (Boston Foundation, 1992), pp. 31, 39, 54-55, 81; Child Care Employee Project, *The National Child Care Staffing Study Revisited* (Oakland, CA: 1993), p. 7; Jane Collins and Deborah Weinstein, *The Poor People's Budget FY93* (Boston: Massachusetts Human Services Coalition, January 1993), pp. 3, 24-25, 60-61; Children's Defense Fund, *State of America's Children 1992*, pp. 18-22; Barbara Presley Noble, "Worthy Child-Care Pay Scales," *New York Times*, April 18, 1993; Carol Stevenson and Marcy Whitebook, "Child Care in America: Is Nap Time Over," *Equal Means*, Fall 1993.

30. U.S. Bureau of the Census, *Workers With Low Earnings: 1964 to 1990* (1992) and *Trends in Relative Income: 1964 to 1989* (1991).

31. Lawrence Mishel and Jared Bernstein, "Declining Wages For High School AND College Graduates: Pay and Benefits Trends by Education, Gender, Occupation, and State, 1979-1991," *Briefing Paper* (Economic Policy Institute, May 1992), pp. 9, 12.

32. John Greenwald, "Bellboys with B.A.s," *Time*, November 22, 1993, p. 36, sidebar to George J. Church, "Jobs in an Age of Insecurity."

33. House Committee on Ways and Means, *1993 Green Book*, p. 539.

34. See, for example, S. C. Gwynne, "The Long Haul," *Time*, September 28, 1992; GAO, *Workers At Risk: Increased Numbers in Contingent Employment Lack Insurance, Other Benefits* (March 1991); Bruce D. Butterfield, "'Leasing' employees: a growing discount service," *Boston Globe*, March 21, 1993; Roger Swardson, "Greetings from the Electronic Plantation," *City Pages* (Minneapolis-St. Paul), October 21, 1992, reprinted in *Utne Reader*, March/April 1993; Camille Colatosi, "A Job without a

Future," *Dollars & Sense,* May 1992; Peter T. Kilborn, "A Disrupting Change Hits Workers After Recession," *New York Times,* December 26, 1992.

35. Lance Morrow, "The Temping of America," *Time,* March 29, 1993, pp. 40-41.

36. Quote from Bruce D. Butterfield, "When work is stripped to the bone," January 17, 1993, and statistics from Butterfield, "Diminished Jobs, Added Worry," March 21, 1993, both articles in the *Boston Globe* series, "Broken Promise: Work in the '90s."

37. Janice Castro, "Disposable Workers," *Time,* March 29, 1993, pp. 43-47.

38. Richard A. Cloward and Frances Fox Piven, "The Fraud of Workfare," *The Nation,* May 24, 1993, p. 525; *Statistical Abstract of the United States 1993,* Tables 625, 629, 635. Also see Andrew Hacker, *Two Nations: Black and White, Separate, Hostile, Unequal* (New York: Charles Scribner's Sons, 1992), pp. 103-04.

39. Peter G. Gosselin, "Poverty traps more workers, study says," *Boston Globe,* May 12, 1992.

40. Robert D. Hershey Jr., "Jobless Rate Underestimated, U.S. Says, Citing Survey Bias," *New York Times,* November 17, 1993.

41. National Urban League, *The State of Black America 1993* (Washington, D.C.: National Urban League, 1993), pp. 251, 259. Digital and BankAmerica data from Elaine Ray, "Another Depression," *Boston Globe,* September 24, 1993 and Meg Vaillancourt, "Figures show large job loss among blacks," *Boston Globe,* September 15, 1993, citing *Wall Street Journal* study. Roxbury figure from Diane E. Lewis, "Rebuild Roxbury," *Boston Globe,* March 30, 1993, citing Boston Redevelopment Authority.

42. Only one out of three of the officially counted unemployed received benefits on average from 1984 to 1989; the figure rose to 42 percent in 1991 and 52 percent in 1992, still much less than the 76 percent who received benefits during the 1975 recession. Eligibility varies by state and benefits typically last only a maximum of 26 weeks, whether or not you've found a job. Isaac Shapiro and Marion Nichols, *Far From Fixed: An Analysis of the Unemployment Insurance System* (Center on Budget and Policy Priorities, March 1992), pp. 1-7, 16; House Committee on Ways and Means, *1993 Green Book,* pp. 490-523. Also see Scott Barancik and Isaac Shapiro, *Where Have All the Dollars Gone: A State-By-State Analysis of Income Disparities Over the 1980s* (Center on Budget and Policy Priorities, August 1992).

43. Shapiro and Nichols, *Far From Fixed,* p. 25.

44. Iris J. Lav, et al., *The States and the Poor: How Budget Decisions Affected Low Income People in 1992* (Washington, D.C.: Center on Budget and Policy Priorities and Albany, NY: Center for the Study of the States, 1993), pp. 44-45, citing Martha Burt, *Over the Edge* (Washington, D.C.: Urban Institute, 1992) and Knud Hansen, *The Impact of Elimination of the General Assistance Program in Michigan,* Center for Urban Studies, Wayne State University, August 1992.

45. There is no federally prescribed minimum for the AFDC benefit, which is set by states. The median monthly benefit for a family of three in 1992 was $372, which at $4,464 a year, is much less than half the official poverty threshold for a family of three that year ($11,280). In high-cost Massachusetts, the maximum 1992-93 AFDC benefit was $579, still much less than the official poverty line. Lav, et al., *The States and the Poor,* pp. 11-14; also see House Ways and Means Committee, *Background Material on Family Income and Benefit Changes,* pp. 7-8.

46. In 40 of 44 metro areas surveyed nationally, the cost of a modest two-bedroom apartment, according to HUD's Fair Market Rent level, is greater than the *entire* AFDC benefit for a family of three with no other income; in 28 metro areas a one-bedroom apartment would cost more than the entire AFDC benefit for a family of three. Leonard and Lazere, *A Place To Call Home,* pp. 1, 5-8, 36-41, "Highlights:

Northeastern Metropolitan Areas, Boston"; House Committee on Ways and Means, *1993 Green Book*, p. 712; U.S. Department of Health and Human Services (HHS), Office of Family Assistance, *Characteristics and Financial Circumstances of AFDC Recipients FY 1991*, p. 8.

47. Most families receiving AFDC will be enrolled for less than two years, if single spells are considered, and less than four years total, if multiple spells over time are considered. The *1993 Green Book* explains variations among different measures of length of time on welfare and why, though over time most recipients are short-term recipients, at any one point in time there will be a large proportion of long-term recipients on the rolls. A minority of families become long-term recipients. Long-term recipients have greater obstacles to getting off welfare such as lacking prior work experience, a high school degree or child care, or having poor health. About 20 percent of female AFDC family heads have a work-limiting disability. See House Committee on Ways and Means, *1993 Green Book*, pp. 685-97, 699, 705, 708, 714-18; Robert Greenstein, "Reducing Poverty," in Citizens Transition Project, *Changing America: Blueprints for the New Administration* (New York: Newmarket Press, 1992), p. 426; *Characteristics and Financial Circumstances of AFDC Recipients: FY 1991*, pp. 1-4; Julie Strawn, "Dispelling the Welfare Myths," *Equal Means*, Spring 1992.

48. As noted by Mimi Abramovitz, "the percentage of children in female-headed households has risen steadily since 1959, but the percentage of children receiving AFDC has remained...at about 12 percent." In 1992, the percentage of all children on AFDC reached 13 percent, much less than the growing percentage of children in poverty. Abramovitz, *Regulating the Lives of Women*, p. 354; House Committee on Ways and Means, *1993 Green Book*, p. 688. "In 1972, all States paid AFDC benefits to a family with wages equal to 75 percent of the poverty threshold; by 1991, only 5 States paid AFDC to such a family. Average tax rates on such earnings increased from 52 to 69 percent from 1972 to 1984, and then fell to 56 percent in 1991." House Ways and Means Committee, *Background Material on Family Income and Benefit Changes*, pp. 7-8.

49. Catherine Lerza, "Sex, Lies & Welfare Reform," *Equal Means*, Spring 1992; Robin Toner, "Politics of Welfare: Focusing on the Problems," *New York Times*, July 5, 1992.

50. Alison Mitchell, "Posing as Welfare Recipient, Agency Head Finds Indignity," *New York Times*, February 5, 1993.

51. Rosemary L. Bray, "So How Did I Get Here?" *New York Times Magazine*, November 8, 1992.

52. Barbara Presley Noble, "An Increase in Bias is Seen Against Pregnant Workers," *New York Times*, January 2, 1993; "Women, Children and Work," *New York Times* editorial, January 12, 1993.

53. Children's Defense Fund, *The State of America's Children 1992*, p. 20; HHS, *Characteristics and Financial Circumstances of AFDC Recipients FY 1991*, pp. 1, 5.

54. Bray, "So How Did I Get Here?" Bray refers to a study of low-wage workers and welfare recipients by Rutgers University Professor Kathryn Edin. Another study of welfare recipients found that four out of ten recipients work at paid jobs, either by simultaneously combining work and welfare benefits (17 percent) or cycling between work and welfare (22 percent). Roberta M. Spalter-Roth, Heidi I. Hartmann and Linda Andrews, *Combining Work and Welfare: An Alternative Anti-Poverty Strategy*, A Report to the Ford Foundation (Washington, D.C.: Institute for Women's Policy Research, 1992). Also see the Institute for Women's Policy Research reports, *The Real Employment Opportunities of Women Participating in AFDC: What the Market Can*

Provide (October 1993) and *Dependence on Men, the Market, or the State: The Rhetoric and Reality of Welfare Reform* (November 1993).

55. Children's Defense Fund, *Leave No Child Behind*, p. 7.

56. Robert B. Reich, *The Work of Nations* (New York: Alfred A. Knopf, 1991), pp. 199, 260.

57. Federal, state, local expenditures. *Statistical Abstract of the United States 1992*, Table 565.

58. John Miller, "The Clinton Budget: New Voodoo and Old Snake Oil," *Dollars & Sense*, November/December 1993, p. 32.

59. As the *Boston Globe* put it in a lengthy series, "As state after state succumbs to the perfume of gambling, the odor of desperation becomes increasingly harder to mask...An exhaustive study by two Duke University economists found that lotteries...rather than being a voluntary tax or even a nontax way to balance state budgets...prey on the poor and make gamblers of people who never before had placed a bet." Mitchell Zuckoff and Doug Bailey, "US turns to betting as budget fix," *Boston Globe*, September 26, 1993, first of five-part series, "Easy Money: America's Big Gamble." On regressive taxes, see, for example, Lav, et al., *The States and the Poor*, pp. 71-76; Bruce L. Fisher and Robert S. McIntyre, eds., *Growth & Equity: Tax Policy Challenges for the 1990s* (Washington, D.C.: Citizens for Tax Justice, 1990).

60. Robert B. Reich, "Secession of the Successful," *New York Times Magazine*, January 20, 1991. Also see Reich, *The Work of Nations*.

CHAPTER 8

1. See Holly Sklar, "Young and Guilty by Stereotype," *Z Magazine*, July/August 1993; "The Upperclass and Mothers N the Hood," *Z Magazine*, March 1993; "These kids have not given up," *The Plain Dealer* (Cleveland), May 18, 1991.

2. Lynne Duke, "But Some of My Best Friends Are...," *Washington Post Weekly*, January 14-20, 1991.

3. Coramae Richey Mann, *Unequal Justice: A Question of Color* (Bloomington, IN: Indiana University Press, 1993), p. 33, citing R. L. McNeely and Carl E. Pope, *Race, Crime and Criminal Justice* (Beverly Hills, CA: Sage Publications, 1981).

4. Handlin, *Boston's Immigrants*, p. 332, fn. 87 and pp. 117-23.

5. Thomas H. O'Connor, "A city of 'foreigners': then and now," *Boston Globe*, January 24, 1993. On the Massachusetts registry, see Dolores Kong, "Vital records speak volumes on tougher times," *Boston Globe*, December 27, 1992.

6. Black per capita income was 58 percent of White in 1992; Latino income was 56 percent of White. U.S. Bureau of the Census, *Money Income of Households, Families, and Persons in the United States: 1992*.

7. Holly Sklar's conversation with Mimi Abramovitz, December 23, 1992. Also see, for example, Ricki Solinger, *Wake Up Little Susie: Single Pregnancy and Race Before Roe V. Wade* (New York: Routledge, 1992); Patricia Hill Collins, *Black Feminist Thought* (New York: Routledge, 1991); Susan Faludi, *Backlash: The Undeclared War Against American Women* (New York: Crown, 1991); Stephanie Coontz, *The Way We Never Were: American Families and the Nostalgia Trap* (New York: Basic Books, 1992); Jewell Handy Gresham and Margaret B. Wilkerson, eds., "Scapegoating the Black Family: Black Women Speak," *The Nation* special issue, July 24-31, 1989.

8. For example, in *The Negro Family*, Daniel Patrick Moynihan, then a Labor Department official, embellished sociologist E. Franklin Frazier's thesis of the Black matriarch in whom "neither economic necessity nor tradition had instilled the spirit

of subordination to masculine authority." Moynihan claimed in his 1965 report that matriarchal families are at the core of a Black "tangle of pathology"—and this, not racism, was the "fundamental source of the weakness of the Negro Community." The civil rights movement was then struggling to dismantle American apartheid. Moynihan's thesis was the antithesis to the Black liberation movement, feminism and the welfare rights movement. The Johnson White House released the report shortly after the Watts riots.

In a 1992 speech at Yale University—mixing laudable calls for expanded economic and educational opportunity with slander of single mother families and affirmative action—liberal Massachusetts Senator John Kerry recycled Moynihan's false choice between patriarchy and pathology: "Twenty-seven years ago, my Senate colleague Daniel Patrick Moynihan warned that: 'from the wild Irish slums of the 19th century eastern seaboard, to the riot-torn suburbs of Los Angeles, there is one unmistakable lesson in American history: A society that allows a large number of young men to grow up in broken families...never acquiring any stable relationship to...authority, never acquiring any rational expectations about the future—that society asks for and gets chaos. Crime, violence, unrest, disorder—more particularly, the furious, unrestrained lashing out at the whole social structure—that is not only to be expected; it is very near inevitable.'" (Ellipses Kerry's.) Senator John Kerry, "Race, Politics and the Urban Agenda," Yale University, March 30, 1992, transcript excerpted in Holly Sklar, "Reaffirmative Action," *Z Magazine,* May 1992.

In a news article better suited to the opinion pages for its one-sided trumpeting of conservative commentary, the *Boston Globe* warned of a growing White "underclass," claiming: "The surge in this fatherless tier of poor white Americans, analysts said, vividly resembles the development of the black underclass 30 years ago, beginning with the rampant growth in young, single-parent households and eventually descending toward a culture of poverty and violence supported largely by government programs [namely welfare]." Brian McGrory, "Sharp rise in births to unmarried whites stirs welfare worries," *Boston Globe,* January 3, 1994. Among the subsequent op-ed pieces countering those views—and others promoting them—was Robert Greenstein, "Critics of welfare are ignoring the data," January 26, 1994.

9. Solinger, *Wake Up Little Susie: Single Pregnancy and Race Before Roe V. Wade,* pp. 41, 148.

10. Coontz, *The Way We Never Were,* p. 223; also see pp. 221-28. Coontz critiques Judith Wallerstein's famous study of divorced parents.

11. Felicia R. Lee, "With No Parents, Ladeeta, 18, Presses On," *New York Times,* April 6, 1993, in the ten-part series, "Children of the Shadows."

12. Also see Chapter 7, fn. 26. Most families on AFDC have one child (42 percent) or two children (30 percent); only 10 percent have more than three children. HHS, *Characteristics and Financial Circumstances of AFDC Recipients FY 1991* and *1990,* pp. 1-4, 42-43; House Committee on Ways and Means, *1993 Green Book,* pp. 696-98, 706, 727-28; Will Marshall and Elaine Ciulla Kamarck, "Replacing Welfare with Work," in Will Marshall and Martin Schram, eds., *Mandate for Change* (New York: Berkeley Books/for The Progressive Policy Institute of the Democratic Leadership Council, 1993), p. 224.

13. On the issue of intergenerational welfare, see, House Committee on Ways and Means, *1993 Green Book,* pp. 721-23. In 1900, Black women's labor force participation rate was 40.7 percent, White women's 16 percent. The 1960 rates were 42.2 percent for Black women and 33.6 percent for Whites; in 1970, 49.5 percent and 42.6 percent; in 1980, 53.2 percent and 51.2 percent; and in 1991 they converged at nearly 58 percent. Teresa L. Amott and Julie A. Matthaei, *Race, Gender & Work: A Multicultural*

Economic History of Women in the United States (Boston: South End Press, 1991), Appendix C, Table C-1; *Statistical Abstract of the United States 1992*, Table 609.

14. On Los Angeles, see, for example, Mike Davis, *City of Quartz: Excavating the Future in Los Angeles* (New York: Vintage, 1990), Chapters 4 and 5.

15. Interview with Deputy Superintendent James Wood, Commander of the Drug Control Unit, Boston Police Department, Neighborhood Crime Watch Program, *The Neighborhood Observer* 1:2, 1992. A similar view from New Haven, Connecticut, was aired on NPR's "Weekend Edition," June 19, 1993, Brenda Wilson reporting.

16. Alan Lupo, "Remember, suburbanites: Drug trafficking is a two-way street," *Boston Globe*, April 27, 1993.

17. U.S. Department of Health and Human Services, *HHS News Release*, May 13, 1992. Also see GAO, *Teenage Drug Use: Uncertain Linkages with Either Pregnancy or School Dropout* (January 1991); Michael Isikoff, "Contrary to Popular Belief: Study finds white students are most likely to use drugs," *Washington Post Weekly*, March 4-10, 1991; and National Institute on Drug Abuse (NIDA), HHS, *National Household Survey on Drug Abuse: Main Findings 1990*; *Population Estimates 1990*; *Highlights 1990*; *NIDA Capsules: Summary of Findings from the 1991 National Household Survey on Drug Abuse*.

18. NIDA estimated that in 1991, 19.5 million Whites had used illicit drugs in the past year compared to 3.6 million Blacks and 1.9 million Latinos. NIDA estimates that in 1992, 5.5 percent of non-Hispanic Whites, 6.6 percent of Blacks and 5.3 percent of Latinos had used an illicit drug in the past month. The percent of the population that currently uses illicit drugs has dropped considerably across race lines. NIDA, *National Household Survey on Drug Abuse: Main Findings 1990*; *Population Estimates 1990* and *1991* (revised November 20, 1992); *Highlights 1990* and *1991*; *NIDA Capsules: Summary of Findings from the 1991 National Household Survey on Drug Abuse*; *Preliminary Estimates from the 1992 National Household Survey on Drug Abuse: Selected Excerpts*, June 1993.

19. Congresswoman Maxine Waters has testified: "A Federal Judicial Center study of federal sentences for drug trafficking and firearms offenses found that the average sentence for blacks was 49% higher than for whites in 1990, compared to 28% in 1984." Waters' testimony before the Senate Banking Committee, May 14, 1992. In 1992, 40 percent of those arrested on illicit drug charges were Black—up from 30 percent in 1984. The arrest rate for possession is twice as high as for sale and/or manufacturing. *Statistical Abstract of the United States 1993*, Table 316; FBI, *Crime in the United States 1991: Uniform Crime Reports* (August 1992), p. 231 and FBI, *Crime in the United States 1992: Uniform Crime Reports* (October 1993), p. 235.

Even mandatory minimum sentences for different drugs are discriminatory. The federal mandatory minimum of five years applies to distribution of 500 grams of powder cocaine, but as little as 5 grams of crack cocaine—nine out of ten persons sentenced for federal crack offenses in 1992 were Black. (In 1990, 500 grams of powder cocaine was worth about $50,000; 5 grams of crack, about $125). There is also a five-year mandatory minimum for simple possession of more than 5 grams of crack (the same minimum, for example, as a second offense for the sexual exploitation of children). In 1991, the Minnesota Supreme Court declared unconstitutional state statutes mandating a sentence of four years in prison for a first-time conviction for possession of 3 grams of crack, but probation for first-time possession of 3 grams of powder cocaine. The evidence showed that in 1988, over 92 percent of all persons convicted of crack possession were Black while 85 percent of those convicted of powder cocaine possession were White. The court found there is no rational basis for distinguishing between crack cocaine and powder cocaine.

A 1991 report to Congress by the United States Sentencing Commission found that most federal mandatory minimum penalties were never or rarely used with the most glaring exception of drug violations, and one-third of mandatory minimum defendants had no prior criminal record. Of those convicted with mandatory sentences, 64 percent were Black or Latino. The Commission concluded, "The disparate application of mandatory minimum sentences in cases in which available data strongly suggest that a mandatory minimum is applicable appears to be related to the race of the defendant, where whites are more likely than non-whites to be sentenced below the applicable mandatory minimum." A Commission survey found that judges, defense attorneys and probation officers responded negatively to mandatory minimum sentencing laws, with the most frequent response being that they are too harsh. United States Sentencing Commission, Special Report to the Congress, *Mandatory Minimum Penalties in the Federal Criminal Justice System* (Washington, D.C., August 1991), pp. ii, 10, 50-54, 76, 82, 91, 107, Appendix A. On crack and powder cocaine sentencing disparities, see Ibid., pp. 9, 31; Campaign For An Effective Crime Policy, "Evaluating Mandatory Minimum Sentences," October 1993, p. 4, citing Dennis Cauchon, "Sentences for Crack Called Racist," *USA Today*, May 26, 1993; Clarence Lusane, *Pipe Dream Blues: Racism and the War on Drugs* (Boston: South End Press, 1991), pp. 44-46; *Los Angeles Times*, April 22, 1990, cited in Davis, *City of Quartz*, p. 288; United States Code, Title 21, Sections 841 and 844 (drug offenses and penalties). On the Minnesota case see, Mauer, *Americans Behind Bars*, p. 12, citing *State v. Russell*, decided December 13, 1991; U.S. Sentencing Commission, *Mandatory Minimum Penalties*, Appendix H-17-19. When crack was introduced, it was purposefully marketed to poor inner city neighborhoods, before the suburbs, and one study found that earlier differences in use between Whites and Blacks were related to availability. The rates of current crack use among Blacks, Whites and Latinos in 1991 were less than 1 percent and past-year use was 1.5 percent or less. Marsha Lillie-Blanton, et al., "Probing the Meaning of Racial/Ethnic Group Comparisons in Crack Cocaine Smoking," *Journal of the American Medical Association* 269:8, February 24, 1993; *HHS News*, December 19, 1991, p. 3; *NIDA Capsules: Summary of Findings from the 1991 National Household Survey on Drug Abuse*, p. 3.

20. American Bar Association (ABA), Section of Criminal Justice, *The State of Criminal Justice: An Annual Report* (Chicago: ABA, February 1993), pp. ii and 11. "The decision of whether to charge a youth with possession is a highly subjective process," reports the National Center on Institutions and Alternatives. "Being labeled a seller as opposed to a user often determines whether the youth is held in detention, dealt with by juvenile justice agencies, prosecuted as an adult, or released to his family." In Baltimore in 1981, before the "drug war" heated up, 15 White juveniles and 86 African American juveniles were arrested for sale of drugs. Look at the numbers gap a decade later: in 1991, 13 White juveniles and 1,304 African American juveniles were arrested for sale of drugs; 159 White juveniles and 470 African American juveniles were arrested for possession. National Center on Institutions and Alternatives, *Hobbling a Generation: Young African American Males in the Criminal Justice System of America's Cities: Baltimore, Maryland* (September 1992), pp. 5-6.

21. Special Series, "Is the Drug War Racist?" Sam Vincent Meddis, "Disparities suggest the answer is yes," *USA Today*, July 23-25, 1993; also see other articles in series. Earlier "drug wars" were also racially biased—the campaigns against Chinese immigrants and opium beginning in the late nineteenth century and the early twentieth-century campaigns against Blacks and cocaine and Mexican immigrants and marijuana. See, for example, Mann, *Unequal Justice*, pp. 58-62.

22. Ira J. Chasnoff, et al., "The Prevalence of Illicit-Drug or Alcohol Use During Pregnancy and Discrepancies in Mandatory Reporting in Pinellas County, Florida," *New England Journal of Medicine*, April 26, 1990, pp. 1202-06; House Committee on Ways and Means, *1992 Green Book*, p. 1120; Katha Pollitt, "Fetal Rights: A New Assault on Feminism," *The Nation*, March 26, 1990; Joseph B. Treaster, "For Children of Cocaine, Fresh Reasons for Hope," *New York Times*, February 16, 1993.

23. America's Black Forum, "America's War on Drugs," August 1, 1992, Journal Graphics transcript.

24. Deborah Prothrow-Stith, *Deadly Consequences: How Violence is Destroying Our Teenage Population and a Plan to Begin Solving the Problem* (New York: Harper Perennial, 1991/1993), pp. 103-06; FBI, *Crime in the United States 1991*, pp. 18-21; *Crime in the United States 1992*, pp. 17-21. Also see Albert J. Reiss Jr. and Jeffrey A. Roth, eds., National Research Council, *Understanding and Preventing Violence* (Washington, D.C.: National Academy Press, 1993), pp. 139-45. According to the FBI, less than 4 percent of the 1992 nationwide homicides for which circumstances are known were juvenile gang-related.

25. Prothrow-Stith, *Deadly Consequences*, p. 14; U.S. Senate Committee on the Judiciary, Majority Staff Report, *Fighting Crime in America: An Agenda for the 1990's* (March 12, 1991); Coontz, *The Way We Never Were*, p. 5.

26. Motor vehicle fatalities are the leading cause of death for people between the ages of 5 and 34—including 40 percent of all teenage deaths—and half of all road deaths are due to drunk drivers. In contrast to drug offenders, who are disproportionately low-income Black and Latino because of the racially biased "War on Drugs," the predominantly White drunk drivers are generally charged with misdemeanors and typically receive sentences involving fines, license suspension, treatment programs and community service. Of the approximately 70,000 deaths due to alcohol and other drug-related overdoses, disease and injury other than drunk driving road crashes, 64,000 are attributed to alcohol. Cathy Shine and Marc Mauer, *Does the Punishment Fit the Crime? Drug Users and Drunk Drivers: Questions of Race and Class* (Washington, D.C.: The Sentencing Project, March 1993), pp. 4, 6, 11, 17, passim. Also see FBI, *Crime in the United States 1992*, p. 235; Prothrow-Stith, *Deadly Consequences*, p. 9; Paul J. Goldstein, et al., "Drug-Related Homicide in New York: 1984 and 1988," *Crime and Delinquency* 38:4, October 1992, pp. 467-68, 473; U.S. Department of Justice, *Drugs and Crime Facts, 1991*, pp. 3-7; Reiss and Roth, eds., *Understanding and Preventing Violence*, pp. 13-14, 182-203.

Studies have found rates of drug-related homicides—variously excluding or including alcohol—ranging from 10 percent nationally to one-fourth to over one-half in particular cities at particular times, such as one-third in Boston in 1988. GAO, *The War on Drugs: Arrests Burdening Local Criminal Justice Systems* (April 1991), pp. 2-3, 47; Reiss and Roth, eds., *Understanding and Preventing Violence*, pp. 187-88; U.S. Department of Justice, Bureau of Justice Statistics, *Drugs, Crime, and the Justice System* (December 1992), pp. 5-6, 59. In a narrower category, the FBI lists 6 percent of homicides as known to be involving narcotics felonies. Public Health Professor Paul Goldstein links peaks in the homicide rates during 1979-1981 and the mid-to-late 1980s to Cocaine Wars I (powder) and II (crack), when "New York City and Washington, D.C. replaced Miami as the nation's murder capitals." Paul J. Goldstein, "Drugs and Homicide: Questions For The Future," *CESAR Reports* (Center for Substance Abuse Research), Winter 1992, p. 3, and conversation with Holly Sklar, March 4, 1993. Also see Goldstein, et al., "Drug-Related Homicide in New York"; Goldstein, "Drugs and Violent Crime," in N.A. Weiner and M.E. Wolfgang, eds, *Pathways to Criminal Violence* (Beverly Hills: Sage Publications, 1989).

27. About a third of all murdered women are killed by husbands, boyfriends and ex-partners (less than a tenth are killed by strangers)—"men commonly kill their female partners in response to the woman's attempt to leave an abusive relationship." Arthur L. Kellermann and James A. Mercy, "Men, Women, and Murder: Gender-Specific Differences in Rates of Fatal Violence and Victimization," *The Journal of Trauma* 33:1, July 1992.

    In the words of a congressional report, "Every week is a week of terror for at least 21,000 American women" of all races, regions, educational and economic backgrounds, whose "domestic assaults, rapes and murders were reported to the police." As many as three million more domestic violence crimes may go unreported yearly. Nationally, it is estimated that a woman has between a one in five and a one in three chance of being physically assaulted by a partner or ex-partner during her lifetime. More than 90 women were murdered every week in 1991. U.S. Senate Judiciary Committee, *Violence Against Women: A Week in the Life of America,* report prepared by the Majority Staff, October 1992, pp. ix, 1-3. The Massachusetts rate for women killed in "domestic violence" went from 55 percent of women who were murdered in 1989 to 63 percent in 1990, 70 percent in 1991 and 72 percent through June 30, 1992. Lynda Gorov and John Ellement, "Most women's deaths laid to intimates," *Boston Globe,* January 3, 1993; Lynda Gorov, "Domestic violence searing many states," *Boston Globe,* January 20, 1993.

28. Between 1986 and 1991, the average length of federal prison sentences for drug offenses increased 22 percent to 85 months (over seven years) while sentences for violent offenses decreased 30 percent to 91 months (seven and a half years). ABA, *The State of Criminal Justice,* p. 5.

    Incredibly, violent offenders, including murderers, rapists and child molesters, are being released early to make way for incoming prisoners in systems bursting with nonviolent drug offenders. See, for example, the report by Leslie Stahl on CBS, *60 Minutes,* April 11, 1993, which highlighted the overcrowding, early release problem while obscuring the cause and pointing only to solutions such as more prisons and more overcrowding. The Boston Bar Association concluded that Boston's criminal justice system was in a "desperate condition." During the 1980s, an estimated 60 to 70 percent of all cases prosecuted by the district attorney's office were drug-related and an estimated 50 to 70 percent of cases tried in the Boston Municipal Court and the Suffolk County Superior Court were drug-related. GAO, *The War on Drugs,* Appendix III, Boston and North Adams, Massachusetts, pp. 48-51.

29. Data compiled for Dudley census tracts by the Massachusetts Department of Public Health, April 1993. Boston had a peak of 152 murders in 1990, 113 in 1991 and 76 in 1992. Boston's homicide rate began rising again in 1993.

30. See Prothrow-Stith, *Deadly Consequences,* p. 136, citing J. T. Gibbs, "The New Morbidity: Homicide, Suicide, Accidents and Life-Threatening Behavior," in Gibbs, ed., *Young, Black Male in America* (Dover, MA: Auburn House, 1988). Also see Carol W. Runyan and Elizabeth A. Gerken, "Epidemiology and Prevention of Adolescent Injury: A Review and Research Agenda," *Journal of the American Medical Association* 262:16, October 27, 1989. Rates from *Statistical Abstract of the United States 1993,* Tables 127-29, 134; Children's Safety Network, *A Data Book of Child and Adolescent Injury* (Washington, D.C.: National Center for Education in Maternal and Child Health, 1991).

31. *Statistical Abstract of the United States 1993,* Tables 134, 138. The age-adjusted Black male homicide and "legal intervention" rate was 82.1 per 100,000 in 1970, 71.9 in 1980, 50.2 in 1985 and 68.7 in 1990. The age-adjusted White male rates in 1970 and 1990 were 7.8 and 8.9 respectively. The age-adjusted Black female homicide rate was

15 per 100,000 in 1970, 13.7 in 1980, 10.9 in 1985 and 13 in 1990. The age-adjusted White female rates in 1970 and 1990 were 2.2 and 2.8. *Statistical Abstract of the United States 1993*, Table 129. Among Black males ages 15-24, homicide rates went from 46.4 in 1960 to 102.5 in 1970 to 84.3 in 1980 and 66.1 in 1985 and 101.8 in 1988. Among Black males ages 25-34, rates went from 92 in 1960 to 158.5 in 1970 to 145.1 in 1980 to 94.3 in 1985 and 108.8 in 1988. After 1988 the rates rose further. Christopher Jencks, *Rethinking Social Policy: Race, Poverty, and the Underclass* (Cambridge, MA: Harvard University Press, 1992), pp. 181-83.

32. Centers for Disease Control, *Homicide Surveillance: High Risk Racial and Ethnic Groups—Blacks and Hispanics, 1970-1983*, Atlanta, November 1986, p. 7. Also see Reiss and Roth, eds., *Understanding and Preventing Violence*, pp. 14-15, 129-33. On overall mortality disparities, see Gregory Pappas, et al., "The Increasing Disparity in Mortality Between Socioeconomic Groups in the United States, 1960 and 1986," *New England Journal of Medicine* 329:2, July 8, 1993.

A report by the Massachusetts Department of Public Health analyzing the period 1977-83, found: "When poor white urban neighborhoods were compared with middle-income neighborhoods, the gaps between murder rates were as dramatic as those between races. For instance, Charlestown, a low-income Boston neighborhood, has a homicide rate 10 times higher than that of nearby Malden, a moderate-income suburban area. Both communities are over 97% white...In fact, South Boston, the most exclusively white neighborhood in Boston, has a homicide rate equal to that of South Dorchester/Mattapan, a poor community that is nearly 50% black." The highest murder rates in that period were in Roxbury and North Dorchester, areas of "staggering poverty and a large youth population." Massachusetts Department of Public Health, *Violence in Massachusetts: The Epidemiology of Homicide in Massachusetts, 1977-1983* (Boston, September 1987), pp. 24-25, 27, 29. This report was still in the process of being updated at the time of this writing.

33. On the profitable, poorly regulated civilian weapons trade, see, for example, the *Boston Globe*'s three-part series, "Guns: aiming for profits," beginning with Gregg Krupa, "Gun firms spur market," December 19, 1993 and ending with Krupa, "Spotty oversight, potential for abuse mark weapons sales," December 21, 1993. Studies have found the risk of murder to be three times higher and the risk of suicide five times higher with a gun in the home. In 1988, 277 children under 15 were killed by unintentional firearm injuries such as "playing" with loaded guns in the home. See Arthur L. Kellermann, et al., "Gun Ownership as a Risk Factor For Homicide in the Home" and Jerome P. Kassirer, "Guns in the Household," editorial, *New England Journal of Medicine*, October 7, 1993; Nancy Gibbs, "Up In Arms," *Time*, December 20, 1993, p. 24, citing remarks by Secretary of Health and Human Services Donna Shalala; GAO, *Accidental Shootings: Many Deaths and Injuries Caused by Firearms Could be Prevented* (March 1991), pp. 2-3; Children's Safety Network, *A Data Book of Child and Adolescent Injury*, p. 30.

34. Quoted in Children's Defense Fund, *The State of America's Children: Yearbook 1994* (prepublication press edition, 1994), p. 6.

35. FBI, *Crime in the United States 1991*, p. 279. Erik Eckholm, "Teen-Age Gangs Are Inflicting Lethal Violence on Small Cities," *New York Times*, January 31, 1993. Also see "Why Johnny Gets a Gun," *Time*, August 2, 1993.

36. Prothrow-Stith, *Deadly Consequences*, pp. 30-31, 34-36.

37. David Barry, "Screen Violence: It's Killing Us," *Harvard Magazine*, November/December 1993. Also see Prothrow-Stith, *Deadly Consequences*; U.S. House of Representatives, Committee on the Judiciary, *Hearings on the issue of violence on television*, witness statements, December 15, 1992; "Violence on TV,"

special report, *TV Guide,* August 22, 1992; "Violence in Our Culture," *Newsweek,* April 1, 1991; Christina Robb, "Are we hooked on media violence? Scientists say yes," *Boston Globe,* July 8, 1991; Reiss and Roth, eds., *Understanding and Preventing Violence,* p. 371.

38. James Alan Fox, "Murder most common," *Boston Globe,* January 31, 1993. Fox highlights a demographic factor in violence rates since males (of all races) between the ages of 15 and 24 are about three times as likely as men over 25 to be arrested for violent crimes; the high murder rates of the 1970s partly echoed the baby boom. Today's rates partly reflect the boomers' children.

39. Fact sheet with Children's Defense Fund, *The State of America's Children: Yearbook 1994;* also see Children's Defense Fund, *The State of America's Children 1992,* p. ix.

40. Prothrow-Stith, *Deadly Consequences,* p. 164.

41. Jonathan Kozol, *Savage Inequalities: Children in America's Schools* (New York: Crown Publishers, 1991) and *Death At An Early Age: The Destruction of the Hearts and Minds of Negro Children in the Boston Public Schools* (New York: Plume/Penguin, 1967).

42. Prothrow-Stith, *Deadly Consequences,* pp. 164-66, 169-71. Also see, for example, Alexis Jetter, "Mississippi Learning," *Boston Globe Magazine,* February 21, 1993, on the Algebra Project led by Bob Moses.

43. Jeff P. Howard, "The Third Movement: Developing Black Children for the 21st Century," in National Urban League, *The State of Black America 1993,* pp. 20-21.

44. Jean Caldwell, "Ending Tracking: Difficult and Controversial," *Boston Globe,* November 14, 1993.

45. The percentage of Blacks (ages 25-29), who are high school graduates or more has steadily climbed from 22.3 percent in 1947 (years before the Supreme Court outlawed school segregation) to 76.6 percent in 1980 to 81.7 percent in 1991, while the percentage of Whites went from 54.9 percent in 1947 to 86.9 percent in 1980 to 85.8 percent in 1991. The percentage of Blacks (ages 25 to 29) with four or more years of college rose from 2.8 percent in 1947 to 11.6 percent in 1980 to 13.4 percent in 1990, and it was 11 and 11.3 percent in 1991 and 1992, while the percentage of Whites rose from 5.9 percent in 1947 to 23.7 percent in 1980, 24.2 percent in 1990 and 24.6 percent in 1991. U.S. Bureau of the Census statistician, February 17, 1993, citing *Current Population Reports; Statistical Abstract of the United States 1993,* Table 230. Boston's highest dropout rates are in two low-income neighborhoods: predominantly White South Boston and predominantly Black Roxbury. Leslie Horst and Maryellen Donahue, *Annual and Cohort Dropout Rates in Boston Public Schools: Focus on Programmatic and Demographic Characteristics 1990-1991,* Boston Public Schools, Office of Research and Development, November 1991; U.S. Department of Education, National Center for Education Statistics, *Dropout Rates in the United States: 1991* (September 1992).

46. Congressional commission, cited in Mary Jordan, *Washington Post,* "Panel to call for new student-aid system," *Boston Globe,* February 3, 1993; Associated Press, "US college costs still rising faster than income," *Boston Globe,* September 22, 1993; Anthony Flint, "Report finds region scrimping on colleges," *Boston Globe,* October 1, 1991. Also see James H. Rubin, "Colleges: Budget cuts will hurt minority enrollment," *Boston Globe,* January 18, 1993; Deborah J. Carter and Reginald Wilson, *Minorities in Higher Education,* 1992 Eleventh Annual Status Report (Washington, D.C.: American Council on Education, January 1993).

47. Diane E. Lewis, "Employment testing: Useful tool, or entrapment?" *Boston Globe,* April 11, 1993.

48. Margery Austin Turner, et al., *Opportunities Denied, Opportunities Diminished: Racial Discrimination in Hiring,* (Washington, D.C.: Urban Institute Press, 1991), pp. 2, 56-57.

49. National Center for Education Statistics, U.S. Department of Education, *Youth Indicators 1993: Trends in the Well-Being of American Youth* (October 1993), p. 140.

50. People for the American Way, *Democracy's Next Generation II: A Study of American Youth on Race* (Washington, D.C.: 1992), pp. 41, 161. Also see Lynne Duke, "Just When You Thought It Was the 20th Century...," *Washington Post Weekly,* January 6-12, 1992; Tom W. Smith, "Ethnic Images in the United States," *The Polling Report* 7:11, May 27, 1991.

51. Mark Muro, "Class Privilege," *Boston Globe,* September 18, 1991.

52. Ellis Cose, "To the Victors, Few Spoils," *Newsweek,* March 29, 1993, p. 54; also see David Gates, "White Male Paranoia," in the same issue; Anne B. Fisher, "When Will Women Get To The Top?" *Fortune,* September 21, 1992; "Corporate Women: Progress?," *Business Week,* June 8, 1992; Judith H. Dobrzynsi, "The 'Glass Ceiling,': A Barrier to the Boardroom, Too," *Business Week,* November 22, 1993.

53. DSNI Human Services Activity Report, August-December 1988.

54. Andrea Nagel and Gail Sullivan, *Youthful Visions: Building a Foundation for Community: A report about Dudley's Young Architects and Planners Project* (Boston: DSNI, 1992), foreword by Ché Madyun.

55. Blumenstock, et al., "Assessing Human Needs: A Report to the Dudley Street Neighborhood Initiative," pp. 19-20; Nagel and Sullivan, *Youthful Visions,* pp. 16-17.

56. Nagel and Sullivan, *Youthful Visions,* pp. 42, 49.

57. Federal spending on "drug control" programs climbed from $1.7 billion in fiscal 1982 to $12 billion in 1992. Despite the proven success of intensive treatment for actual drug addiction, the portion of the federal drug budget going to treatment dropped from 25 to 14 percent during 1981-91. Less than 15 percent of those needing publicly funded treatment are able to get it at any one time. Six of seven imprisoned addicts will leave prison or jail without receiving any drug treatment, much less the kind of intensive treatment that shows success. Without treatment and other services such as education and job assistance, many end up back in prison. Meanwhile, the courts, juvenile facilities, jails and prisons are jammed and "corrections" spending is the fastest growing part of state budgets, including in Massachusetts where the corrections budget has more than doubled while drug treatment and social services have been slashed. Mathea Falco, "Toward A New National Drug Strategy," in Citizens Transition Project, *Changing America,* pp. 366-68; GAO, *ADMS Block Grant: Women's Set-Aside Does Not Assure Drug Treatment for Pregnant Women* (May 1991), p. 1; U.S. Senate Committee on the Judiciary, *Fighting Crime in America,* p. 22; Sean P. Murphy, "Few inmates get drug rehab," *Boston Globe,* January 8, 1993; Drugs and Crime Data Center & Clearinghouse, U.S. Department of Justice, *Fact Sheet: Drug Data Summary,* November 1992; GAO, *The War on Drugs,* Appendix III, Boston and North Adams, Massachusetts, p. 46.

58. Quoted in Diego Ribadeneira, "Students on the run: Track program helps youths clear inner-city hurdles," *Boston Globe,* March 24, 1990.

59. John Barros, "Personal and Present," St. Patrick's newsletter.

60. The Boston Police Department Management Review Committee headed by James St. Clair of the law firm Hale and Dorr found that nearly a third of the misconduct complaints made against members of the Boston Police Department in 1989 and 1990 alleged physical abuse of citizens and there was "a disturbing pattern of violence

toward citizens by a small number of officers" with a history of prior complaints—a pattern also documented nationally. Area B, which includes Dudley, generated the highest number (26 percent) of the complaints while Area D, which includes Allston/Brighton, the South End, Fenway and Back Bay generated the second highest (19 percent). A review of 1989-90 cases found that 50 percent of the complainants were Black and 9 percent were "non-black racial and ethnic minorities." In 1989, the Police Department sustained only 6.6 percent of the complaints it resolved and in 1990, even less, 4.4 percent. Of the allegations sustained, a disproportionate share are those brought by the Department itself for violation of departmental rules. The St. Clair Commission recommended establishment of a Community Appeals Board. An NAACP report of police misconduct reviewed similar patterns around the country and noted the finding of the commission headed by Warren Christopher—now U.S. secretary of state—that three of the four police officers indicted in the Rodney King beating had been the subjects of prior excessive force complaints. See *Report of the Boston Police Department Management Review Committee,* James D. St. Clair, Esq. Chairman, Submitted to Mayor Raymond L. Flynn, January 14, 1992, pp. 106-15, 128-33; National Association for the Advancement of Colored People, *Beyond the Rodney King Story: NAACP Report on Police Conduct and Community Relations,* prepared by the Criminal Justice Institute, Harvard Law School and the William Monroe Trotter Institute, University of Massachusetts-Boston (Baltimore, MD: NAACP, March 1993), p. 63; Gary Indiana, "Closing Time: Double Jeopardy? Apocalypse Again? L.A. Waits," *Village Voice,* April 20, 1993, pp. 26-27.

61. Quotes from unofficial statements written by those involved and author interviews with John Barros and "Tony." The authors were also at DSNI when the young men came by to tell what happened.

62. Marc Mauer, *Americans Behind Bars: One Year Later* (Washington, D.C.: The Sentencing Project, February 1992).

63. The number of those convicted of a drug offense in the federal prison system more than doubled in the 1980s to 59 percent of inmates in 1992 and is expected to grow to 69 percent by 1995. Between 1979 and 1991, the percentage of drug offenders in state prisons jumped from 6 percent to 22 percent; among women state prisoners, a third are serving time for drug offenses. For prison composition and drug offender data: U.S. Department of Justice, Bureau of Justice Statistics, *Survey of State Prison Inmates, 1991* (March 1993); U.S. Department of Justice statisticians, March 1 and 5, 1993, citing 1993 federal statistics; U.S. Department of Justice, *Drugs and Crime Facts, 1992,* p. 18; Mauer, *Americans Behind Bars,* p. 7, citing *Washington Post,* April 25, 1991; *The World Almanac and Book of Facts 1993* (New York: Pharos Books, 1992), p. 950. For historical data, see Patrick A. Langan, U.S. Department of Justice, Bureau of Justice Statistics, *Race of Prisoners Admitted to State and Federal Institutions, 1926-86* (May 1991).

64. The figures for women were 1 in 37 Blacks, 1 in 56 Latinas and 1 in 100 Whites. Mark Mauer, *Young Black Men and the Criminal Justice System* (The Sentencing Project, 1990).

65. Jerome C. Miller, *Hobbling A Generation: Young African American Males In Washington, D.C.'s Criminal Justice System* (Alexandria, VA: National Center on Institutions and Alternatives, April 17, 1992), pp. 1, 5; National Center on Institutions and Alternatives, *Hobbling a Generation: Baltimore, Maryland,* pp. 1-4.

66. Carol Stocker and Barbara Carton, "GUILTY...of being black," *Boston Globe,* May 7, 1992. Also see ABC News, *20/20,* "Presumed Guilty," November 6, 1992, on Los Angeles.

67. James M. Shannon, Stephen A. Jonas and Marjorie Heins, *Report of the Attorney General's Civil Rights Division on Boston Police Department Practices,* December 18, 1990, pp. 14-15, citing Judge Mather in *Commonwealth v. Phillips & Woody.* Also see *Commonwealth v. Carr et al.*

68. Shannon, et al., *Attorney General's Report,* p. 36.

69. Prothrow-Stith, *Deadly Consequences,* pp. 33-34.

70. Shannon, et al., *Attorney General's Report,* pp. 60-61, 66-67. Also see Daniel Golden, "A Failure to Communicate," *Boston Globe Magazine,* February 17, 1991, p. 44; Citizens for Public Safety/Youth Congress Task Force, *Survey: 1991/92 Police/Youth Relations,* Boston, 1992. A civil rights investigation by the U.S. Attorney's Office also "disclosed evidence of police misconduct directed against civilian witnesses, and individuals who were targets of the Stuart homicide investigation." U.S. Department of Justice, U.S. Attorney, District of Massachusetts, press release summarizing the results of the U.S. Attorney/FBI investigation, July 10, 1991, p. 19. The Boston Police Department denied almost all the findings in Superintendent Ann Marie Doherty, Chief, Office of Internal Investigations, A Report to Police Commissioner Francis M. Roache, *The Stuart Investigation: A Response to the U.S. Attorney's Report.*

71. Mike Davis, *City of Quartz: Excavating the Future in Los Angeles* (New York: Vintage, 1990), p. 284, citing *Los Angeles Times,* May 8, 1988. Gates has also said that a disproportionate number of Blacks died as a result of police chokeholds because they didn't have veins in their necks "like normal people." See Mann, *Unequal Justice,* p. 152.

72. Mann, *Unequal Justice,* p. 188, citing Joan Petersilia, "Racial Disparities in the Criminal Justice System: A Summary," *Crime and Delinquency* 31:1, 1985.

73. Mann, *Unequal Justice,* pp. 167-71, 181-84, 213-14. Also see Jill Smolowe, "The Trials of the Public Defender," *Time,* March 29, 1993.

74. Hubert Williams and Patrick V. Murphy, "The Evolving Strategy of Police: A Minority View," *Perspectives on Policing,* U.S. Department of Justice (January 1990), p. 2. Also see National Minority Advisory Council on Criminal Justice, *The Inequality of Justice: A Report on Crime and the Administration of Justice in the Minority Community* (U.S. Department of Justice, January 1982).

75. *New York Times* editorial, "Young Black Men," May 7, 1992.

76. Quoted in Derrick Z. Jackson, "Showing youth a new destiny," *Boston Globe,* March 23, 1990.

CHAPTER 9

1. Mike Davis, "In L.A., Burning All Illusions," *The Nation,* June 1, 1992, p. 743. Also see Davis, *City of Quartz,* and Don Hazen, ed., *Inside the L.A. Riots* (New York: Institute for Alternative Journalism, 1992). The majority of those arrested on riot-related charges were Latino and African American, but over one out of eight were Anglo. See Davis, *L.A. was Just the Beginning* (Westfield, NJ: Open Magazine Pamphlet Series, 1992), p.1, citing Sheriff's Department analysis.

2. Rep. Maxine Waters, testimony before the Senate Banking Committee, May 14, 1992.

3. Ibid.

4. Eric Mann, "The Poverty of Corporatism: Los Angeles—A Year After (1)," *The Nation,* March 29, 1993. Also see Mann's follow-up article, "The Left and the City's Future," May 3, 1993.

5. Marc Cooper, "Falling Down," *Village Voice*, March 23, 1993.

6. Mike Davis, "Who Killed L.A.?: The War Against the Cities," *Crossroads*, June 1993, pp. 3, 17.

7. Rubén Martínez, "1 Quake, 2 Worlds," *New York Times*, January 20, 1994.

8. Tom Mashberg, "Tensions rise in LA," *Boston Globe*, December 20, 1992.

9. About 90 percent of DSNI's voting membership comes from the core area, which has a population of about 12,000, of whom more than one-third (nearly 4,400) are under 18 years old. So, the adult core area share of DSNI's voting membership (members must be at least 18 years old to vote in DSNI elections) represents more than 20 percent of the adult core population.

10. William H. Harrison, "Dudley group starts first development," *Boston Globe*, March 28, 1993. Unfortunately, this article was buried inside the limited-circulation City Weekly section. Also see *Boston Globe* editorial, "A new face on Dudley Street," April 1, 1993 and Lynda Morgenroth, "Neighborhood group breaks ground on new housing," *Boston Globe*, September 12, 1993.

11. John McKnight, Speech to Massachusetts Foundations, April 22, 1992.

12. John McKnight, *The Future of Low-Income Neighborhoods And the People Who Reside There: A Capacity-Oriented Strategy for Neighborhood Development* (Evanston, IL: Center for Urban Affairs and Policy Research, Northwestern University, undated), p. 18.

13. John McKnight, "Services are Bad for People: You're either a citizen or a client," *Organizing*, Spring/Summer 1991, p. 41.

14. Thomas F. Jackson, "The State, the Movement, and the Urban Poor: The War on Poverty and Political Mobilization in the 1960s," in Katz, ed., *The 'Underclass' Debate*, pp. 419-21.

15. See Neal R. Peirce and Carol F. Steinbach, *Corrective Capitalism: The Rise Of America's Community Development Corporations* (New York: Ford Foundation, 1987); W. Dennis Keating, "The Emergence of Community Development Corporations: Their Impact on Housing and Neighborhoods," *Shelterforce*, February 1989.

16. William Traynor, "Community Development: Does It Need To Change?" *The Neighborhood Works*, April/May 1992.

17. Ricanne Annik Hadrian, *Combining Organizing and Housing Development: Conflictive Yet Synergistic*, Masters Thesis, MIT Department of Urban Studies and Planning, May 6, 1988, p. 107.

18. DAC International, *A Proposal to Develop a Comprehensive Plan for the Dudley Street Neighborhood*, October 13, 1986.

19. Memo from Bill Traynor and John Vaughn, CTAC, to DSNI/DNI staff and board, October 6, 1993.

20. Edward Skloot, address to Conference of Local Development Corporations, sponsored by New York University and the Coalition for Neighborhood Economic Development, New York, May 30, 1991.

21. The four other groups are Germantown Settlement, Philadelphia; Marshall Heights Community Development Corporation, Washington, D.C.; NEWSED Community Development Corporation, Denver; and Warren/Conner Community Development Coalition, Detroit.

22. Arlene Eisen, *A Report On Foundations' Support Of Comprehensive Neighborhood-Based Community-Empowerment Initiatives*, sponsored by East Bay Funders, Ford Foundation, The New York Community Trust, Piton Foundation, Riley Foundation, March 1992, p. 5.

23. Ibid., pp. 5, 39-40.
24. Ibid., p. 40.
25. Flather quoted on catalytic role in Ibid.
26. Ibid.
27. Ibid.
28. Jeff Faux, "As Our Cities Go, So Does America," in Hazen, ed., *Inside the L.A. Riots*, p. 141.
29. Lynn A. Curtis and Vesta Kimble, *Investing in Children and Youth, Reconstructing Our Cities: Doing What Works to Reverse the Betrayal of American Democracy* (Washington, D.C.: The Milton S. Eisenhower Foundation, 1993), pp. 12-14, 157-58.
30. Testimony of Howard Leibowitz before the Boston City Council Special Committee on Intergovernmental Relations, February 26, 1991.
31. Todd Schafer, "Still Neglecting Public Investment: The FY94 Budget Outlook," *Briefing Paper*, Economic Policy Institute (September 1993). Also see Miller, "The Clinton Budget"; Robert Greenstein and Paul Leonard, *A New Direction: The Clinton Budget and Economic Plan* (Center on Budget and Policy Priorities, March 1993).
32. *New York Times*, March 24, 1982.
33. Curtis and Kimble, *Investing in Children and Youth, Reconstructing Our Cities*, pp. 214-17.
34. Mann, "The Poverty of Corporatism," p. 409.
35. President Eisenhower said in his Farewell Radio and Television Address to the American People, January 17, 1961: "This conjunction of an immense military establishment and a large arms industry is new in the American experience...In the councils of government, we must guard against the acquisition of unwarranted influence, whether sought or unsought, by the military-industrial complex. The potential for the disastrous rise of misplaced power exists and will persist."

    Instead of curtailing weapons proliferation and supporting military-civilian conversion at home and abroad, the United States is strengthening its position as the world's leading arms dealer and its already overwhelming capacity for military intervention. The retired military officers of the Washington-based Center for Defense Information (CDI) are among the many voices for military reform, with clear programs providing for the nation's defense with much less than the Cold War levels of spending perpetuated by the Bush and Clinton administrations. In CDI's words, the Clinton "administration wants to spend an astounding $1.3 Trillion on the military over a period of just 5 years. In the final year of the plan, the downward trend will be reversed as military spending rises again." CDI warns that "Pentagon 5-year plans have long been grounded in overstated threats and understated costs." CDI urges politicians not to rationalize military spending as "a welfare program," noting that "money spent on real needs will generate more jobs than are currently wasted on unneeded military programs." Center for Defense Information, "Cutting Unnecessary Military Spending: Going Further and Faster," *The Defense Monitor* XXI: 3, 1993. Also see "President Clinton and the Military," *Defense Monitor* XXII: 2; "President Clinton's First Military Budget," *Defense Monitor* XXII: 4; "America's Military Role in the New World Order: Have Guns, Will Travel," *Defense Monitor* XXII: 7; "The Military and American Society: A Clash of Values," *Defense Monitor* XXII: 8; "International Arms Sales: Race to Disaster," *Defense Monitor* XXII: 9.
36. Children's Defense Fund, *The State of America's Children: Yearbook 1994*, p. 29.
37. Martin Luther King Jr., *Where Do We Go From Here: Chaos or Community?* (Harper & Row, 1967).

INTERVIEWS

Najwa Abdul-Tawwab, resident and teacher; chair, DSNI Human Development Committee

Nancy Andrews, deputy director, Office of Program and Managed Investment, Ford Foundation; program related investment officer, Ford Foundation

John Barros, resident; cochair, DSNI Youth Committee; DSNI board

Sue Beaton, DSNI deputy director/development director; DSNI board; DSNI Development Committee; development director, Project Hope

Rebecca Black, director of planning, Public Facilities Department

Paul Bothwell, resident; DSNI board; DSNI Development Committee

Kelley Brown, DSNI development director

Shirley Carrington, executive director, Roxbury Multi-Service Center; DSNI Executive and Planning Committees

Lisa Chapnick, commissioner, Inspectional Services; director, Public Facilities Department

Melvyn Colón, executive director, Nuestra Comunidad Development Corporation; DSNI president; DSNI vice president; DSNI Executive, Development and Planning Committees; DSNI board

Andrea D'Amato, planner, Boston Redevelopment Authority

Carline Dorcena, resident; DSNI board; DSNI Organizing Committee; cochair, DSNI Youth Committee

Ros Everdell, DSNI organizing director

Jessie Farrier, resident; DSNI member; Mt. Pleasant-Vine Neighborhood Association

Gertrudes Fidalgo, resident; DSNI organizer

Maria-Goreth Fidalgo, resident; DSNI board; cochair, DSNI Human Development Committee

Newell Flather, administrator, Riley Foundation; cofounder, Grants Management Associates

Sarah Flint, resident; chair, Orchard Park Tenants Association

Raymond Flynn, mayor of Boston

Deborah Goddard, deputy director, Public Facilities Department

Nancy Green, acting executive director, Orchard Park Tenants Association

Bob Haas, resident; planning director, Dorchester Bay Economic Development Corporation; DSNI Development and Planning Committees; DNI and DSNI boards; DSNI vice president

Stephen Hanley, executive director, WAITT House; DSNI Executive and Human Development Committees; DSNI board, board clerk

Laura Henze, staff, Riley and Boston Foundations Monitoring Project

Robert Holmes Jr., trustee, Riley Foundation; lawyer, Powers & Hall

Shelley Hoon, development director, Roxbury Multi-Service Center; DSNI board, board clerk

Linda Joyce, resident; Orchard Park Tenants Association; DSNI Organizing Committee; DSNI board

Sue Karant, DSNI fundraiser

Positions listed are those held during interviewee's association with DSNI. Where multiple positions are listed, they are given in chronological order, from most recent to past.

Gail Latimore, resident; head of planning, Action for Boston Community Development; DSNI Executive and Planning Committees; DSNI board

Ché Madyun, resident; president of DSNI and DNI; DSNI Executive and Organizing Committees; DSNI board

Sophia McCarthy, resident; DSNI Organizing Committee; DSNI board

Peter Medoff, first DSNI executive director

Nelson Merced, director of technical assistance, YouthBuild USA; MA state representative; deputy director for policy and planning, Public Facilities Department; DSNI president; DSNI founding cochair; executive director, La Alianza Hispana

Peter Munkenbeck, development director, The Community Builders

Andrea Nagel, DSNI human development director; first DSNI organizer

Eugene "Gus" Newport, second DSNI executive director

Mary Nee, director, Public Facilities Department

Tubal Padilla, resident; DSNI Planning Committee; DSNI board

Stephen Plumer, vice president, DAC International

Luis Prado, executive director, La Alianza Hispana; DSNI board; DSNI treasurer

David Rockwell, vice president of community lending, Shawmut Bank; DSNI development director

Gareth Saunders, Boston City Council member; treasurer, DNI; cochair, Roxbury Neighborhood Council

Bill Slotnik, executive director, Community Training and Assistance Center

Arnaldo Solís, resident; deputy director, Children's Services of Roxbury; DSNI Executive, Development and Human Development Committees; DSNI board, board clerk; director of counseling and social services, La Alianza Hispana

Lessie Spann, resident; DSNI Organizing Committee; DSNI board

Margarita Sturniolo, resident; DSNI Organizing Committee; DSNI board

Gail Sullivan, architect; coordinator, Dudley's Young Architects and Planners

Marcia Szymanski, DSNI economic development staff

Adalberto Teixeira, resident; Cape Verdean and Roxbury liaison, Mayor's Office of Neighborhood Services; DSNI organizer

Bob Terrell, cochair, Greater Roxbury Neighborhood Authority

Henry Thayer, lawyer, Rackemann, Sawyer & Brewster

"Tony," resident

Bill Traynor, community development consultant; director of community development, Community Training and Assistance Center

Clayton Turnbull, resident; DSNI vice president; DSNI Executive, Development and Economic Development Committees; DNI and DSNI boards

Ken Wade, cochair, Greater Roxbury Neighborhood Authority; Roxbury Neighborhood Council

Father Walter Waldron, pastor, St. Patrick's church; DSNI board

Jason Webb, resident; DSNI Organizing and Youth Committees

Rogelio "Ro" Whittington, resident; third DSNI executive director; treasurer, DSNI; DNI and DSNI boards

Paul Yelder, director, DNI; deputy director, DSNI; treasurer, DNI and DSNI; DSNI Executive and Development Committees; DSNI board; development director, Roxbury Multi-Service Center

APPENDIX

TABLE 1
POPULATION BY RACE & ETHNICITY, 1990*

	DSNI Whole	DSNI Core	Boston
Total Number	24,068	12,018	574,282
		(in percent)	
White (non-Hispanic)	6.1	6.8	59.0
Black (non-Hispanic)	60.9	50.0	23.8
Hispanic	23.3	29.2	10.8
Asian & Pacific Islander	.9	.9	5.3
Am. Indian, Eskimo, Aleut	.5	.7	.3
Other (non-Hispanic)	8.5	12.7	1.0
		(estimates)	
Cape Verdean	N.A.	25	N.A.
Black (non-Cape Verdean, non-Hispanic)	N.A.	37	N.A.

* These figures differ from Table 6 because they are based on census block groups, which delineate the DSNI whole and core areas more precisely than do larger census tracts. In the DSNI core, the primary non-Hispanic "Other" category is Cape Verdean. Many Cape Verdeans identify themselves for the census as Black. See Chapter 1, fn. 21, for explanation of estimates.

TABLE 2
POPULATION BY AGE AND GENDER, 1990

	DSNI Core	Boston
	(in percent)	
Female	53.6	52.0
Male	46.4	48.0
Under 18 years old	36.5	19.1
Ages 18-64	56.0	69.4
Ages 65 & over	7.5	11.5
	(in years)	
Median age	27.3	30.8
White	31.6	32.5
Black	25.7	28.2
Hispanic*	22.3	25.1

* Unless otherwise specified in tables, White and Black includes Hispanics. Hispanics may be of any race.

TABLE 3
PERCENT BELOW OFFICIAL POVERTY LINE, 1989

	DSNI Whole	DSNI Core	Boston
Total population	32.4	35.2	18.7
White	32.9	31.8	13.9
Black	29.6	35.8	24.2
Other	40.3	36.2	34.1
Hispanic	50.0	46.6	33.9
Under 18 years	44.8	49.3	28.3
65 & over	21.6	25.8	15.3
Female Householder Family with related children under 18 (no spouse present)	51.5	57.8	44.0
Male Householder Family with related children under 18 (no spouse present)	35.2	44.4	15.6
Married-Couple Family with related children under 18	18.9	23.2	9.4

TABLE 4
PER CAPITA INCOME, 1989
(Universe: Total persons or persons 15 years & over)

	DSNI Whole	DSNI Core	Boston
All persons	$8,631	$7,634	$15,581
White	$9,937	$9,264	$18,939
Black	$9,306	$7,902	$10,420
Asian & Pacific Islander	$7,676	$6,819	$9,406
Am. Indian, Eskimo, Aleut	$7,154	$6,942	$9,319
Other	$6,162	$6,559	$7,959
Hispanic	$5,508	$5,593	$8,364

TABLE 5
PERCENT UNEMPLOYMENT 1960-1990

	DSNI Core	Boston
1960	6.1	5.0
1970	6.5	4.3
1980	12.4	6.1
1990	16.3	8.3

* Official figures for civilians 16 years and over for 1970-90; 14 years and over for 1960. Does not count discouraged workers or involuntary part-timers. See Chapter 7.

TABLE 6
POPULATION BY RACE & ETHNICITY 1950-1990*
DSNI CORE

	1950	1960	1970	1980	1990 by census tracts
Total	38,674	28,246	21,187	15,214	15,488
		(in percent)			
White	94.8	79.4	45.1	16.4	14.2
Black	4.8	20.0	52.6	53.8	54.4
Other	N.A.	N.A.	N.A.	29.0	29.2
Hispanic	N.A.	N.A.	12.2	27.8	29.7

* These 1950-1990 population figures are derived from census tract data. Table 1 and other tables use the more precise census block-group method for 1990.

SOURCES FOR TABLES

Tables prepared by Holly Sklar, with assistance from Jarrett Barrios, using these sources:

Rolf Goetze, with the assistance of Mark R. Johnson, *Dudley Triangle Area: U.S. Census (STF1) 1990 Population & Housing Tables, with comparisons to City of Boston*, Boston Redevelopment Authority (BRA) Policy Development & Research Department, assisted by Massachusetts State Data Center, Massachusetts Institute for Social and Economic Research (MISER), University of Massachusetts/Amherst, May 1992.

BRA Special Files: *DSNI Core, DSNI Whole* and *DSNI Triangle*. Created from 1990 Census of Population and Housing, Summary Tape File 3, Prepared by the Massachusetts State Data Center/MISER, using software provided by the California State Data Center.

City of Boston 1990 Census of Population and Housing Summary Tape File 3, U.S. Census Bureau, printed by the Massachusetts State Data Center/MISER, available through the BRA Policy Development & Research Department, July 1992.

Rolf Goetze, *City of Boston Income, Employment and Housing Changes Revealed by the 1990 U.S. Census, Summary Tape File 3*, BRA Policy Development & Research Department, July 1992.

1950-1990 census tract data compiled by Jarrett Barrios.

DECLARACIÓN DE DERECHOS COMUNITARIOS

Nosotros, la juventud, los adultos, los ancianos de descendencia Africana, Latinoamericana, Indioamericana, Caribeña, Asiática y Europea, somos la comunidad de Dudley. Hace nueve años eramos el basurero de Boston y uno de los más olvidados vecindarios. Hoy, nos estamos alzando. Estamos reclamando nuestra dignidad, reconstruyendo nuestras viviendas y reparando el tejido social de nuestra comunidad. Mañana, haremos realidad nuestra visión de un barrio de vibrante diversidad cultural, donde cada uno de sus habitantes es valorado por su talento y contribución a la comunidad. Nosotros, los residentes de Dudley, nos comprometemos a la siguiente declaración de derechos:

1. Tenemos el derecho de darle forma a todos los planes de desarrollo, programas e iniciativas que puedan afectar la calidad de nuestras vidas como residentes del barrio.

2. Tenemos el derecho a una atención médica que a la vez que es accesible a todos los residentes de la comunidad, es también sensible a la diversidad cultural de los usuarios.

3. Tenemos el derecho a controlar la urbanización de los terrenos del vecindario de tal forma que nos aseguremos de la existencia de espacios abiertos para parques, jardines, parques infantiles y una serie de elementos para uso recreacional.

4. Tenemos el derecho a vivir en un ambiente libre de peligro, que sea positivo para la salud y la seguridad de nuestras familias.

5. Tenemos el derecho a celebrar la vibrante diversidad cultural de nuestro barrio por medio de todas las formas de expresión artística.

6. Tenemos el derecho a educación y entrenamiento que propicie el que nuestros niños, nuestros jóvenes, nuestros adultos y ancianos puedan alcanzar su máximo potencial.

7. Tenemos el derecho a una porción de los trabajos y la prosperidad creada por las iniciativas económicas del area metropolitana de Boston en general y de nuestro vecindario en particular.

8. Tenemos el derecho a viviendas de buena calidad y al alcance de nuestros medios económicos en el vecindario tanto en calidad de inquilinos como de dueños de propiedad.

9. Tenemos el derecho a cuidado infantil y al alcance de nuestros medios económicos que dé respuesta a nuestras necesidades particulares tanto del niño como de su familia, disponible en centros o en hogares.

10. Tenemos el derecho a transportación pública accesible y segura que sirva a todo el vecindario.

11. Tenemos el derecho al gozo de servicios y productos de buena calidad, que se ponga a disposición de todos por medio de un distrito comercial basado en el vecindario.

12. Tenemos el derecho al gozo de una vida religiosa y espiritual en lugares apropiados de ejercicio religioso.

13. Tenemos el derecho tener tranquilidad y seguridad en nuestros hogares y en nuestro barrio.

DECLARAÇÃO DE DIREITOS DA COMUNIDADE

Nós, os jovens, adultos e velhos de ascendência Africana, Latinoamericana, Caribena, Indioamericana, Asiatica e Europea do tá formâ comunidade de Dudley. Nove ano passado nós eramos um bairro esquecido e lugar de despejo; hoje do stâ tá lebantá! Nós do stá tá exigir nós dignidade, reconstrui nos casas e compô nós comunidade. Amanhã, do tá bem realiza visão duma vizinhança culturalmente diversa undi nós é avaliado pá nós talentos e contribuicão na comunidade. Nós, residentes da área de Dudley ta exigi e declara o seguinte:

1. Nós do tem direito de difini todos os planos de desenvolvimento, programas e leis qui podê afectâ qualidade de vida como residentes do bairro.

2. Nós do tem direito a qualidade de saúde na alcance de todos os residentes do bairro, e qui ê sensivel as culturas de cada um.

3. Nós do tem direito de controlâ desenvolvimento dos terrenos do bairro na maneira adequada de espaços vazios pá parque, jardins e outros usos de recreação.

4. Nós do tem direito de viver num zona livre de perigos e que tá ofereçé segurança e estabilidade pá nós familias.

5. Nós do tem direito de celebrar nós diversidades culturais de nós vizinhança através de expressões artisticas.

6. Nós do tem direito a educação e treinos que ta encorajar nós crianças, jovens, adultos e velhos a alcança sês maxima potência.

7. Nós do tem direito de participâ na trabadjo criado pela iniciativa de desenvolvimento econômico na região de Boston e na vizinhança em particular.

8. Nós do tem direito a casas de boa qualidade e preços baixos no bairro tanto como rendeiros ou donos de casas.

9. Nós do tem direito a qualidade de cuidados de crianças, responsáveis para diferentes tipos de necessidade da criança e familia em casa ou em centros.

10. Nós do tem direito a meios de transportes públicos que são seguros e acessiveis pá servi comunidade.

11. Nós do tem direito de desfrutar de serviços e mercadorias de qualidade através de uma base comercial activa do bairro.

12. Nós do tem direito de practicar vida religiosa e Espiritual em lugares apropriados para tal.

13. Nós do tem direito a segurança na nós casas e na nós bairros.

INDEX

A

Abandoned cars, 73-74
Abdul-Tawwab, Faridah, 214-15, 225
Abdul-Tawwab, Fatimah, 214-15
Abdul-Tawwab, Najwa, 180-81, 200-201, 255, 258; on education, 214-16; and human development, 171, 172-73; on youth involvement, 225, 241
Abdul-Tawwab, Qasim, 54
Abramovitz, Mimi, 206
Abromowitz, David, 127
ACORN (Association of Community Organizations for Reform Now), 74-75
AFDC (Aid to Families with Dependent Children). *See* Welfare system
Affirmative action, 217, 229
AFL Disposal Company, 82, 83, 85, 181
African Americans. *See* Blacks; Racism
Agency Collaborative, 175-79, 255
AGM. *See* Associated Grantmakers of Massachusetts
Aid to Families with Dependent Children (AFDC). *See* Welfare system
Alcohol and other drugs, 19, 82; drunk driving, 210, 211 308n26; and Mary Hannon Park reclamation, 225, 226; stereotypes, 71, 205-06, 208-10; treat-

ment shortage, 226, 312n57; White use, 79, 208-10, 306n18. *See also* "War on drugs"
Alianza Hispana, La, 38-39, 40, 41-44, 47, 103
Alonso, Carla, 100
Alves, Tony, 183
Ambush, Steve, 81
Andrews, Nancy, 147-48, 149, 155, 157
Annie E. Casey Foundation, 271, 273
Anti-Semitism, 9-10, 206
Arson, 2, 12, 30-31, 33, 68
Asian Americans, 23
Associated Grantmakers of Massachusetts (AGM), 79
"At risk" label, 169, 206, 214, 255
Attucks, Crispus, 10

B

Bailey, Andrew, 40, 41
Banker & Tradesman, 142
Banking discrimination. *See* Housing discrimination; Redlining
Barros, Casimiro, 183, 232, 235, 237, 242, 259
Barros, John, 227-31, 232-37, 242, 246, 259

Barros, Jose, 82, 84

Barros, Olivia, 82, 85

Bauman, Robert, 82, 84, 85

BBURG. *See* Boston Banks Urban Renewal Group

Beaton, Sue, 111, 220, 250, 286; and eminent domain campaign, 120-21, 133, 135, 139; hiring, 183-84, 258; on housing construction, 152, 251

Bird Street Community Center, 175, 178, 227

Black, Rebecca, 123, 143, 151, 152

Blacks: Black-Latino tension, 47-48, 56-57, 77-78; causes of death, 211, 309-10n31; demographics, 10, 13; and DSNI formation, 47-48, 56-57; education, 216, 311n45; employment, 24, 196, 207, 305n8; and Greater Roxbury Neighborhood Authority, 94; infant mortality, 170, 299n5; Moynihan theory, 304-5n8; poverty among, 13, 23, 192-93; and urban renewal, 17, 19. *See also* Economic development; Housing discrimination; Racism; Segregation; *specific people*

Blockbusting, 26-27, 68

Bolling, Bruce, 71, 77, 84, 127, 133, 135

Bolling, Royal, Jr., 127

Boston. *See specific topics*

Boston Arson Prevention Commission, 30-31, 68

Boston Banks Urban Renewal Group (BBURG), 25-27

Boston Foundation, 115-16, 273, 274

Boston Globe. See Media coverage

Boston Herald. See Media coverage

Boston Housing Authority (BHA), 51, 163

Boston Natural Areas Fund, 78-79, 182, 183

Boston Redevelopment Authority (BRA), 22, 23, 24; abandonment study, 32-33; and community planning process, 102; Dudley Square Plan, 50-52, 53, 68, 92, 163; Finn study, 27, 28-29; and Greater Roxbury Neighborhood Authority, 93; South End urban renewal, 19-22; Washington Park urban renewal, 18-19. *See also* City government; Eminent domain campaign

Boston Safe Deposit and Trust Company, 18, 40

Boston Urban Gardeners, 79, 182

Bothwell, Paul, 5-6, 33-35, 70, 249, 262

BRA. *See* Boston Redevelopment Authority

Brandão, Miguel, 191

Bray, Rosemary, 198, 199

Brickley, Betty, 60

Brown, Dee, 238

Brown, Kelley, 155

Brown, Prudence, 272

Bush administration. *See* Reagan-Bush administrations

Businesses, 14, 110, 252. *See also* Economic development

Busing. *See* School desegregation

Bynoe, Edna, 81

C

Cape Verdean Community House, 44, 86

Cape Verdeans, 13-14, 44, 83, 86-87, 291n21

Cardoso, Adilson, 232, 233, 237, 242, 259

Carr, M. L., 227

Carrington, Shirley, 98, 102, 103

Carroll, Harold, 135

Casa Esperanza, 122, 226

Casey Foundation. *See* Annie E. Casey Foundation

Catholic Church, 11-12, 116, 120. *See also* St. Patrick's Church; *specific people*

CAUSE. *See* Community Assembly For a United South End

CCCD. *See* Coalition for Community Control of Development

CDC. *See* Community development corporations

Celester, William, 239

Census data. *See* Demographics

Champion, Hale, 21

Chapnick, Lisa: and community planning process, 90-91, 99, 112; and eminent domain campaign, 123, 124-25, 129-30, 135, 139, 264, 278; and housing construction, 152-53, 251; on Los Angeles riots, 247; on organizing, 262; and town common, 128, 129

Chapter 121A. *See* Eminent domain campaign

Charles Stuart Mott Foundation, 116

Child care, 51, 174, 193, 198-99, 289n2

Children's Defense Fund, 4, 212-13, 285

CIC. *See* Community Investment Coalition

Cintrón, Jenny, 174

City government: and Arson Commission report, 68-69; and community planning process, 112; and eminent domain campaign, 121-25, 127, 129-32, 134, 148, 278; and environmental organizing, 71-73, 74, 82, 83, 84-86; and Greater Roxbury Neighborhood Authority, 92-94, 95, 96; and housing construction, 252; lack of city services, 3, 32-33, 35, 75, 180-81; and organizing, 263-64; partnership role, 64-65, 276-81; and vacant land disposal, 74-75, 91, 92, 95; youth programs, 227. *See also* Boston Redevelopment Authority; Criminal justice system; Public Facilities Department; Urban renewal; *specific people*

City Year, 175, 251, 283

Civil War, 10

Clark, Shirley, 136

Clinton administration, 199, 252, 283, 284, 285, 316n35

Coalition for a Better Acre, 261

Coalition for Community Control of Development (CCCD), 94

Coleman, Earl, 53, 54, 58, 60, 257

Collins, Chuck, 127

Collins, John, 18, 121

Colón, Melvyn, 65, 77, 100, 124; and DSNI founding, 48, 60; and Riley Foundation, 41, 42

Combined Jewish Philanthropies, 270

Commission for Racial Justice (United Church of Christ), 181

Community activism: Bothwell group, 33-35; RCC survey, 37-38; and urban renewal, 20-21, 22. *See also specific groups and topics*

Community Assembly For a United South End (CAUSE), 20-21

Community Builders, The (TCB), 116, 117, 148, 149

Community development corporations (CDCs), 260. *See also specific organizations*

Community Facilities Planning Group, 178-79

Community gardens, 78-79, 182-83

Community Investment Coalition (CIC), 164, 165. *See also* Community Investment and Economic Development Coalition

Community Investment and Economic Development Coalition, 167

Community land trust. *See* Dudley Neighbors, Incorporated; Eminent domain campaign

Community planning process, 89-113; charettes, 104-5; consultant hiring, 96-99; Greater Roxbury Neighborhood Authority efforts, 92-96; human service agency survey, 102-3; master plan, 108-11; PFD participation, 90-91, 99; plan presentation, 111-13; process, 99-103; resident-agency tension in, 98-99, 106-7; town common, 128-29; vs. traditional approach, 89-90, 263; Triangle build-out plan, 150-54; urban village concept, 105-6. *See also* Eminent domain campaign

Community Reinvestment Act (1977), 27, 28, 29

Community Search Conference, 39

Community Summerfest, 226-27, 230

Community Training and Assistance Center (CTAC), 45, 270

Comunitas, 150

Condit, Nancy, 43-44

Condominium conversions, 28-29, 51, 54-55, 163

Connolly, John, 140

Consumers United Insurance Company (CUIC), 100, 147

Contingent workers, 194-95

Corporate strategies. *See* Economic development; Employment

Cottage Brook Apartments improvement, 161-62

Coyle, Steve, 93, 122, 123, 125, 135, 140, 141

Criminal justice system: prison building, 282-83; racism in, 232-41, 312-13n60, 314n70, 314n71; Stuart murder case, 239-40, 314n70. *See also* "War on Drugs"

Critical mass, 108

CTAC. See Community Training and Assistance Center

CUIC. See Consumers United Insurance Company

"Culture of poverty," 3-4, 205-6, 305n8

D

DAC International, 97-98, 99-100. See also Community planning process

Dacia-Woodcliff Community Garden, 182-83

D'Amato, Andrea, 123, 132, 136-37, 142-43, 154

Daniels, Mildred, 69, 242

Danner, Douglas "Doad," 40, 41

Davis, Mike, 248

DEC. See Digital Equipment Corporation

Defenders of the Faith Church, 226

Demographics, 9-10, 11-14, 156, 291n21, 292n33. See also specific groups

Digital Equipment Corporation (DEC), 189-90, 196, 284

DiMambro, Antonio, 150-51

Discrimination. See Gender; Housing discrimination; Racism

Disinvestment, 2, 14, 23-24, 247-48, 281-83. See also Redlining

Displacement. See Disinvestment; Urban renewal

DNI. See Dudley Neighbors, Incorporated

Domestic violence, 210, 309n27

Donlan, Michael, 141

"Don't Dump On Us" campaign, 70-74, 81-86, 90, 180

Dorcena, Carline, 204-05, 218, 231, 242-43, 259

Dorcena, Linda, 242

Dorcena, William, 242

Dorchester, 7, 8, 9, 10, 11. See also specific topics

Dorchester Bay Economic Development Corporation, 162, 178

Douglass, Frederick, 10, 277

Drugs. See Alcohol and other drugs

Drumlin Farm, 183

Drunk driving, 210, 211, 308n26

DSNI founding, 37-65; Black-Latino tension, 47-48, 56-57, 77-78; board formation, 57-58, 60-62; boundary

definitions, 47-48; Community Search Conference, 39; Dudley Advisory Group formation, 44-46, 295n10; Dudley Neighborhood Coalition, 38; first elections, 58-60; From the Ground Up study, 38-39, 41; governance structure, 49-50, 56-58, 256; initial community meeting, 52-56; initial neighborhood survey, 69-70; leadership changes, 65; Riley Foundation involvement, 39-44, 61-62; Shirley-Eustis House meeting, 45-46; staff hiring, 62-64. See also Resident-agency tension

DSNI housing construction: DSNI role, 158-61, 268-70; Dudley List, 160-61; groundbreaking, 251-52, 253; jobs policy, 188; Triangle build-out plan, 150-54, 158-61. See also Dudley Neighbors, Inc.; Eminent domain campaign; Housing

Dudley, Joseph, 45

Dudley, Thomas, 7, 45

Dudley Advisory Group, 44-46, 47, 48, 60, 295n10. See also specific topics

Dudley Initiative, The (Flather & Condit), 43-44

Dudley Neighborhood Coalition, 38

Dudley Neighbors Business Alliance, 186, 188

Dudley Neighbors, Incorporated (DNI), 126-27, 147, 158-59

Dudley PRIDE, 111, 179-81, 242

Dudley Square Plan, 50-52, 53, 68, 92, 163

Dudley Station, 2, 106

Dudley Street Neighborhood Initiative (DSNI): ACORN conflicts, 74-75; arson meeting, 68-69; Black-Latino tension, 47-48, 56-57, 77-78; celebration (1992), 245, 246; community ownership, 286-87; community revitalization, 266-68; Declaration of Community Rights, 200-202, 287; as family, 184, 203, 250-51; Flather-Condit report, 43-44; intergenerational nature of, 4, 258; legal support, 116-17; Local 26 conflicts, 75-77; membership, 250-51, 315n9; multicultural festivals, 78, 111, 226-27, 241-42; organizational capacity, 266-68; and other groups, 78-79; staff transitions,

145-47, 183-85, 258; success of, 1, 4-5, 248-50, 253-54. *See also* DSNI founding; Funding; *specific people; specific topics*
Dudley Street Neighborhood Initiative Revitalization Plan, The: A Comprehensive Community Controlled Strategy, 108-11. *See also* Community planning process
Dudley Triangle. *See* Triangle build-out plan
Dudley's Young Architects and Planners project, 219-24
Durazo, María Elena, 247-48

E

East Brooklyn Churches, 261
Economic development, 110, 185-200; contract access, 187-88; and corporate strategies, 189-92; and drug treatment, 226; Dudley Neighbors Business Alliance, 186; economic summit, 187; enterprise zone approach, 190, 283-85; need for, 185-86; youth involvement, 188-89
Economic Opportunities Act, 260
Economy. *See* Economic development; Employment; Poverty; Unemployment
Education, 311n45; DSNI agenda, 174-75, 216; racism in, 63, 213-16, 228-30
Eisen, Arlene, 271-72, 275, 276
Eisenhower, Dwight D., 285, 316n35
Eisenhower Foundation. *See* Milton S. Eisenhower Foundation
Emergency Tenants Council, 20, 21. *See also* Inquilinos Boricuas en Acción
Eminent domain campaign, 117-44; BRA decision, 139-42; BRA hearing, 135-39; and city government, 121-25, 127, 129-32, 134, 148, 278; delays, 154-57; DNI formation, 126-27; DNI role, 158-59; financing, 147-50, 154-56; Ford Foundation closing, 157-58; housing design, 159-60; importance of, 264-66; initial distrust of, 119-21, 126; legal background, 118-19; and Mandela reincorporation movement, 131-32; and Minority Developers Association, 127-28, 137, 138; neighborhood rally,

132-34; precedent concerns, 142-44; title searches, 155-56. *See also* DSNI housing construction
Employment: Blacks, 24, 196, 207, 305n8; contingent workers, 194-95; and corporate strategies, 189-92, 194-95; declining wages, 192-95; discrimination in, 216-17; and disinvestment, 23-24; and gender, 196, 217, 292n34; and Los Angeles riots, 247-48; and segregated suburbanization, 16; and welfare system, 198-99, 303n54. *See also* Economic development; Poverty; Unemployment
Empowerment zones, 284-85
Enterprise zones, 190, 283-85
Environmental organizing: "Don't Dump On Us" campaign, 70-74, 90, 180; Dudley PRIDE, 179-81; need for, 2, 32; neighborhood greening, 78-79, 181-83; trash transfer station campaign, 81-86
Environmental racism, 181
Equal Credit Opportunity Act (1976), 27
Eustis, William, 8
Everdell, Ros, 146, 173, 208, 261, 280; on environmental organizing, 181, 182-83; on housing construction, 161, 164; on housing discrimination, 165, 166-67; on tenant organizing, 161, 162; on youth involvement, 219, 221, 225, 228, 230, 236

F

Family Support Act, 199
Farrell, Robert, 141-42
Farrier, Jessie, 2, 69
Federal Housing Administration (FHA), 14, 15, 25, 27
Federal policy: community-government partnership, 281-86; disinvestment, 281-83; military spending, 282, 285, 316n35; official poverty line, 289-90n2; and redlining, 28; and resource limitations and priorities, 199-200, 263, 282-83, 285; segregated suburbanization, 14-16; taxation, 199-200, 282, 283, 304n59; and urban renewal, 22-23, 293n54; welfare system, 197-

99, 302n45. *See also* Criminal justice system; "War on drugs"; *specific laws*
Federal Reserve Bank of Boston, 29, 164
Felix, Patricia, 242, 259
Ferrara, Anthony, 195
FHA. *See* Federal Housing Administration
Fidalgo, Gertrudes, 145-46, 250-51, 280; on housing construction, 154, 161; on youth involvement, 207, 228, 230
Fidalgo, Maria-Goreth, 83, 146, 173
Financing. *See* Funding
Finn, Charles, 25, 27, 28-29
Fitzgerald, John "Honey Fitz," 9
Flather, Newell, 61, 62, 128, 246; on community-foundation partnership, 274, 275; and DSNI founding, 40-41, 42-44, 45-46, 48
Flint, Sarah, 51, 65, 81, 84, 85, 104, 162-63
Flynn, Ray: 63-64, 252; on arson, 68-69; and community planning process, 112; and community-government partnership, 277, 278, 281; and eminent domain campaign, 129-32, 134, 139-40, 141-42, 144, 148; and environmental organizing, 72, 73, 74, 82, 84-85; and Greater Roxbury Neighborhood Authority, 92, 94; and vacant land disposal, 91, 152. *See also* City government
Ford Foundation, 147-50, 154-56, 157-58, 271, 272
Fox, James Alan, 212
Framework for a Human Development Agenda (DSNI), 171
From the Ground Up (Total Studio), 38-39, 41
Funding, 79-80, 115-16, 273; agency competition, 79-80, 94-95, 177-78, 275; community-foundation partnerships, 271-76, 315n21; housing, 147-50, 153-56; and human development, 177-78; and resident-agency tension, 255. *See also* Riley Foundation; other *specific foundations*

G

G.I. Bill (1944), 14
Gambling, 200, 304n59
Gangs, 207-8, 212

Gans, Herbert, 17
Garritty, Arthur, 63
Gates, Daryl, 240, 314n71
Gender: and employment, 196, 292n34; and poverty, 193, 300n25, 301n26; stereotypes about, 206-7, 304-5n8. *See also* Single mothers
Gentrification, 21-22, 28-29, 51-52. *See also* Urban renewal
Gentry, Albert, 137
Gillis, Don, 130
Glover, Danny, 246
Goddard, Deborah, 280
Goldstein, Paul J., 308n26
Gomes, Alice, 83
Gonçalves, Manuel, 60
Gonçalves, Ulisses, 60
Goodwin, Proctor and Hoar, 236
Gottin, Pio, 13
Goulston & Storrs, 116, 127
Greater Roxbury Incorporation Project, 131
Greater Roxbury Neighborhood Authority (GRNA), 53, 92-96, 132, 161, 164, 176
Green, Nancy, 163, 206
Green Team, 183
Gregory, Valerie, 44
GRNA. *See* Greater Roxbury Neighborhood Authority
Guns. *See* Violence
Gutensohn, James, 128, 129

H

Haas, Bob, 30, 60, 73-74, 100
Hadrian, Ricanne, 261
Haitians, 204, 205
Hanley, Stephen, 173, 177-78, 246
Harding, Lloyd, 60
Harmon, Lawrence, 25-26, 27
Henríquez, Julio, 227
Henze, Laura, 274
Hernández, José, 224
Hispanic Office of Planning and Evaluation (HOPE), 38, 219
Hispanics, *See* Latinos
Historical background, 7-35; Bothwell activism, 33-35; disinvestment, 23-24; early development, 8-10; housing ar-

son and abandonment, 2, 30-33; population, 9-10, 11-14; Puritans, 7-8; redlining, 24-30; segregation, 14-17; urban renewal, 17-23

Holmes, Robert, Jr., 40, 205, 236, 274-75; and DSNI founding, 41, 42, 43, 46, 55, 56

Home Mortgage Disclosure Act (1975), 27, 29

Homer, Ron, 238

Homicide. *See* Violence

Hoon, Shelley, 47, 60

HOPE. *See* Hispanic Office of Planning and Evaluation

Hotel and Restaurant Employees International Union. *See* Local 26 (Hotel and Restaurant Employees International Union)

Housing: arson and abandonment, 2, 30-33; cooperatives, 3, 161, 162; cost of, 289-90n2, 300n21, 302n46; homebuyer training, 163-64; speculation, 185-86; tenant organizing, 161-63. *See also* Community planning process; DSNI housing construction; Eminent domain campaign; Gentrification

Housing Act (1949), 17

Housing and Community Development Act (1987), 153

Housing and Urban Development, U.S. Department of (HUD), 16, 22, 153, 289-90n2

Housing discrimination: BBURG, 25-27; blockbusting, 26-27, 68; condominium conversions, 28-29, 51, 54-55, 163; current, 15-16, 28-29; FHA, 14-15; mortgage discrimination, 164-67; redlining, 1, 15, 24-25, 29-30

Houston, John, 99-100

Howard, Jeff, 213-14

Hoyte, Jamie, 129

HUD. *See* Housing and Urban Development, U.S. Department of

Hughey, Harold, 113

Human development, 169-81; Agency Collaborative, 175-79, 255; defining, 171-73; education agenda, 174-75

Human Services. *See* Human development; Social services

Hyams Foundation, 96, 273

I

IBA. *See* Inquilinos Boricuas en Acción

Immigrants, 9, 11, 13-14, 205-06, 241

Income/wealth inequality, 170, 192, 193-95, 199-200, 206, 293n54, 299n3, 300n24. *See also* Economic development; Employment; Poverty

Infant mortality, 170, 212-13, 299n5

Inquilinos Boricuas en Acción (IBA), 20, 21

Institute for Community Economics, 127, 158, 270

Insurance discrimination. *See* Housing discrimination; Redlining

Interim Roxbury Planning Advisory Committee (PAC), 93

Irish immigrants, 9, 11, 19, 205-6, 305n8

Italian immigrants, 206

J

Jacobs, Jane, 105

Jews, 9-10, 26, 206, 270

Job training/placement, 51. *See also* Economic development; Employment

Johnson, Alex, 182, 252

Johnson, Stephen, 53

Joint Disposition Committee (JDC), 138-39, 151-53

Jones, Andrew, 131

Jones, Clarence "Jeep," 141

Jones, Della, 100

Jones, Nolando, 222-23, 224

Jones, Willie, 92

Judd, Dennis, 15

K

K & C Disposal, 83, 85

Karant, Sue, 270, 273

Keeping Track: How Schools Structure Inequality (Oakes), 214

Ken, Bostian, 10

Kenealy, Joseph, 27

Kennedy, Joseph, 29

Kennedy, Robert, 245-46, 259-60

Kerner Commission, 282

Kerry, John, 305n8

King, Martin Luther, Jr., 246, 248, 285-86
King, Mel, 13, 21, 63-64, 92
King, Rodney, 238, 313n60. See also Los Angeles riots
Know-Nothing Party, 11
Koebert, Cynthia, 64

L

Land development. See Community planning process; DSNI housing construction; Eminent domain campaign
Latimore, Gail, 58, 60, 100, 106
Latino Youth AIDS Education Project, 219
Latinos, 13; Black-Latino tension, 47-48, 56-57, 77-78; current housing discrimination, 28, 29; organizing difficulties, 77-78; poverty among, 23, 192-93; and urban renewal, 21. See also Racism; specific people
Lee, Tunney, 38, 96
Leibowitz, Howard, 283
Leonard, Sister Margaret, 253
Lepardo, Anthony, 82, 85
Levine, Hillel, 25-26, 27
Lewis, Oscar, 205
Lewis, Reggie, 242
Leyland Street Crime Watch, 79
Lipman, Mark, 246
Local 26 (Hotel and Restaurant Employees International Union), 75-77, 164
Logue, Ed, 18, 22, 121
Lopes-Jefferson, Cynthia, 79, 112
Los Angeles riots, 238, 241, 245-46, 247-48, 314n1
Lupo, Alan, 208-9
Lyons, Tom, 11-12

M

McCarthy, Sophia, 12, 22, 69, 85-86, 242, 252
McKnight, John, 254, 255
Madyun, Ché, 2-3, 161, 219-20, 246, 250, 261; board presidency, 65, 257; and community planning process, 108, 113; and DSNI founding, 54-55, 56, 56-57, 60, 65; and eminent domain campaign, 124, 126, 134, 135, 139;

and housing construction, 251, 252; and human development, 169, 171-72
Madyun, Yaqana, 183
Magnolia Cooperative Housing, 161
Mahan, Leah, 246
Malcolm X, 13
Mandela reincorporation movement, 131-32
Mann, Eric, 247, 284
Marrero, Gevel, 225
Martin, Marvin, 82-83
Martínez, Bob, 210
Martínez, Rubén, 248
Mary Hannon Park, 33, 225-27
Massachusetts Affordable Housing Alliance Home Buyers Union, 164
Massachusetts Bay Transportation Authority (MBTA), 75
Massachusetts Commission Against Discrimination (MCAD), 216
Massachusetts Fair Share, 74
Massachusetts Horticultural Society, 182, 183
Mathers, Cortland, 239
Mayol, Ricardo, 226
MBTA. See Massachusetts Bay Transportation Authority
MCAD. See Massachusetts Commission Against Discrimination
MDA. See Minority Developers Association
Media coverage, 113, 129, 207-08, 252; criminal justice system, 209-10, 238, 240; eminent domain campaign, 126, 134, 138; trash transfer station campaign, 84, 85. See also specific topics
Medoff, Peter, 62, 67, 100, 146, 148; and eminent domain campaign, 117, 122, 124, 135; hiring of, 62-63, 64
Menino, Tom, 252
Merced, Nelson, 38, 45, 46, 65; board membership, 60, 257; and eminent domain campaign, 133, 135; and governance structure, 49-50, 57, 58; and initial community meeting, 52, 53-54; and Riley Foundation funding, 39, 41-42, 44
METCO. See Metropolitan Council for Educational Opportunity
Metropolitan Council for Educational Opportunity (METCO), 54

Millett, Ricardo, 44, 47, 48, 50, 53
Milton S. Eisenhower Foundation, 282-83, 284
Minority Developers Association (MDA), 127, 137, 138
Mollenkopf, John, 20, 22
Morgan Memorial Goodwill Industries, 80-81, 172
Morrow, Lance, 195
Moynihan, Daniel Patrick, 304-5n8
Mt. Pleasant Neighborhood Association, 38, 69
Muhammad, Fadilah, 54, 55-56, 60, 65, 252
Munkenbeck, Peter, 117, 135, 154-55

N

NAFTA. *See* North American Free Trade Agreement
Nagel, Andrea, 67-68, 81, 82, 101-2, 250, 254, 263; and human development, 173, 176-77; and youth involvement, 221, 225
National Commission on Urban Problems (1968), 15
National Night Out Against Crime, 219
Native Americans, 7, 8
Nee, Mary, 279
Nehemiah Housing Opportunity Program, 153
Neighborhood control principle, 108
Neighborhood greening, 78-79, 181-83
Neighborhood leadership, 256-58. *See also* Resident-agency tension
Nesbitt, David, 99, 251
New Federalism, 22
Newport, Eugene "Gus," 146-47, 184-85, 246, 250, 256; and eminent domain campaign, 150, 154, 155, 157, 160, 264; on funding, 272; and housing construction, 151, 152-53, 251; on mortgage discrimination, 165; on organizing, 261; and youth involvement, 224, 243
1965-1975 General Plan for the City of Boston (BRA), 18, 20
Nixon administration, 22
North American Free Trade Agreement (NAFTA), 192

Nuestra Comunidad Development Corporation, 38, 39, 42, 44, 76, 77, 153, 176, 178, 269

O

Oakes, Jeannie, 214
O'Brien, Hugh, 9
O'Brien, Quinn, 216
Ogletree, Charles, 238-39
O'Leary, Sister Pauline, 44, 60
Orchard Park Tenants Association, 38, 51, 81, 104, 162-63, 176, 178, 206
Orchard Park United Tenants Association. *See* Orchard Park Tenants Association
Organizing: building on neighborhood assets, 170-71, 254-57; vs. developer role, 268-70; importance of, 5, 62, 67, 69, 259-61; and political will, 262-64. *See also* specific campaigns

P

Padilla, Tubal, 60, 98-99, 100-101, 111
Pereira, Joseph, 191
PFD. *See* Public Facilities Department
Phillips, Mary, 40
Pierce, Glen, 240
Planning. *See* Community planning process; Urban renewal
Plumer, Stephen, 99, 100, 102, 111, 251
Police. *See* Criminal justice system
Porter, Joan, 72
Poverty: and disinvestment, 23-24; extent of, 3, 4, 23, 170, 192, 299n2, 299n3, 300n21, 300n24, 300n25; and federal tax policy, 199-200, 304n59; and gender, 193, 300n25, 301n26; and human development, 169-70; official vs. alternative definitions of, 199, 289-90n2; and race, 13, 23, 192-93; stereotypes about, 3-4, 51, 169-70, 204-6, 207, 254-55, 304-5n8; welfare system, 197-99, 302n45, 303n47, 303n48
Powers & Hall, 40, 116
Pradhan, Geeta, 128-29, 153-54
Prado, Luis, 102, 103, 107
Project Hope, 111, 133, 161, 176

Project 747, 123
Proposition 2½, 122
Prothrow-Stith, Deborah, 212, 213
Public Facilities Department (PFD): and community planning process, 90-91, 99; and eminent domain campaign, 123-25, 138-39; and Triangle build-out plan, 151-52. See also City government; specific people
Public transportation, 9, 75
Puritans, 7-8

Q

Quakers, 7, 9
Quiroga, Ricardo, 122

R

Racism: criminal justice system, 232-41, 312-13n60; in education, 63, 213-16, 228-30; in employment, 216-17; stereotypes, 3-4, 13, 73, 204, 205-6, 207, 228-29, 235, 304-5n8; and "war on drugs," 209-10, 238, 306-7n19, 307n20, 307n21, 308n26. See also Blacks; Housing discrimination; Latinos; Los Angeles riots; Segregation
Rackemann, Sawyer & Brewster, 116-17, 118, 121-22, 135
Rankin, Dorothy, 106
Rappaport, Jerome, 292n38
RCC. See Roxbury Community College
Reagan-Bush administrations, 22-23, 283, 316n35
Real estate market. See Eminent domain campaign; Gentrification; Housing; Housing discrimination; Speculation
Rebuild L.A., 247, 248
Redlining, 1, 15, 24-25, 29-30, 164-65
Reich, Robert, 199, 200
Reid, Ala, 40, 45
Resident-agency tension, 52-58, 65, 255; and coalition work, 270-71; and community planning process, 98-99, 106-7; and funding, 255; and governance structure, 49-50, 56-58, 256, 257; and staff hiring, 62. See also Neighborhood leadership

Riggs, Herbert, 163, 167
Riley, Mabel Louise, 39-40
Riley Foundation, 39-44, 62, 79, 80, 96; and board formation, 57, 61-62; community-foundation partnership, 271-74, 275-76; and Morgan Memorial Goodwill Industries headquarters, 80-81. See also Dudley Street Neighborhood Initiative; specific people
RMSC. See Roxbury Multi-Service Center
RNC. See Roxbury Neighborhood Council
Rockwell, David, 149, 155, 165-66, 258
Rodriguez, Sol Angel, 135
Rogers, Sister Mary, 44
Roxbury, 7, 8-9, 10; secession movement, 131-32. See also specific topics
Roxbury Community College (RCC), 37-38
Roxbury Multi-Service Center (RMSC), 38, 44, 47-48, 103, 176
Roxbury Neighborhood Council (RNC), 94, 95, 265
Roxbury YMCA, 176, 178, 179
Ruggles, Patricia, 289n2

S

Salerno, Rosaria, 133, 135
Saunders, Gareth, 166
Say Brother, 138
School desegregation, 63
Schools. See Education
Schwarz, John, 289n2
Scondras, David, 68-69, 135
Segregation, 1, 10, 14-17, 241. See also School desegregation; Racism
Shames, Ervin, 191
Shelley v. Kraemer, 15
Shirley, William, 8
Shirley-Eustis House, 45, 79
Single mothers, 51, 193, 206-7, 301n26, 305n8. See also Gender; Welfare system
Sisters of Charity, 44
Skloot, Edward, 271
Slavery, 10, 206, 241
Slotnik, Bill, 45, 262, 265, 274; on boundary definitions, 47-48; on first elections, 59, 60; on initial community

meeting, 52, 53, 55, 56; on neighborhood leadership, 256, 257
Smith, Carole, 99, 102
Smith, Larry, 162
Smith, Lorraine, 252
Sobel, Barbara, 198
Social services: Agency Collaborative, 175-79, 255; and community planning process, 102-3; vs. organizing, 259; and poverty, 169-70. *See also* Human development; Resident-agency tension
Socioeconomic status, 211, 310n32. *See also* Employment; Income/wealth inequality; Poverty
Solinger, Ricki, 206
Solís, Arnaldo, 78, 173, 177, 250, 252
Soto, Esteban, Jr., 60
South End Tenants Council, 20
South End urban renewal, 19-22, 186
Southwest Corridor Project, 31
Spann, Lessie, 60
Speculation, 185-86, 264, 265
St. Patrick's Church, 11, 13, 38, 43-44, 52, 120, 231
Stereotypes, 19, 218; and banking, 165-66; "culture of poverty," 3-4, 205-6, 305n8; drugs, 71, 208-10; and education, 213-14, 217, 228-30; and employment, 192, 217; gender, 206-7, 304-5n8; poverty, 3-4, 51, 169-70, 204-6, 207, 254-55, 304-5n8; racial, 13, 73, 204, 205-6, 207, 228-29, 235, 238-41; 304-5n8; and speculation, 186; violence, 205, 210, 305n8, 308n26; welfare system, 197-99, 207
Stewart, Maria, 10
Strand Theatre, 11, 48, 176, 246
Streetcar Suburbs (Warner), 9
Stride Rite Corporation, 189-91, 284
Stuart murder case, 239-40, 314n70
Stull and Lee, 97, 98, 104-5
Sturniolo, Margarita, 12, 69, 106
Suburbanization, 1, 14-17
Sullivan, Gail, 221, 222-24, 225
Sullivan, Louis, 209
Sullivan, Neil, 130, 140
Szymanski, Marcia, 190

T

Tandem strategy, 108
Taylor, Janet, 45
Taylor, Richard, 138
TCB. *See* Community Builders, The
Teixeira, Adalberto, 86-87, 126, 145
Teixeira, Gino, 252
Teixeira, Maria "Uia," 165
Teixeira, Peter, 165
Teklamariam, Azalech "Azi," 172, 177, 219
Tenant organizing, 161-63. *See also* Orchard Park Tenants Association
Tenants Development Corporation, 20
Tent City, 21
Terrell, Bob, 92, 132
Thayer, Henry, 116, 155-56
Total Studio, 38-39
Town common, 128-29, 153-54
Tracking, 213-14
Trash transfer station campaign, 81-86
Traynor, Bill, 260, 268
Triangle build-out plan, 150-54, 158-61
Tufts University, 173
Turnbull, Clayton, 185, 190, 252, 280; on community ownership, 286-87; on Dudley PRIDE, 179-80; and eminent domain campaign, 126, 133-34, 137-38, 139, 147; and neighborhood leadership, 257-58
Turner, Chuck, 92, 132

U

Ueberroth, Peter, 247, 248
"Underclass," 3-4, 305n8
Unemployment, 3, 51, 195-96; benefits, 196-97, 302n42; and disinvestment, 23, 293n55; and race, 23, 216-17; and segregated suburbanization, 16-17. *See also* Employment; Poverty
Uphams Corner, 8, 11, 48
Urban Institute, 216
Urban renewal, 1, 17-23, 292n38; activist opposition to, 20-21, 22; Dudley Square Plan, 50-52, 53, 68, 92, 163
Urban Villagers, The (Gans), 17
UrbanArts, 183
Uriarte, Miren, 21, 77-78

V

VA. *See* Veterans Administration
Vacant land reclamation: conflict with
  ACORN, 74-75; *From the Ground Up*
  report, 38-39; moratorium agreements, 91, 92, 95. *See also* Community gardens; Community planning
  process; "Don't Dump On Us" campaign; DSNI housing construction;
  Eminent domain campaign; Neighborhood greening
Vance, Darryl, 216
Vaughn, John, 268
"Vault, The," 18
Veterans Administration (VA), 14, 156
Villa Victoria, 21
Violence: 162-63; 211-13, 310n33; against
  women, 210, 309n27; and age,
  311n38; economic, 212-13, 245-46;
  and race, 211, 309-10n31; and socio-
  economic status, 211, 310n32; stereotypes about, 205, 210, 239-40, 305n8,
  308n26; and "war on drugs," 211,
  309n28
Volgy, Thomas, 289n2

W

Wade, Ken, 92-93, 94-95, 99, 132, 133,
  138, 143, 144
WAITT House, 38, 44, 176
Waldron, Father Walter, 43-44, 60, 84, 86,
  120, 154
WANA. *See* Woodville Area Neighbor-
  hood Association
"War on Drugs": and prison system, 238,
  309n28, 312n57, 313n63; racism of,
  209-10, 238, 306-7n19, 307n20,
  307n21, 308n26; *See also* Alcohol and
  other drugs; Violence
War on Poverty, 259-60
Warner, Sam, 9, 30
Washington Park Urban Renewal project,
  18-19
Washington Street Corridor Coalition, 94
Waters, Maxine, 245-46, 306n19
Webb, Jason, 203-4, 208, 225, 242, 259
Weld, William, 138, 153, 198

Welfare system, 302n45, 303n47, 303n48;
  stereotypes, 197-99, 205, 207
West End urban renewal, 17-18, 292n38
*Where Do We Go From Here: Chaos or
  Community?* (King), 285-86
White, Kevin, 20-21, 31
Whites: affirmative action for, 217;
  causes of death, 211, 309-10n31;
  demographics, 12; drug/alcohol use,
  79, 208-10, 306n18; education,
  311n45; employment, 23, 305n8;
  gang violence, 212; and Los Angeles
  riots, 314n1
Whittington, Rogelio "Ro," 164, 231, 252;
  on economic development, 185-86,
  187; hiring, 183-84, 258
Wilkins, Lauress, 61
Williams, Jacqui Cairo, 174-75
Williams, Tony, 123, 138, 154
Wilson, Laval, Jr., 136
Winthrop, John, 7-8
Women: and criminal justice system, 210,
  238, 313n64; domestic violence, 210,
  309n27. *See also* Gender
Wood, James, 208-9
Woods, Robert, 19
Woodville Area Neighborhood Associa-
  tion (WANA), 79
World War I, 11

Y

Yancey, Charles, 135
Yelder, Paul, 100, 224, 246, 258; and
  DSNI housing construction, 150, 152,
  159-60, 269; and eminent domain
  campaign, 124, 139, 140, 149
Youth: employment discrimination, 196,
  216-17; stereotypes, 204-12, 218,
  220, 228-30, 232-40, 241. *See also*
  Criminal justice system; Education;
  Violence; "War on Drugs"; Youth involvement
Youth involvement, 4, 203-43, 258-59;
  John Barros story, 227-31; DSNI
  board membership 230; Dudley's
  Young Architects and Planners project, 219-25; and economic development, 188-89; environmental
  organizing, 182, 183; focus group,

218-19; Mary Hannon Park reclamation, 225-27; mural, 241-42; neighborhood festivals, 78; Youth committee founding 230-31
YouthBuild, 176, 189, 251, 283

Z

Zoning. *See* Community planning process; Urban renewal

ABOUT THE AUTHORS

Peter Medoff, a leading consultant on community development for foundations, community groups and government, died shortly after *Streets of Hope* was published in 1994. Medoff served as DSNI's first executive director during 1986-89. Before that he was director of the Citizens Research Education Network, which provided research and organizing assistance to community groups in the Greater Hartford area of Connecticut, and he worked as a tenant organizer in New York City. He also served as a consultant to groups developing housing for people with AIDS. He received a masters in Urban Planning from Columbia University. The Peter Medoff Dudley Youth Scholarship Fund awards college scholarships to Dudley neighborhood youth.

Holly Sklar is a writer whose commentaries on current affairs have appeared in well over 150 newspapers nationwide as well as numerous magazines and anthologies. Her latest book, *Chaos or Community? Seeking Solutions, Not Scapegoats for Bad Economics,* has been hailed as a "tour-de-force" and "essential reading for anyone who wants to know what's really going on." She is a contributor to the new book, *Stone Soup for the World: Life-Changing Stories of Kindness & Courageous Acts of Service.* Sklar's other books include the best-selling *Trilateralism: The Trilateral Commission and Elite Planning for World Management,* which foretold the global corporate economy, and *Poverty in the American Dream* (co-authored). She has a masters in Political Science from Columbia University.

FOR MORE INFORMATION ABOUT DSNI

Dudley Street Neighborhood Initiative (DSNI) can be reached at: DSNI, 504 Dudley Street, Roxbury, MA 02119-2767. Phone: (617) 442-9670. Fax: (617) 427-8047. Or visit http://www.dsni.org/.

To learn more about DSNI, see the award-winning documentary *Holding Ground: The Rebirth of Dudley Street*, produced by Leah Mahan and Mark Lipman. For ordering information, contact New Day Films. Toll-free number: 888-369-9154. Or write: New Day Films, 22-D Hollywood Avenue, Ho-ho-kus, NJ 07423-1437. Phone: (201) 652-6590. Fax: (201) 652-1973. E-mail: curator@newday.com. Or visit the New Day web site: http://www.newday.com/holdingground/newsletter.html.

The address for the Peter Medoff Dudley Youth Scholarship Fund is: Medoff Scholarship Fund, c/o WAITT House, 117 Mount Pleasant Avenue, Roxbury, MA 02119-3351.

ABOUT SOUTH END PRESS

South End Press is a nonprofit, collectively run book publisher with more than 200 titles in print. Since our founding in 1977, we have tried to meet the needs of readers who are exploring, or are already committed to, the politics of radical social change. Our goal is to publish books that encourage critical thinking and constructive action on the key political, cultural, social, economic, and ecological issues shaping life in the United States and in the world. In this way, we hope to give expression to a wide diversity of democratic social movements and to provide an alternative to the products of corporate publishing.

Through the Institute for Social and Cultural Change, South End Press works with other political media projects—Z Magazine; Speakout, a speakers' bureau; and Alternative Radio—to expand access to information and critical analysis.

DUDLEY STREET NEIGHBORHOOD INITIATIVE YOUTH COMMITTEE MURAL

"At a time when others are writing off our inner cities and writing off inner city youth, *Streets of Hope* challenges and inspires us with the brilliance of the Dudley Street neighborhood example. This eloquent book reveals the respect, dignity and love – *respeto, dignidad y cariño* – of people for their neighborhood, their diverse cultures and their shared vision of change."

Frieda Garcia, chair of the board, The Boston Foundation and executive director, Harriet Tubman House/United South End Settlements

"This is one of the best books ever on neighborhood organizing and community development. What makes *Streets of Hope* stand out is both the boldness of the story and the sophistication with which Medoff and Sklar conceptualize it. Using the Dudley Street Neighborhood Initiative in Boston's most impoverished neighborhood as a case study, the authors show how effective organizing reinforces neighborhood leadership, encourages grassroots power and leads to successful public-private partnerships and comprehensive community development. *Streets of Hope* should be greeted warmly by planners and policymakers, urban historians, community activists and all those who care about the restoration of inner city neighborhoods."

Professor Norman Krumholz, formerly president of the American Planning Association and Cleveland planning director

"Whatever your political views or policy ideas, if you care about the future of the inner city and the country, read this powerful book. It goes behind the headlines and stereotypes to show how people of all races, religions and ages can work together to achieve shared dreams for their families and their community. It spotlights the economic trends imperiling our livelihoods, our neighborhoods and our children's future. *Streets of Hope* is about saying 'No' to self-fulfilling prophecies of despair and 'Yes' to can-do problem solving. It's about hope and pride and partnership. It's about making the impossible – possible."

Jesse Jackson, president, National Rainbow Coalition

"*Streets of Hope* is an inspiring 'Must read' for everyone engaged in the struggle to turn around low-income urban neighborhoods. Residents, organizers, policymakers, educators, funders – anyone who wants to be part of the solution should read this wonderfully informative and encouraging book."

Stephen Perkins, associate director, Center for Neighborhood Technology, Chicago

South End Press
Current Affairs/Urban Affairs